CW00933265

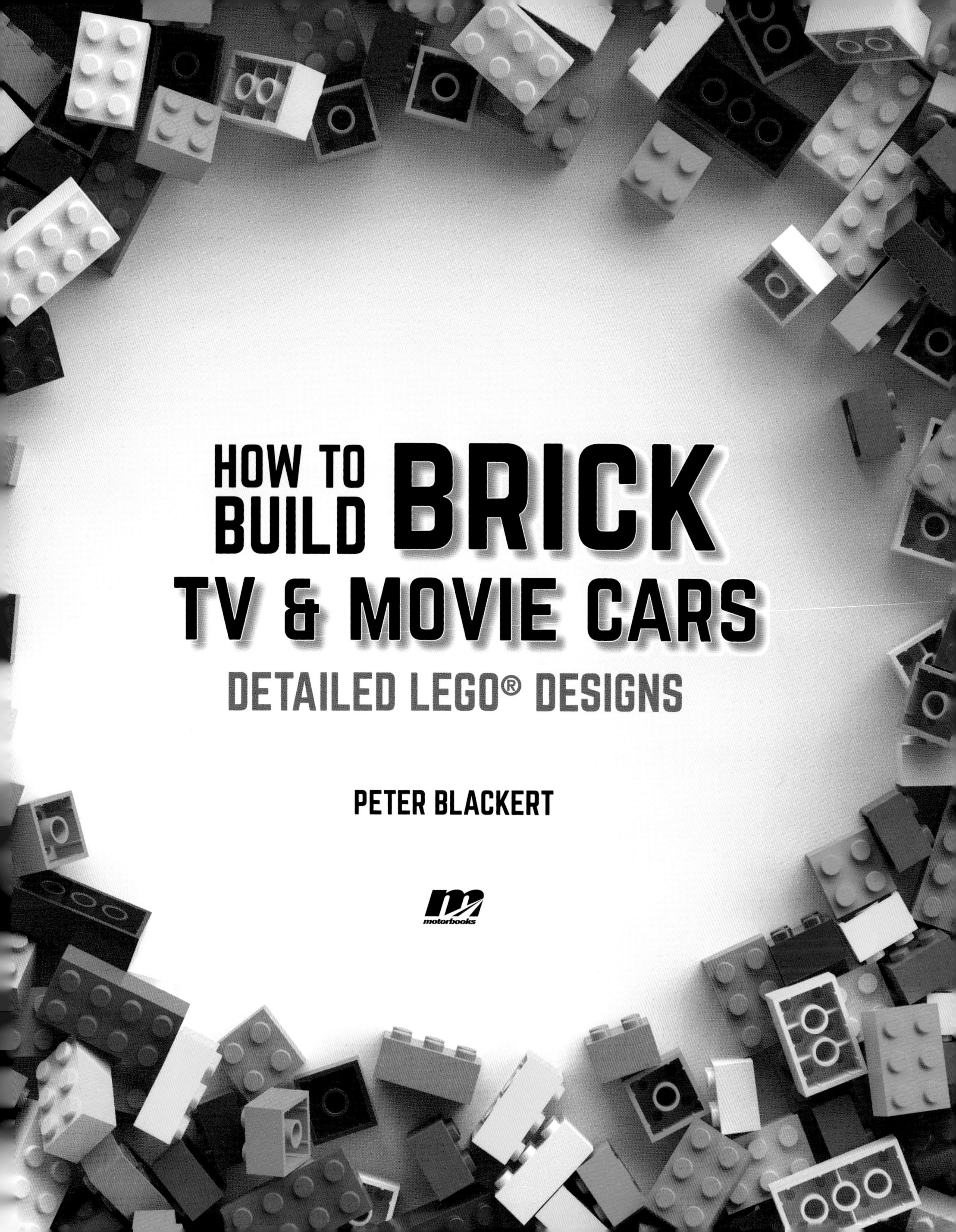

HOW TO BUILD BRICK TV & MOVIE CARS

DETAILED LEGO® DESIGNS

PETER BLACKERT

motorbooks

First Published in 2019 by Motorbooks, an imprint of The Quarto Group,
100 Cummings Center, Suite 265-D, Beverly, MA 01915, USA.
T (978) 282-9590 F (978) 283-2742 QuartoKnows.com

23 22 21 20 19 1 2 3 4 5

ISBN: 978-0-7603-6588-5
Digital edition published in 2019
eISBN: 978-0-7603-6589-2

Library of Congress Cataloging-in-Publication Data

Names: Blackert, Peter, 1972- author.
Title: How to build brick TV and movie cars / Peter Blackert.
Description: Beverly, MA, USA. : Quarto Publishing Group USA, Inc., [2019] | Includes bibliographical references and index. |
Identifiers: LCCN 2019017367 (print) | LCCN 2019018537 (ebook) | ISBN 9780760365892 (E-Book) | ISBN 9780760365885 | ISBN 9780760365892 (eISBN)
Subjects: LCSH: Automobiles--Models. | Stage props--Models--United States. | Television programs--United States. | LEGO toys.
Classification: LCC TL237 (ebook) | LCC TL237 .B533 2019 (print) | DDC 629.22/12--dc23
LC record available at https://lccn.loc.gov/2019017367

Acquiring Editor: Jordan Wiklund
Art Director: Cindy Samargia Laun
Page Layout: Kim Winscher

Printed in China

CONTENTS

PREFACE

Motorbooks has invited me to create a third LEGO instruction book title. This time the subject is Cars of Film and Television. We learned a few things in putting the first two books together—things that went well and some that went less well.

We found that the listing of parts in the first car book was really difficult to interpret and unfortunately was a source of most of the errors in the book. The solution we implemented for the aircraft book is again found here. First we have included a visual map of every part used in the book, colored white to be as clear as possible. Second, we've included a list of each part code and color code for all the equipment needed for the car builds. Many of the cars are able to be built in more than one color, and I encourage you to explore this option. The colors that are required to build the external body color are highlighted, along with a set of icons to show what alternative combinations are possible.

I have been approached with questions concerning where to get parts. It is clear from conversations with people that the official LEGO site didn't help much. Bricklink really is the only way to go. People also have asked for some help on the part orders, as manually inserting the codes into the various stores isn't so much fun. The plan is to have all the models from the book hosted on Rebrickable; the parts lists will be downloadable but can also be automatically directed to Bricklink against purchase and shop criteria, automating almost the entire process. Look out for some additional free model instructions to build your collection further, along with a few projects that were too big to fit in the book available at extra cost. Search for me under the Designer name lego911.

To add a bit of extra pizazz to the Aircraft book, we printed some of the aircraft insignias, along with nameplates to add to the microplane stand (available as a free additional model on Rebrickable). This time around we are doing the same thing—licence plates and other small prints for most models. Thanks to The Big Brick here in Melbourne for helping out with this. Look for details in Appendix III and the prints that are associated with each model.

Thanks to the Motorbooks team for the opportunity to do the book, along with the resources to develop the copy and to set out the thousands of images that make up the book. In particular, to my Editor and Publisher Zack Miller, art director Cindy Laun, and designer Kim Winscher.

As with the other books, I love to see the models people build themselves. Please tag your creations on social media with the publication title HTBBTVAMC and let me know about them too. I am often in a number of the groups that these may be uploaded and viewed in, and it's always great to see them.

INTRODUCTION

My first book, *How to Build Brick Cars*, was a toe-in-the-water exercise to see if we were able to put together a book with a wide range of 'performance' vehicles in instruction form (yes, I know, what was the 2CV in there for then?).

For this book, the clear focus is cars from film and television. The cars here are not necessarily fast or beautiful—they are part of a story-telling narrative. In researching cars for this book, it became clear that cars are an integral part of 20th-century culture. What also became clear is that the vehicles that most strongly make this cultural impact were made from 1950–1990. Even looking at films and television series made today, a majority of the lead-role vehicles come from this classic period. The oldest car featured in the book is from 1932—the first Ford V8, a model that was popular when new and formed the basis for a car-modifying culture after World War II. The storyline that reflects this is seen in the George Lucas film *American Graffiti* (1973) set in 1962 Modesto, California. The newest car featured as a build here is the 1983 Toyota AE86 Trueno, a seemingly humble hatchback transformed into a Japanese youth icon in the anime *Initial D.*

In my first book I also mention "STEAM"—Science, Technology, Engineering, Arts & Mathematics. Film and television definitely fall into the 'Arts' category of this acronym, but our emotional engagement with art creates the value in much of the other (STEM) work that goes into the creation of cars and films. Herbie is not loved because of his engineering but because of his soul. Similarly each car here is central to its story, whether it be tales of the recklessness of youth, violence, stealing gold bullion, chasing or escaping baddies, or being popular with the ladies.

The book is broken into three sections: Beginner, Intermediate, and Advanced. The Beginner cars are all smaller scale, mostly 1:28, and able to seat standard LEGO minifigs. The Intermediate section cars are built at the larger miniland-scale (1:21) and introduce features such as suspension and brick-built engine models. The Advanced section retains this scale but adds functional LEGO technic piston engines to the model design.

As with the first and second books, I strongly urge you to start at the beginning and work your way through. Necessarily for book space reasons, the instructions are compacted, and it is worthwhile experiencing the progression of complexity and design method that each section builds upon.

Finally, I was struck as an adult by the violent or disturbing themes in many of the films and TV shows these cars are drawn from, even the Herbie franchise. If you are into cinema, I encourage you to experience the media to contextualize the story and the cars, but they may not be appropriate viewing for everyone who buys this book.

Thanks for reading. I hope you enjoy building the cars as much as I enjoyed designing them.

HOW TO USE THIS BOOK

Designing LEGO cars is a skill set that has taken me a great many pleasurable years of building to master. In writing this book through the detailed instructions, I have endeavoured to provide inspirational material to aid builders, new or experienced alike, with design techniques and solutions that they can use to create their own model vehicles.

The selection of cars spans the 1930s to today and covers the evolution of a number of engineering technologies including vee-engines, all-wheel-drive, independent suspension, mid-engine layouts, and other real-life features scaled down to model size.

On first reading, a new builder may find some of the advanced designs beyond their LEGO parts collection, building experience, or comfort zone. I hope that a slow progression through the Beginner and Intermediate designs, and experimenting with some of the techniques introduced into their own building, will give them the confidence to move to the more advanced designs when they are ready for those challenges.

Build Introduction	Symbol/Nomenclature/ Technique	What does it mean? What should I do?
Chapter 1	**1** **29**	The large, bold numbers for the instructions start at 1 and increase progressively. This helps keep track of the stage that the build is in overall and provides some guidance to the next instruction step when alternative designs can be chosen.
Chapter 1	**1** **4**	The small, bold numbers included in the colored box fields show the step level when creating an assembly. An assembly is a collection of parts that create a cohesive structure prior to being joined to the main model.
Chapter 1		This symbol indicates that the assembly or model should be rotated to aid the next step or to see what it looks like from the reverse side.
Chapter 1	**2** ×	A number followed by a lowercase 'x' indicates that the builder should assemble that number of common assemblies. This is usually the case for wheels, seats, and engine parts.
Chapter 1	**9** LHS	This symbol indicates that the following assembly steps show how to build the left-hand side (LHS) of the model. It also indicates that this assembly stage should additionally be built in a reflected right-hand side assembly. **It is recommended to assemble the LHS and RHS assemblies at the same time as mirrors of each other.**
Chapter 1		Arrows (red, black, or orange) indicate the position for smaller assemblies to be placed on the main model, where this might be difficult to see clearly.

For the advanced builder, I hope that the less complex models are nonetheless a rewarding building exercise at a smaller scale, and that the more complex models reveal a more intricate world of model building—one that more closely reflects the challenges and rewards of designing and engineering real cars for the real world.

INSTRUCTIONS AND SYMBOLS

The following pages of building instructions introduce various symbols and nomenclature progressively through the chapters, allowing for the instruction set to be condensed in the available pages while still maintaining instruction clarity. The following symbols and typography are there to aid the builder in selecting the correct parts at each building stage, preparing intermediate assemblies, and connecting to the base model architecture.

Please check through these instruction symbols before you start building, and feel free to return to check what they mean at any time.

Chapter Introduction	Symbol/Nomenclature/ Technique	What does it mean? What should I do?
Chapter 2		Many of the car models have brick-built windows. The instructions to build these can be quite confusing. To aid the process, the parts to be added at each instruction stage are colored pale yellow.
Chapter 2	17	Similar to the red arrow symbol—the arrow followed by a number, i.e. [17] indicates that the main instruction stage 17 is the assembly that should be attached at the position indicated by the arrow.
Chapter 6	4	This symbol indicates the length (in standard bricks) of the LEGO Technic axle to be used at this assembly stage.
Chapter 11	4x Wheel Trim	For parts where there is no easy indication as to which part exactly is required, a word description is used to make this clear.

DETAILS AND CUSTOMIZATION

As you progress through the models, you will observe that they have employed different part and assembly solutions for systems that might be common between vehicles. In particular, LEGO has wheel and tires that are available in close approximate geometric measurements. Though these wheels have a specific millimetric measure, it is much simpler to refer to them by their approximate LEGO part dimension.

For this book, most of the smaller models use wheel and tire combinations approximating 3-studs (24mm) diameter and in various widths. Unfortunately, this does not quite mean that they will fit inside a 3-stud gap, so creative solutions are required to provide close fitting wheel arches that nonetheless allow the wheel to spin freely. For the larger Miniland-scale cars, wheel and tire combinations approximating 4-studs (32mm) are used in this case, as they closely fit a 4-stud gap. When building any of these models, please use the wheels and tires you have available. Additionally, there are a variety of creative ways of designing fancy wheel trims or hubcaps, and I encourage the builder to select designs that suit their style, as would a customizer in real life.

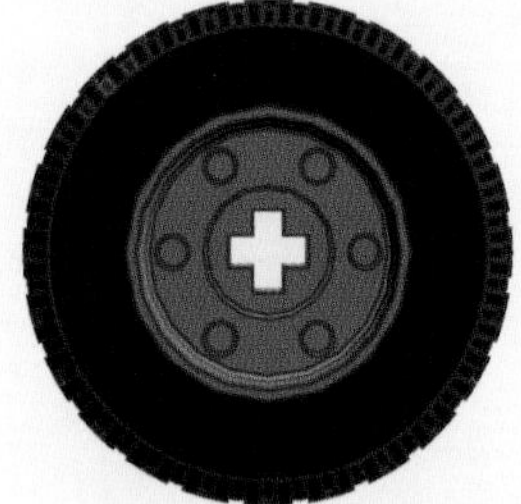

32mm: 55982 & 58090

24mm: 18976 & 18977

Most of the models in this book have been created to an exact specification of vehicle. The Mini is a case in point. There has been a great variety of Minis over nearly 40 years of its production history. Each model changes by a little or a lot. Even within a single year of production there will be considerable variation in details such as wheels, spoilers, light units, seat designs, rear view mirror placement, and antennae. If you want to follow the instructions precisely, enjoy. If you want to build the model with your own eye for customization—be my guest!

I DON'T HAVE ANY TECHNIC—HOW CAN I BUILD THE COMPLEX MODELS?

To this good question, I have two hopefully helpful answers:

1. If your LEGO collection lacks any of the pieces required to build the model, never fear; there are ways and means of obtaining these parts. It does involve making purchases over the internet, and this is best done by a trusted adult. You can buy parts directly from the LEGO Company via the LEGO Shop@Home service—a place to purchase full LEGO sets and also spare parts. This website is available across most of Europe, Asia, and the Americas.
2. Alternatively, the preferred option is to purchase online via a service called Bricklink. Bricklink is a web portal for thousands of individual stores around the world. Most will be able to supply common parts while some others also will be able to supply special and rare parts. The LEGO Company has no affiliation with the Bricklink service, so there are more risks associated with pricing, purchase, and shipping.

PART SUBSTITUTIONS

As you build through the book you may find other parts are unavailable in your LEGO collections and via online retailers. If this is the case, remember, LEGO is a pretty adaptable building medium—there is always another way to build an assembly of parts other than the one shown. Use your imagination and try with the parts you do have. This is what expert MOC builders do every time they design their own models. It is the essence of their creativity.

COLORS

One of the most fun things about LEGO is the vibrancy and range of colors. Models in this book have been selected on color to satisfy a generally available palette. In each chapter, a color guide will indicate what colors that model can be built in from the many available. Unfortunately not every part is available in each of the LEGO colors, and often the hinges, wedge plates, headlight bricks, wheel arches, and other specialist bricks may limit the option to build exactly from the instructions. But remember, with just a slight part substitution, many more colors may be available, perhaps even your favorites!

SECTION 1

FOUNDATION

The Section 1 models represent a first step to building some cool Hollywood cars. Though small, each car has some pretty tricky design solutions that belie their size.

These models are not generic LEGO cars for kids. They are detail-modeled at a smaller scale (1:28), take less time to build, and do not require many specialist pieces. Most of the models here can seat LEGO minifigs.

If you have my first book, *How to Build Brick Cars*, or collect the official LEGO SpeedChampions line, the cars here will fit with your collection of minifig-scale vehicles. As you build the models you will find that even at this scale, the models can incorporate many cool features.

PONTIAC FIREBIRD—K.I.T.T.
KNIGHT RIDER

Fancy a car that can talk and even drive by itself? Today this technology seems to be just around the corner, but in 1982 when NBC launched *Knight Rider*, a TV show starring a computerized Pontiac Trans Am and an open-shirted, skinny-jeaned David Hasselhoff as the seat-warming sidekick, the future had arrived.

The star of the show was K.I.T.T., short for Knight Industries Two Thousand, voiced by William Daniels. K.I.T.T. was a crime-fighting machine full of advanced technology that for some reason had been installed in a 1982 Pontiac coupe.

In the fantasy world of the show, K.I.T.T. had a turbojet engine with modified afterburners fitted to an eight-speed microprocessor-controlled turbodrive transmission—with autopilot for driverless operation. Off screen, Pontiac's 1982 Trans Am shared a platform with the Chevrolet Camaro. The car could be fitted with one of two versions of the Chevrolet 305 cubic-inch V8, producing 165 hp (123 kW) in fuel-injected form and 145 hp (108 kW) carburetted. In reviewing the show today, the ability to drive at very high speed across the desert utilizing K.I.T.T.'s gas-turbine engine seems fun, but it might not help crime-fighting in areas with traffic.

COUNTRY OF ORIGIN:	United States
PRODUCTION:	Third Generation 1982–1992
NUMBER MADE:	840,669
LAYOUT/DRIVE:	Front engine, Rear-wheel-drive
ENGINE:	5.0 liter, 8 cylinders, Vee
POWER TORQUE:	165 hp (123 kW) / 240 lb-ft (325 Nm)
CONSTRUCTION/DOORS:	Steel Monocoque / two-door Coupe
TV/FILM APPEARANCE:	*Knight Rider* (1982–1986)

Joking aside, K.I.T.T. did preview many technologies that very soon will be common in production cars. K.I.T.T. could drive and park by itself, make phone calls and download data (prior to the invention of the public internet), receive voice commands and respond, and navigate via maps and the prevailing traffic conditions.

The original *Knight Rider* was broadcast for four seasons (1982–1986) and was reprised in 1997 and 2008 each for a single, poorly received season.

Knight Rider and K.I.T.T. made a lasting cultural impact, having been referenced in dozens of TV shows and movies because of their reflection of 1980s pop culture, the stunts performed during the series, and the futuristic technology featured in the car.

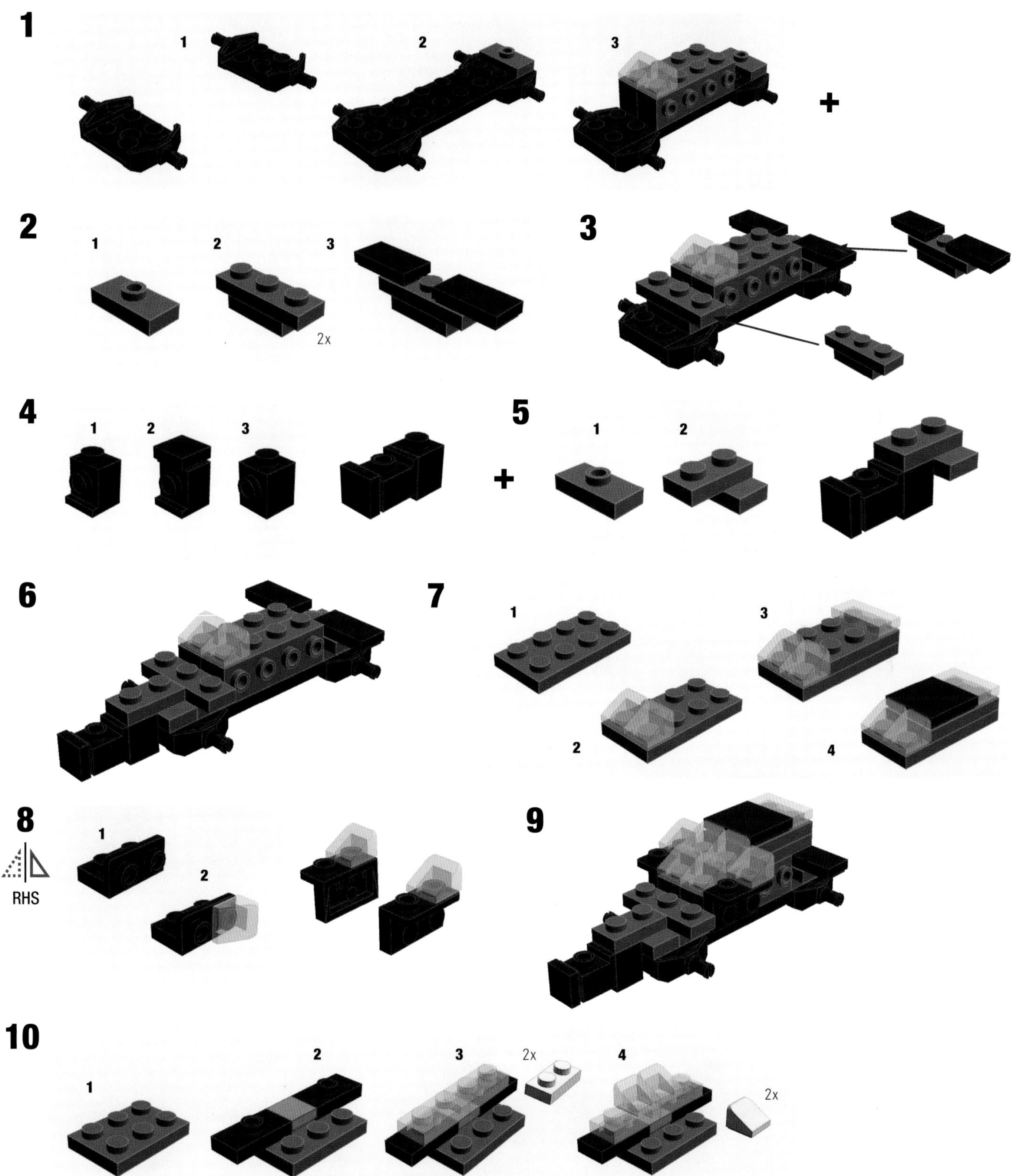

1
1
2
3
+
2
1
2
3
2x
3
4
1
2
3
+
5
1
2
6
7
1
3
2
4
8
1
2
RHS
9
10
1
2
3
2x
4
2x

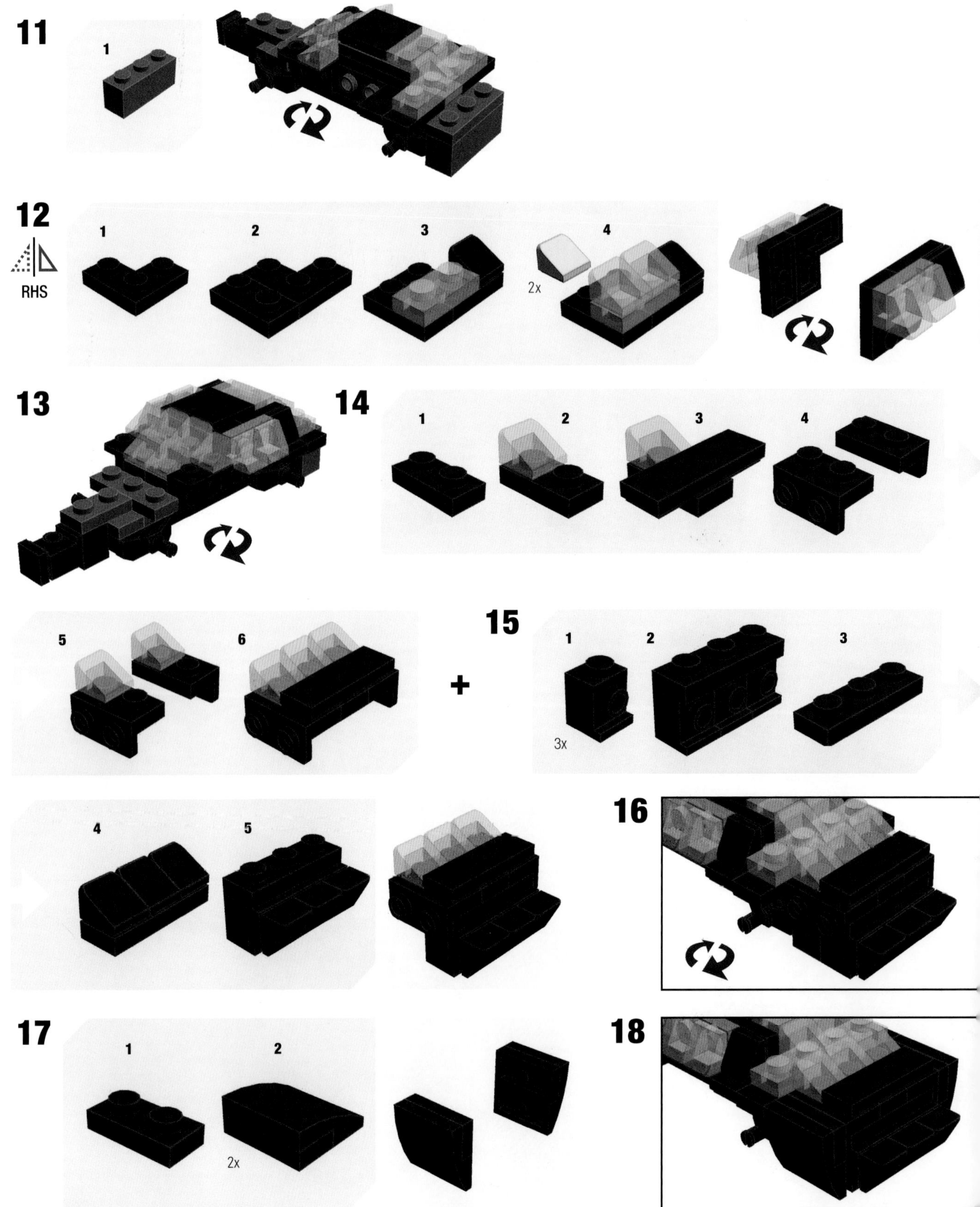

11
1
12
RHS
1
2
3
4
2x
13
14
1
2
3
4
5
6
+
15
1
2
3
3x
4
5
16
17
1
2
2x
18

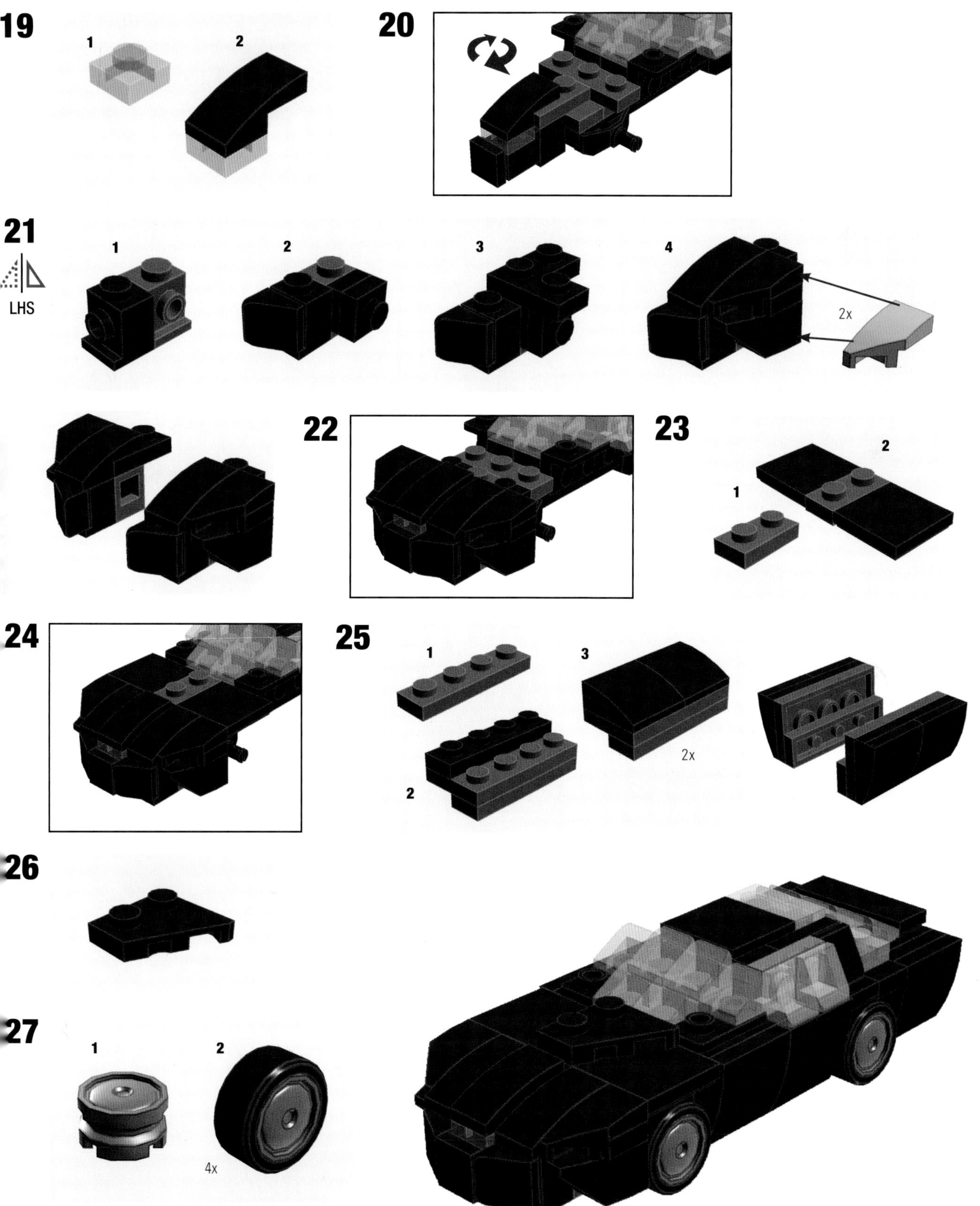
19
1
2
20
21
LHS
1
2
3
4
2x
22
23
2
1
24
25
1
3
2x
2
26
27
1
2
4x

FERRARI 250 GT SWB CALIFORNIA SPYDER

FERRIS BUELLER'S DAY OFF

Any Ferrari 250 GT SWB California Spyder today is probably worth more than $2 million. Some have sold at auction for nearly $20 million. You could imagine, then, how it would feel if, as a 17-year-old, you smashed one that your father owned. This could spell trouble.

In the 1986 film *Ferris Bueller's Day Off*, the car in question fortunately was one of three replica cars built for the film by Modena Design and Development. The real car was rare—only 56 were built—and extremely valuable.

The California Spyder was built in two configurations from 1957 to 1963. The original long-wheelbase (LWB) convertible was produced from 1957 to 1960. The short-wheelbase (SWB) version reproduced for the film was made from 1960 to 1963. The SWB California was fitted with an evolution of Ferrari's 3.0 L "Colombo" V12, producing 276 hp (206 kW), just 20 hp shy of the racing GTO model.

Only three examples of the already lightweight SWB California were fitted with even lighter aluminum bodywork in place of steel.

The magic, though, was the Pininfarina styling—open topped and classically beautiful. As Ferris, played by Matthew Broderick, exclaims, "It is so choice. If you have the means, I highly recommend picking one up."

The Ferrari in the context of the film was owned by the father of Ferris's best friend Cameron (played by Alan Ruck). While trying to wind the mileage back by running the car in reverse gear whilst up on axle stands, Cameron kicks the front of the car, angry at his father's life priorities. One last nudge and the Ferrari falls off the stands and sails out of the window of the mid-century Ben Rose House in Highland Park, Illinois, crashing into the valley floor below.

As Ferris says to Cameron, "No, you don't want this much heat."

COUNTRY OF ORIGIN: Italy

PRODUCTION: 1960–1963

NUMBER MADE: 56

LAYOUT/DRIVE: Front engine, Rear-wheel-drive

ENGINE: 3.0 liter, 12 cylinders, Vee

POWER TORQUE: 276 bhp (206 kW) / 206 lb-ft (280 Nm)

CONSTRUCTION/DOORS: Tubular Steel / two-door Spyder

TV/FILM APPEARANCE: *Ferris Bueller's Day Off*

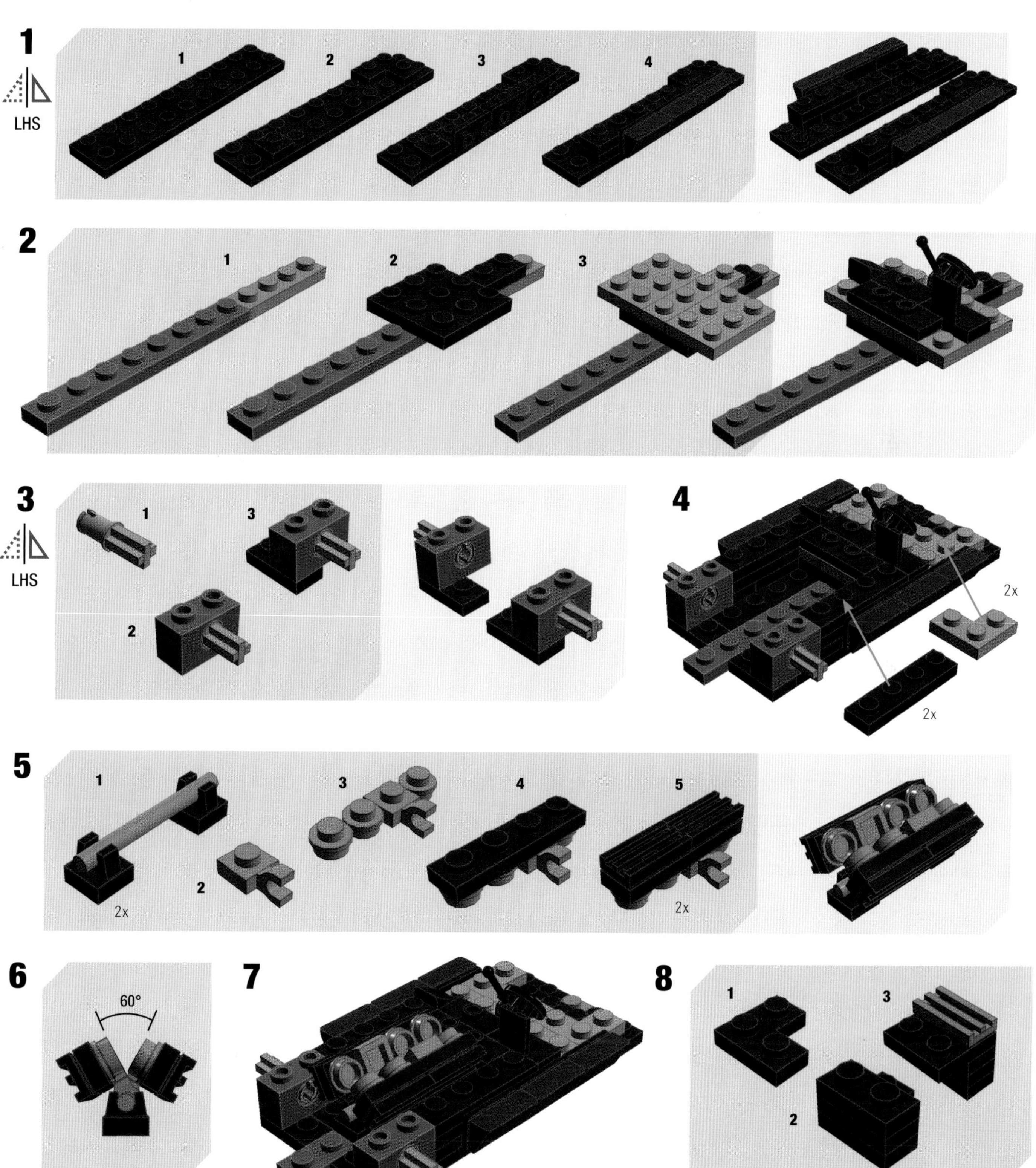
1
LHS
1
2
3
4
2
1
2
3
3
LHS
1
3
2
4
2x
2x
5
1
3
4
5
2x
2
2x
6
60°
7
8
1
3
2

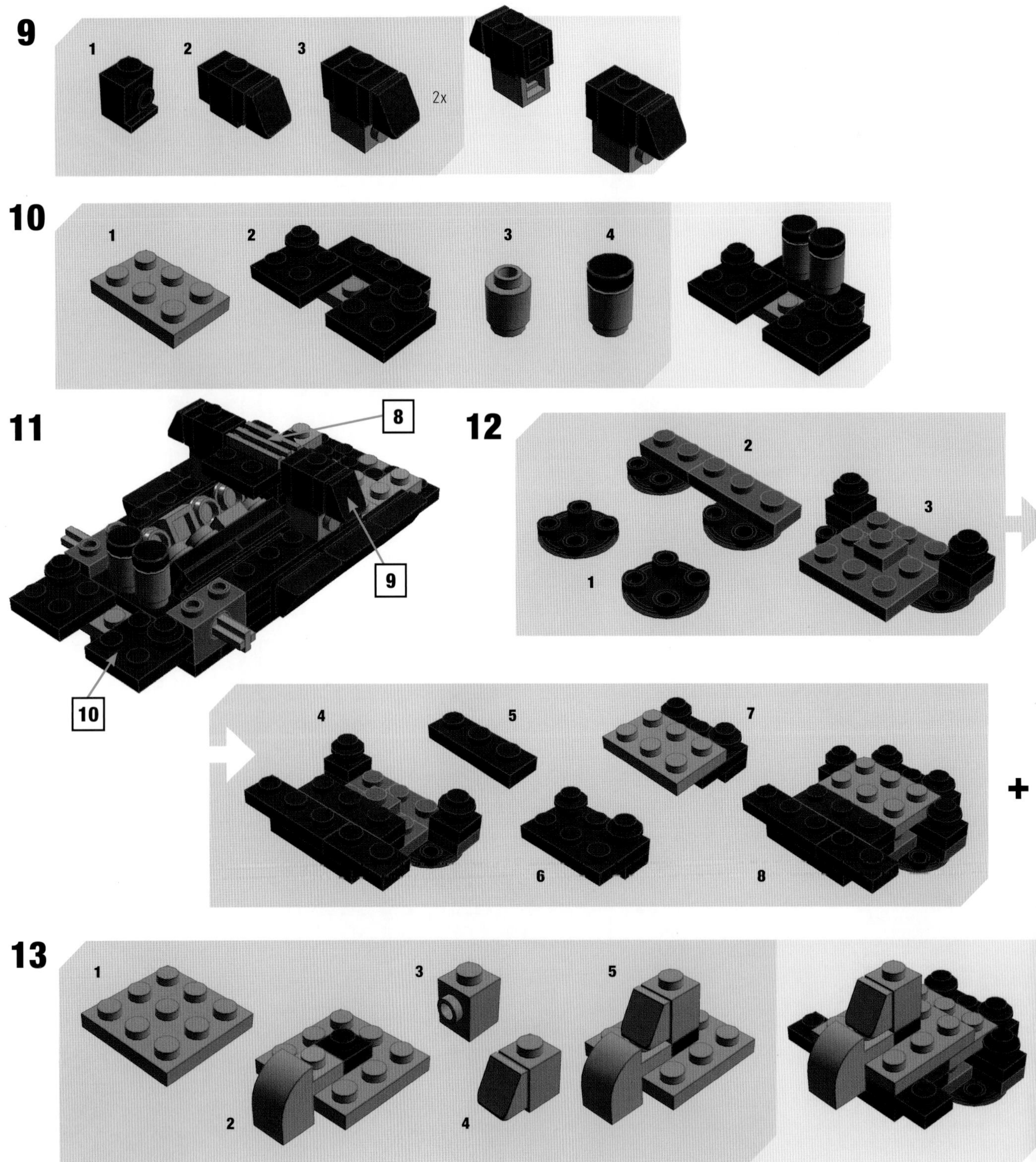
9
1
2
3
2x
10
1
2
3
4
11
8
9
10
12
2
3
1
4
5
7
6
8
+
13
1
3
5
2
4

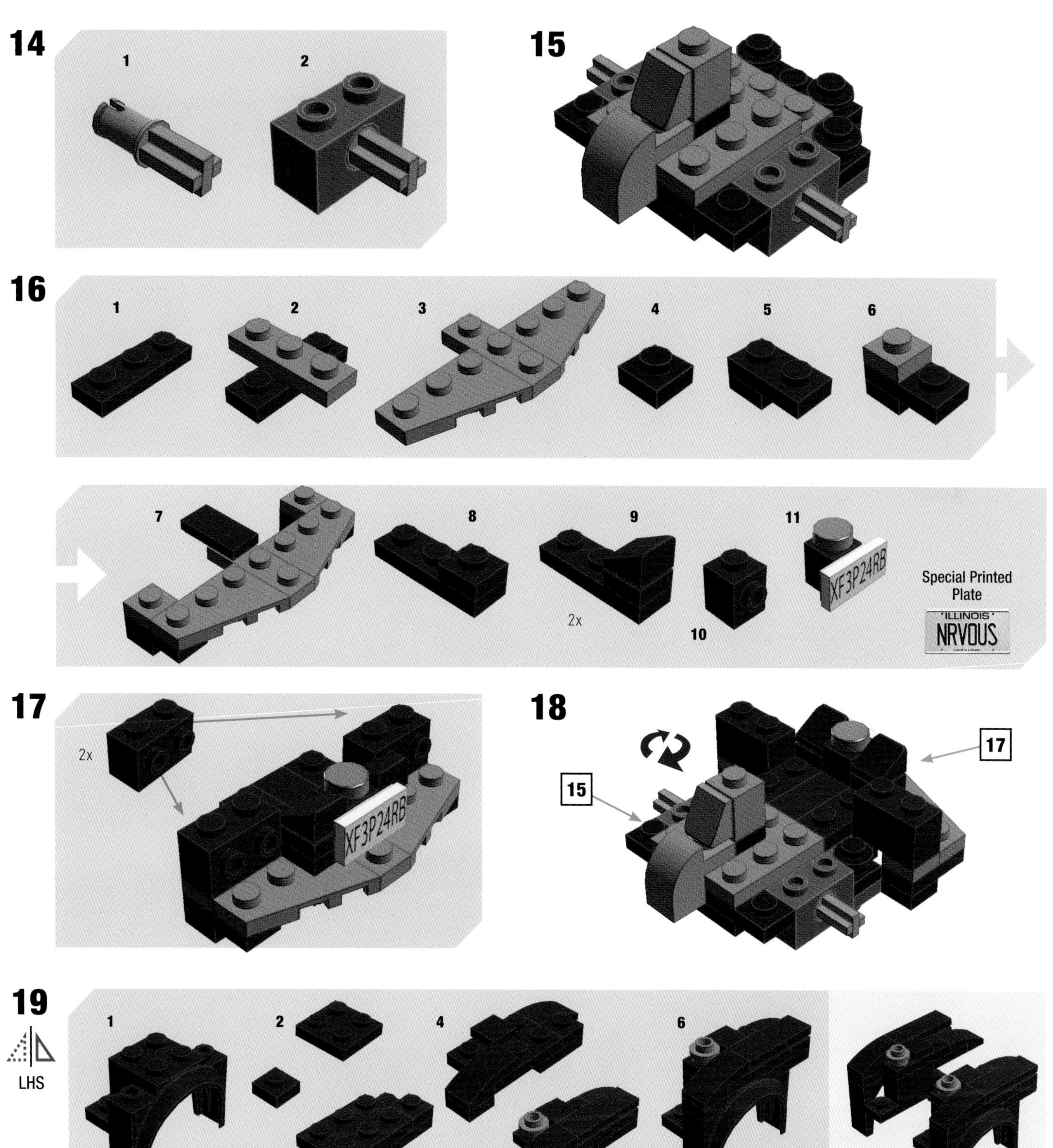
14
1
2
15
16
1
2
3
4
5
6
7
8
9
11
2x
10
Special Printed Plate
XF3P24RB
ILLINOIS
NRVOUS
17
2x
XF3P24RB
18
17
15
19
LHS
1
2
4
6
3
5

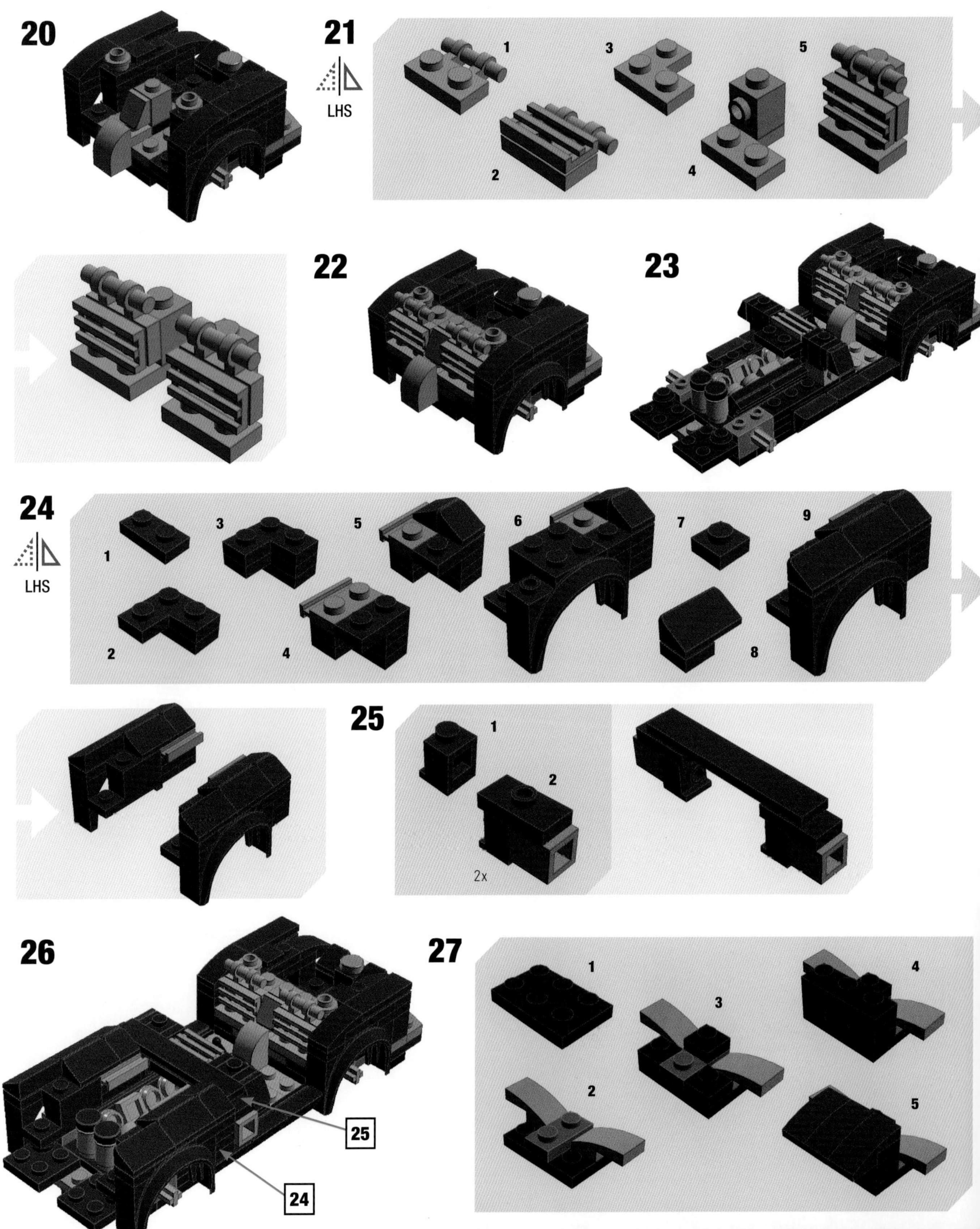
20
21
LHS
1
2
3
4
5
22
23
24
LHS
1
2
3
4
5
6
7
8
9
25
1
2
2x
26
25
24
27
1
2
3
4
5

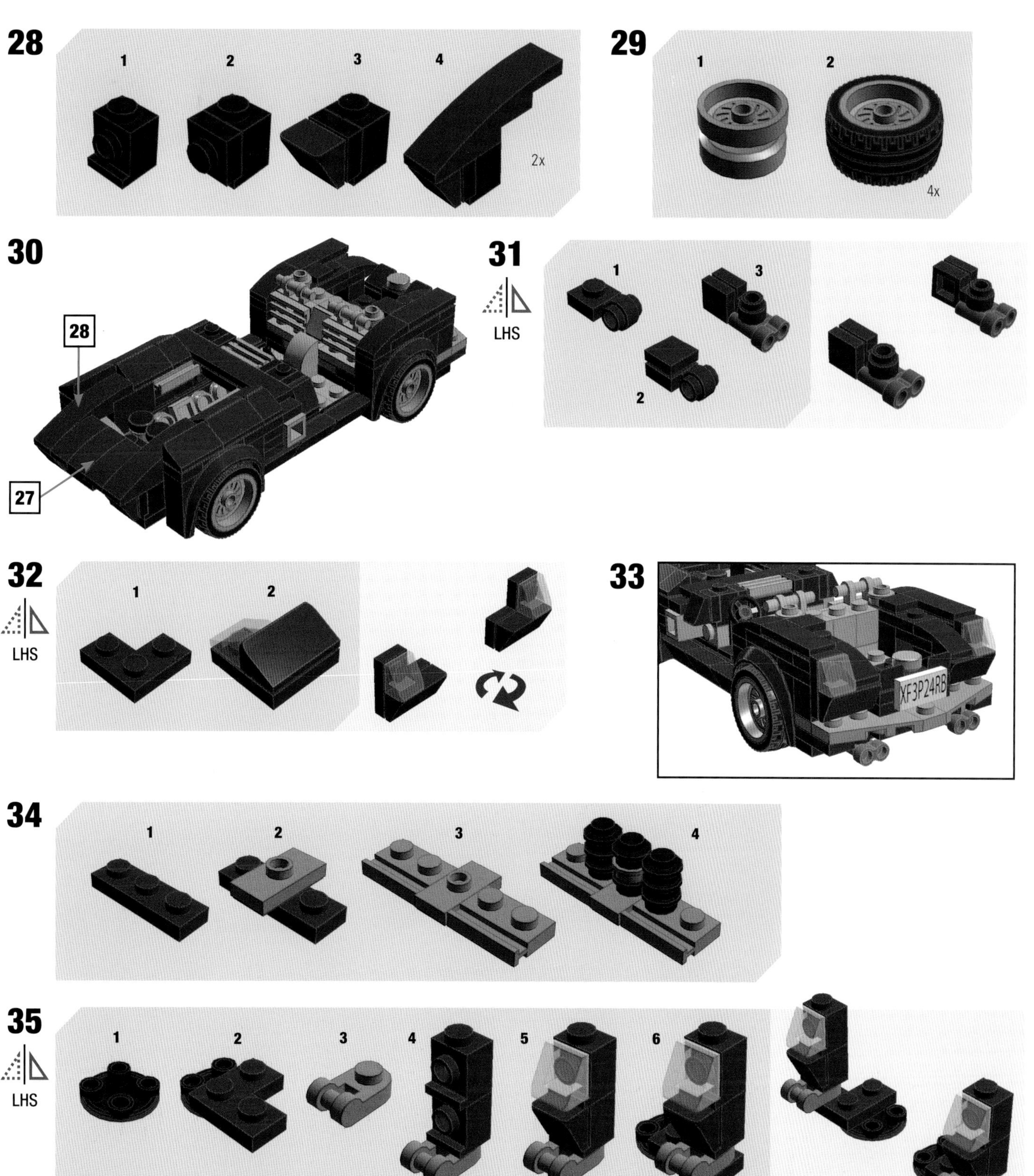
28
1
2
3
4
2x
29
1
2
4x
30
28
27
31
LHS
1
3
2
32
LHS
1
2
33
XF3P24RB
34
1
2
3
4
35
LHS
1
2
3
4
5
6

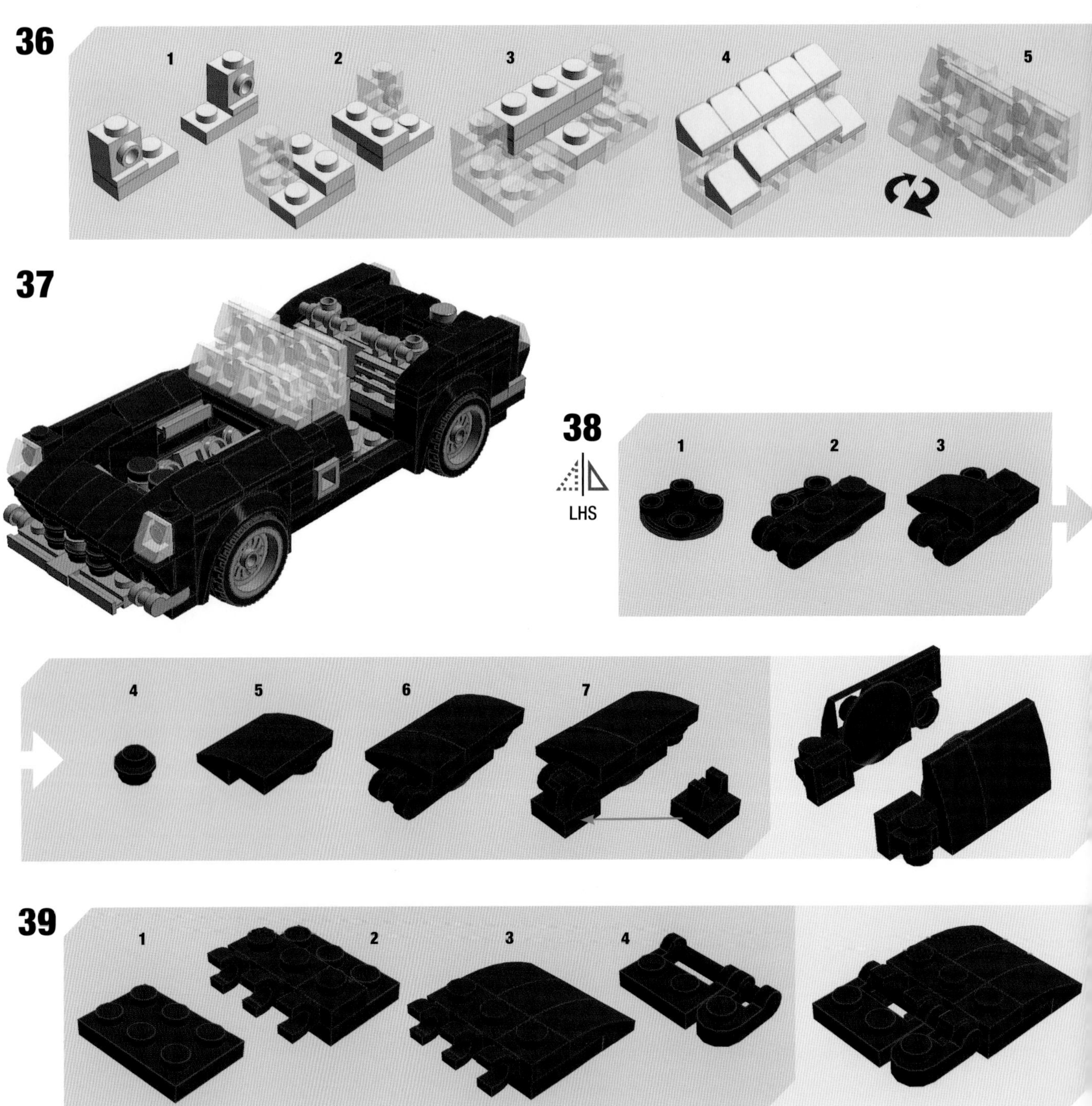
36
1
2
3
4
5
37
38
LHS
1
2
3
4
5
6
7
39
1
2
3
4

40

41

CHAPTER 3

FERRARI 365 GTS/4 SPYDER
MIAMI VICE

They say that imitation is the sincerest form of flattery. Ferrari didn't quite see it this way when NBC launched the 1984 show *Miami Vice*. The beautiful 1972 Ferrari 3z65 GTS/4 Spyder featured in the show was a fake—a replica car, built by McBurnie Coachcraft over a Chevrolet C3 Corvette frame and engine, that wore Ferrari insignia.

You might be curious as to why TV cops would be driving a rare and expensive Ferrari, but that was all part of the show. Set in neon 1980s Miami, the show's Vice division dealt with narcotics, money laundering, and other organized crime, all taking place under sunny Florida skies. The logic behind the fancy cars was a legal statute regarding asset forfeiture that permitted law enforcement agencies to confiscate the property of drug dealers for official use. The Ferrari 365 GTS/4 was a perfect prop for law men negotiating elicit deals—though surely word would get around that the guys in the black Daytona were actually cops.

That said, a real Ferrari Spyder was probably out of budget for the show—only 122 open cars officially were built from the total of 1,406 Daytonas. Many Berlinettas have subsequently been converted to open cars, though these have less value than authentic Spyders. The Daytona is a brutally fast car, hurled by its 347 hp (259 kW) 4.4 L V12 to a top speed of 174 mph (280 km/h). The car is also stunning to behold—classic proportions draped in distinctive bodywork by Pininfarina under the pen of Leonardo Fioravanti.

Despite the car being a fake, the profile and success of *Miami Vice* led to a compromise. During the third season, the fake Daytona disappeared in a fiery inferno, only to be replaced by the then brand-new Ferrari Testarossa—a real one provided courtesy of Ferrari North America.

COUNTRY OF ORIGIN: Italy

PRODUCTION: 1971–1973

NUMBER MADE: 122 Spyders (1,406 total Daytonas)

LAYOUT/DRIVE: Front engine, Rear-wheel-drive

ENGINE: 4.4 liter, 12 cylinders, Vee

POWER TORQUE: 347 hp (259 kW) / 318 lb-ft (431 Nm)

CONSTRUCTION/DOORS: Tubular Steel / two-door Spyder

TV/FILM APPEARANCE: *Miami Vice* (1984–1985)

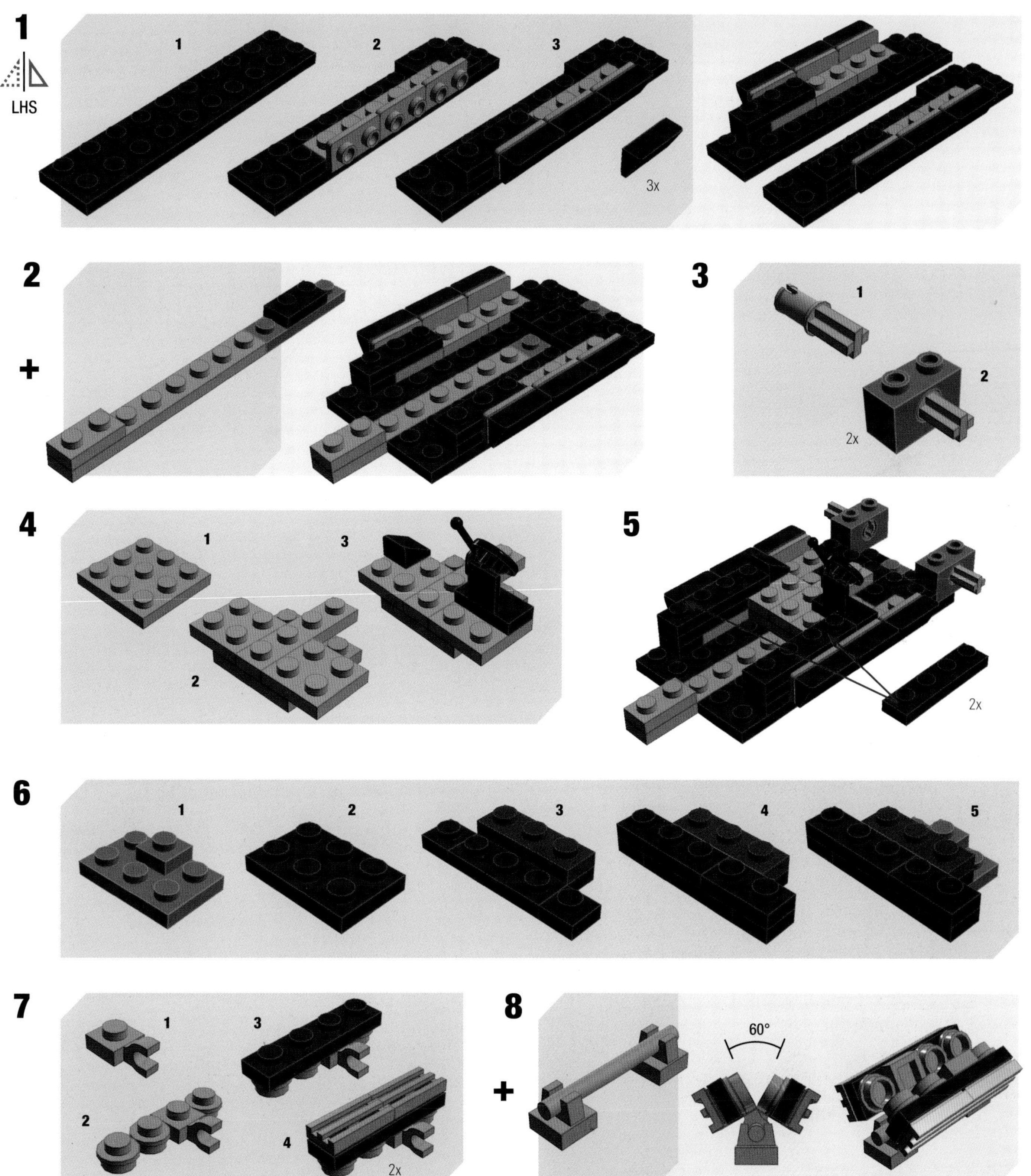
1
LHS
1
2
3
3x
2
+
3
1
2
2x
4
1
3
2
5
2x
6
1
2
3
4
5
7
1
3
2
4
2x
8
+
60°

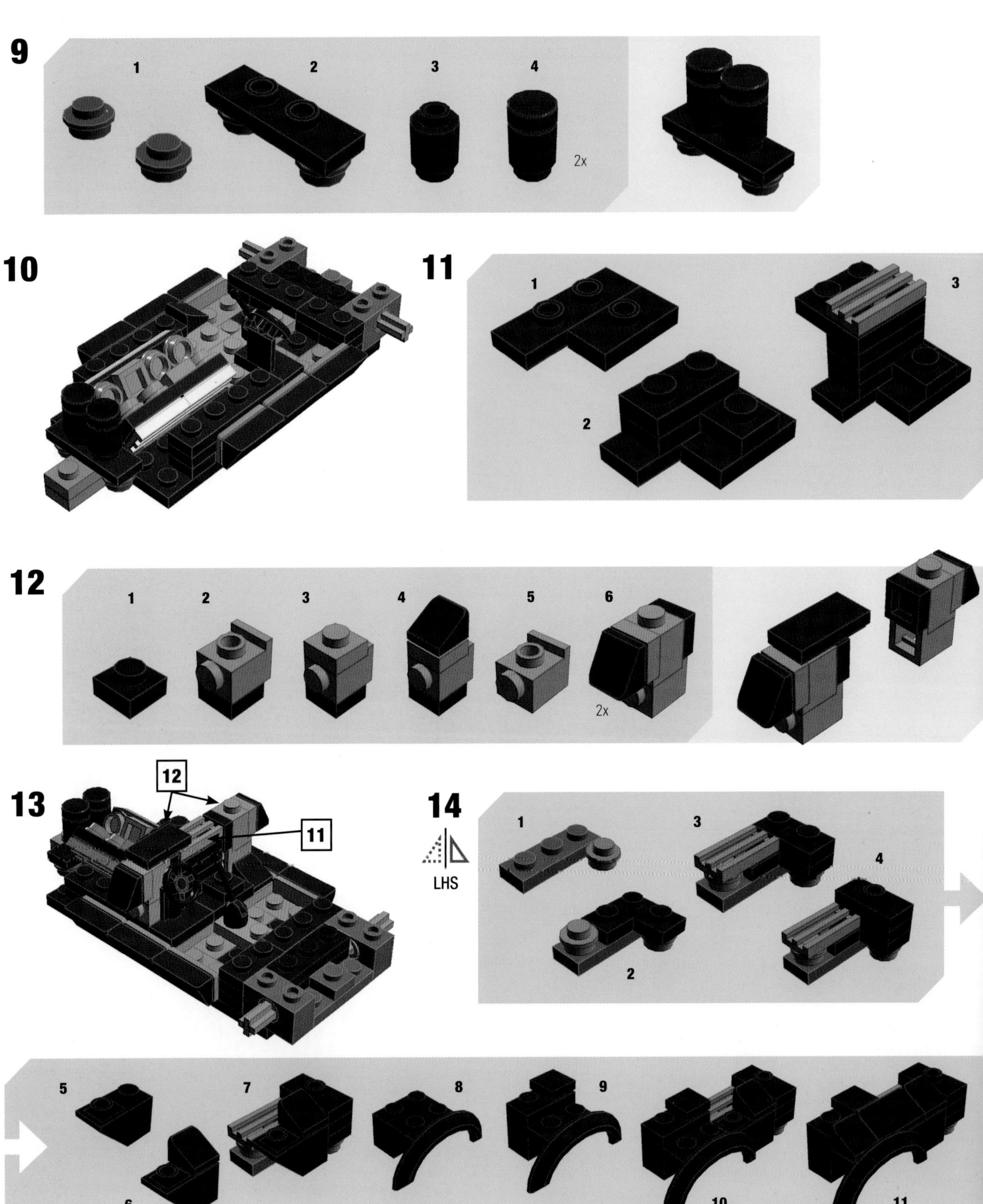
9
1
2
3
4
2x
10
11
1
2
3
12
1
2
3
4
5
6
2x
13
12
11
14
LHS
1
2
3
4
5
6
7
8
9
10
11

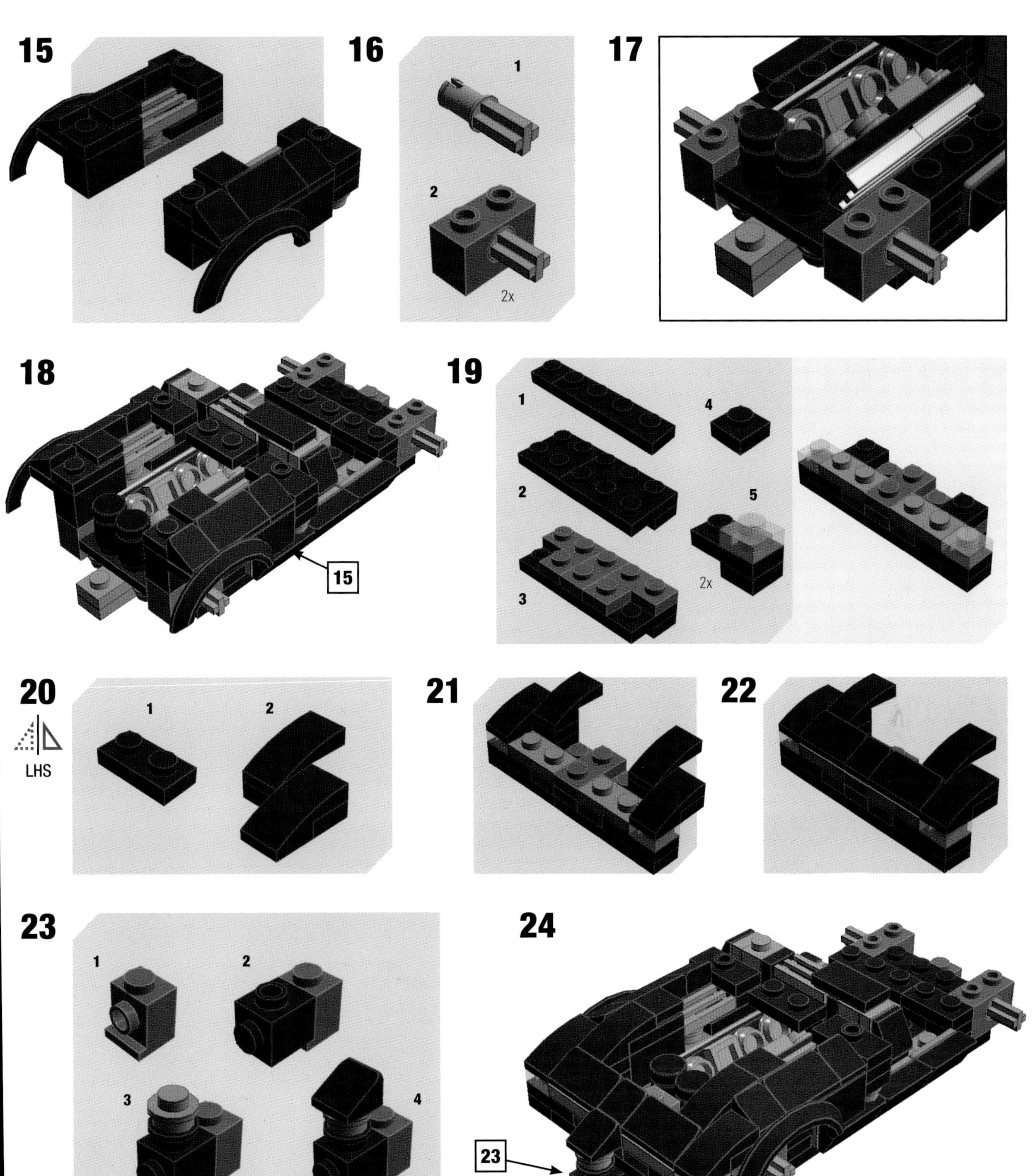
15
16
1
2
2x
17
18
15
19
1
4
2
5
3
2x
20
1
2
LHS
21
22
23
1
2
3
4
24
23

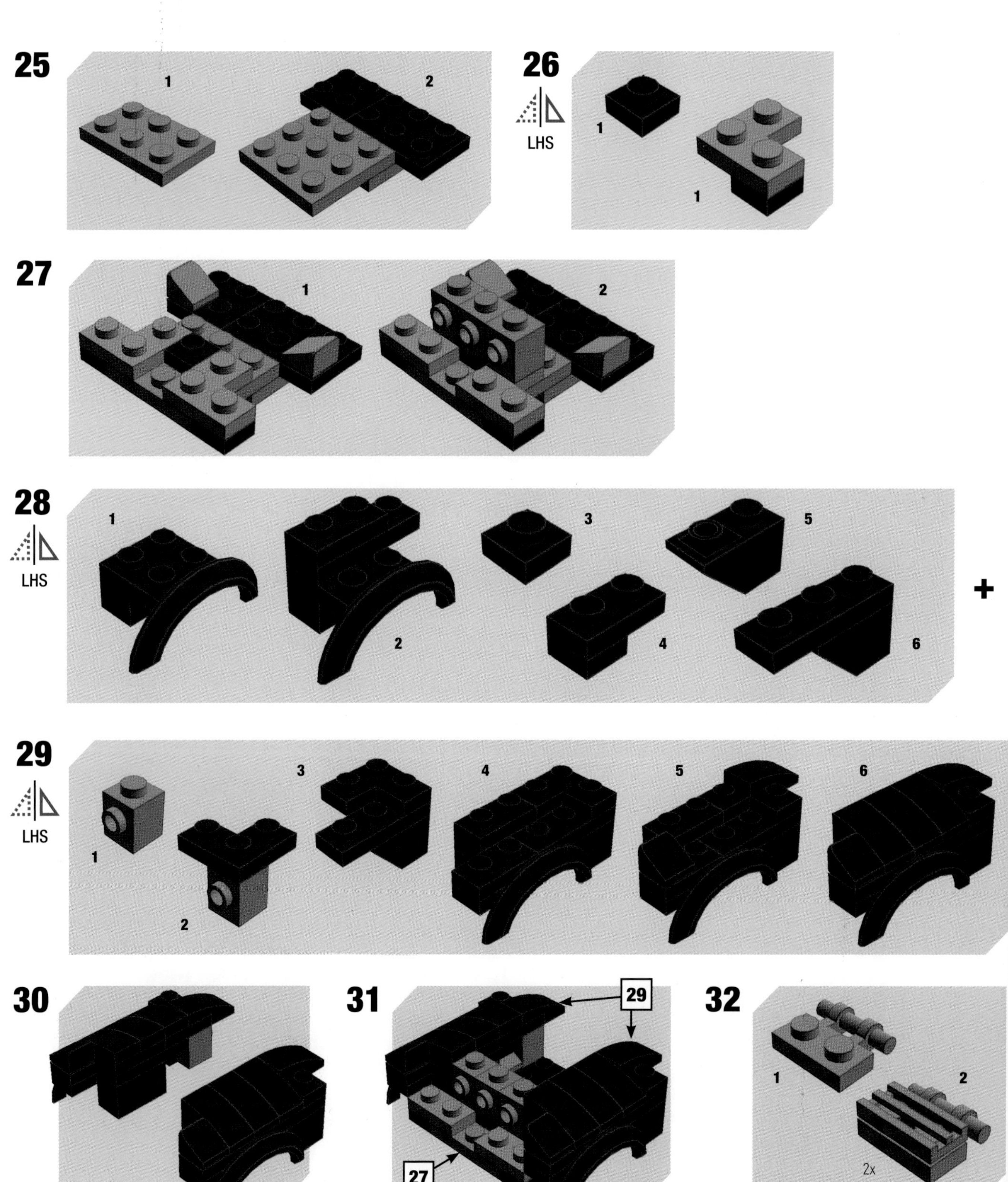
25
1
2
26
LHS
1
1
27
1
2
28
LHS
1
2
3
4
5
6
+
29
LHS
1
2
3
4
5
6
30
31
29
27
32
1
2
2x

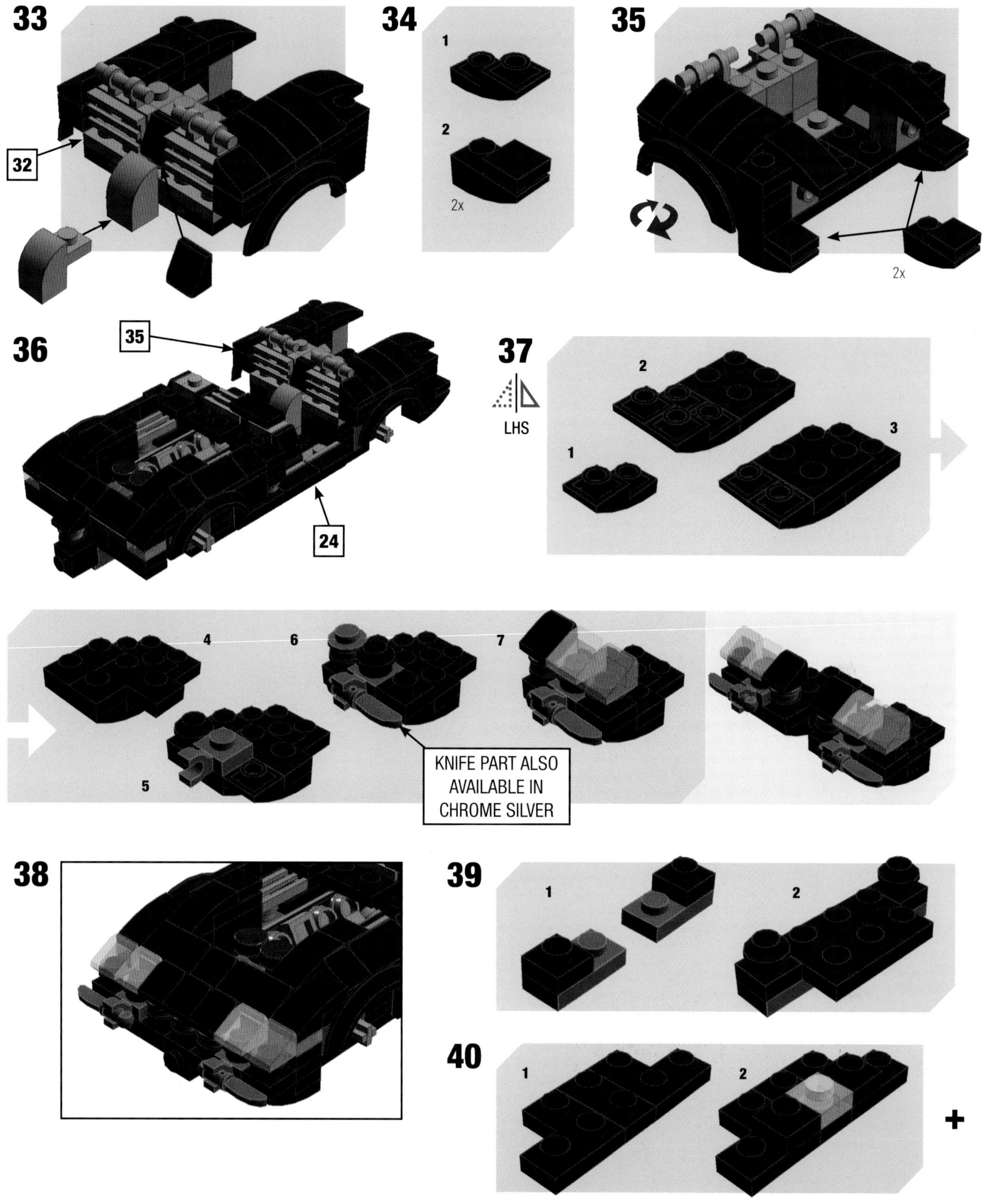
33
32
34
1
2
2x
35
2x
36
35
24
37
LHS
2
1
3
4
6
7
5
KNIFE PART ALSO
AVAILABLE IN
CHROME SILVER
38
39
1
2
40
1
2
+

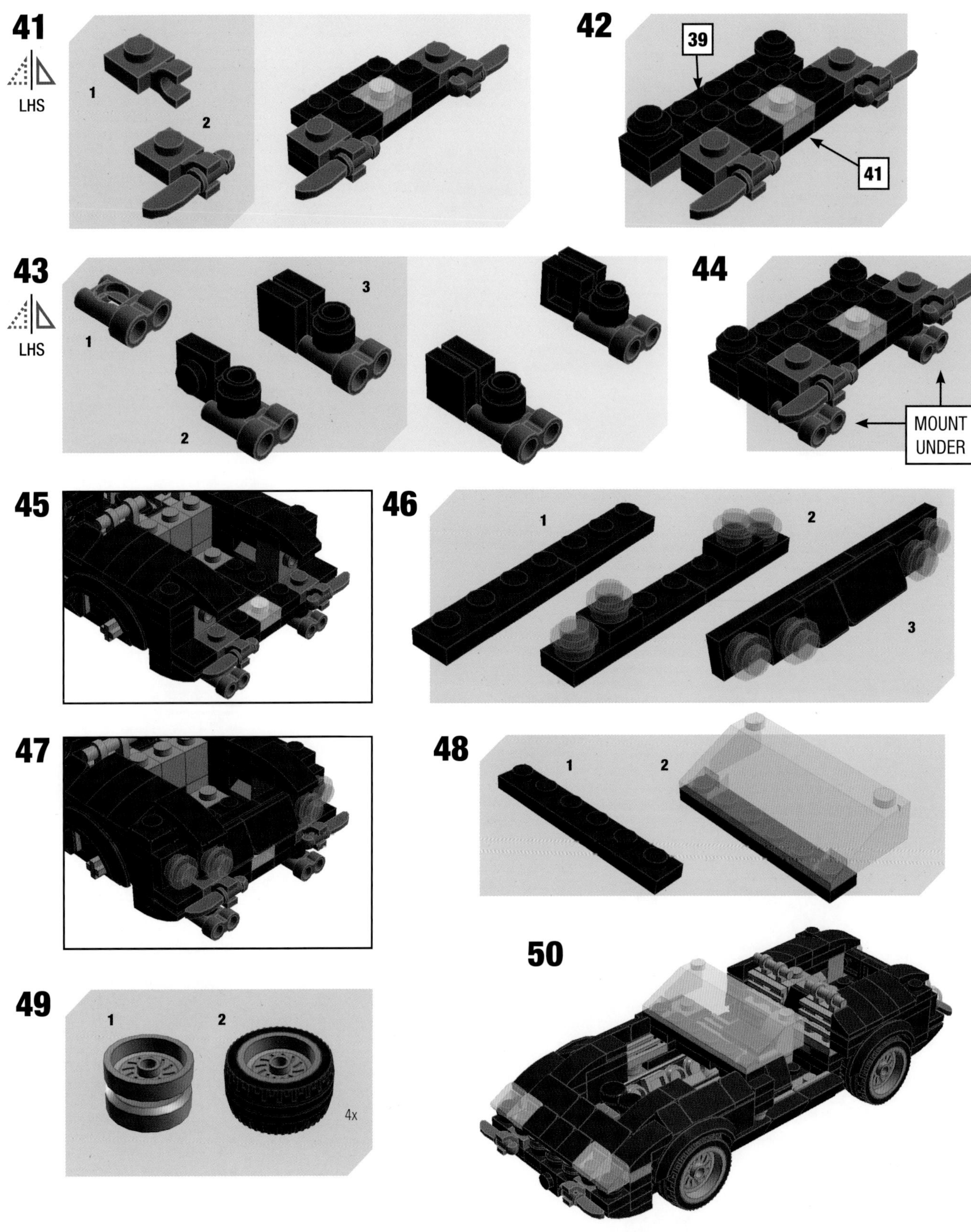
41
LHS
1
2
42
39
41
43
LHS
1
2
3
44
MOUNT
UNDER
45
46
1
2
3
47
48
1
2
49
1
2
4x
50

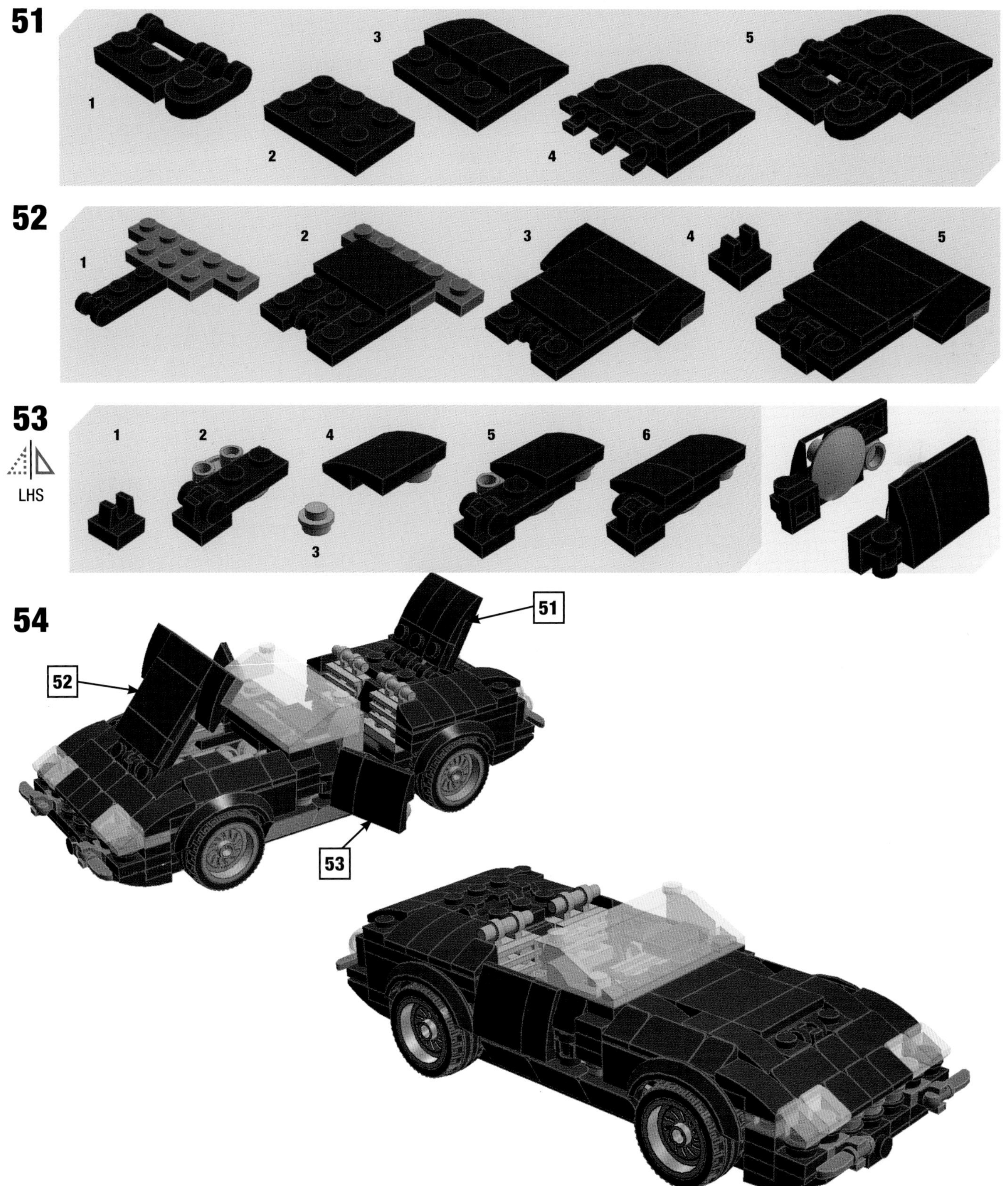
51
1
2
3
4
5
52
1
2
3
4
5
53
LHS
1
2
3
4
5
6
54
51
52
53

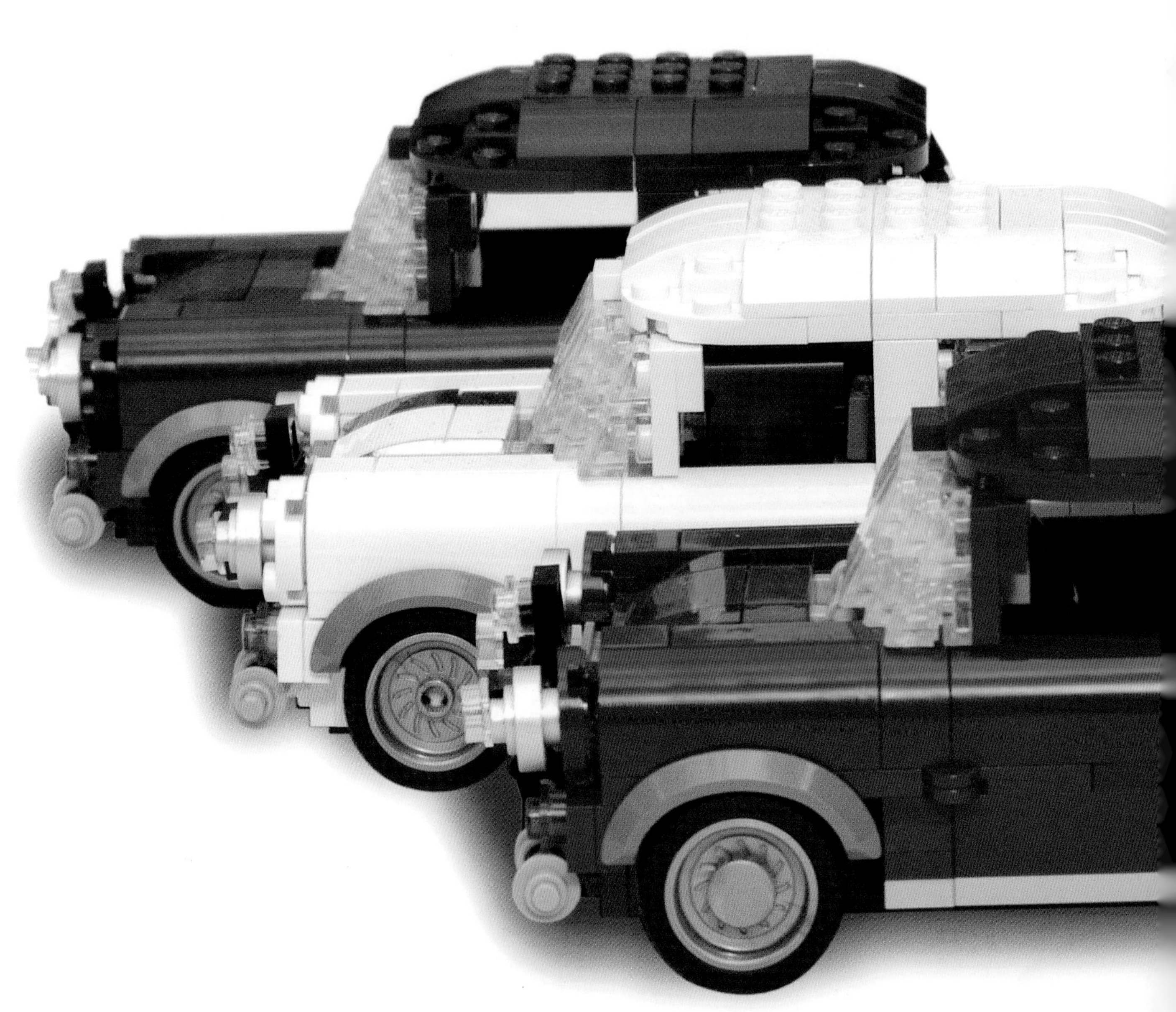

SECTION 2

INTERMEDIATE

Many of the models in this section are movie favorites known for their distinctive shapes and colors. They often appeared in different form in more than one movie, so look out for the alternative colors that can be used along with customizations to build them as a seen in a different film or context.

The models in Section 2 move to a larger scale—Miniland (1:20)—the scale used in the Legoland theme parks across the globe. The larger scale allows scope for introducing more advanced LEGO modeling techniques.

Most of these cars include suspension systems, and there are a couple of different design solutions within the models that can be adapted to other vehicles.

At this scale, the models can also include added details like brick-built engines, engine compartments, doors, luggage compartments, and interiors. Though these models include some very specific details, I encourage the builder to see them as a basis for creating models personalized to their own taste.

CHAPTER 4

MINI COOPER S
THE ITALIAN JOB

At the start of the 1969 film *The Italian Job*, one is led to believe that the automotive star of the film will be a brand new orange Lamborghini Miura being driven through curvaceous mountain passes in northern Italy. This notion is brought to an abrupt halt when the car collides with a bulldozer and is pushed over the edge of the road into the chasm below.

The film, released by Paramount Pictures, is a comedy caper about a crew of British crooks trying to steal gold bullion. Our characterful felons hatch a plan to steal the gold from the FIAT factory in Turin, Italy. The real automotive stars, the three Minis (red, white, and blue), are modified to carry the gold through the streets of Turin; the police and mafia are unable to catch them due to the traffic chaos caused by a deliberate misprogramming of the city's traffic signals. The small size of the Minis allows them to navigate through shopping arcades and even the sewer system (filmed in the UK) before the gold is transferred to a soccer tour bus.

No more spoilers though, in case you haven't seen the film.

The Mini was, by this stage, ten years old, but *The Italian Job* cemented the Mini in popular culture just as much as the car's association with the Beatles and its placement as street furniture in almost every British film during the decade. When BMW sought to create a new Mini in 2001, a remake of the film shot in the United States in 2003 was a key ingredient in bringing back some of the nostalgic Mini magic.

COUNTRY OF ORIGIN: United Kingdom
PRODUCTION: 1959–2000
NUMBER MADE: Cooper S 26,870 (5,387,862 total Mini)
LAYOUT/DRIVE: Front engine, Front-wheel-drive
ENGINE: 1,275 cc, 4 cylinders
POWER TORQUE: 76 hp (56.7 kW) / 80 lb-ft (108 Nm)
CONSTRUCTION/DOORS: Steel Monocoque / two-door Sedan
TV/FILM APPEARANCE: *The Italian Job* (1969)

ITLN JOB
GPF 146G
HMP 729G
LGW 809G
GB

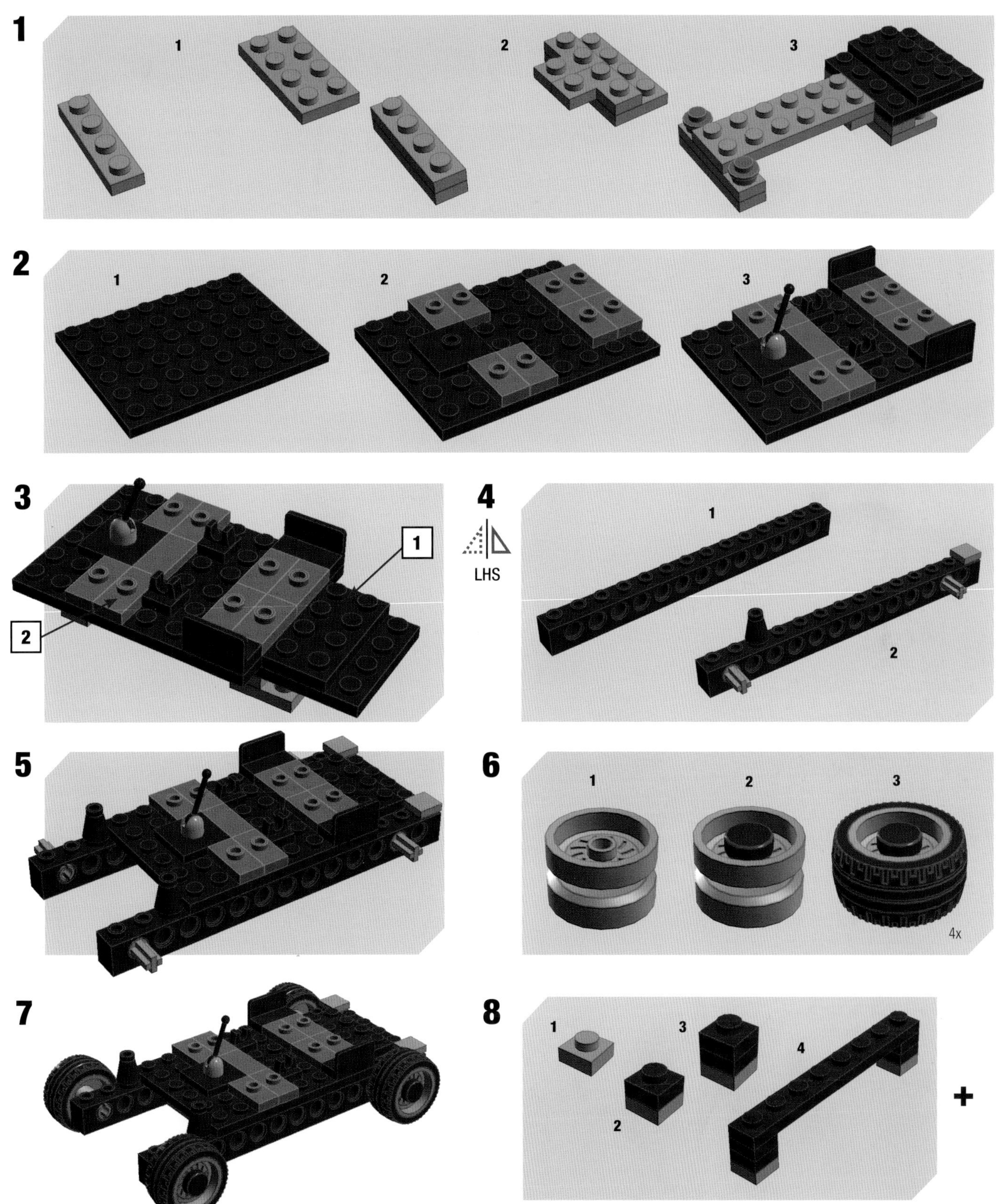
1
1
2
3
2
1
2
3
3
1
2
4
LHS
1
2
5
6
1
2
3
4x
7
8
1
3
4
2
+

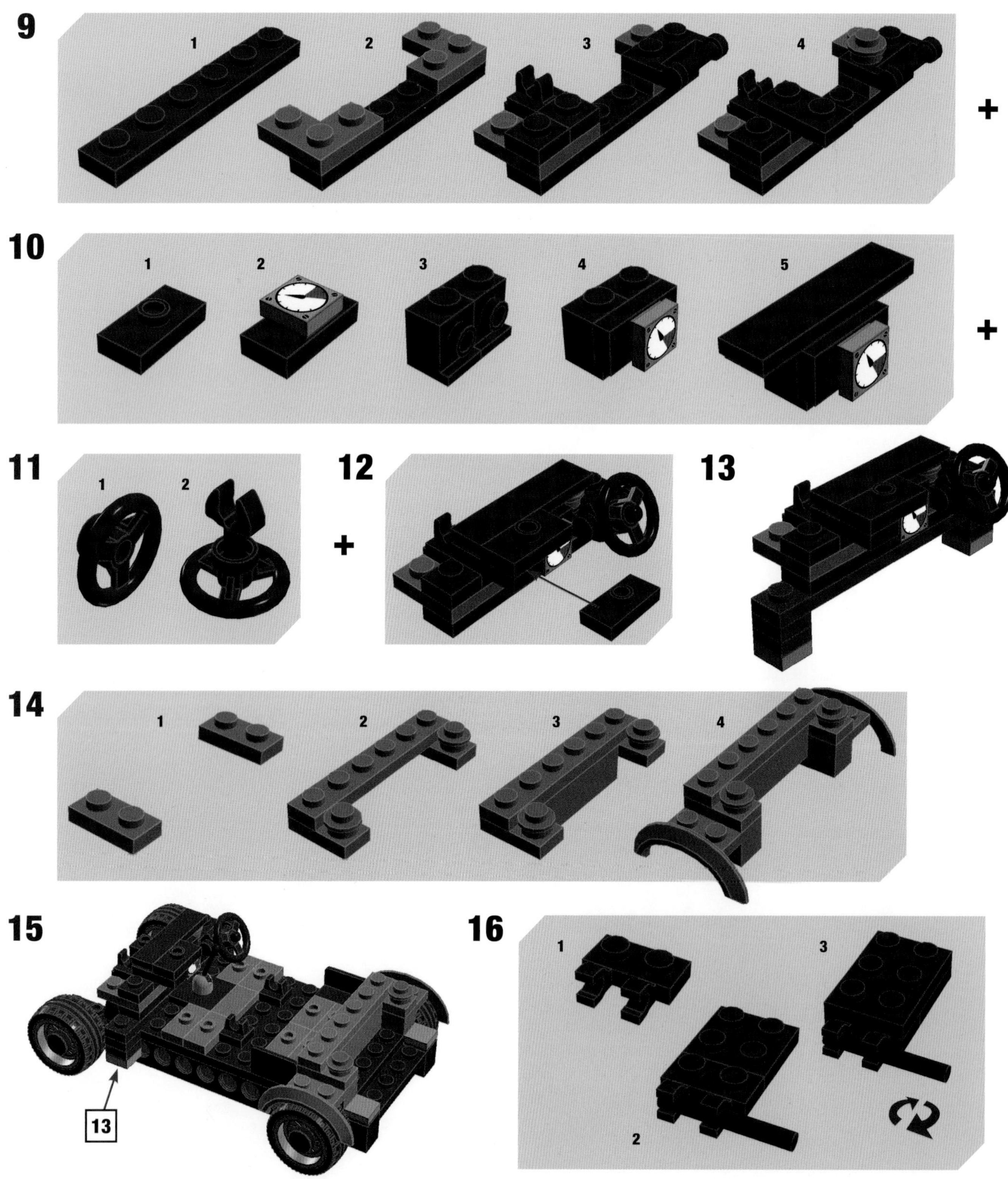
9
1
2
3
4
+
10
1
2
3
4
5
+
11
1
2
+
12
13
14
1
2
3
4
15
13
16
1
3
2

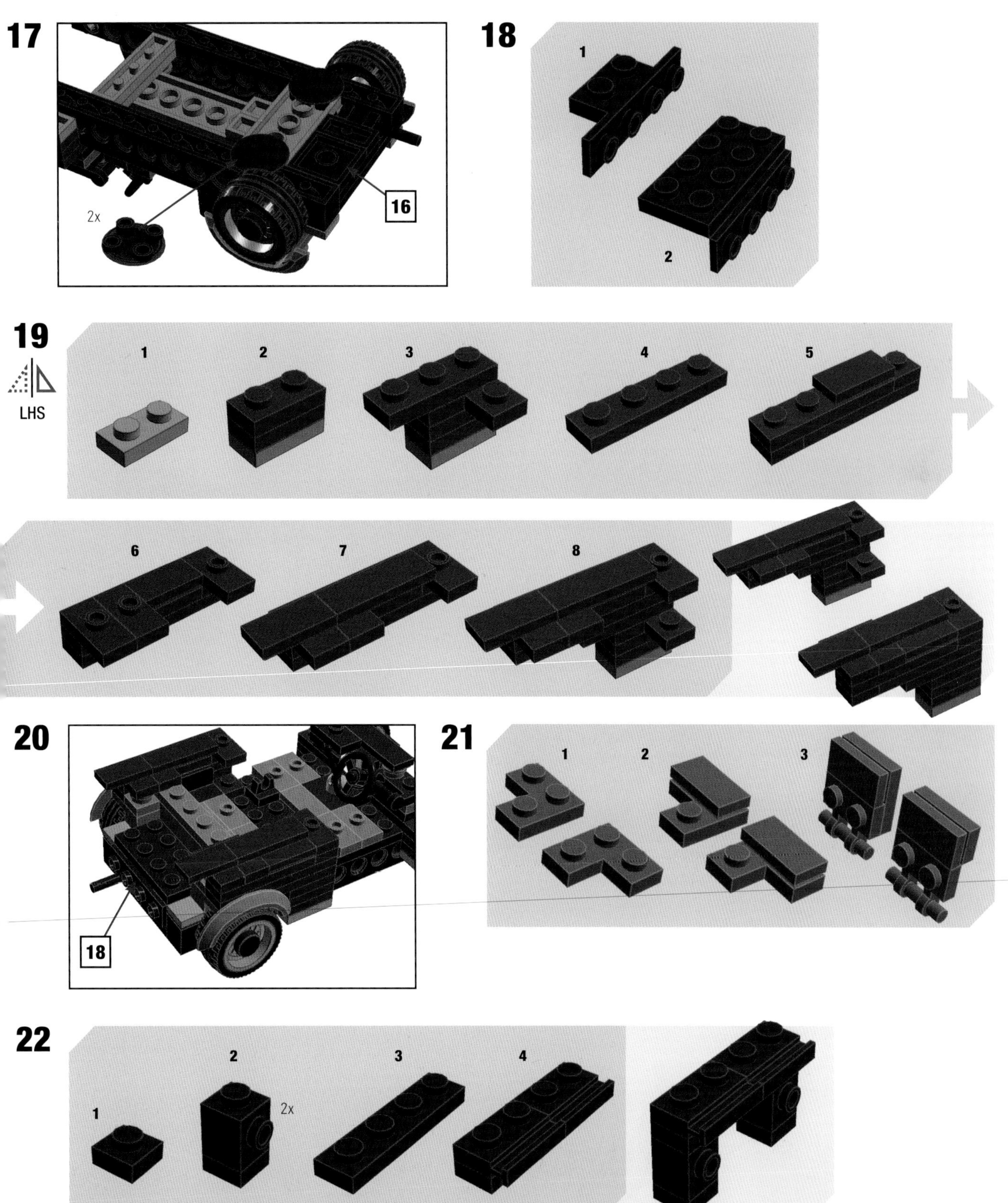
17
16
2x
18
1
2
19
LHS
1
2
3
4
5
6
7
8
20
18
21
1
2
3
22
1
2
2x
3
4

23

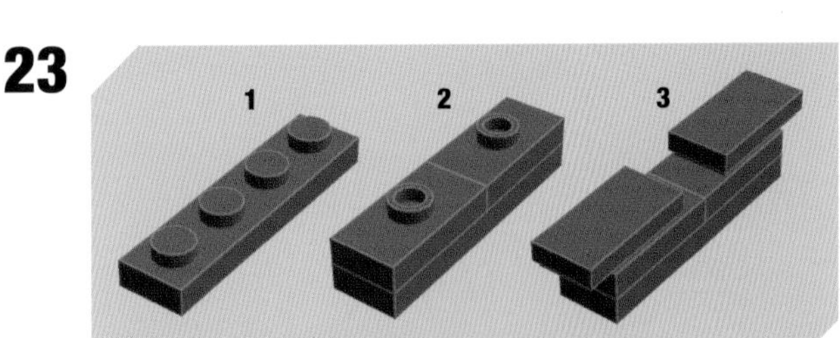

24

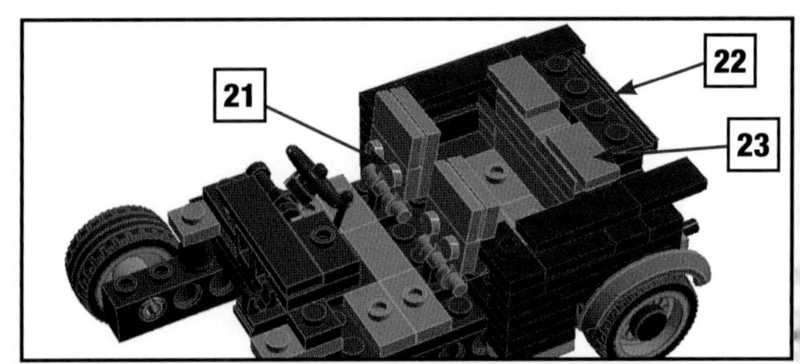

25

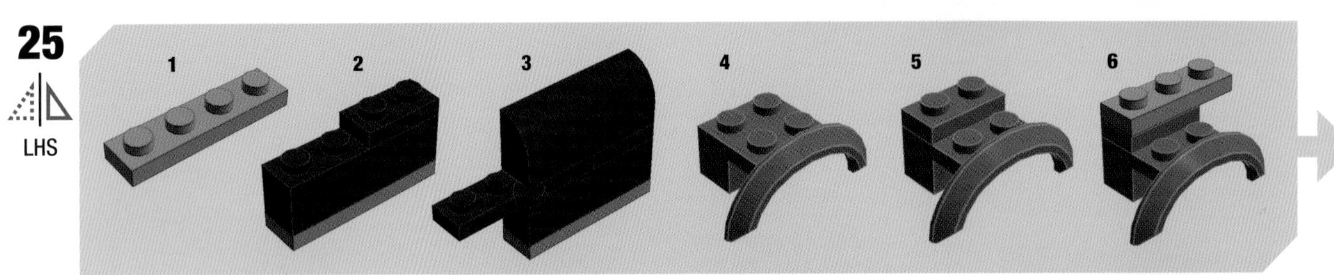

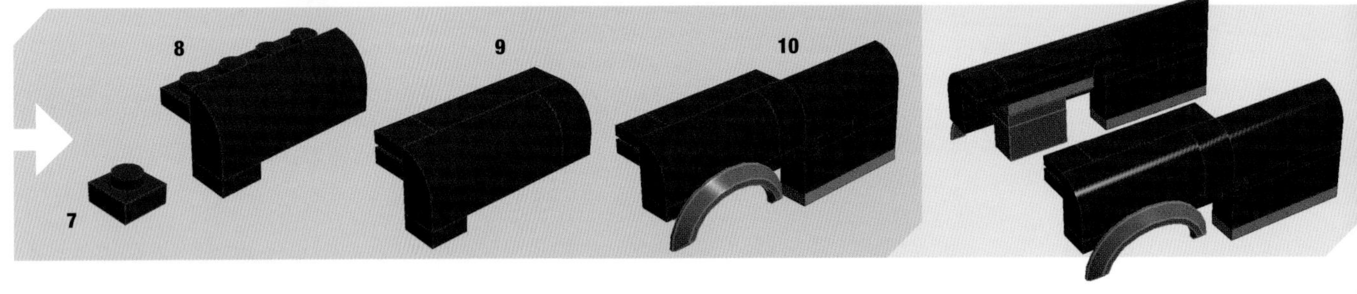

26

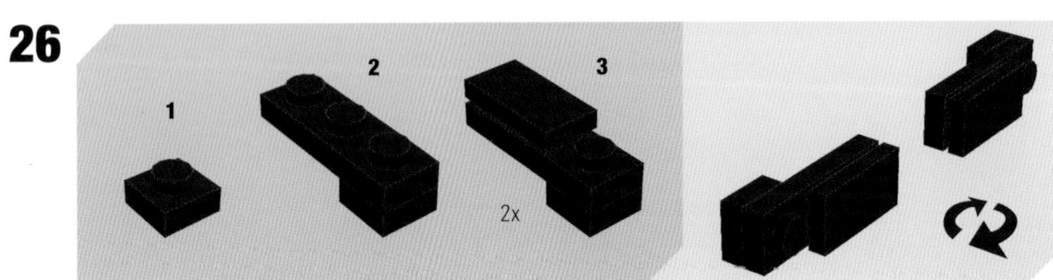

27

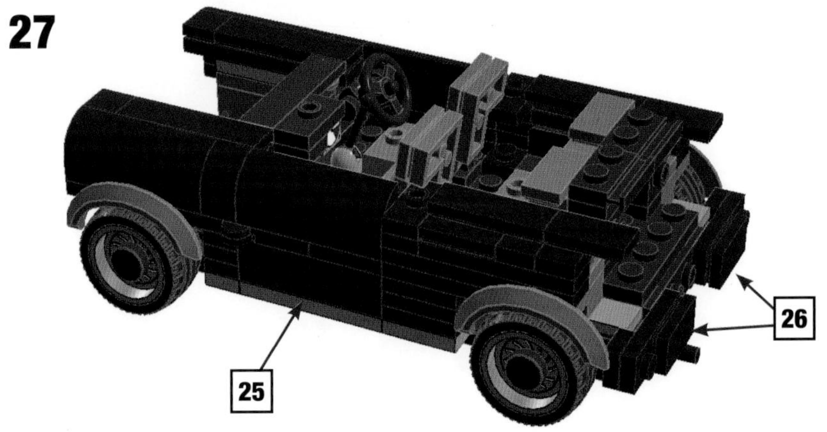

28

1 2 3 4 5 6

7

29

1 2

+

30

1 2 3 4 5

31

32

1 2 3 4

33

34

LHS

1 2 3

35

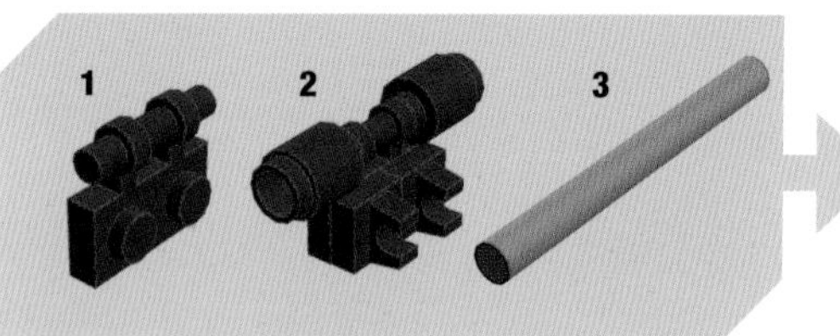

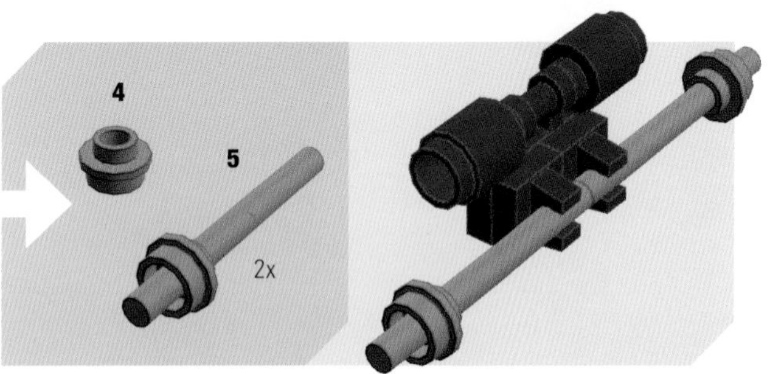

36

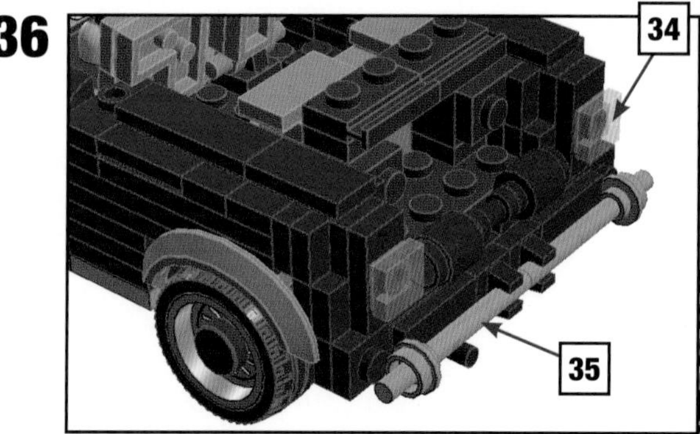

37

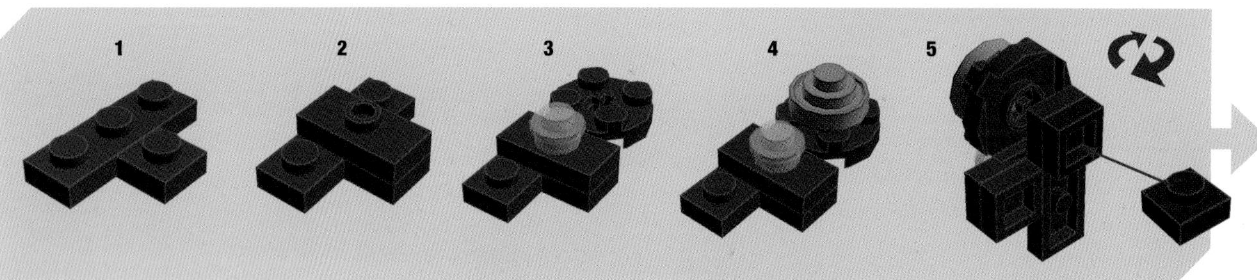

38

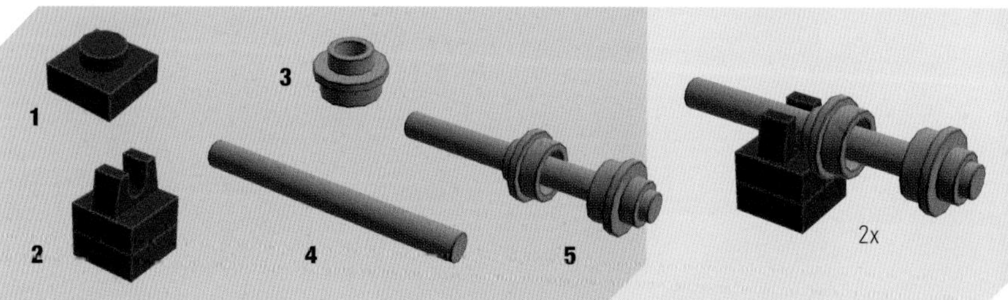

39

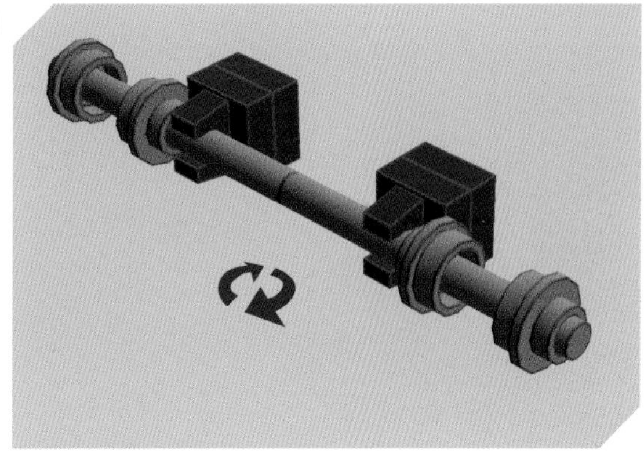

40

41

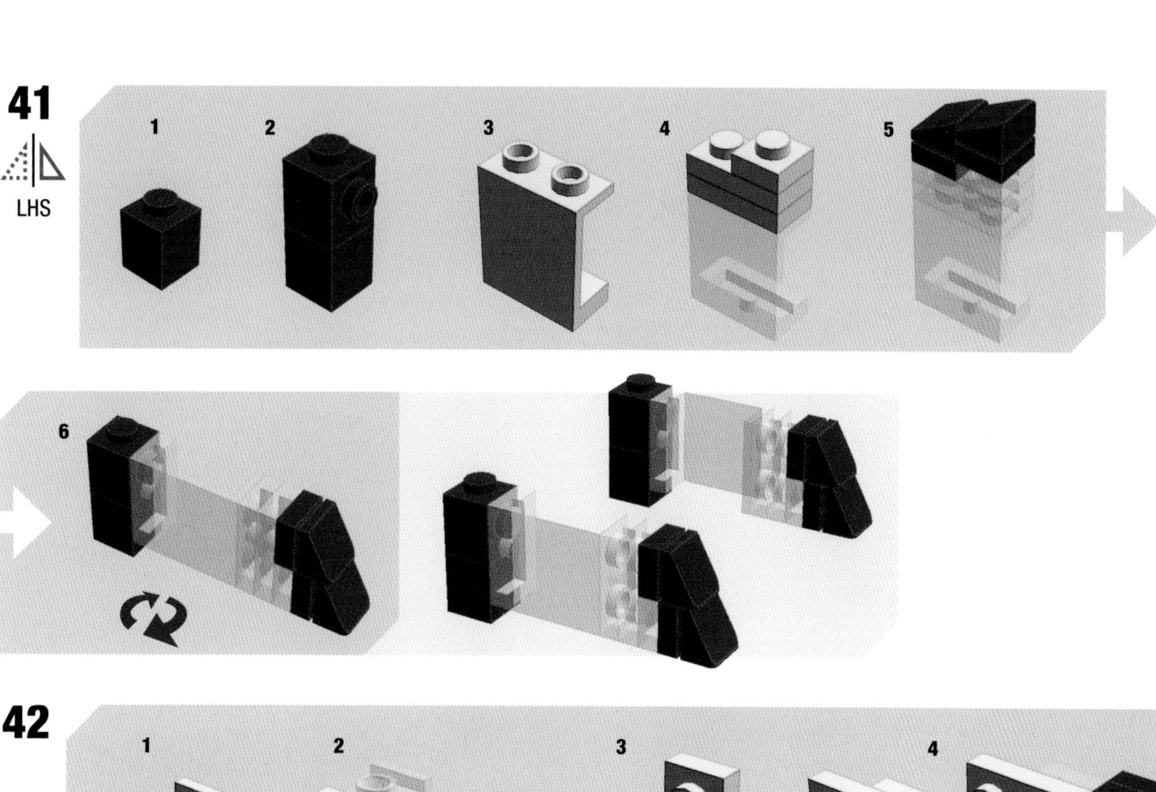

42

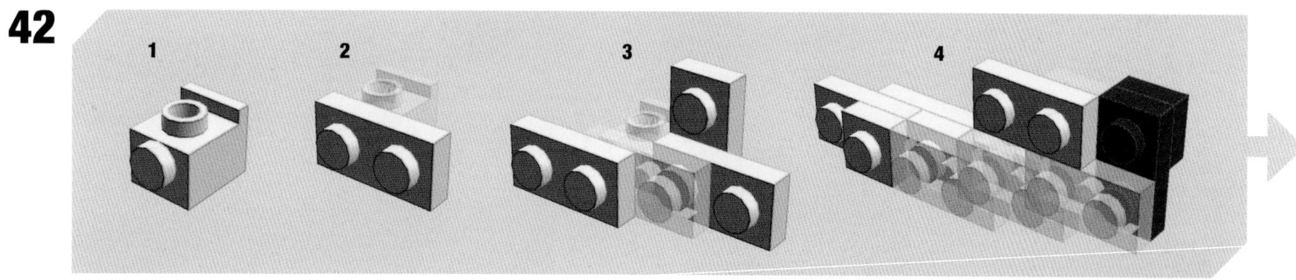

43

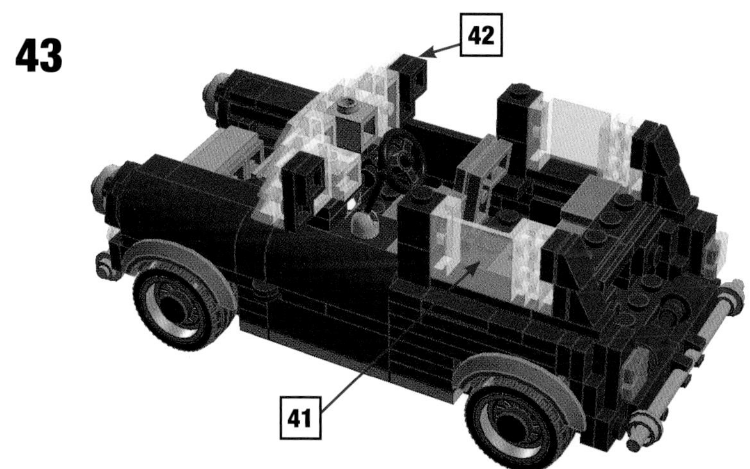

44

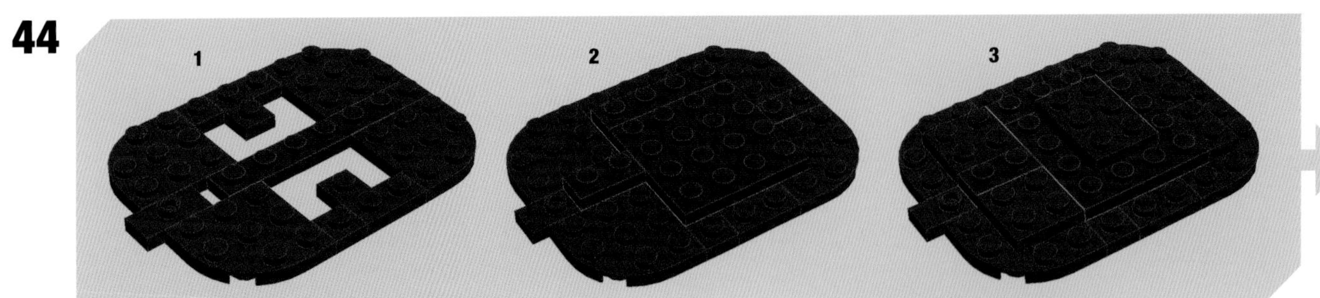

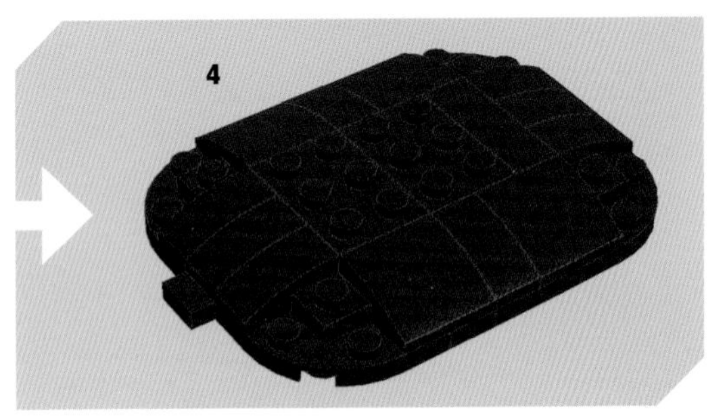

45

46

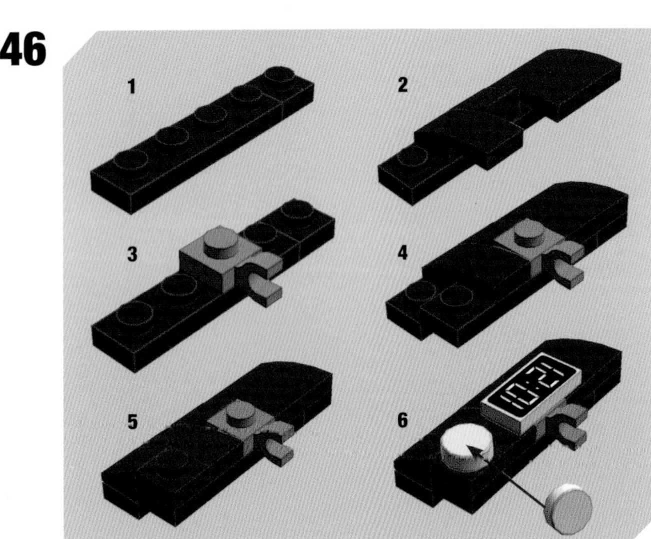

47

48

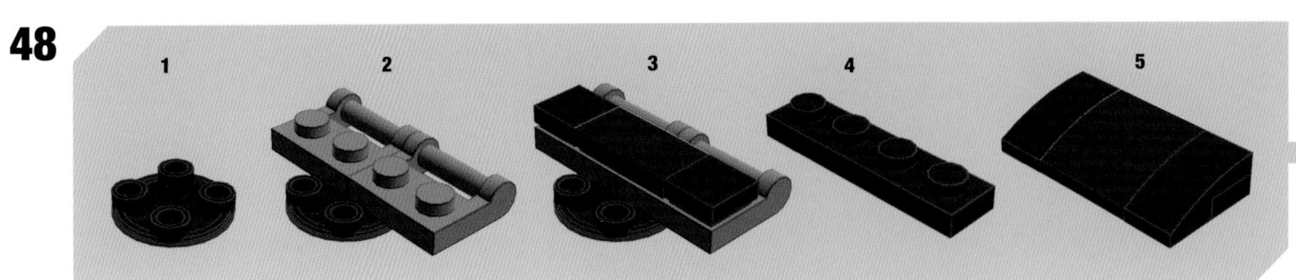

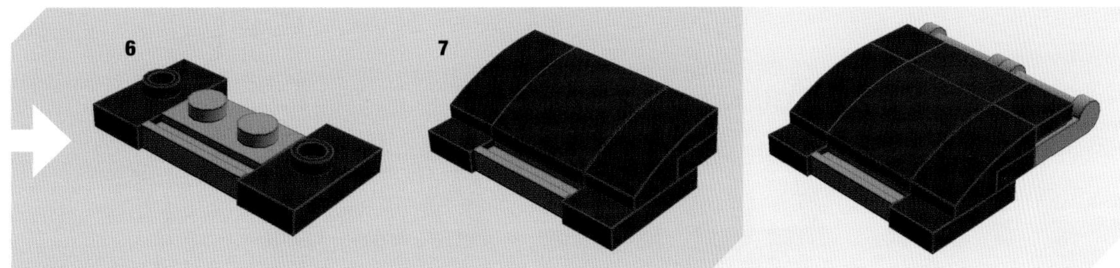

49

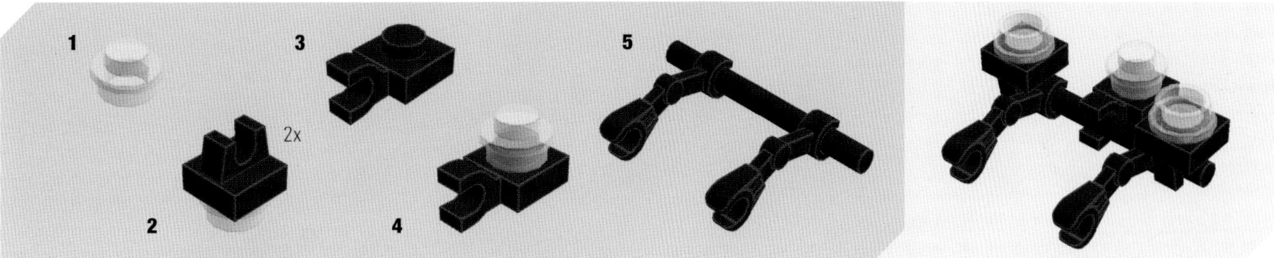

50

CHAPTER 5

VOLKSWAGEN BEETLE
THE LOVE BUG

Herbie probably is the most famous film car of all time, starring in six films after premiering in 1968. The first film *The Love Bug* follows the exploits of racer Jim Douglas, played by Dean Jones, who rescues the car named Herbie from an exclusive car dealership, where it had been rejected by a rich client for the use of one of their domestic staff. Herbie responds to this act of kindness, demonstrating his (its?) sentience by driving without input from Douglas.

Douglas is a race driver, and, as unlikely as this seems, Herbie becomes his race car, competing in and winning auto races through the film wearing the famous number 53. If you like rare and fancy cars, *The Love Bug* is a car-spotter's delight, with various Ferrari, Porsche, and Lotus cars as well as a variety of others competing alongside this humble VW Beetle.

All is not as it seems, though; the original car built for the film is a special "fast" car. Fitted with the engine from a Porsche 356 Carrera, the "fast" Herbie would have dusted most of the competition.

All the Herbie films have somewhat unbelievable plots mixed in with some kooky stunts and Disney Studio special effects. Such is the enduring fondness for the franchise that Herbie reappeared in 2005 in the film *Herbie: Fully Loaded*, staring Lindsay Lohan, though the car in this film was newly built and featured numerous period-specific modifications.

The model featured in the build here shows Herbie as we see him in the second and third films, featuring red and navy stripes, black running boards, and the asymmetrical fitment of the Carello fog light. The model can be easily reconfigured, however, to any of the various movie iterations. If you look carefully in the first film, the VW logos have been removed from the car to avoid copyright infringement. Subsequent film cars were officially endorsed by Volkswagen and have the features reinstated.

COUNTRY OF ORIGIN: West Germany

PRODUCTION: 1938–2003

NUMBER MADE: 21,529,464

LAYOUT/DRIVE: Rear engine, Rear-wheel-drive

ENGINE: 1,192 cc, 4 cylinders, Boxer (horizontally opposed)

POWER TORQUE: 40 hp (30 kW) / 65 lb-ft (88 Nm)

CONSTRUCTION/DOORS: Steel Platform Chassis, two-door Sedan

TV/FILM APPEARANCES: *The Love Bug* (1968), *Herbie Rides Again* (1974), *Herbie Goes to Monte Carlo* (1977), *Herbie Goes Bananas* (1980), *The Love Bug*–TV (1997), *Herbie Fully Loaded* (2005)

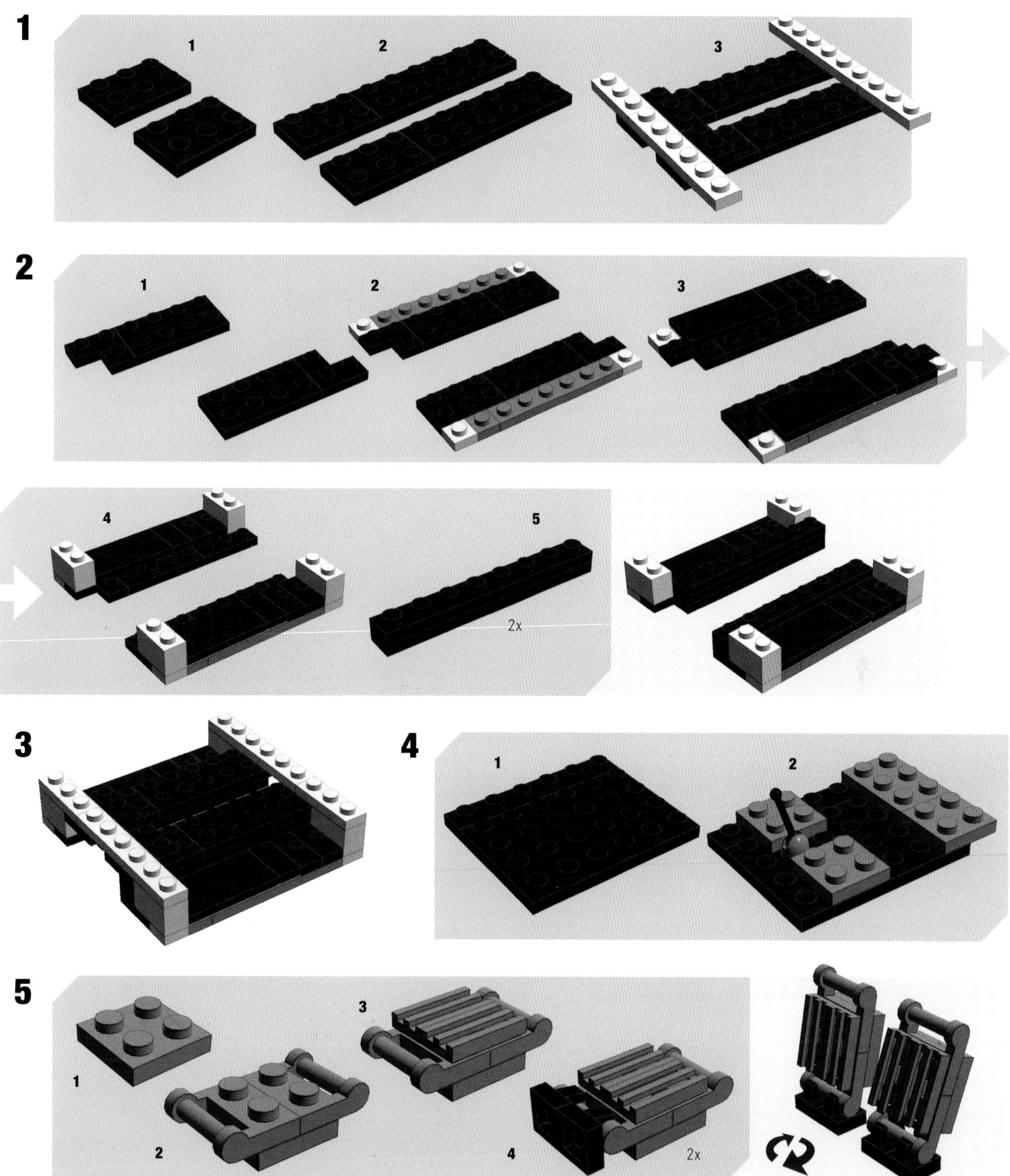
1
1
2
3
2
1
2
3
4
5
2x
3
4
1
2
5
1
2
3
4
2x

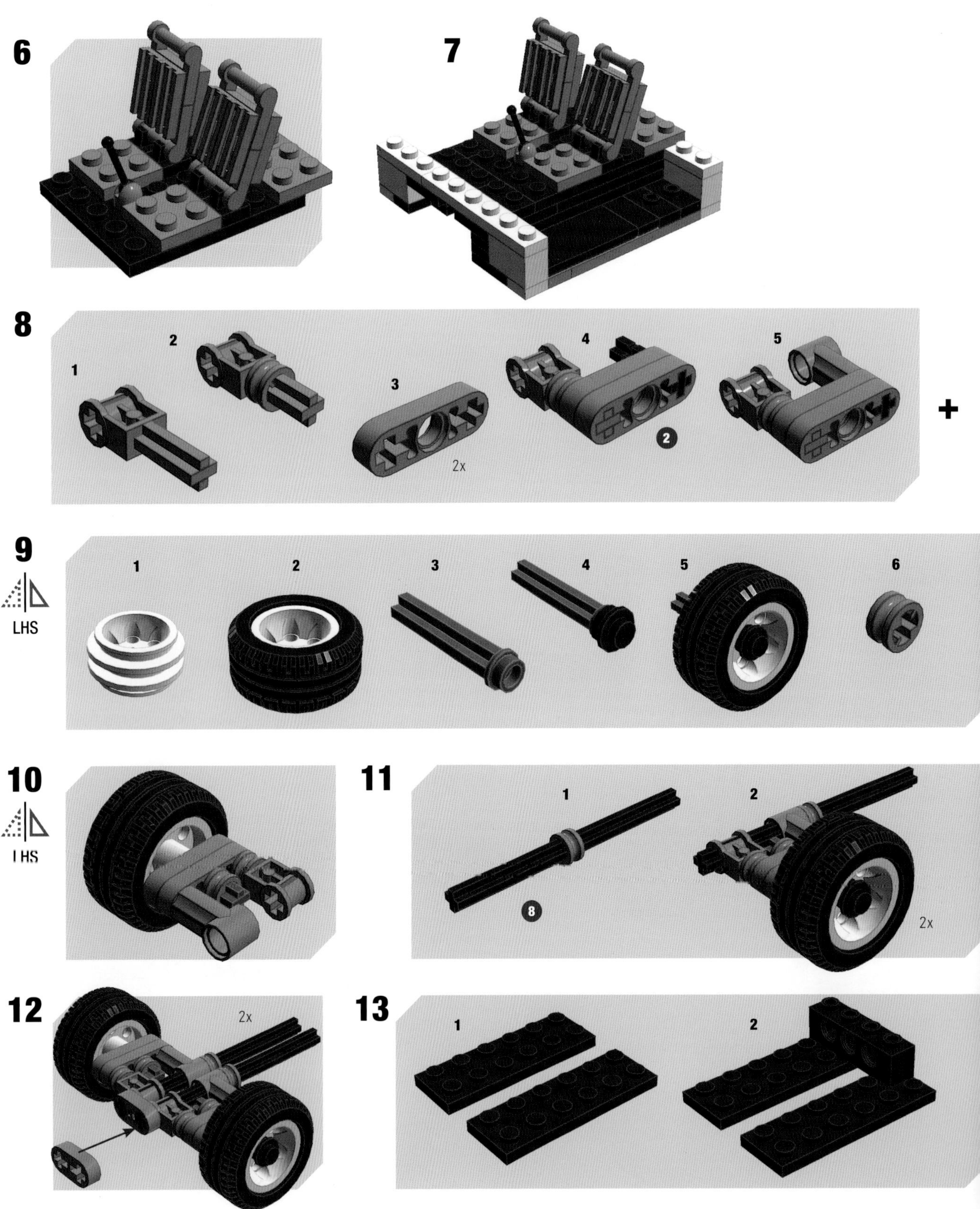

6
7
8
1
2
3
2x
4
2
5
+
9
LHS
1
2
3
4
5
6
10
LHS
11
1
8
2
2x
12
2x
13
1
2

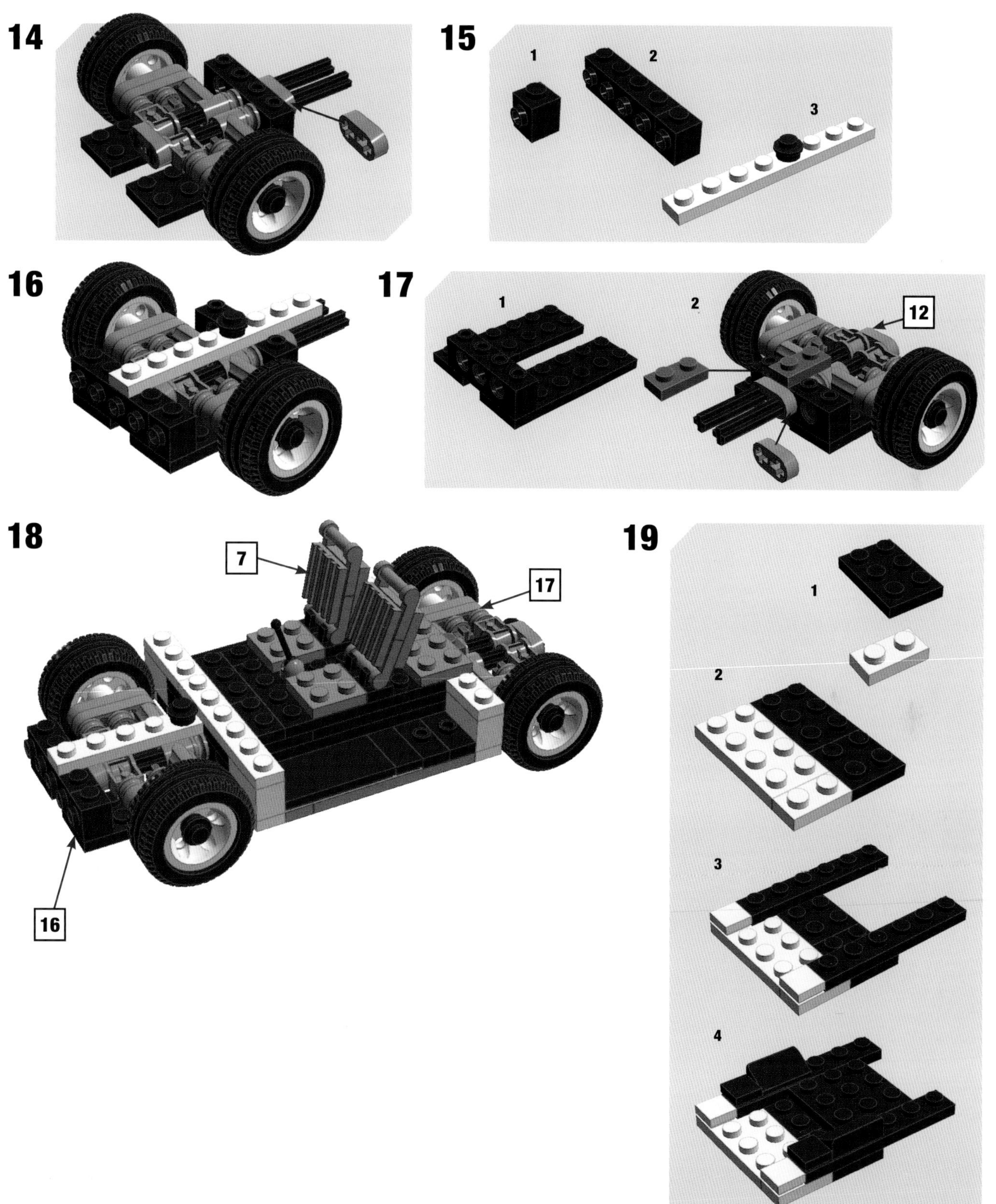
14
15
1
2
3
16
17
1
2
12
18
7
17
16
19
1
2
3
4

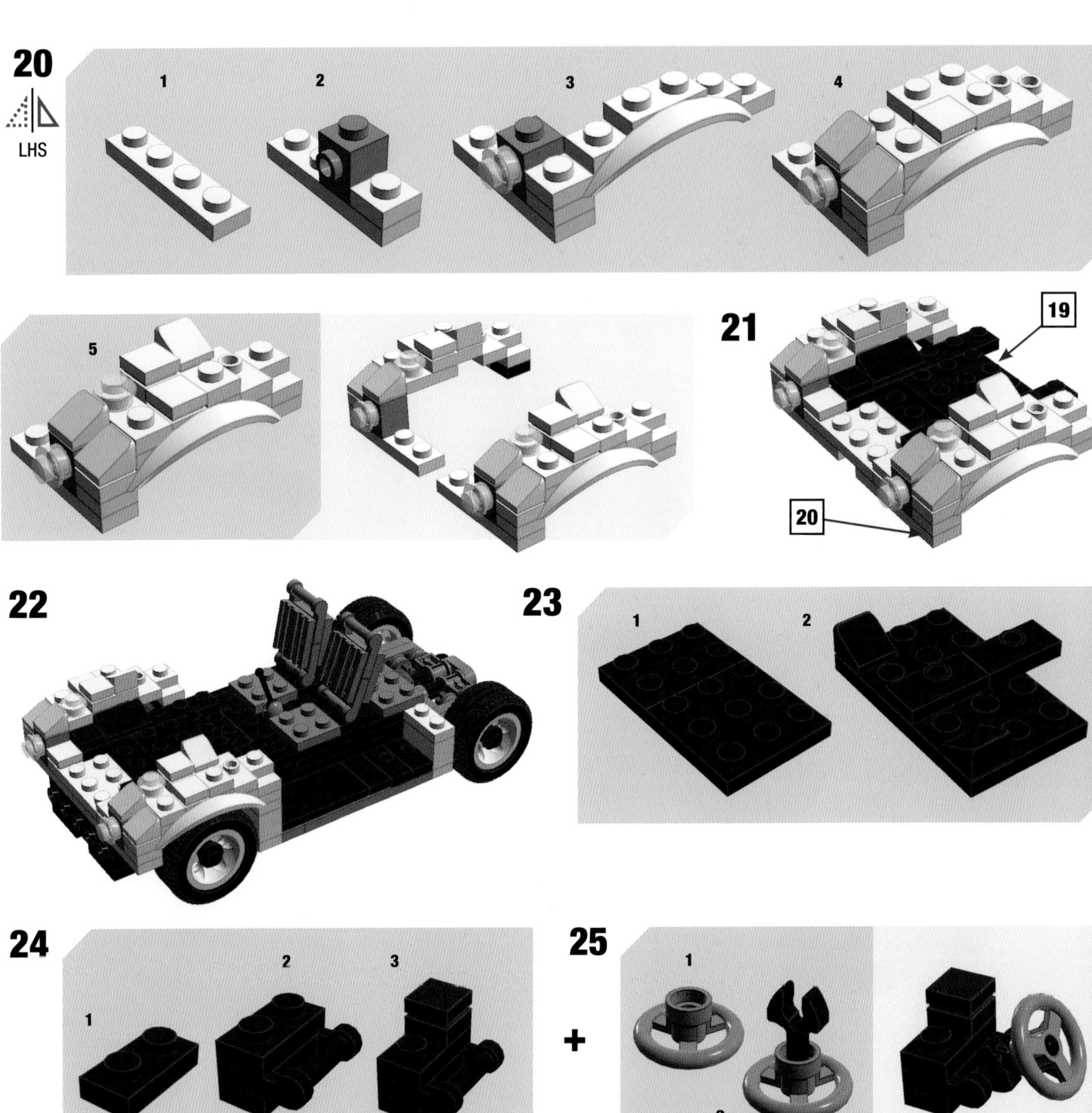
20
LHS
1
2
3
4
5
21
19
20
22
23
1
2
24
1
2
3
+
25
1
2

26

1 2 3

27

1 2

28

1 2

29

1 2

3

30

LHS

1

2 3 4

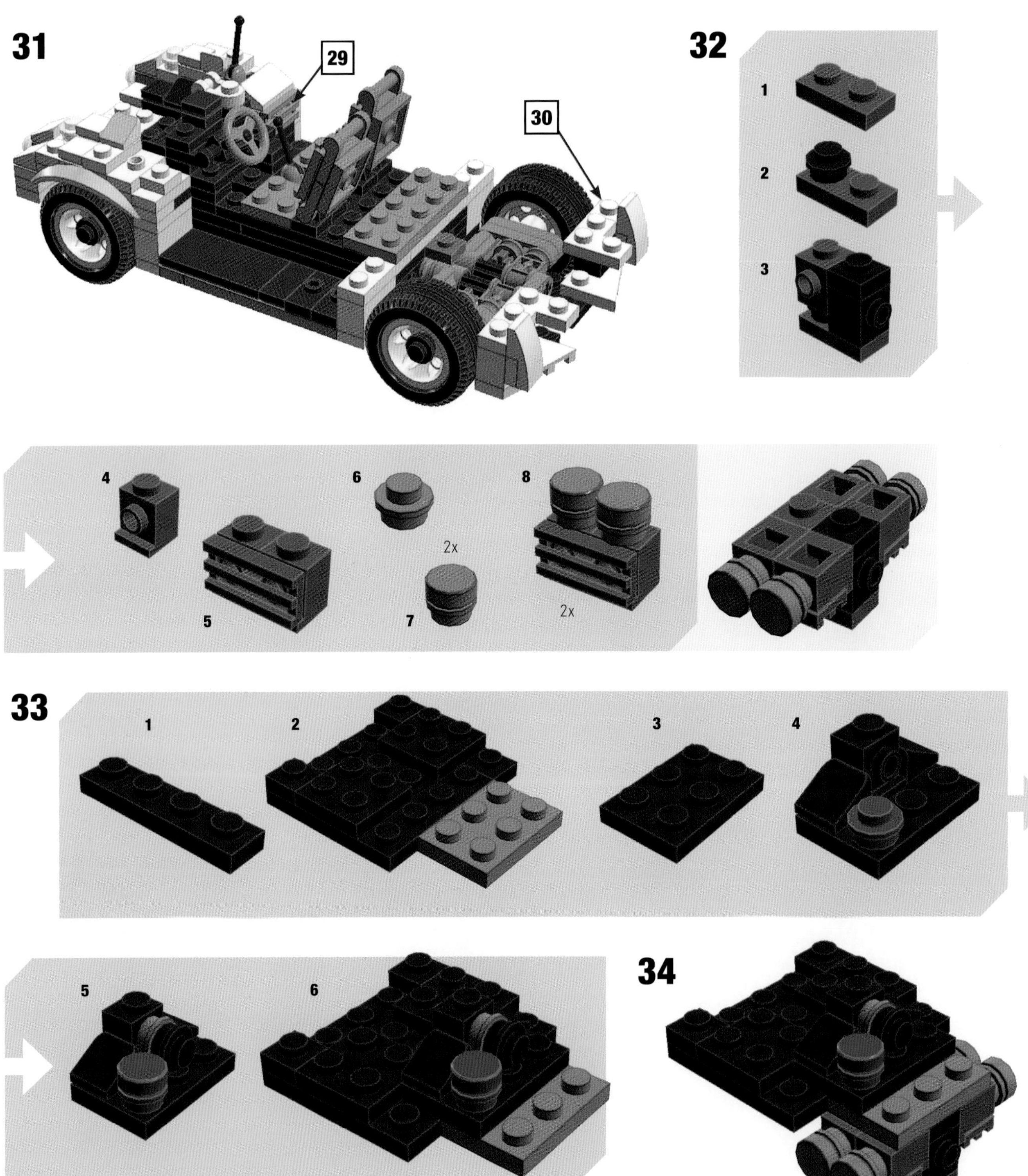
31
29
30
32
1
2
3
4
5
6
2x
7
8
2x
33
1
2
3
4
5
6
34

35

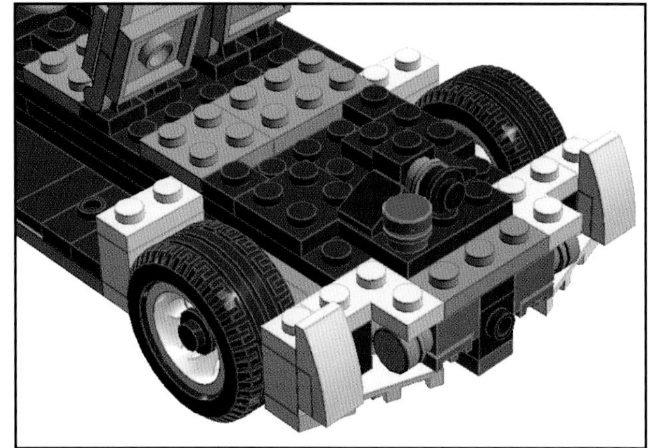

36

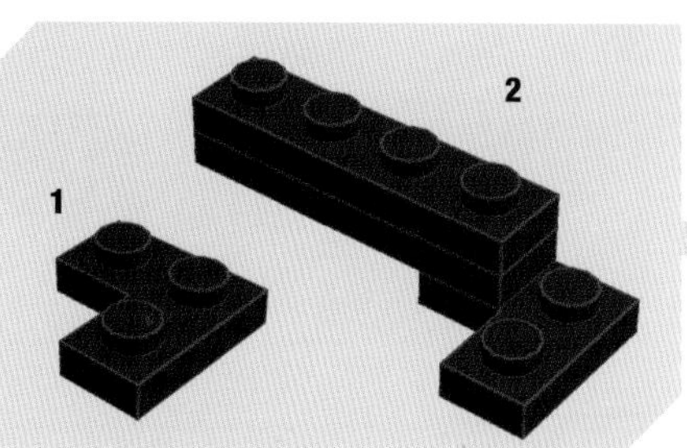

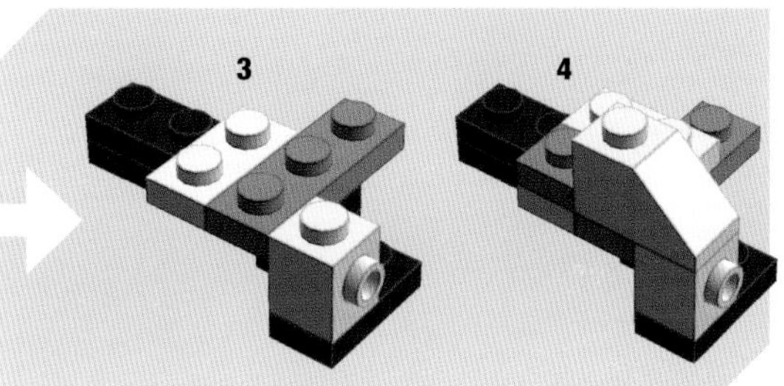

+

36

LHS

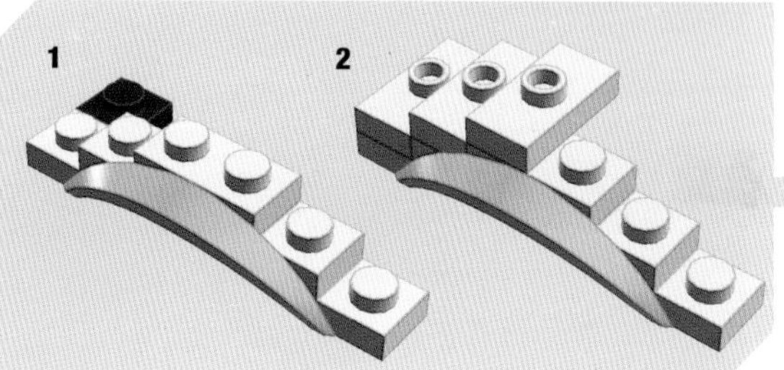

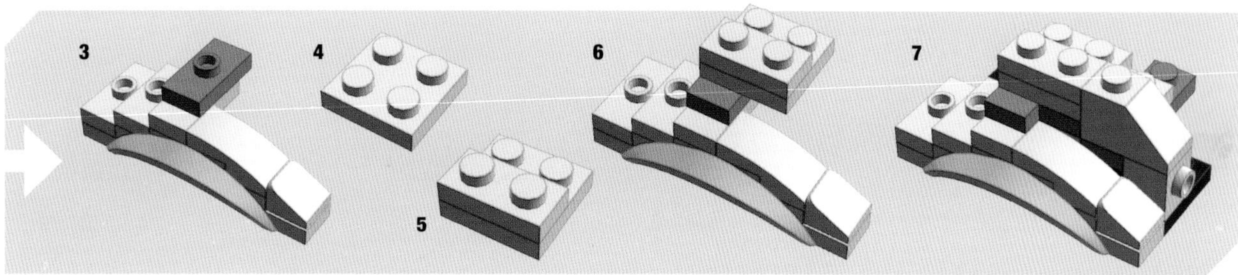

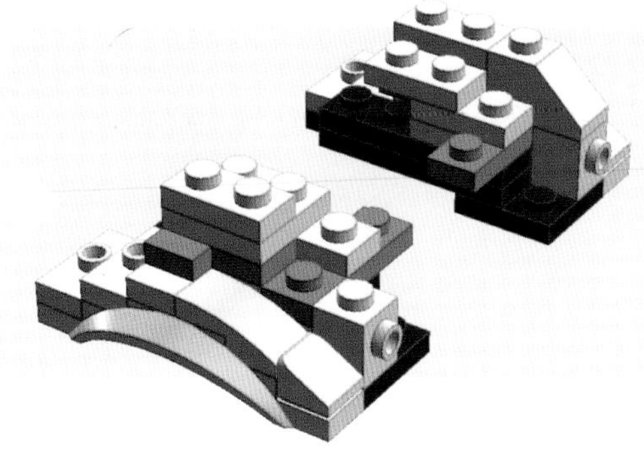

37

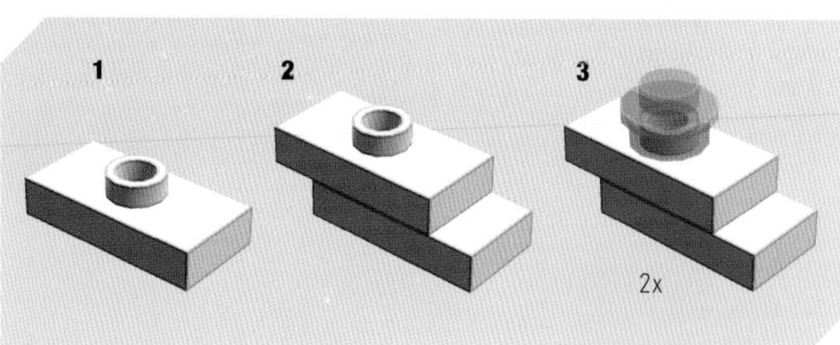

38

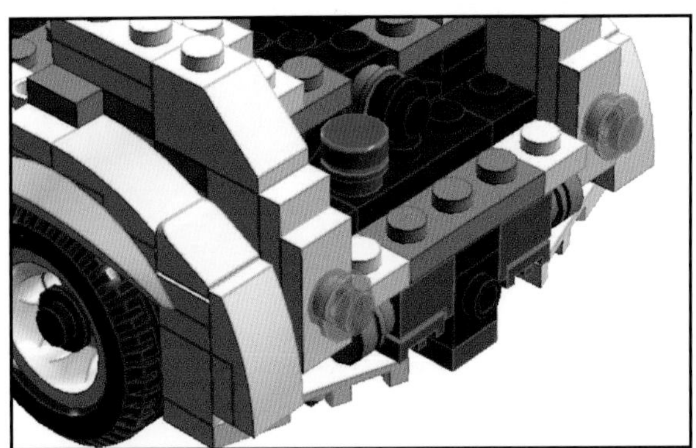

39

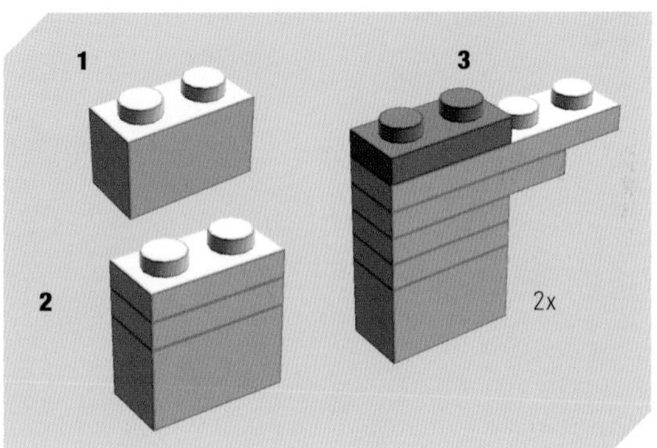

40

41

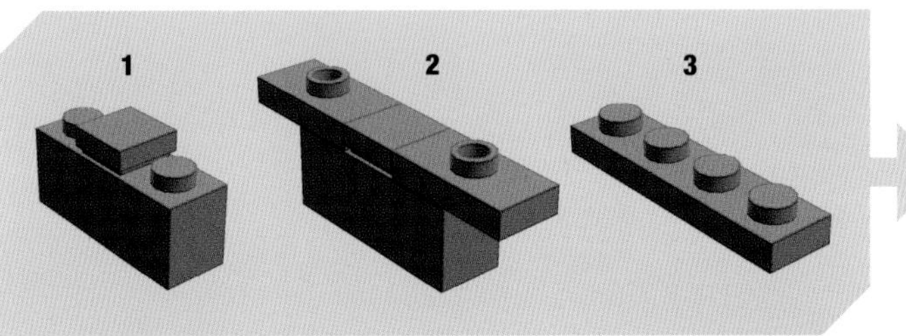

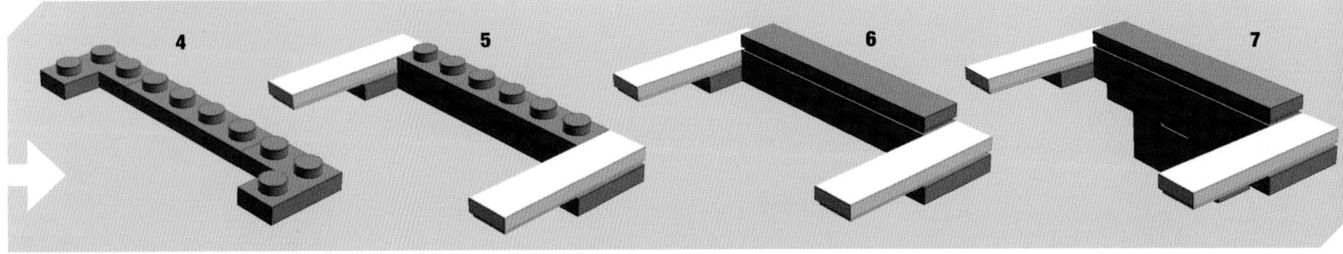

42

43

LHS

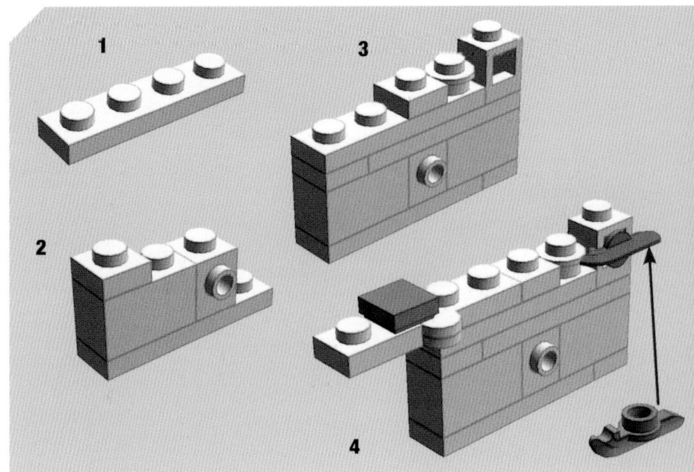

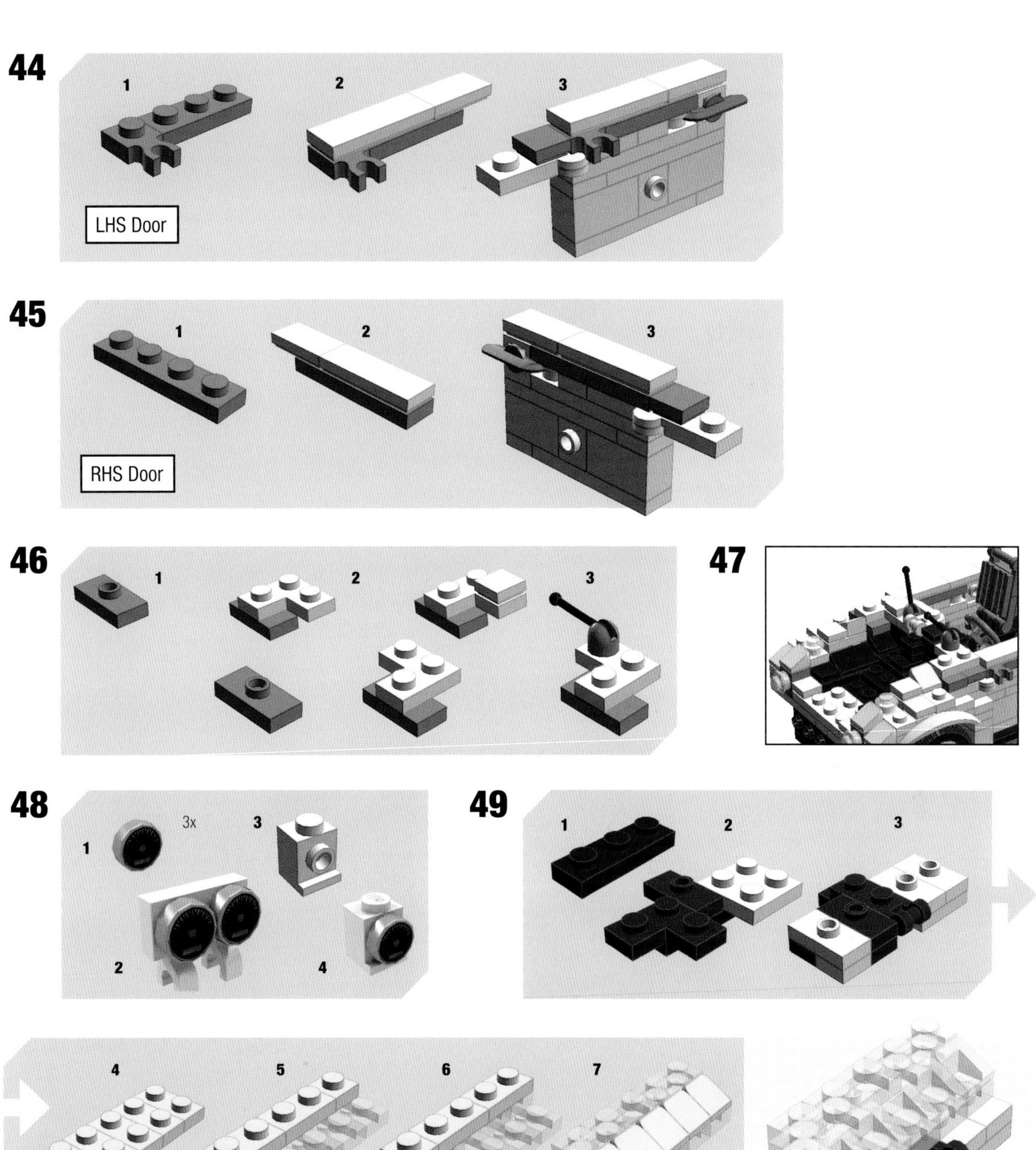
44
1
2
3
LHS Door
45
1
2
3
RHS Door
46
1
2
3
47
48
1
3x
3
2
4
49
1
2
3
4
5
6
7

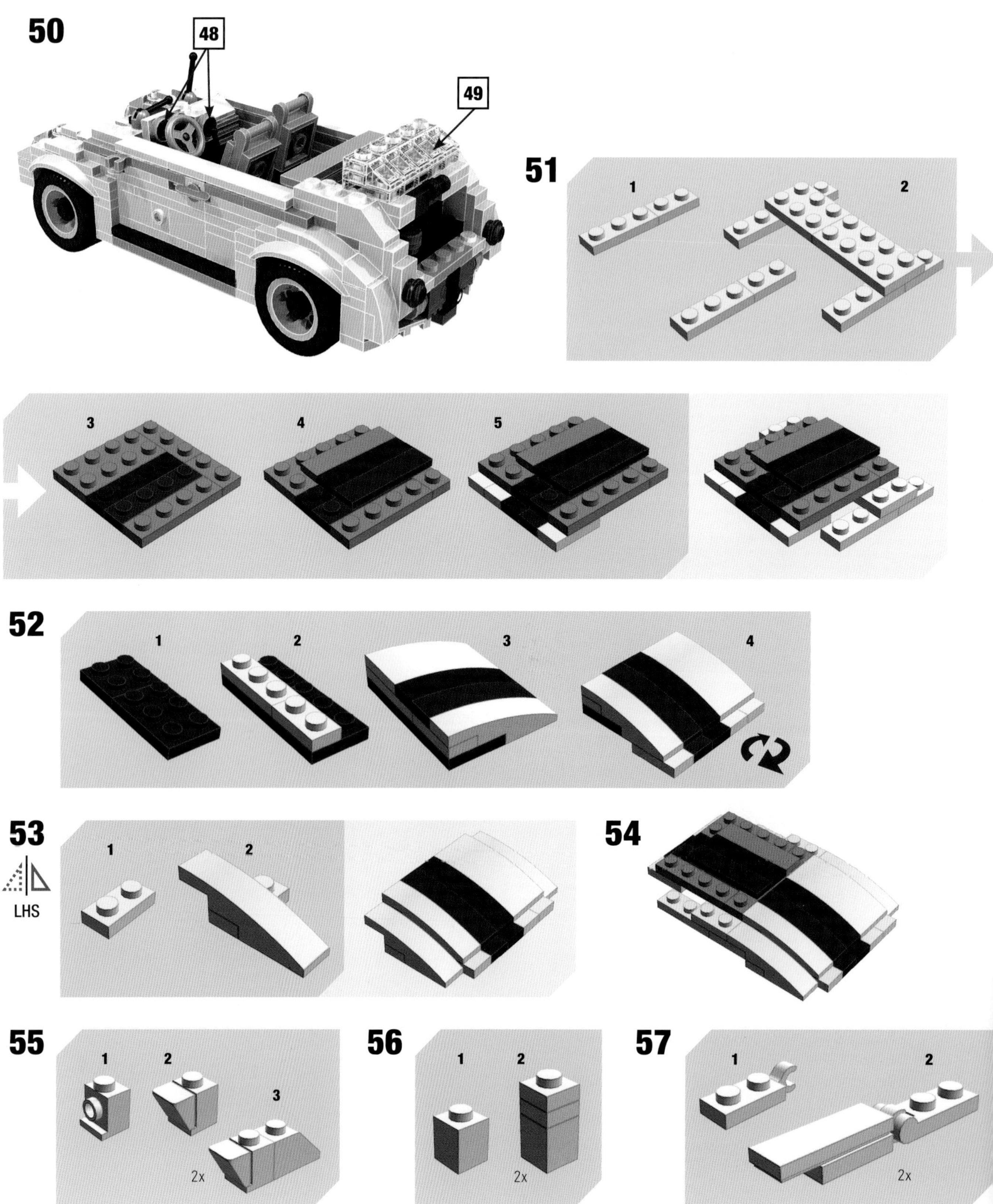
50
48
49
51
1
2
3
4
5
52
1
2
3
4
53
1
2
LHS
54
55
1
2
3
2x
56
1
2
2x
57
1
2
2x

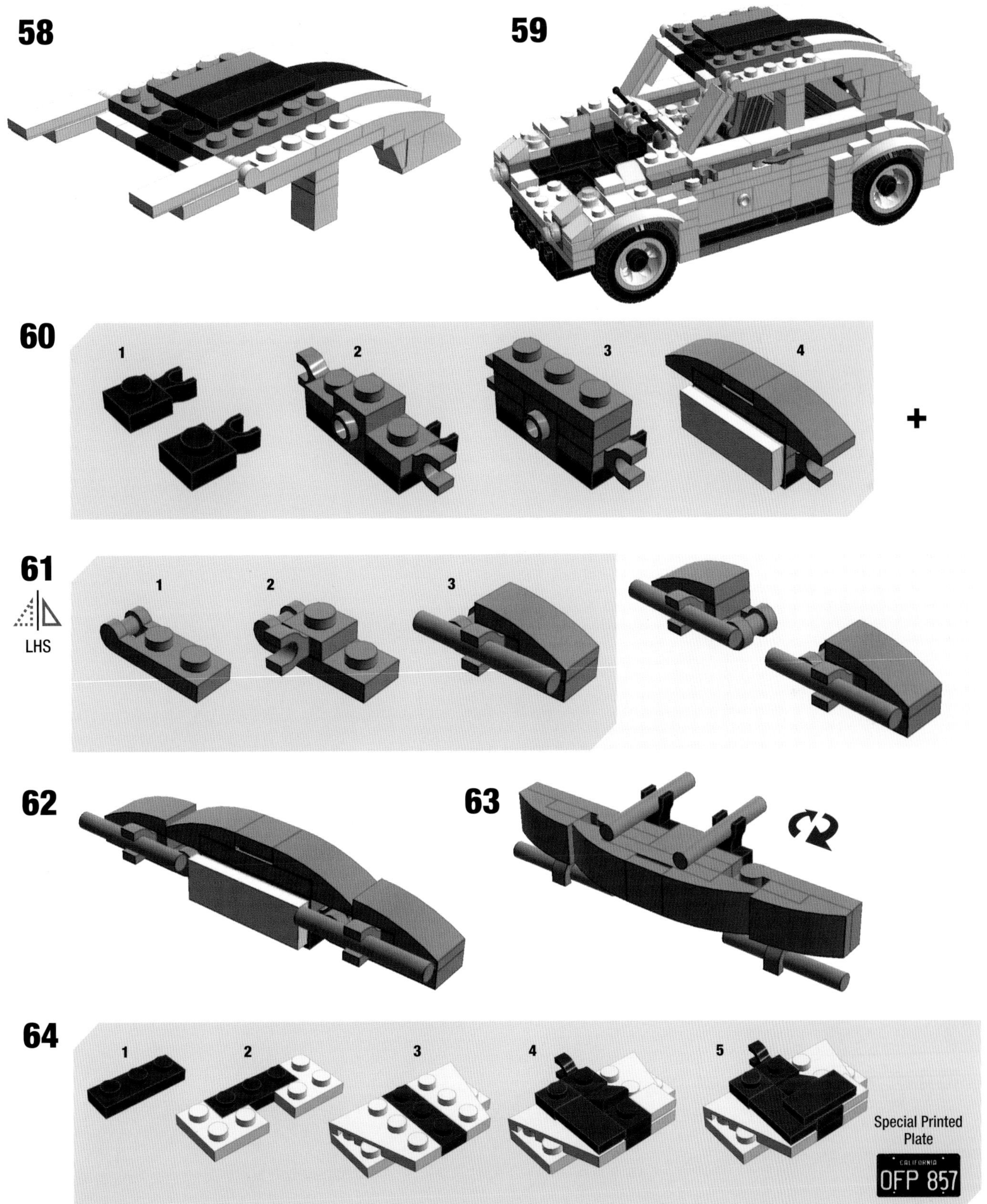
58
59
60
1
2
3
4
+
61
LHS
1
2
3
62
63
64
1
2
3
4
5
Special Printed Plate
CALIFORNIA
OFP 857

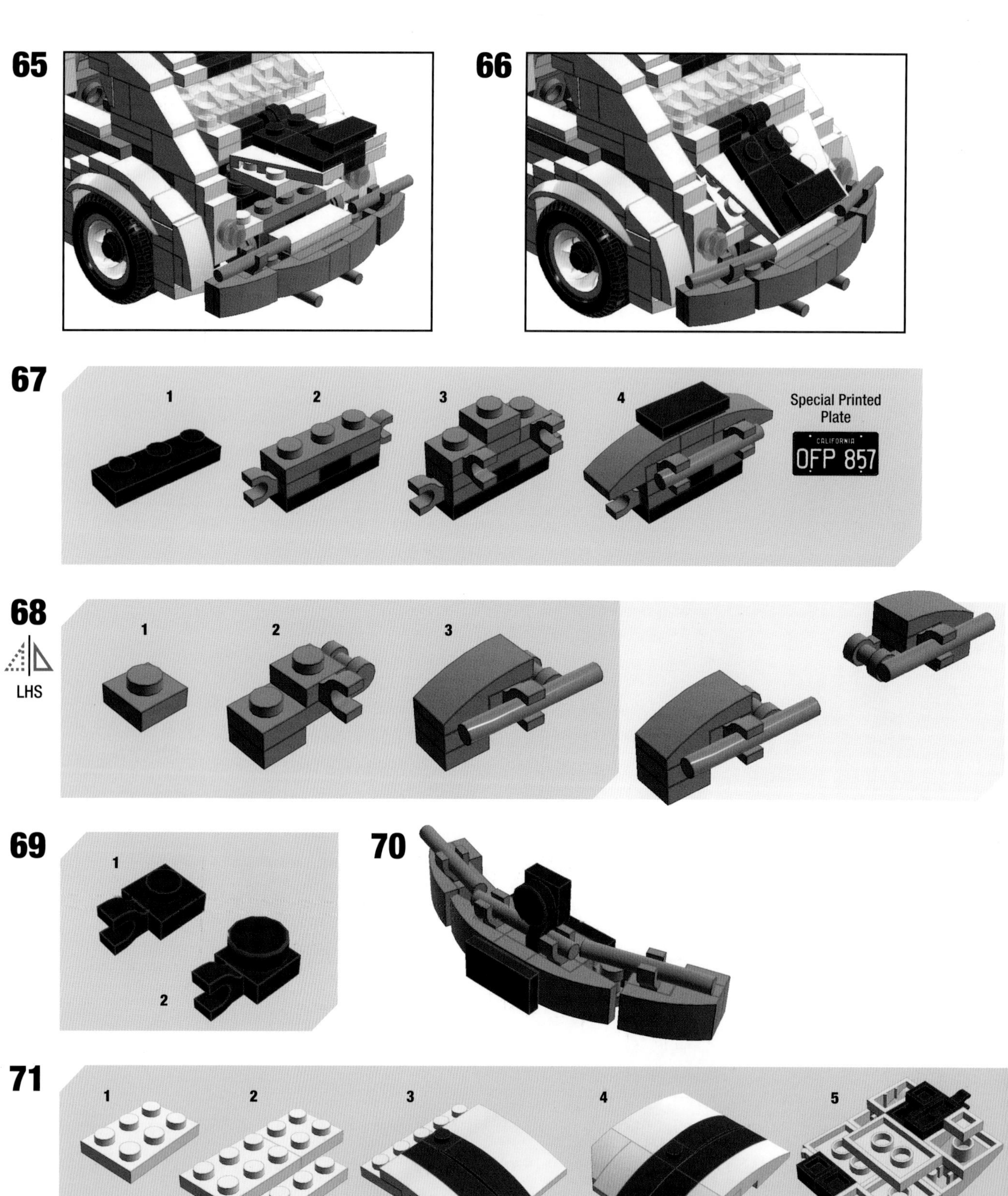
65
66
67
1
2
3
4
Special Printed Plate
CALIFORNIA
OFP 857
68
LHS
1
2
3
69
1
2
70
71
1
2
3
4
5

66

Note: This is a rare part.

53

Four Instances:
- Hood
- Engine Cover
- RHS Door
- LHS Door

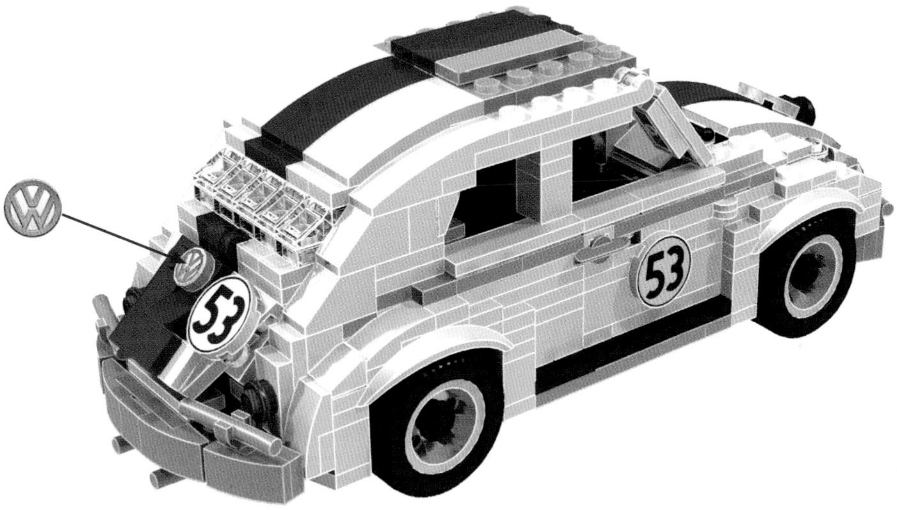

CHAPTER 6

FORD MUSTANG
BULLITT

Bullitt, like many Steve McQueen films, is not an easy first-time watch. If you like cars, it's great, but even then you will be waiting a long time for the iconic car chase through the hilly streets of San Francisco.

McQueen films tend to be short on dialogue and long on mood, meaning that this film is generally appreciated more after a second or third viewing. By that stage, though, you are left thinking "How many hubcaps does that car have?" or "How many times was that green VW Beetle overtaken?" These minor continuity errors can be forgiven for what is arguably one of the greatest car chase sequences in cinema.

At the end of the chase, the two cars head out of San Francisco city and into the hill country around Brisbane, a journey that takes only five minutes in movie time, though much longer in reality.

Car aficionados contend that even equipped with the big 390 cubic inches V8, producing 325 hp (242 kW), the *Bullitt* Mustang would not have been a match for the 375 hp 440-Magnum powered Dodge Charger. Though original guidance indicated that the sequence should have speeds of only 75–80 mph (121–129 km/h), the chase stuntmen exceeded 110 mph (177 km/h) at times—a range more representative of what these two muscle cars were capable of.

The film is not solely about the chase. Like many period movies, it is about power, corruption, and the powerlessness of the average man and woman.

The *Bullitt* mystique, though, is irresistible. The Ford Motor Company returns to the well every five years or so to dress up their current Mustang model in dark green paint and rerun the famous chase sequence for promotional purposes.

COUNTRY OF ORIGIN: United States

PRODUCTION: 1964½–1973 (First Generation)

NUMBER MADE: 317,404 (1968)

LAYOUT/DRIVE: Front engine, Rear-wheel-drive

ENGINE: 390ci (6.4 liter), 8 cylinders, Vee

POWER TORQUE: 325 bhp (242 kW) / 427 lb-ft (579 Nm)

CONSTRUCTION/DOORS: Steel Monocoque, two-door fastback Coupe

TV/FILM APPEARANCE: *Bullitt* (1968)

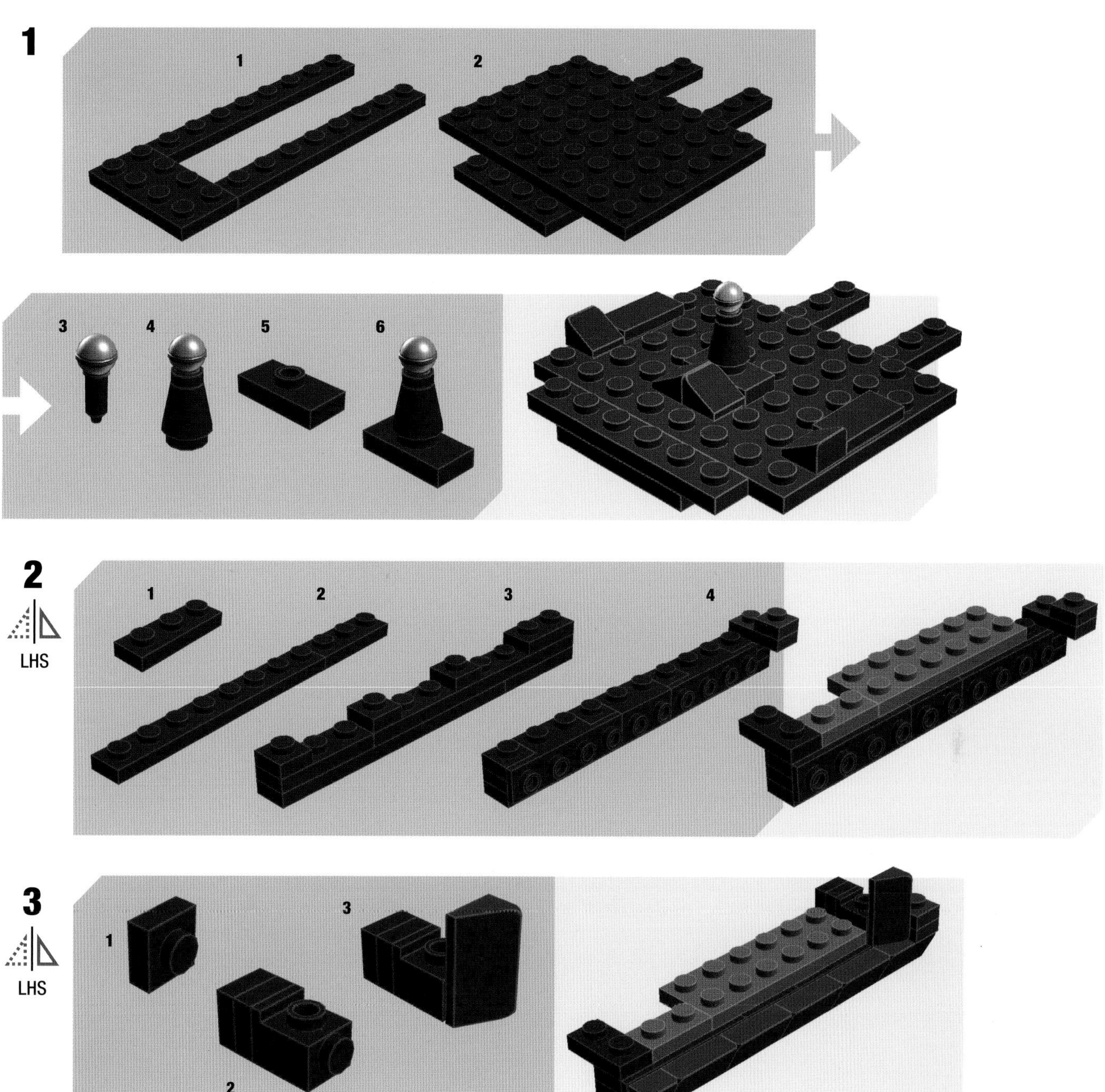
1
1
2
3
4
5
6
2
LHS
1
2
3
4
3
LHS
1
2
3

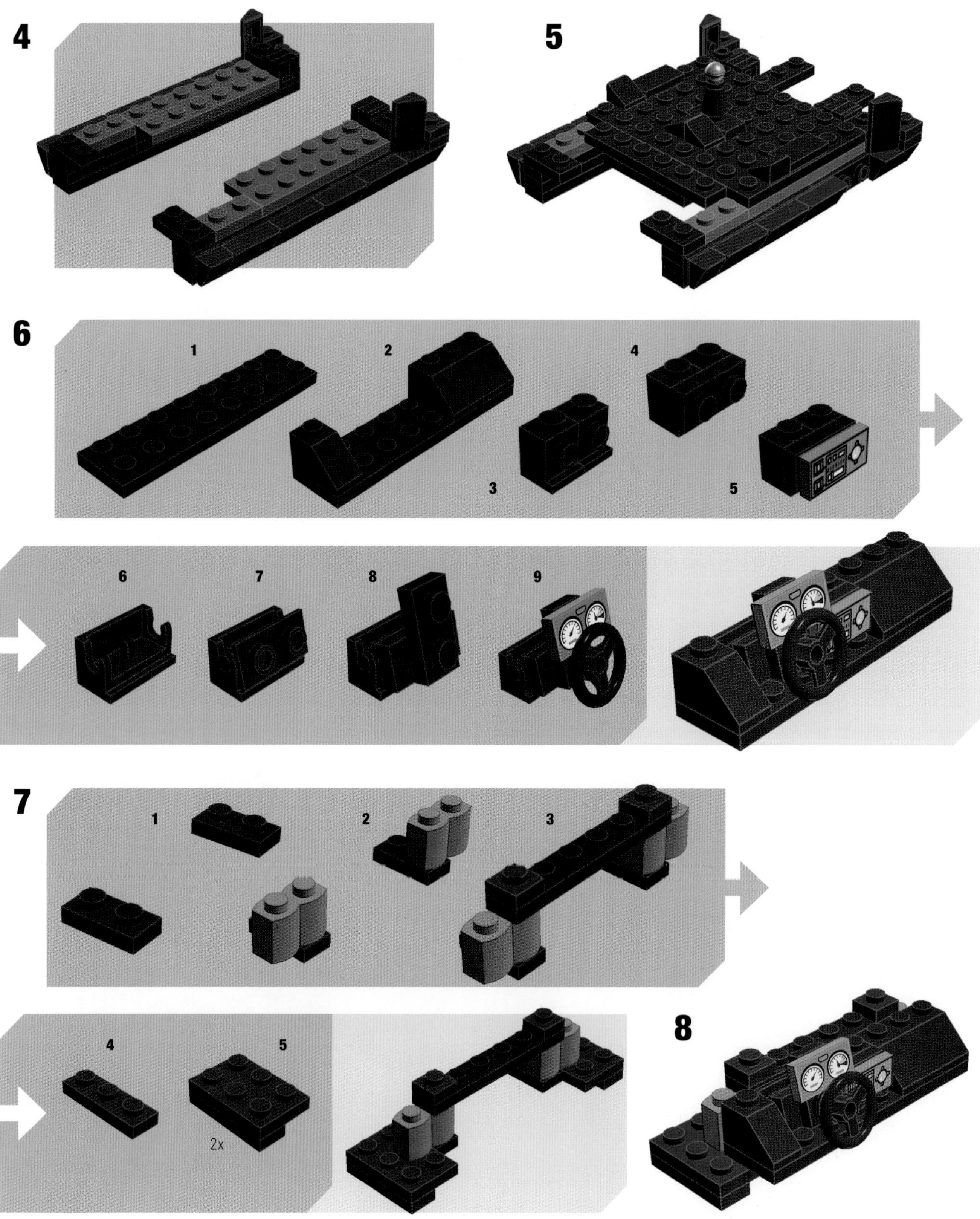
4
5
6
1
2
3
4
5
6
7
8
9
7
1
2
3
4
5
2x
8

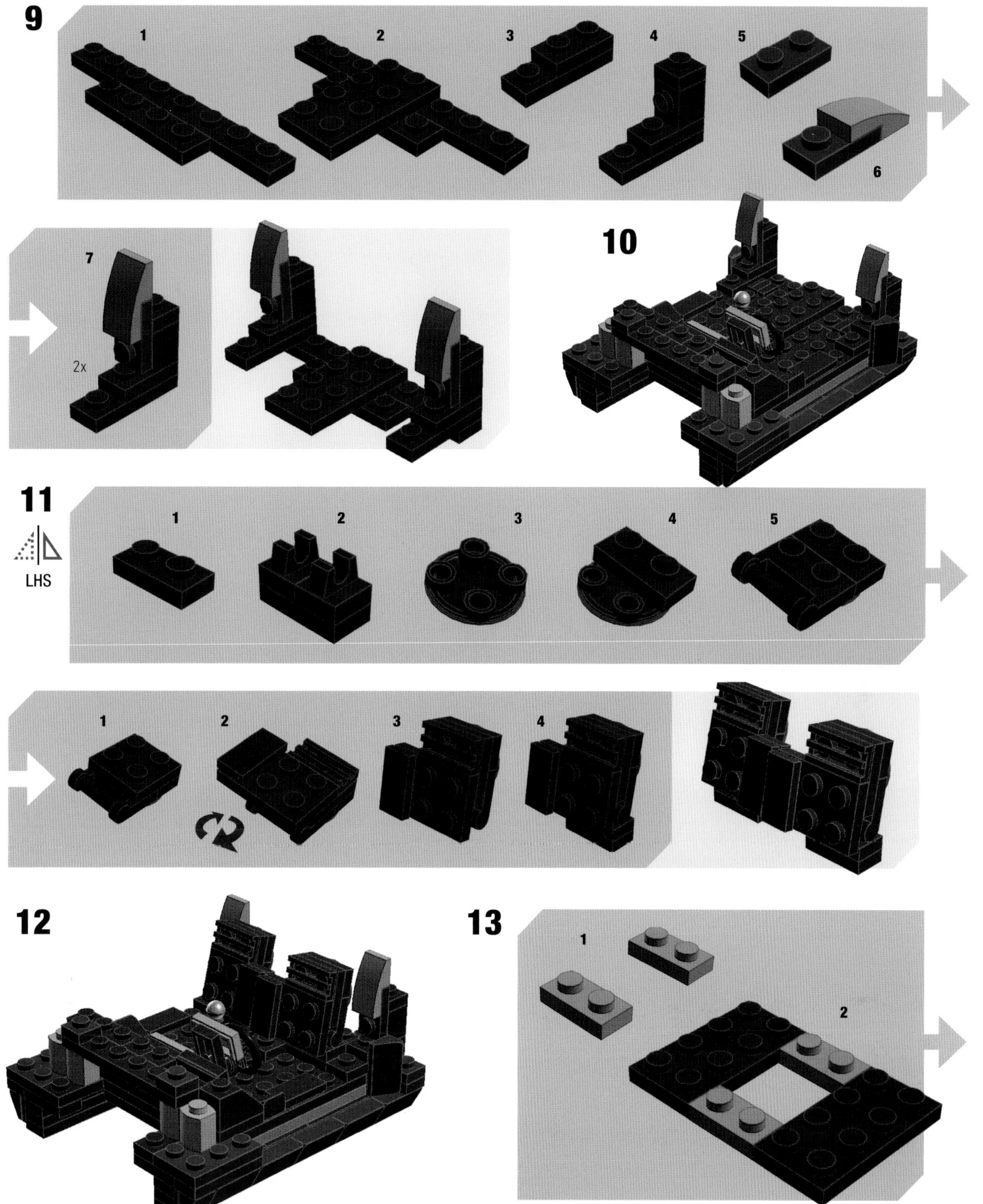
9
1
2
3
4
5
6
7
2x
10
11
LHS
1
2
3
4
5
1
2
3
4
12
13
1
2

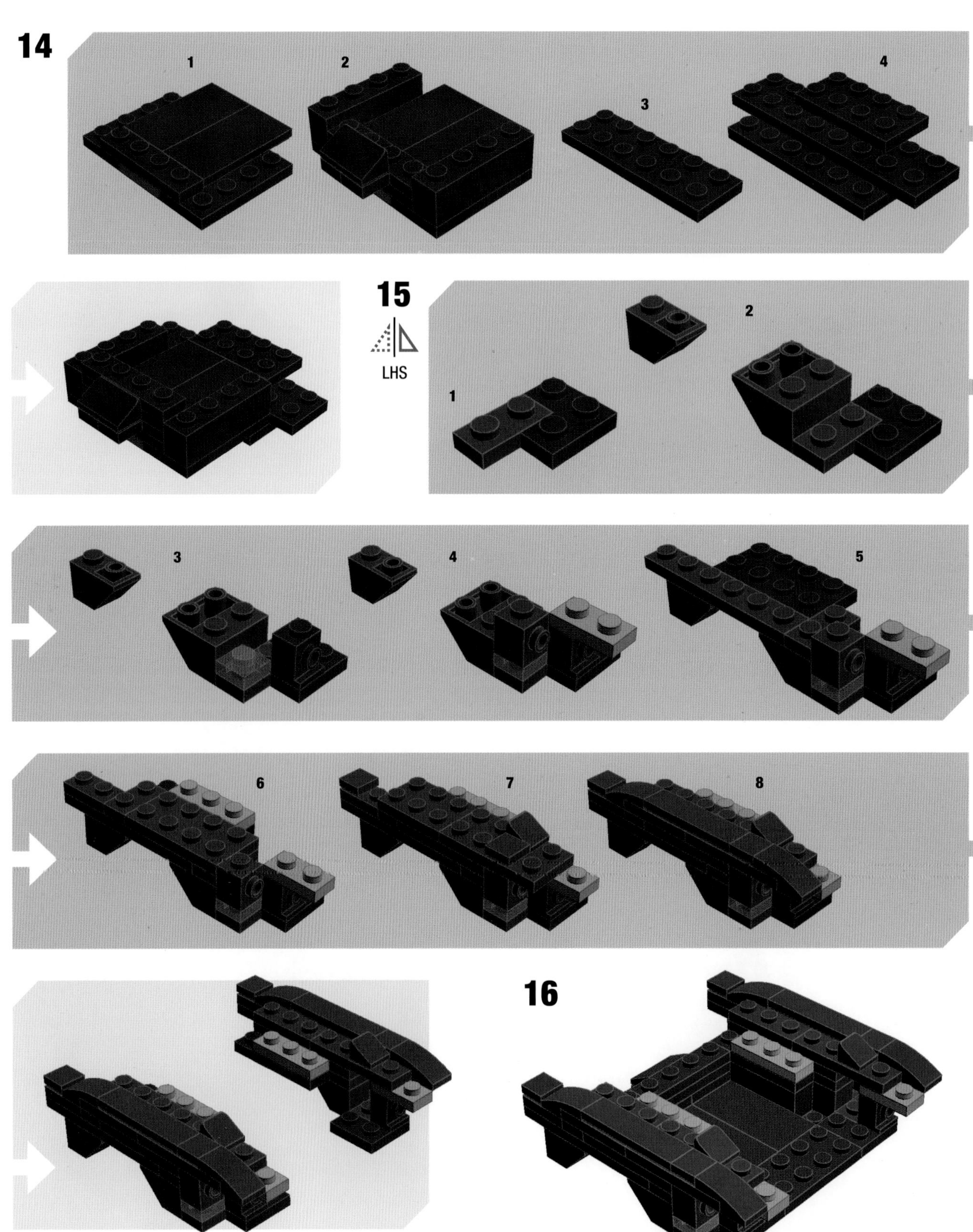
14
1
2
3
4
15
LHS
1
2
3
4
5
6
7
8
16

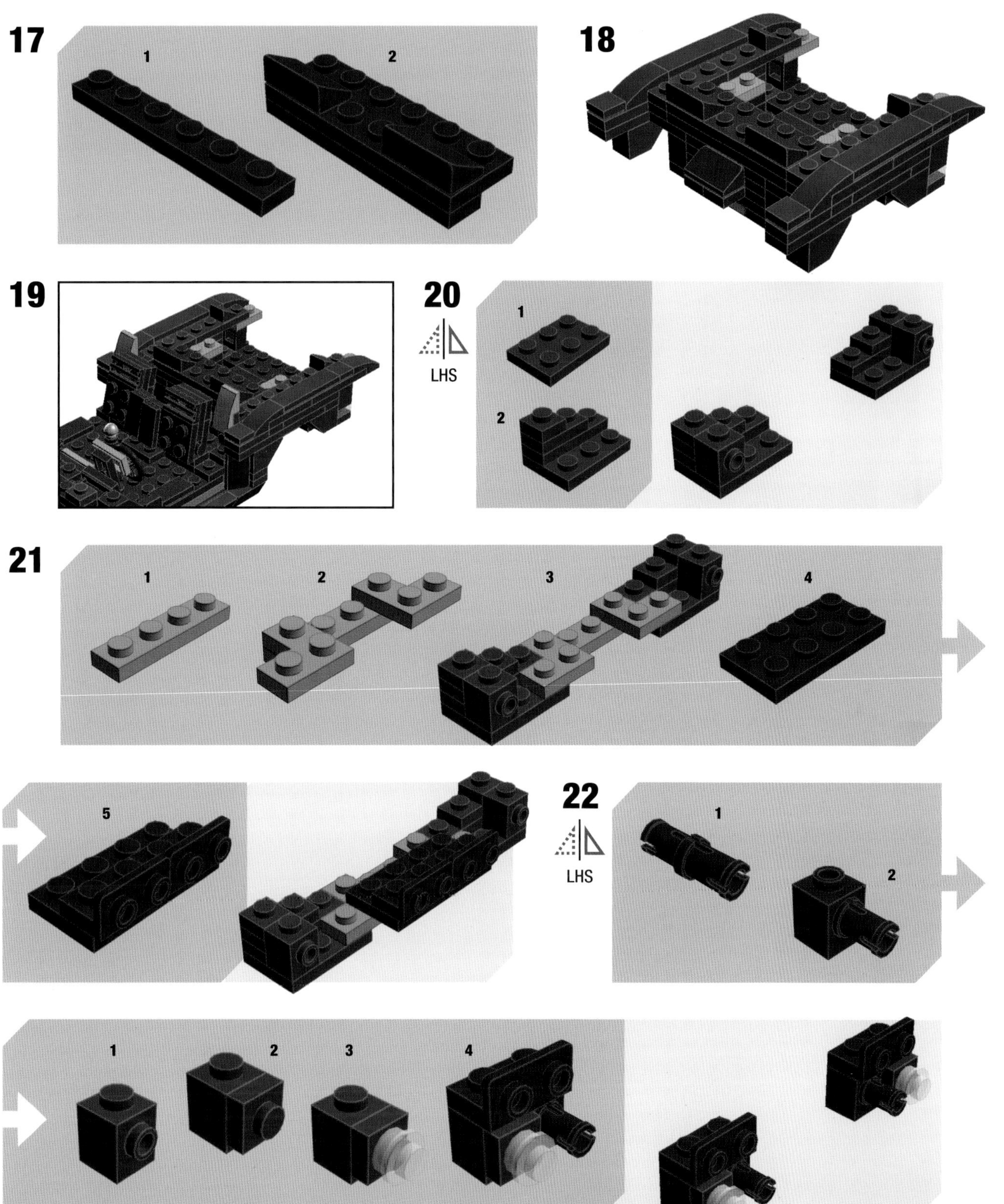
17
1
2
18
19
20
LHS
1
2
21
1
2
3
4
5
22
LHS
1
2
1
2
3
4

23

24

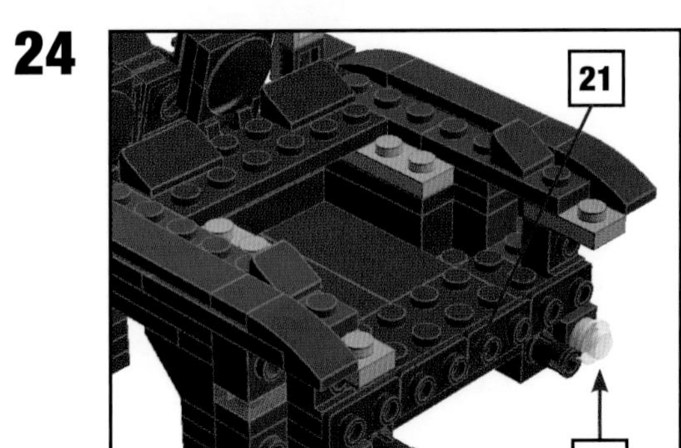

25

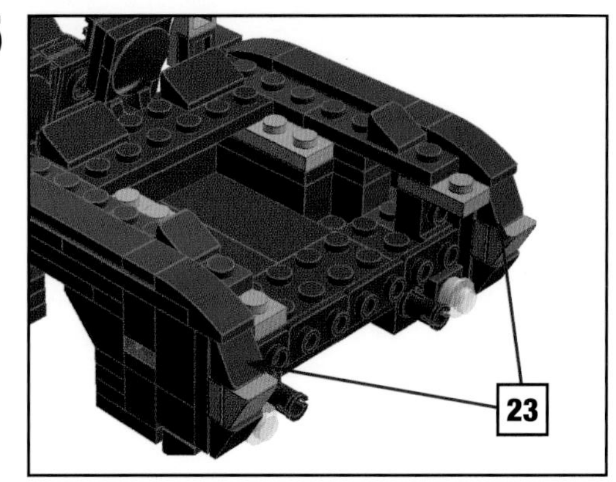

26

LHS

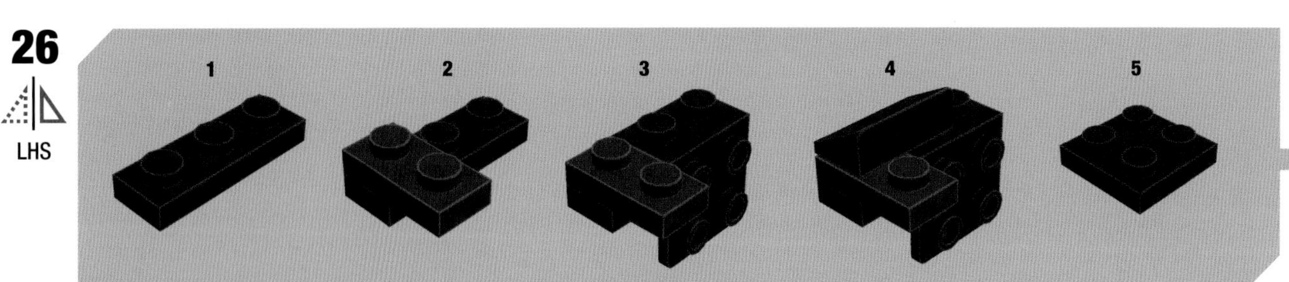

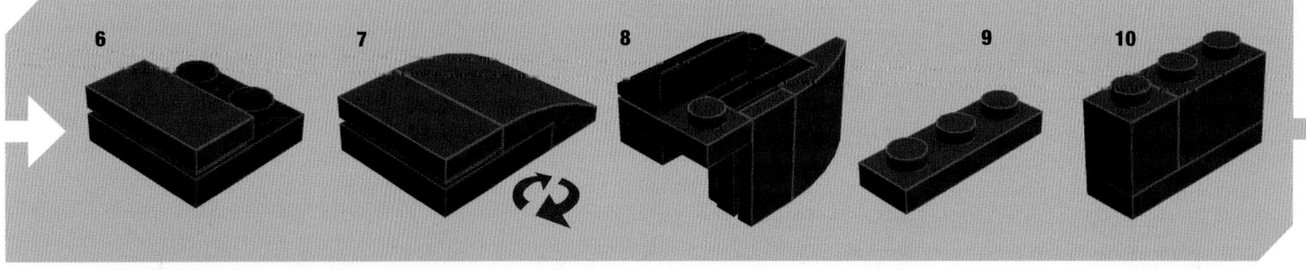

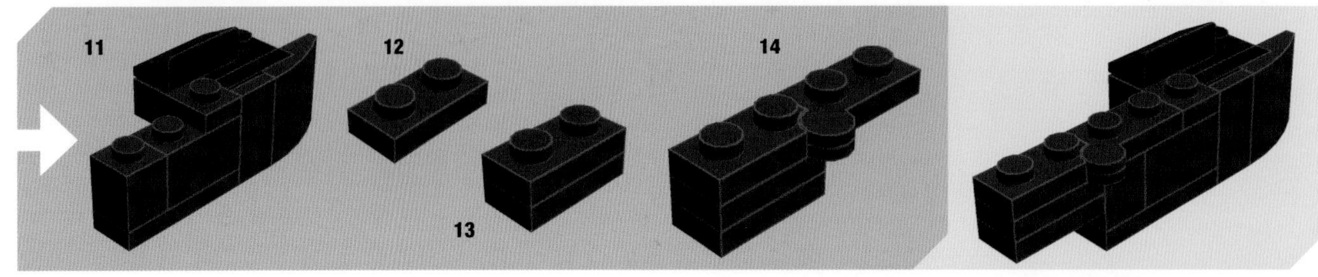

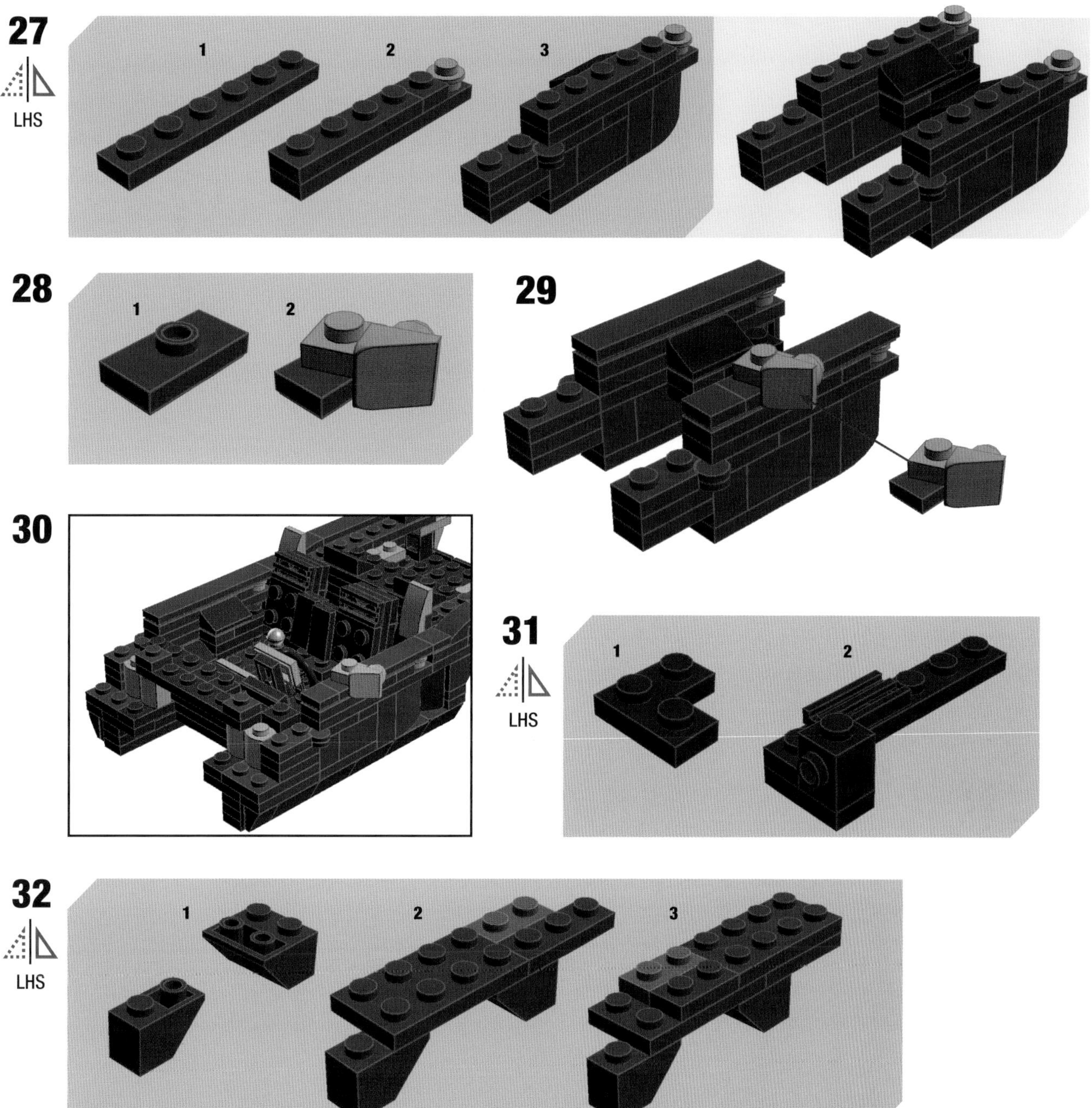
27
LHS
1
2
3
28
1
2
29
30
31
LHS
1
2
32
LHS
1
2
3

33

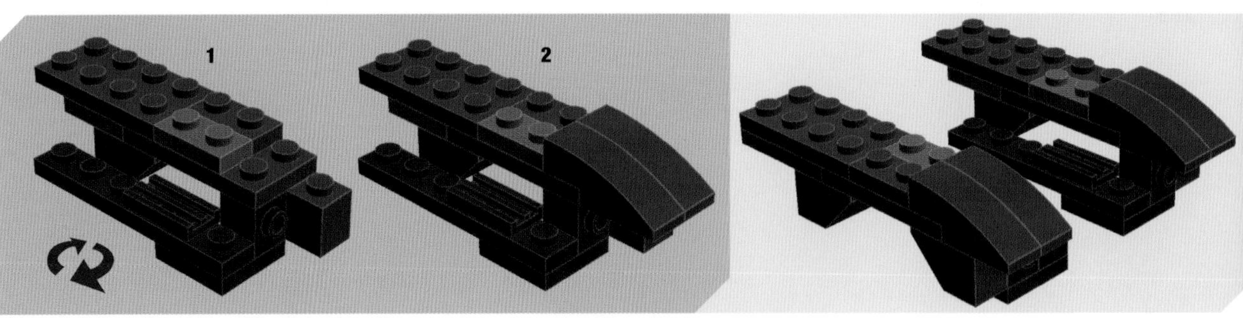

34

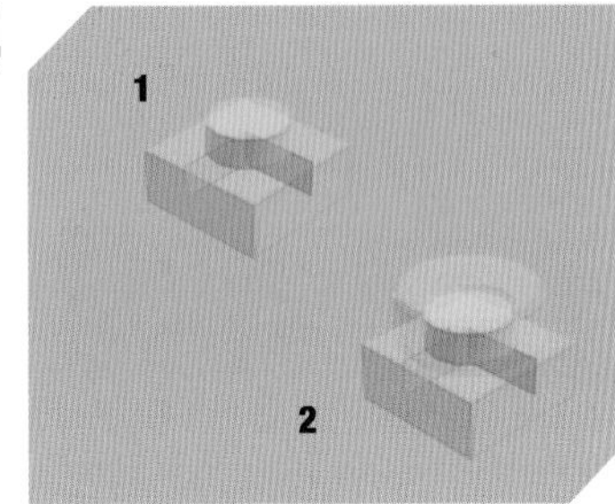

35

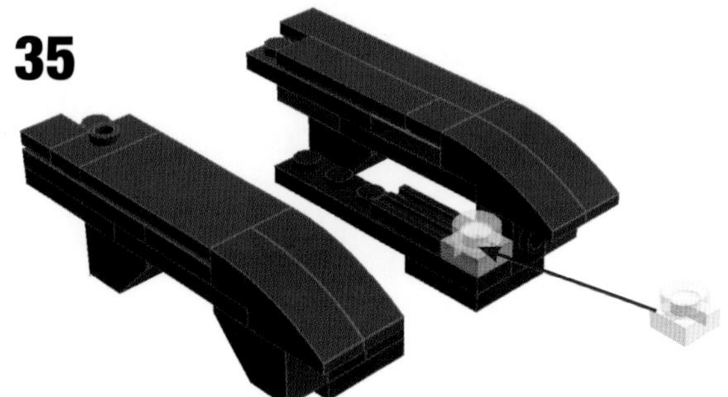

36

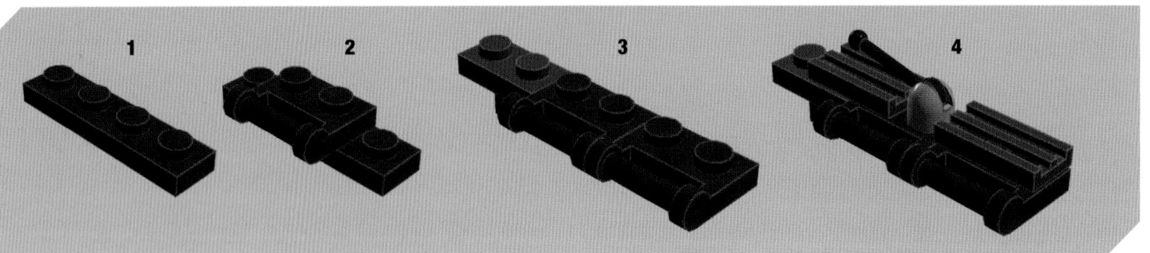

37

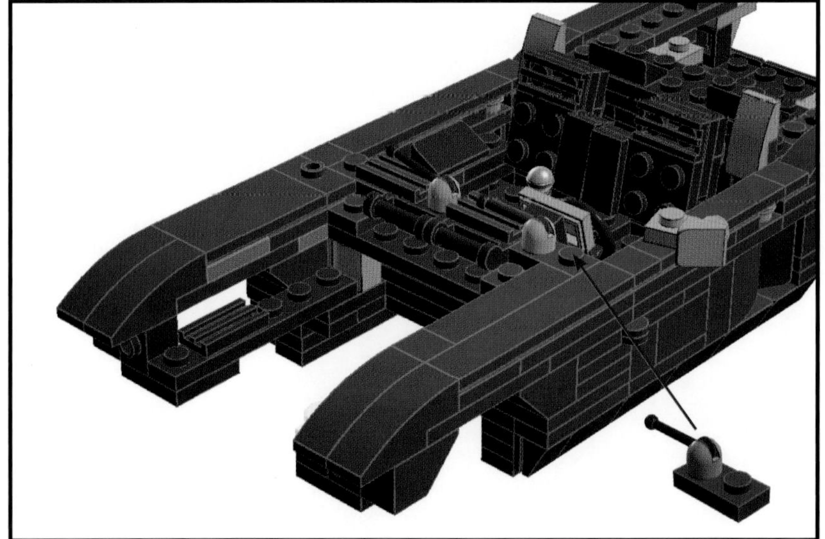

38

1 2 3 4 5

39

LHS

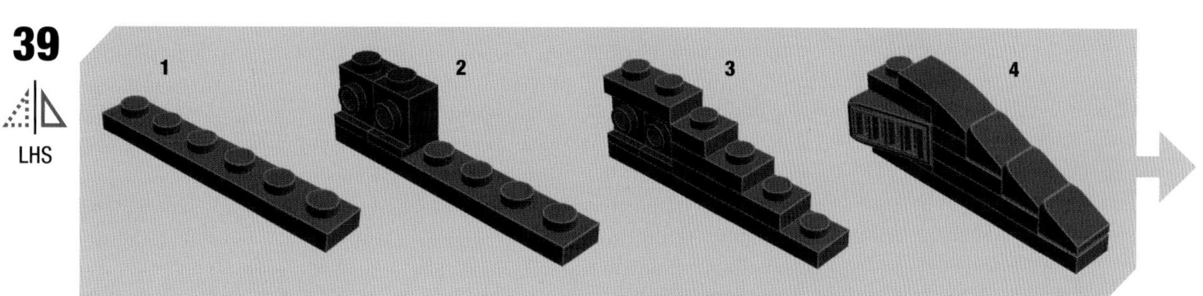

40

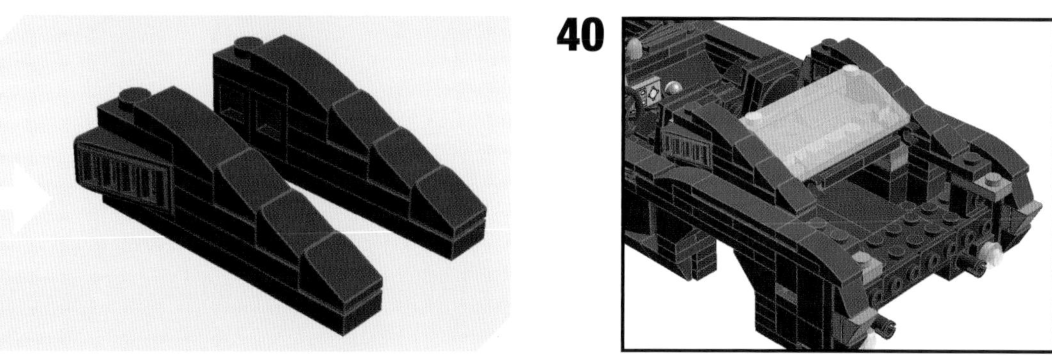

41

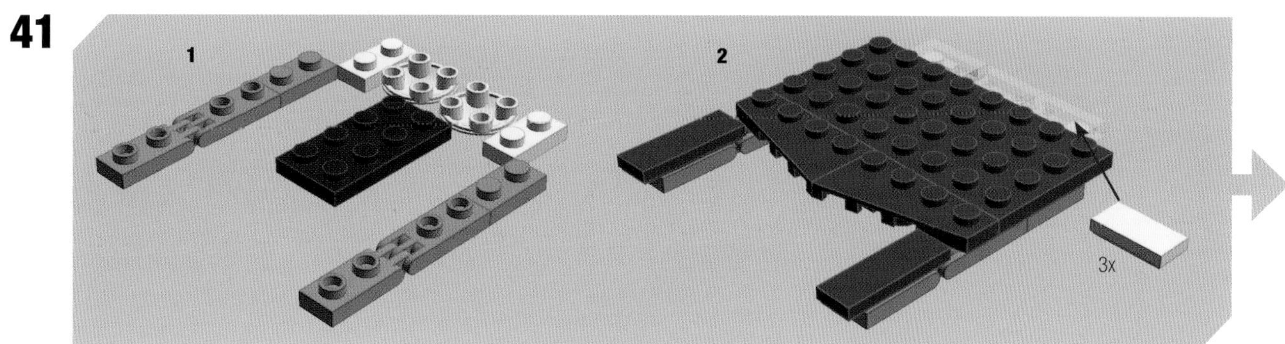

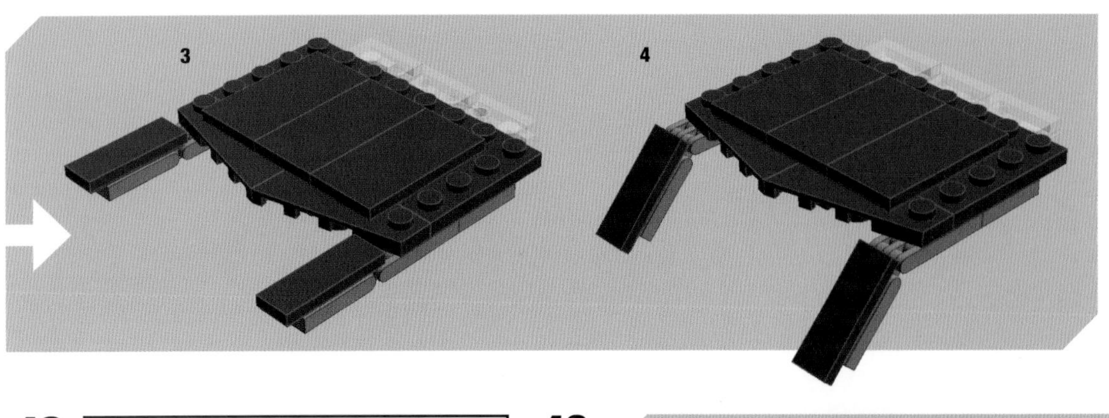

42

43

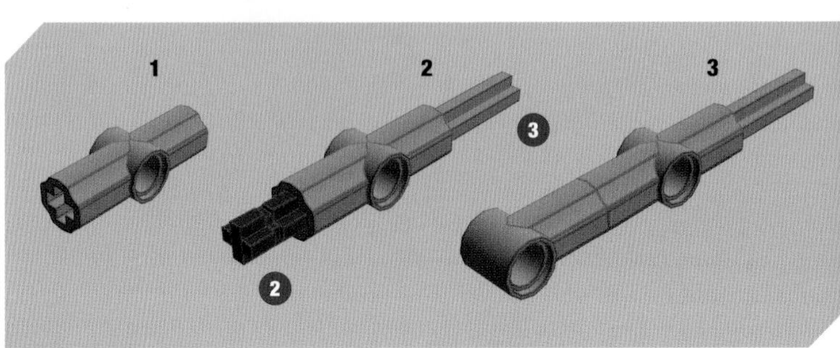

44

LHS

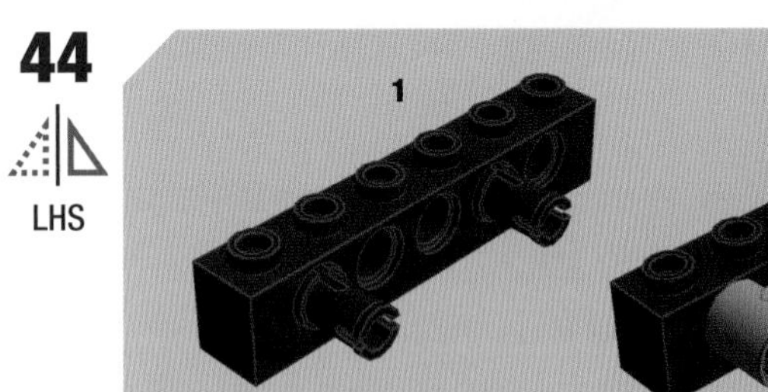

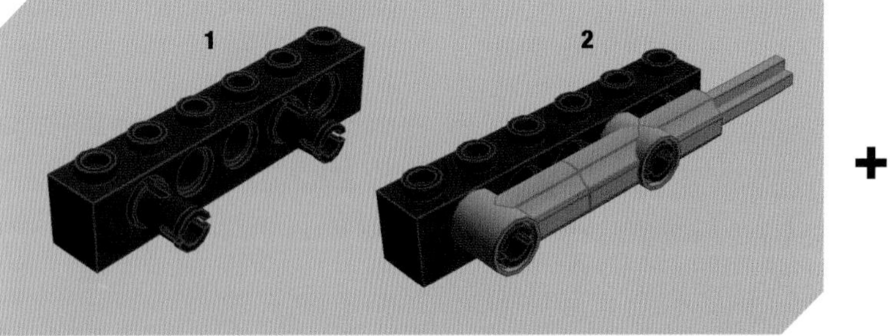

+

45

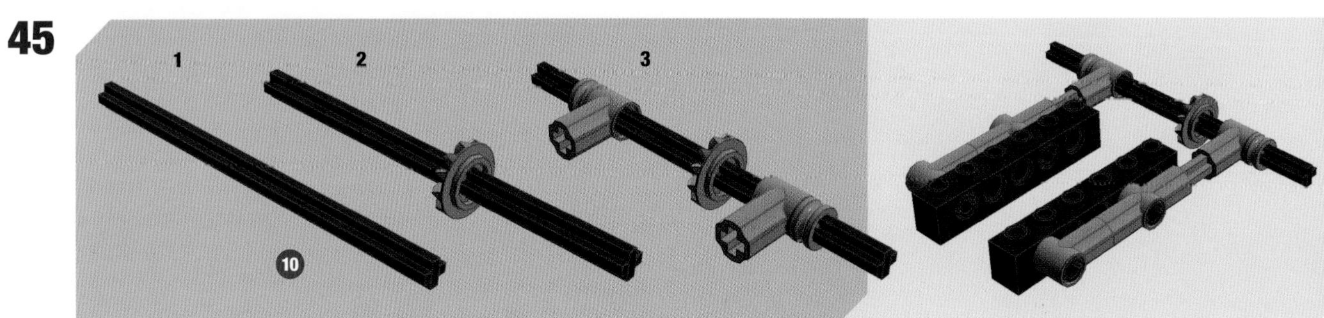

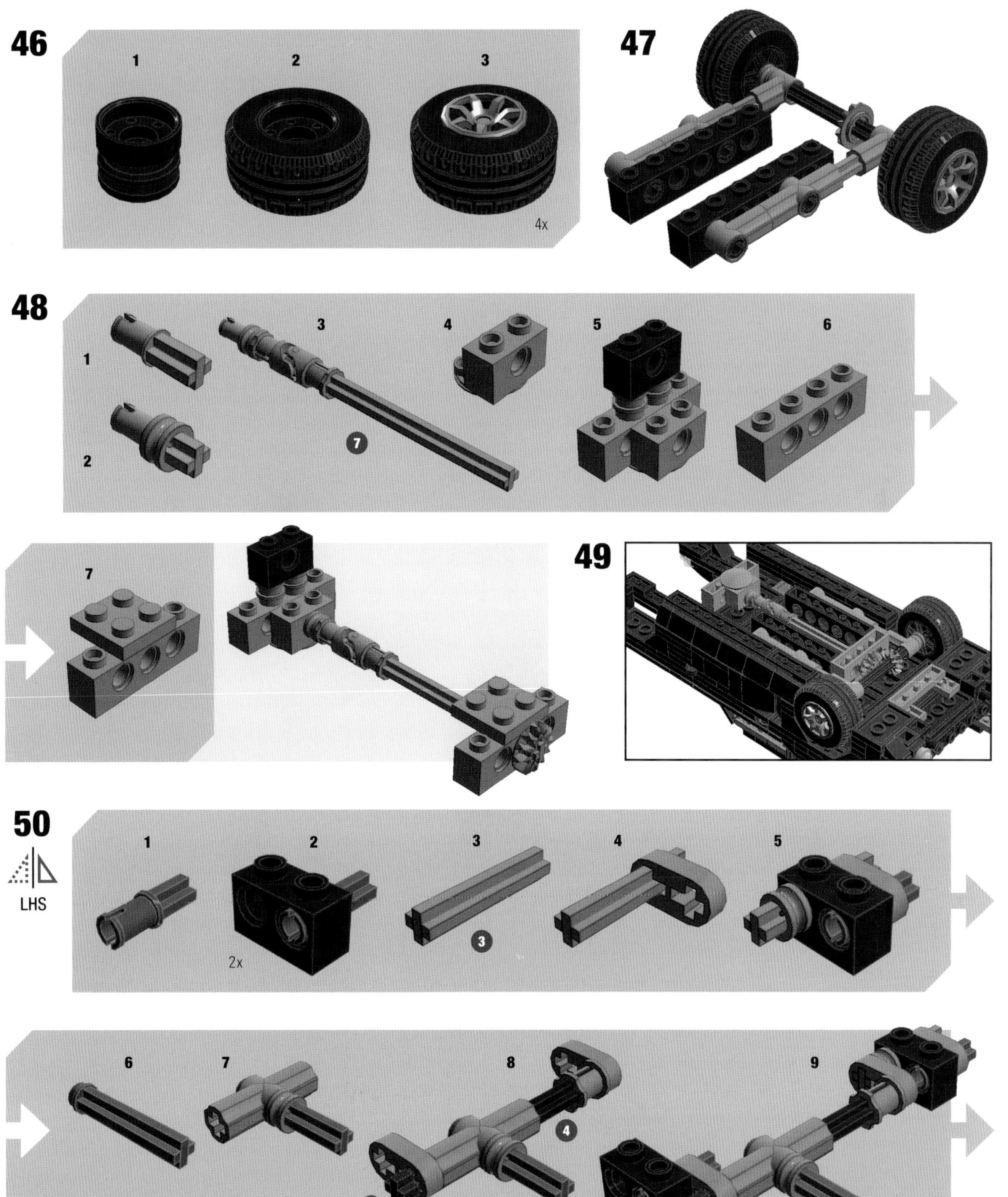
46
1
2
3
4x
47
48
1
2
3
4
5
6
7
7
49
50
LHS
1
2
3
4
5
2x
3
6
7
8
9
4
2

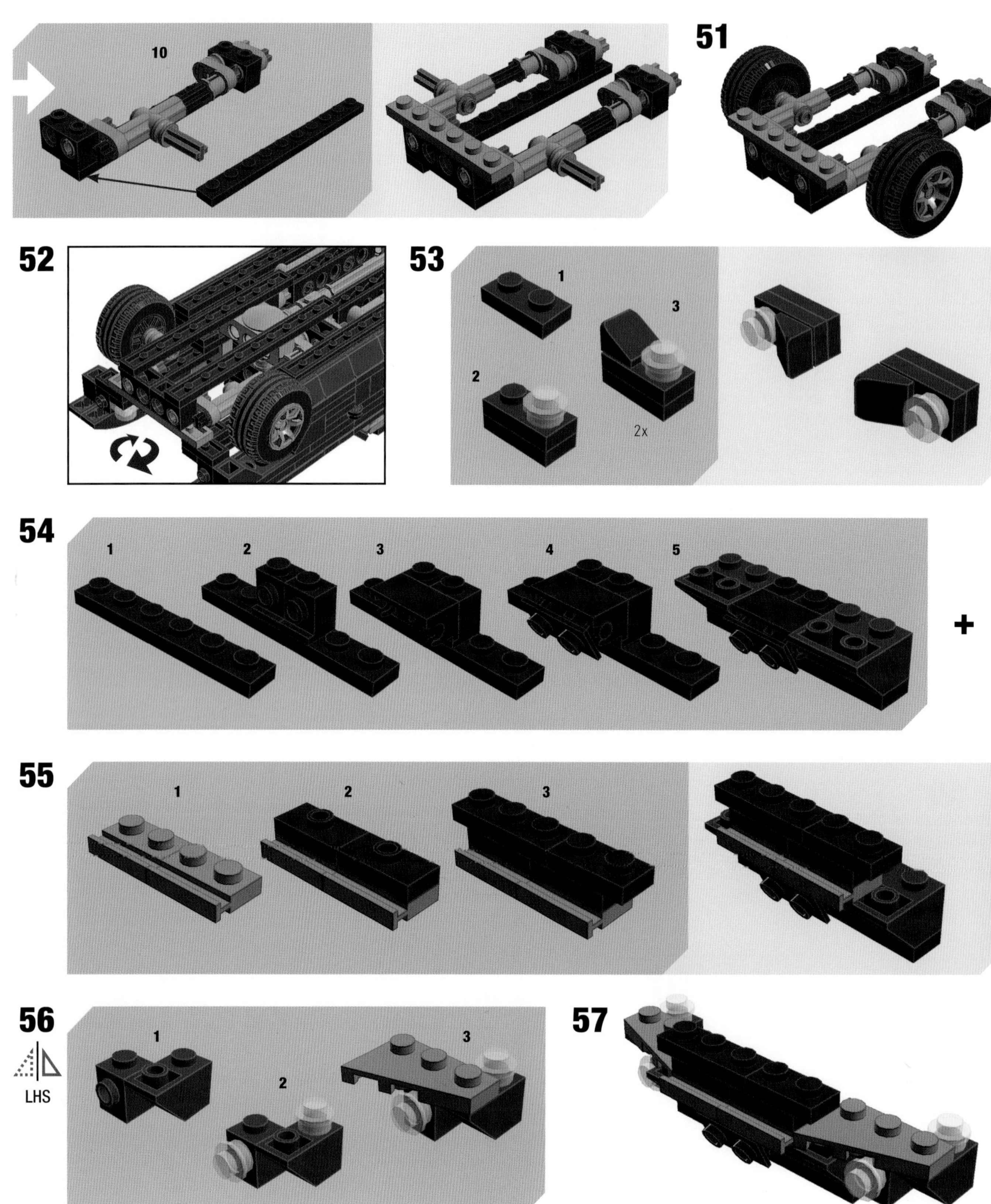
10
51
52
53
1
3
2
2x
54
1
2
3
4
5
+
55
1
2
3
56
LHS
1
3
2
57

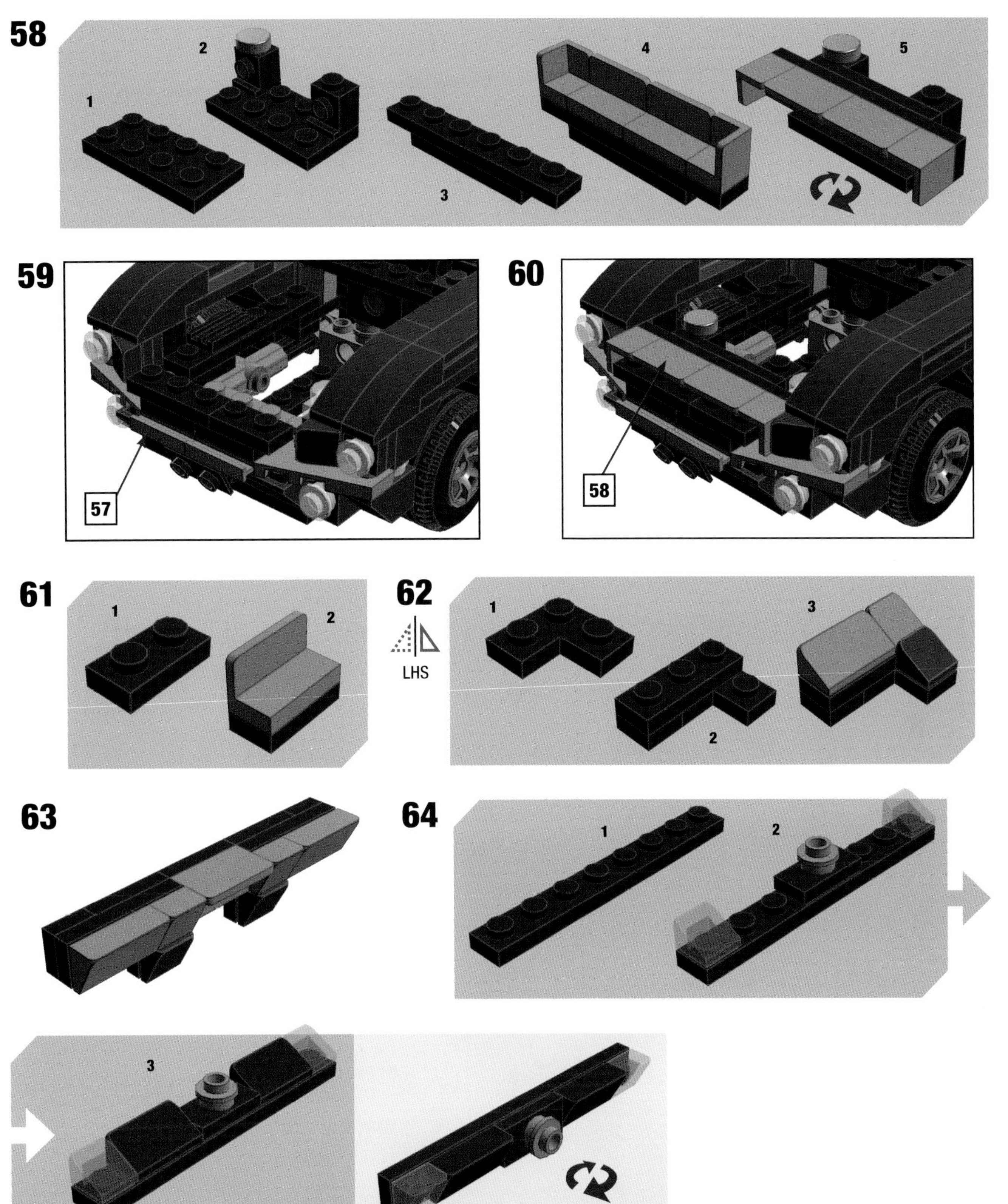
58
1
2
3
4
5
59
57
60
58
61
1
2
62
LHS
1
2
3
63
64
1
2
3

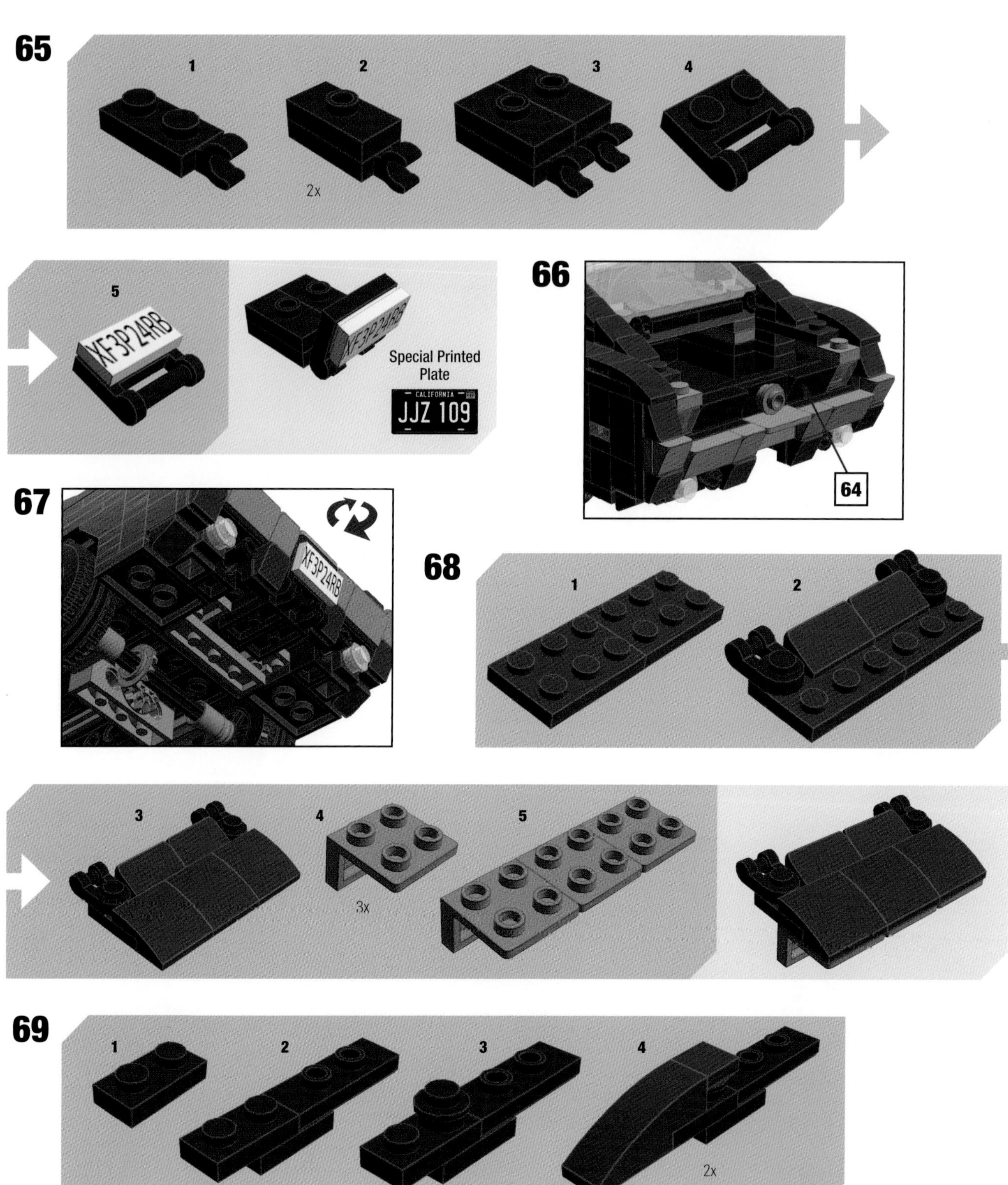
65
1
2
3
4
2x
5
XF3P24RB
Special Printed Plate
CALIFORNIA
JJZ 109
66
64
67
68
1
2
3
4
5
3x
69
1
2
3
4
2x

70

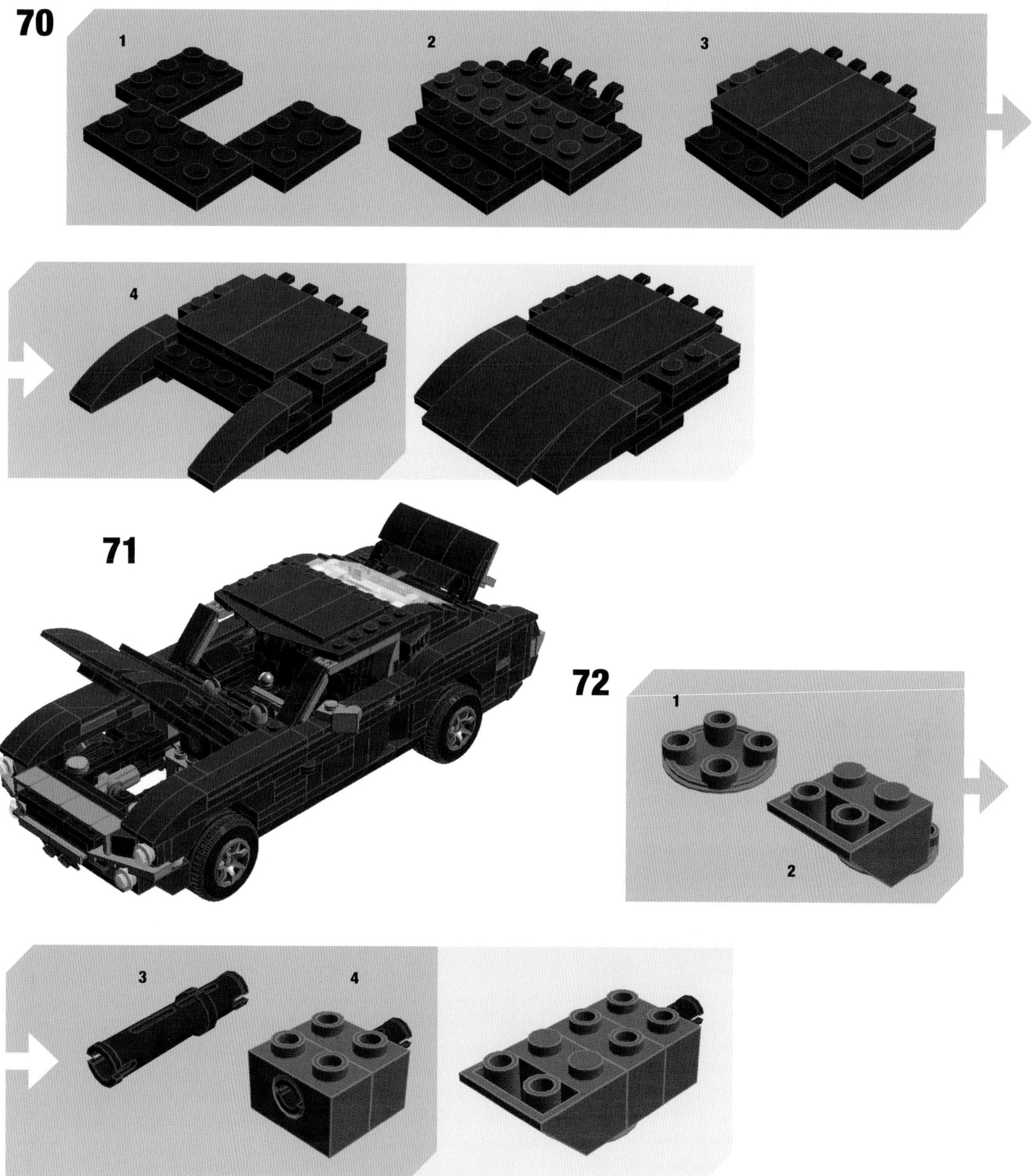

73

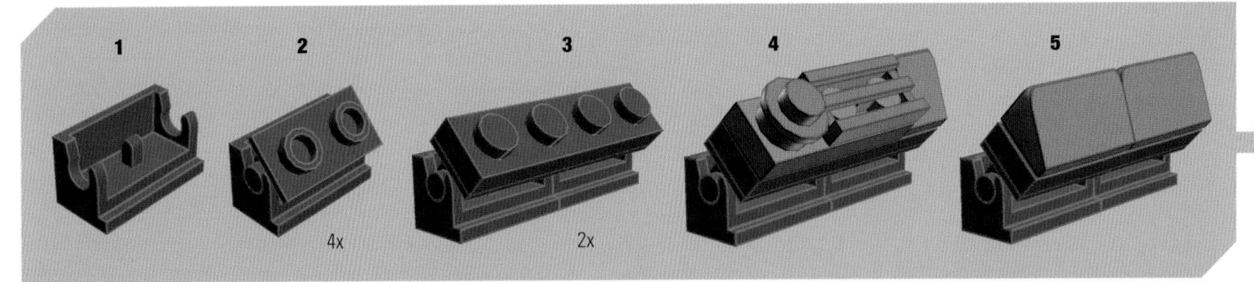

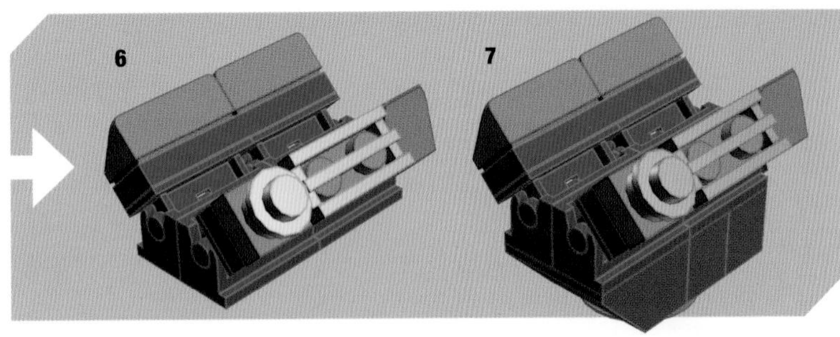

74

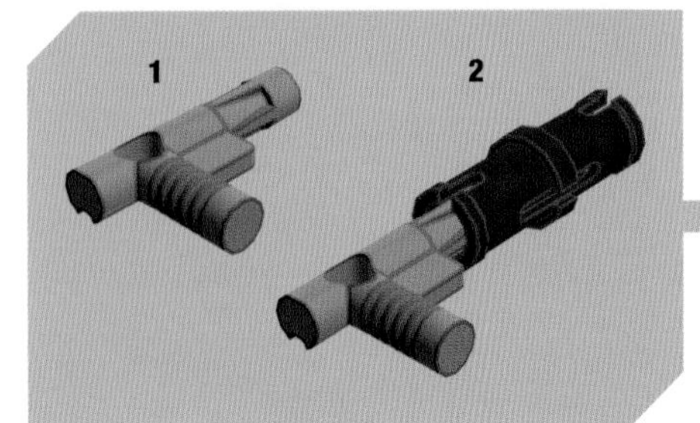

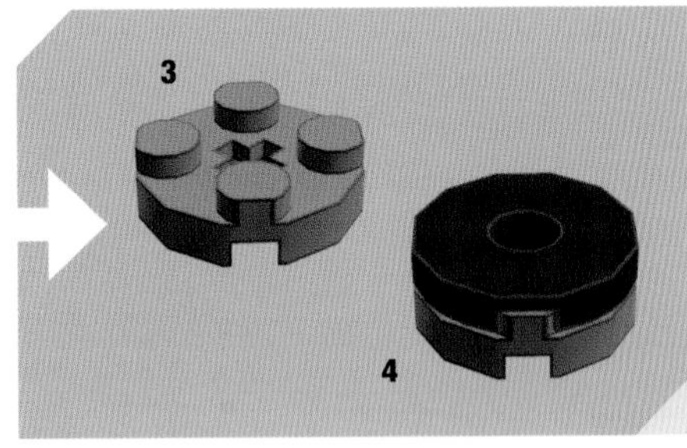

75

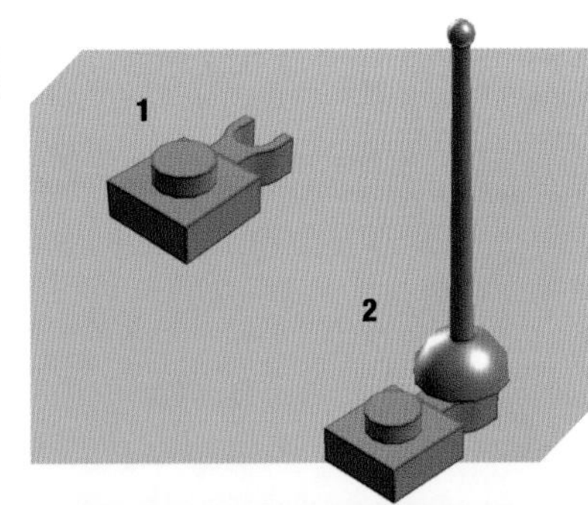

76

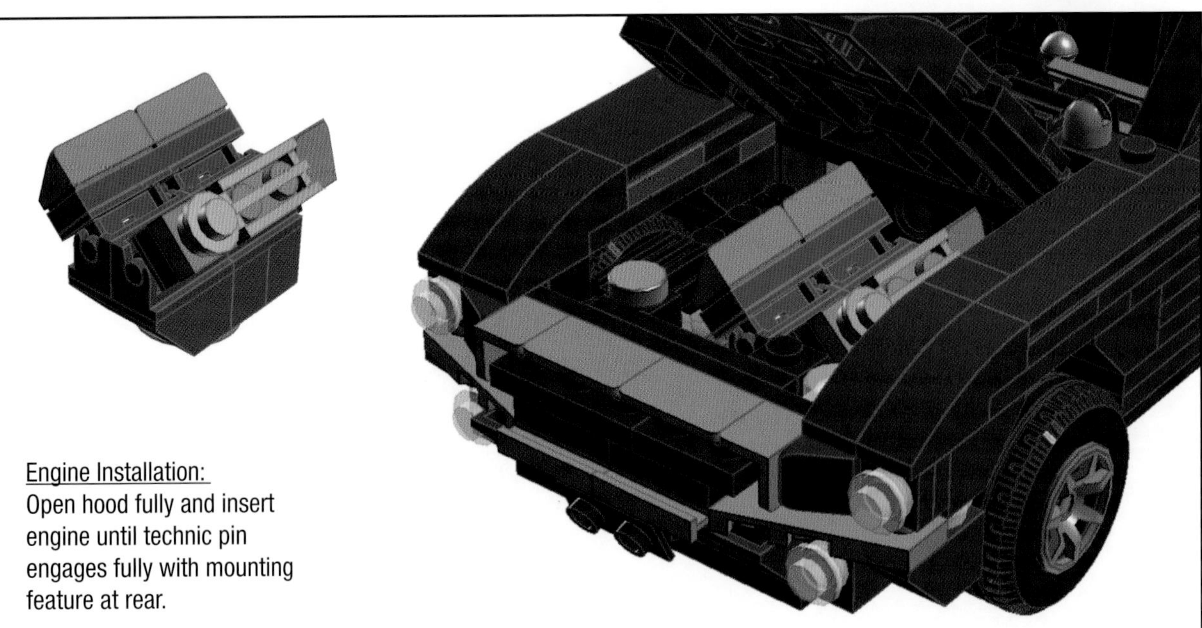

Engine Installation:
Open hood fully and insert engine until technic pin engages fully with mounting feature at rear.

77

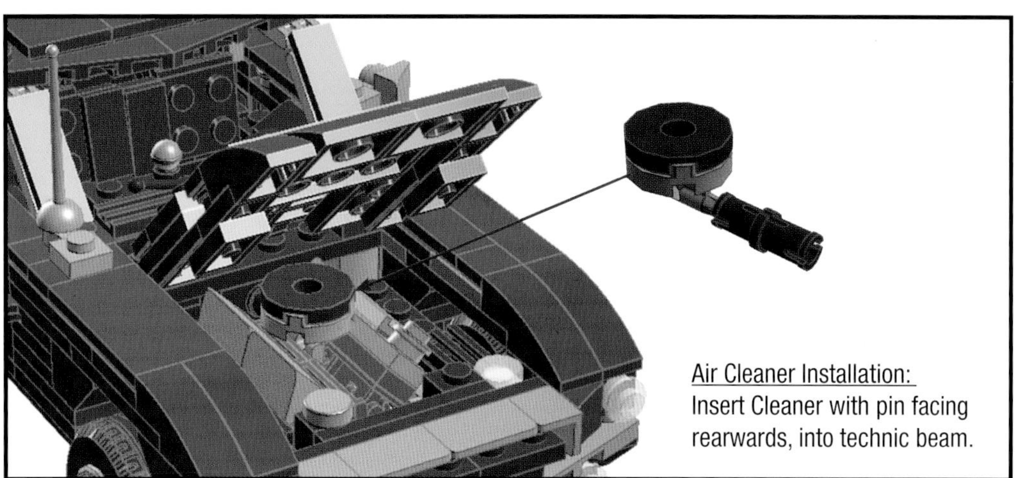

Air Cleaner Installation:
Insert Cleaner with pin facing rearwards, into technic beam.

CHAPTER 7

TOYOTA AE86 TRUENO SPRINTER
INITIAL D

What is the deal with the AE86 Corolla?

Nowadays the car is considered the quintessential Japanese classic, but the reality is that the car was the last vestige of the old rear-wheel-drive (RWD) Corolla genes. Even stranger still, the car was not considered particularly special when new—after a few years and a few dozen thousand miles, was just another used car.

The kind of car that might be driven by a student with a delivery food run.

If that take-out food was in Japan, it might just be tofu being delivered, and as with all "first" cars, the ability to be independently mobile was more important than any objective faults the car may have had. The driver could now play at being a race driver.

And thus: *Initial D*—the story of 18-year-old Takumi Fujiwara, a high-school student who delivers tofu in his father's 1985 Toyota Sprinter Trueno GT Apex AE86 coupe. *Initial D* was originally an illustrated manga in *Weekly Young Magazine* from 1995 to 2013 but was adapted to anime in 1998. Though legendary in native Japan, *Initial D* also has a cult following outside of the country, with English-language distribution through Tokyopop and latterly Funimation.

COUNTRY OF ORIGIN: Japan

群馬55
お 13-954

PRODUCTION: 1983–1987

NUMBER MADE: No data available

LAYOUT/DRIVE: Front engine, Rear-wheel-drive

ENGINE: 1.6 liter, 4 cylinders

POWER TORQUE: 118 hp (88 kW) / 105 lb-ft (142 Nm)

CONSTRUCTION/DOORS: Steel Monocoque, three-door Liftback

TV/FILM APPEARANCE: *Initial D* (1999)

I relate to the story, having delivered takeaway food in my own RWD Corolla during the same period. I did not have the benefit of the punchy fuel-injected 4A-GE 1.6 DOHC inline four cylinder—but then, I didn't have to race through mountain passes in the Kanto region of Japan up against Mazda RX7s. What all RWD Corollas do, though, is go sideways, and in a front-wheel-drive world, that still is a big deal.

The name "AE86" has so much cachet that when Toyota released a new RWD sportscar in conjunction with Subaru, they named it the "86".

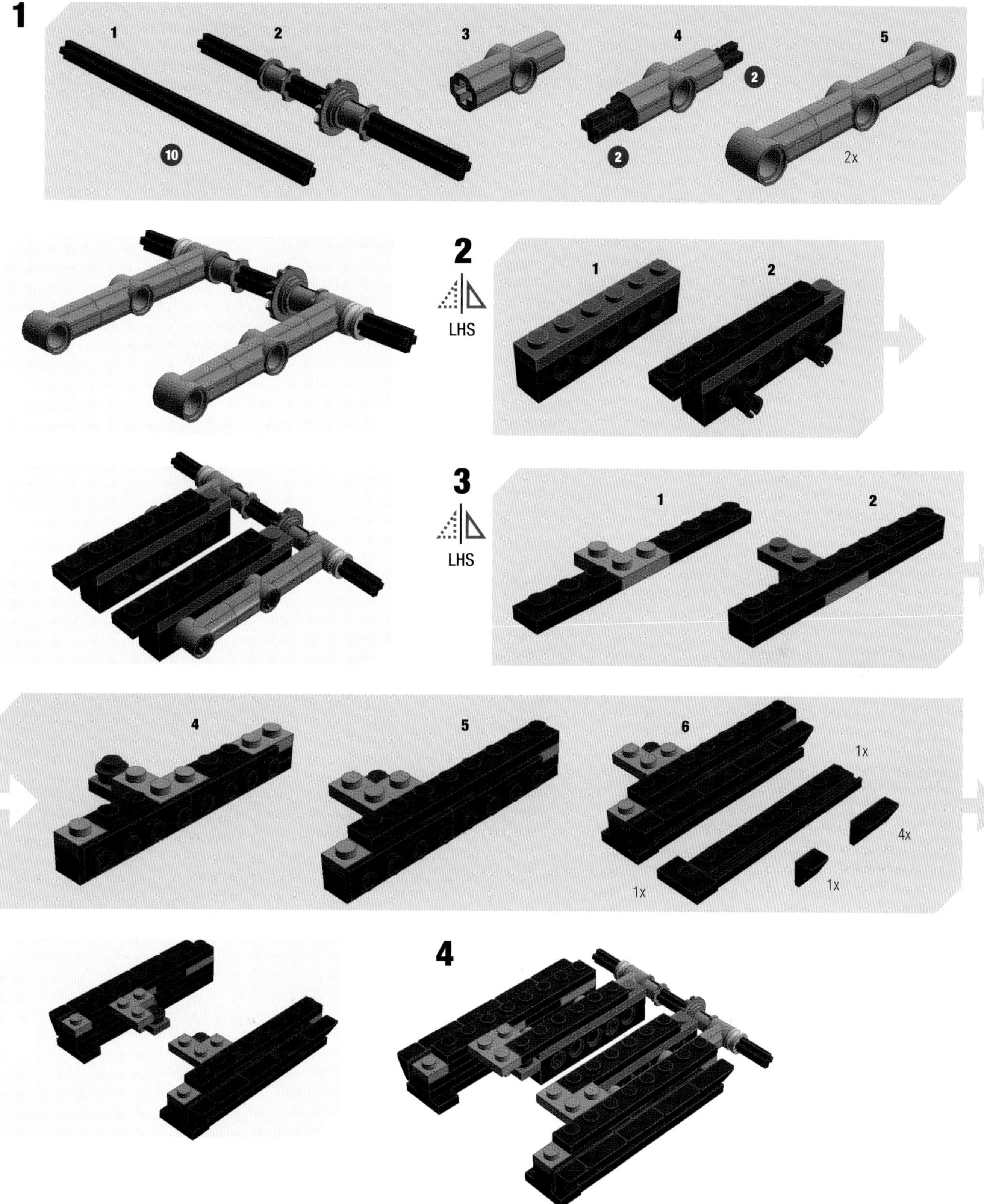
1
1
2
3
4
5
10
2
2
2x
2
LHS
1
2
3
LHS
1
2
4
5
6
1x
4x
1x
1x
4

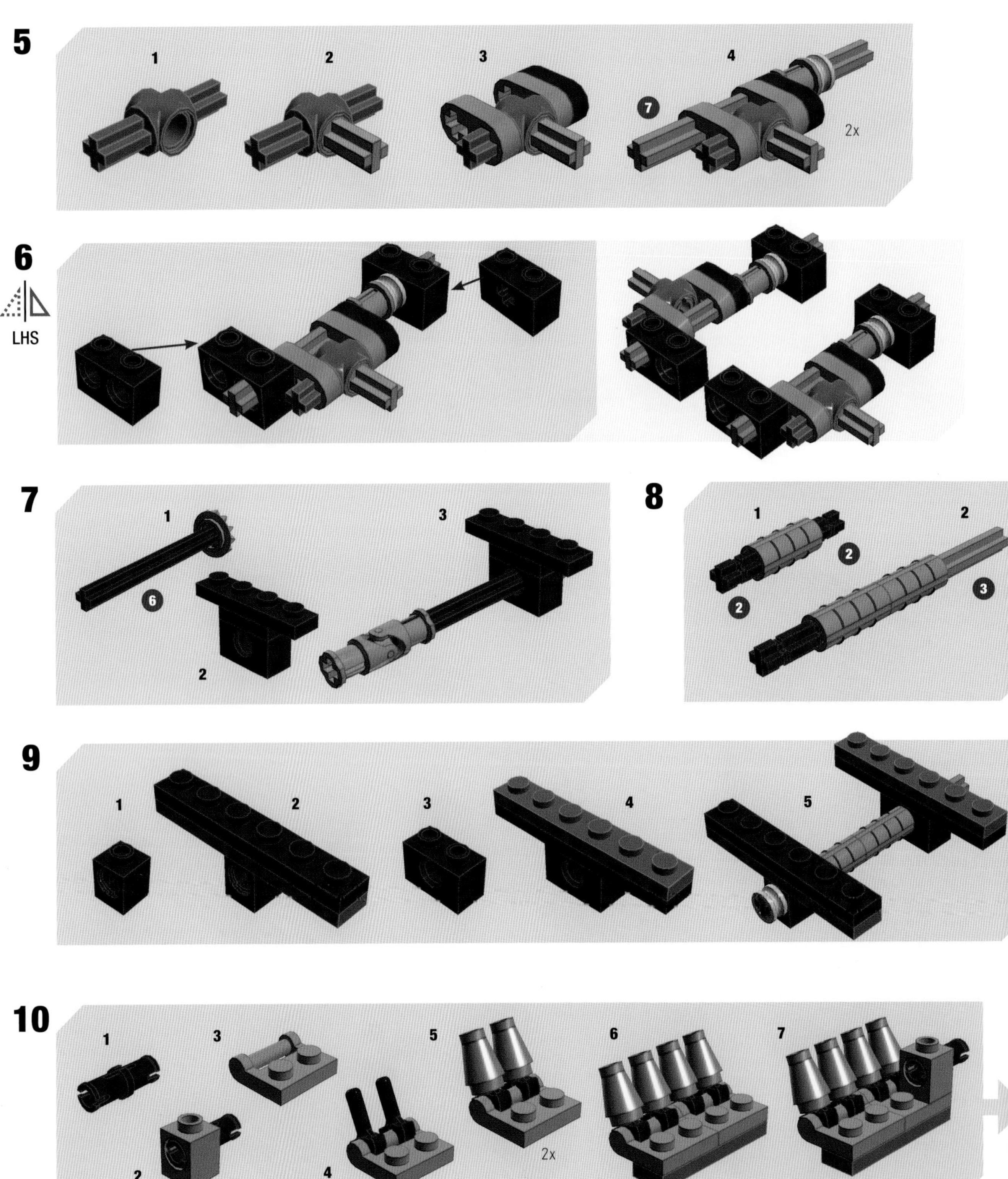
5
1
2
3
4
7
2x
6
LHS
7
1
6
2
3
8
1
2
2
2
3
9
1
2
3
4
5
10
1
2
3
4
5
2x
6
7

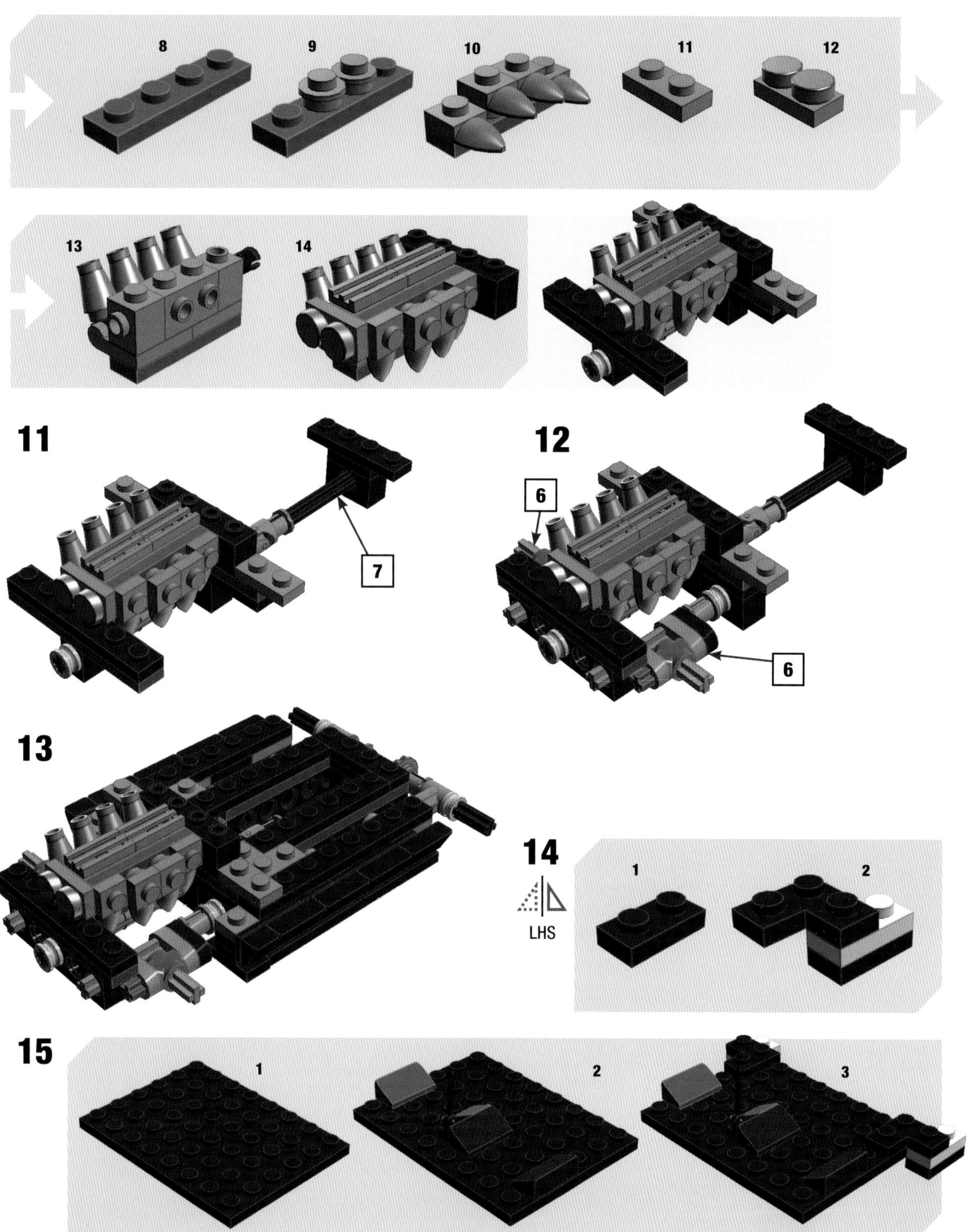
8
9
10
11
12
13
14
11
7
12
6
6
13
14
1
2
LHS
15
1
2
3

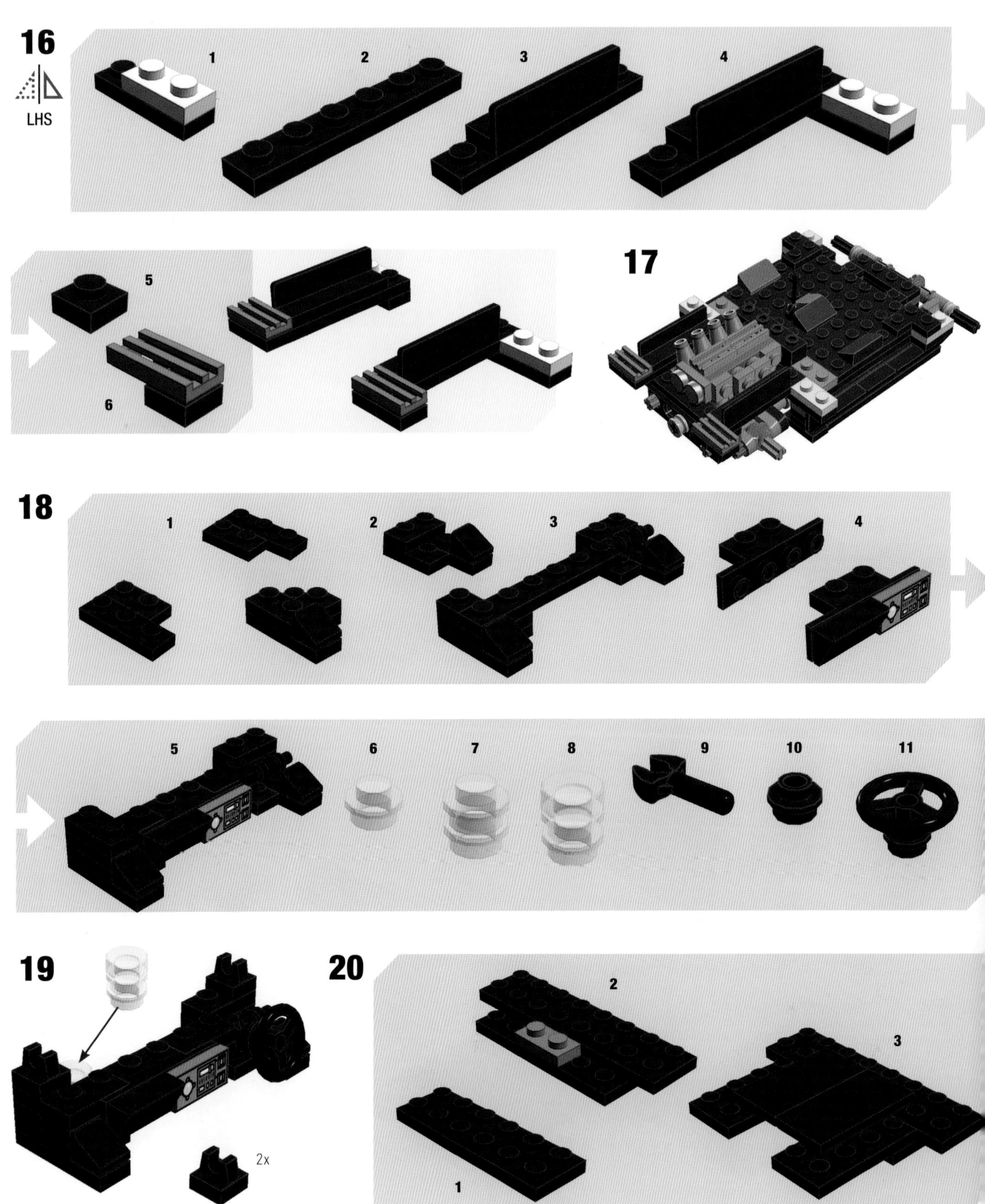
16
LHS
1
2
3
4
5
6
17
18
1
2
3
4
5
6
7
8
9
10
11
19
2x
20
1
2
3

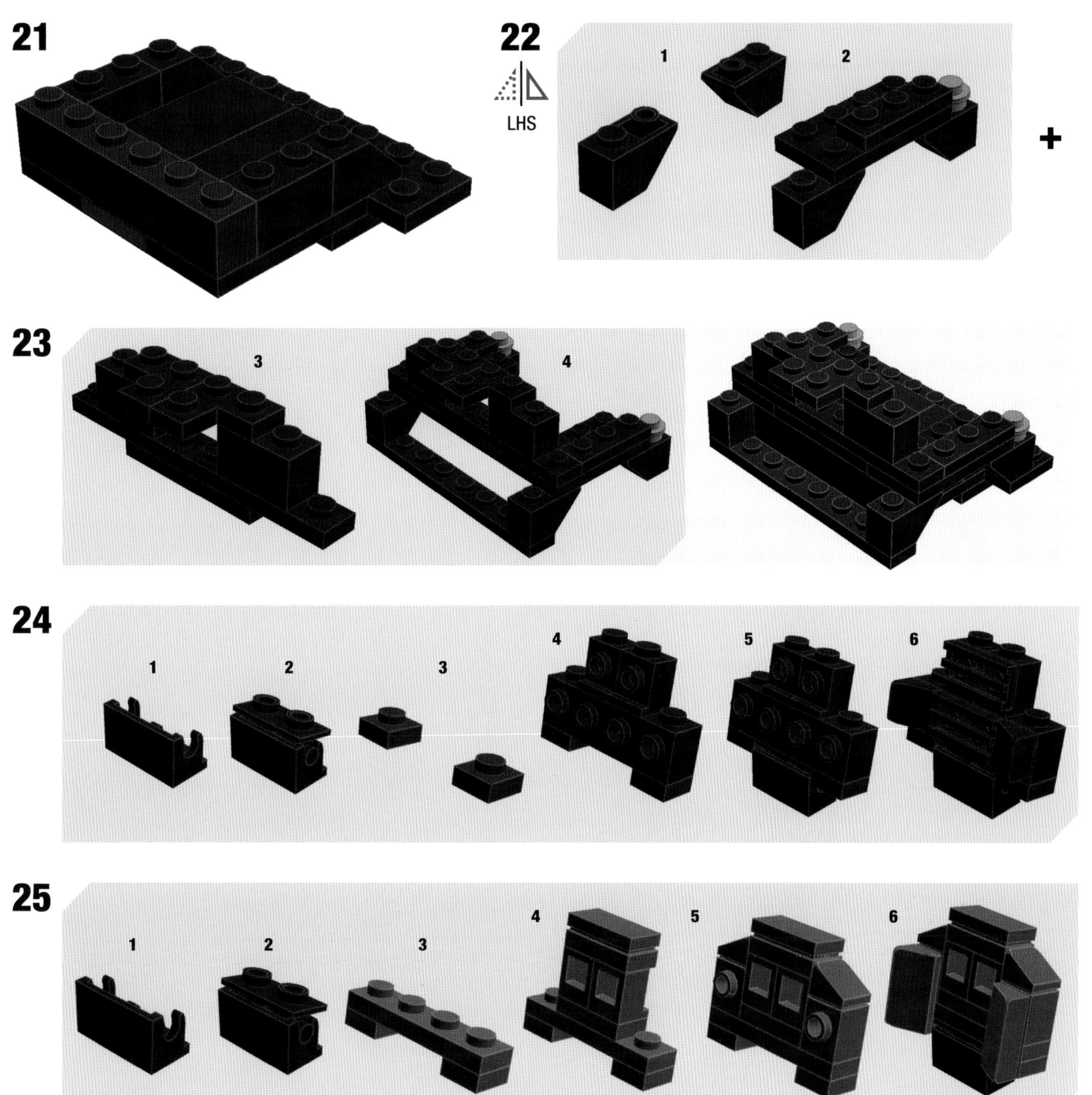
21
22
LHS
1
2
+
23
3
4
24
1
2
3
4
5
6
25
1
2
3
4
5
6

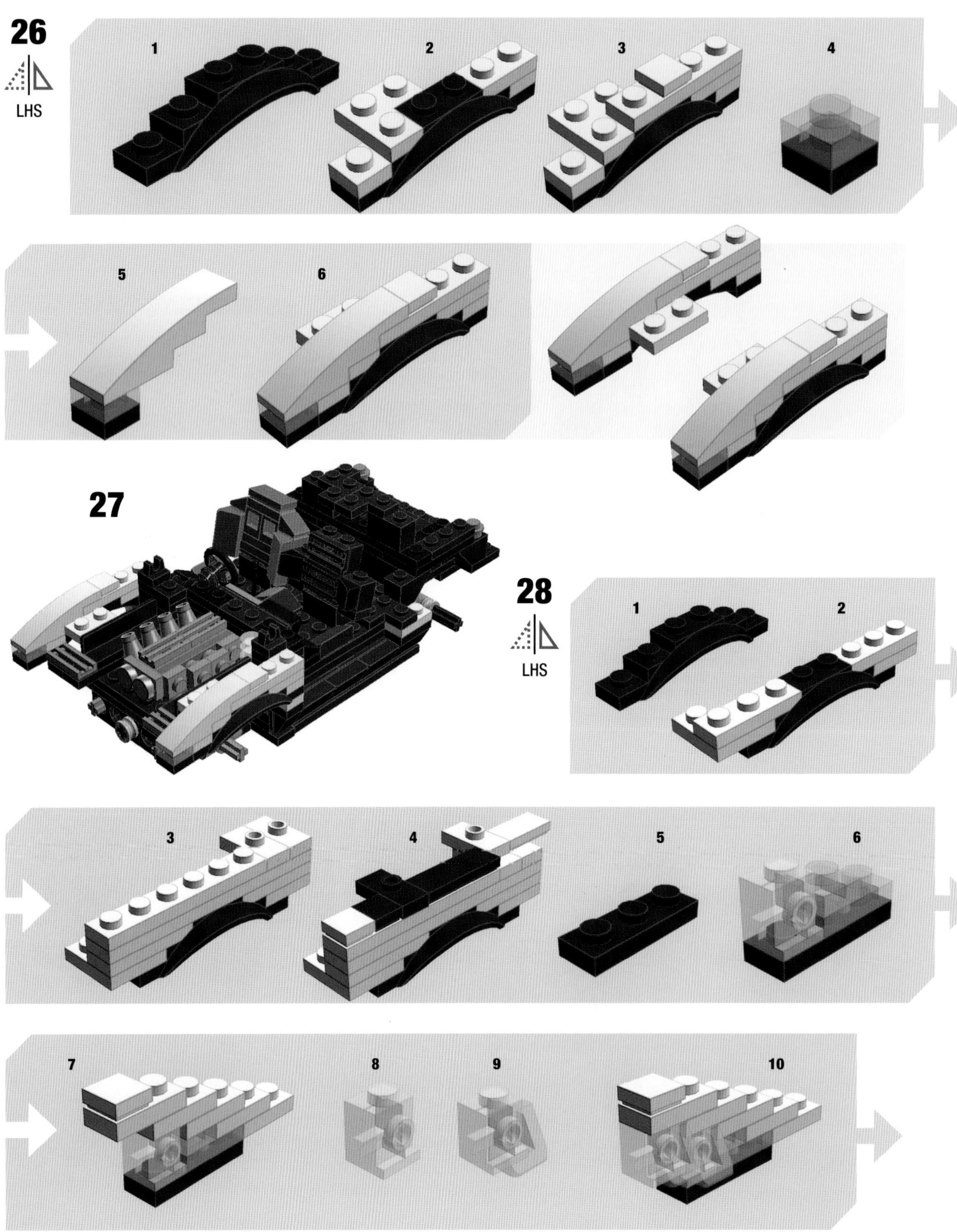
26
LHS
1
2
3
4
5
6
27
28
LHS
1
2
3
4
5
6
7
8
9
10

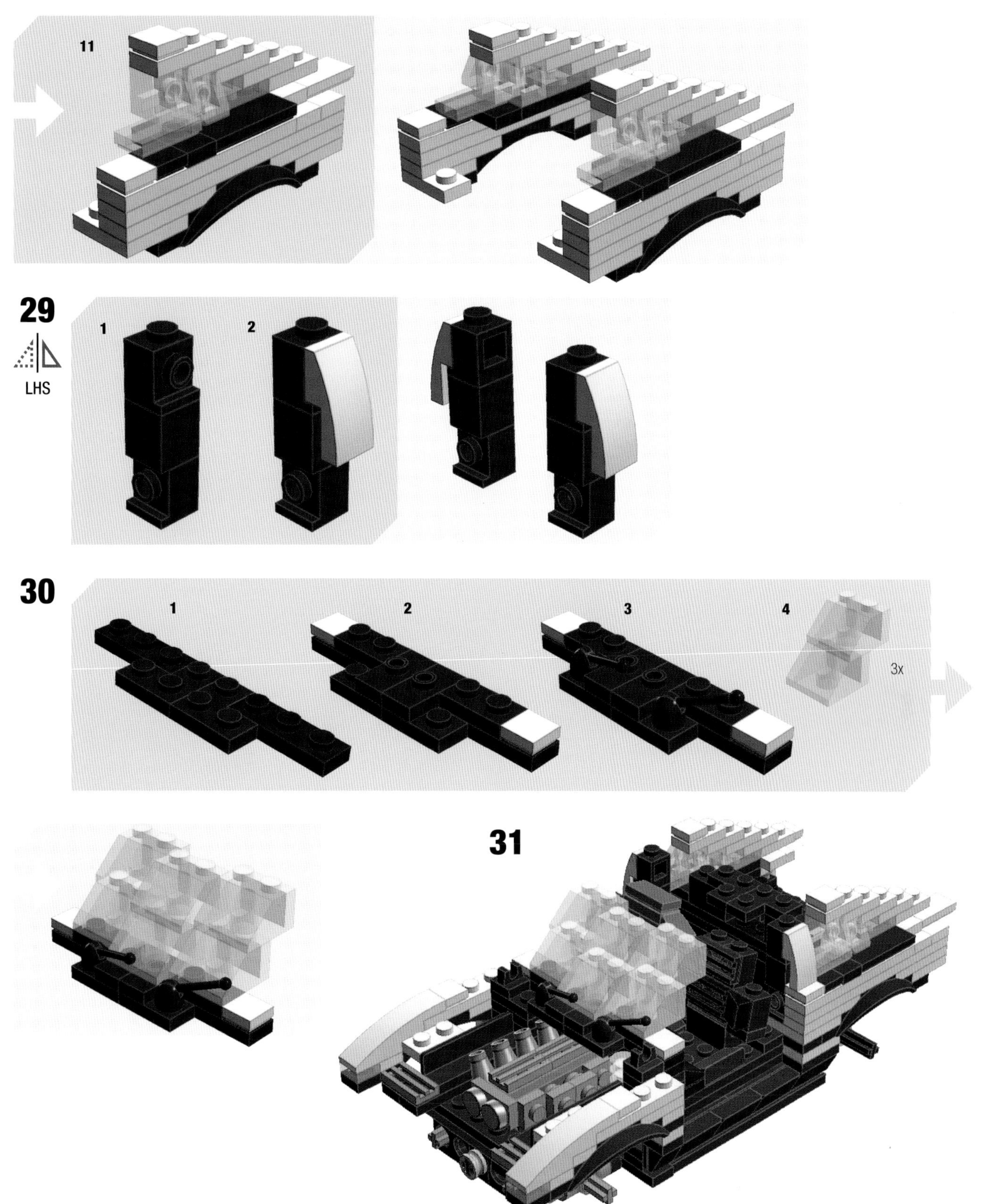
11
29
1
2
LHS
30
1
2
3
4
3x
31

32

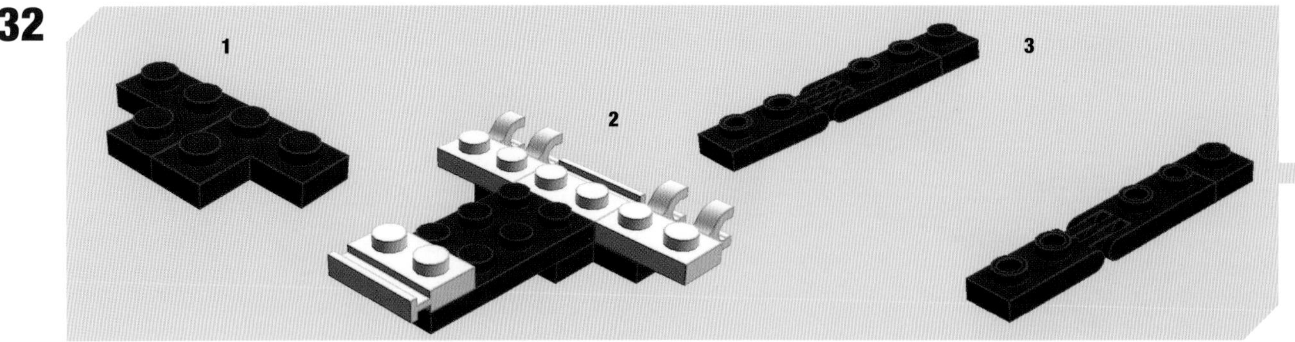
1
2
3

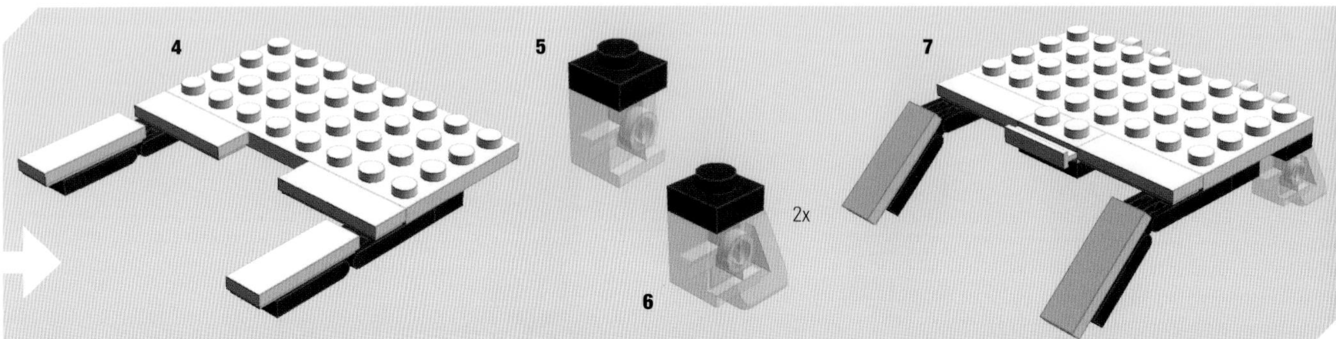
4
5
2x
6
7

33

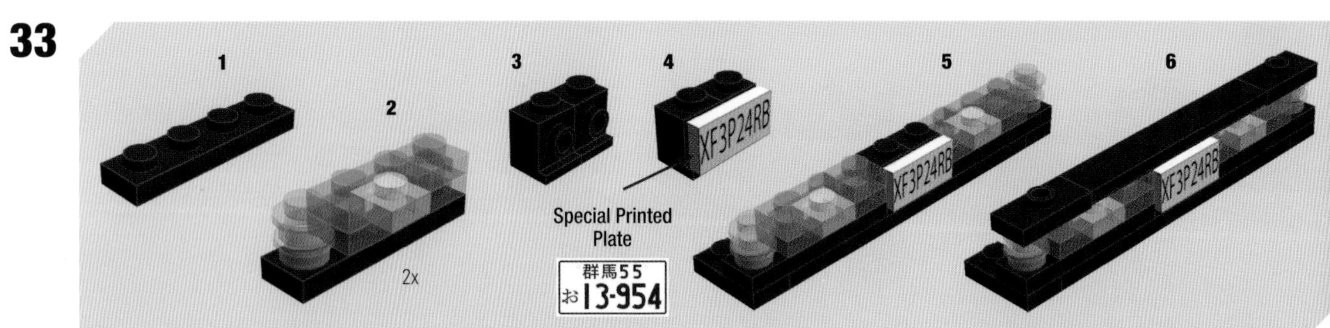
1
2
2x
3
4
XF3P24RB
Special Printed
Plate
群馬55
お 13-954
5
XF3P24RB
6
XF3P24RB

34

LHS

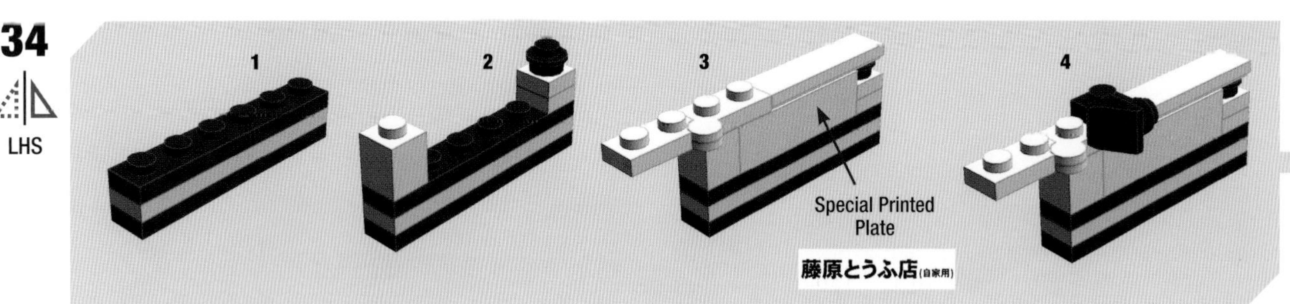
1
2
3
Special Printed
Plate
藤原とうふ店(自家用)
4

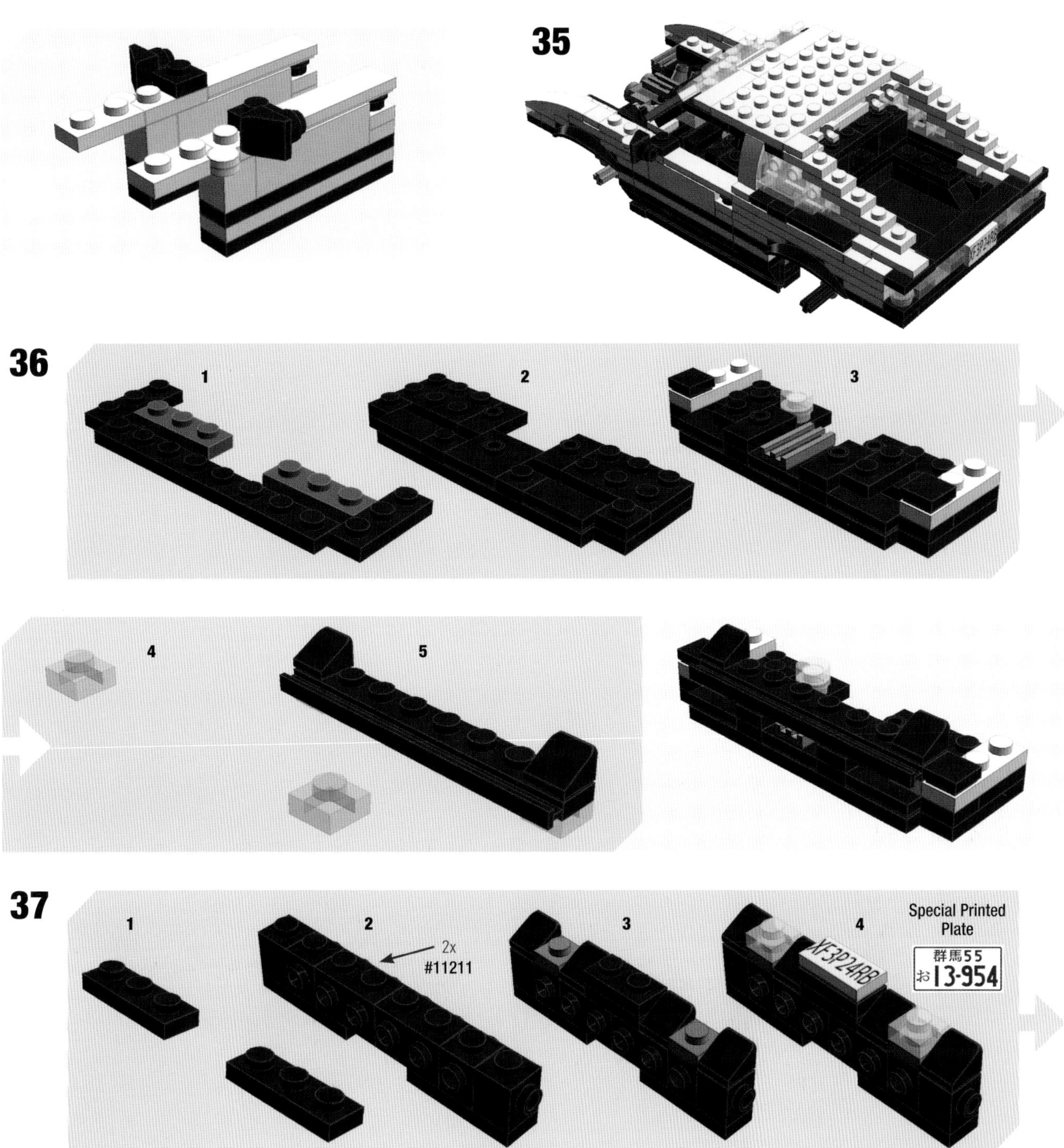
35
36
1
2
3
4
5
37
1
2
3
4
2x
#11211
Special Printed Plate
群馬55
お 13-954
XF3P24RB

38

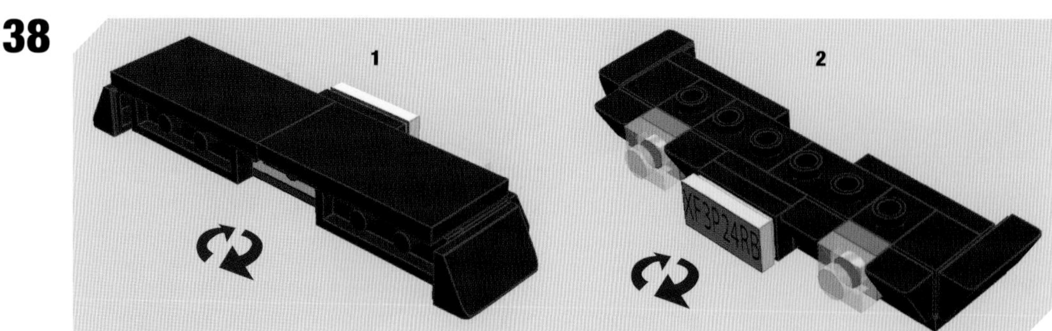

39 **40**

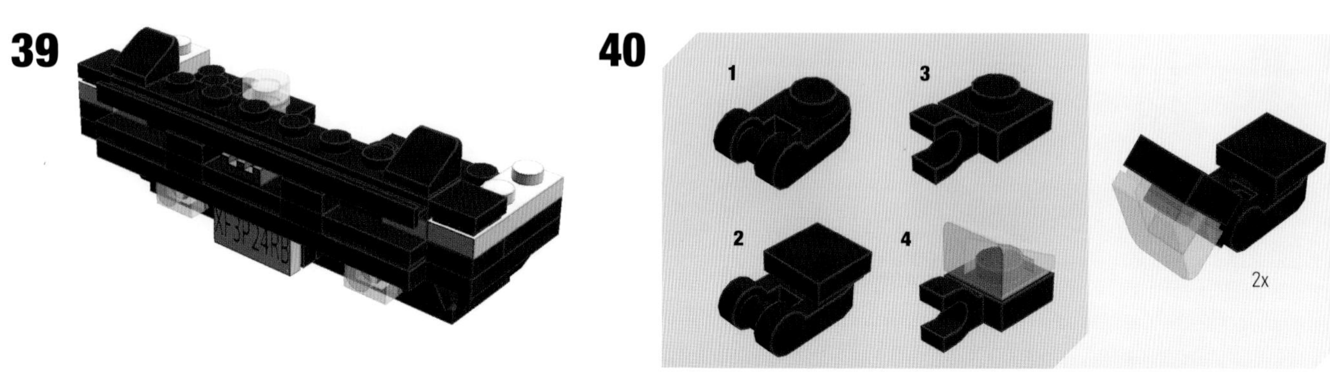

41

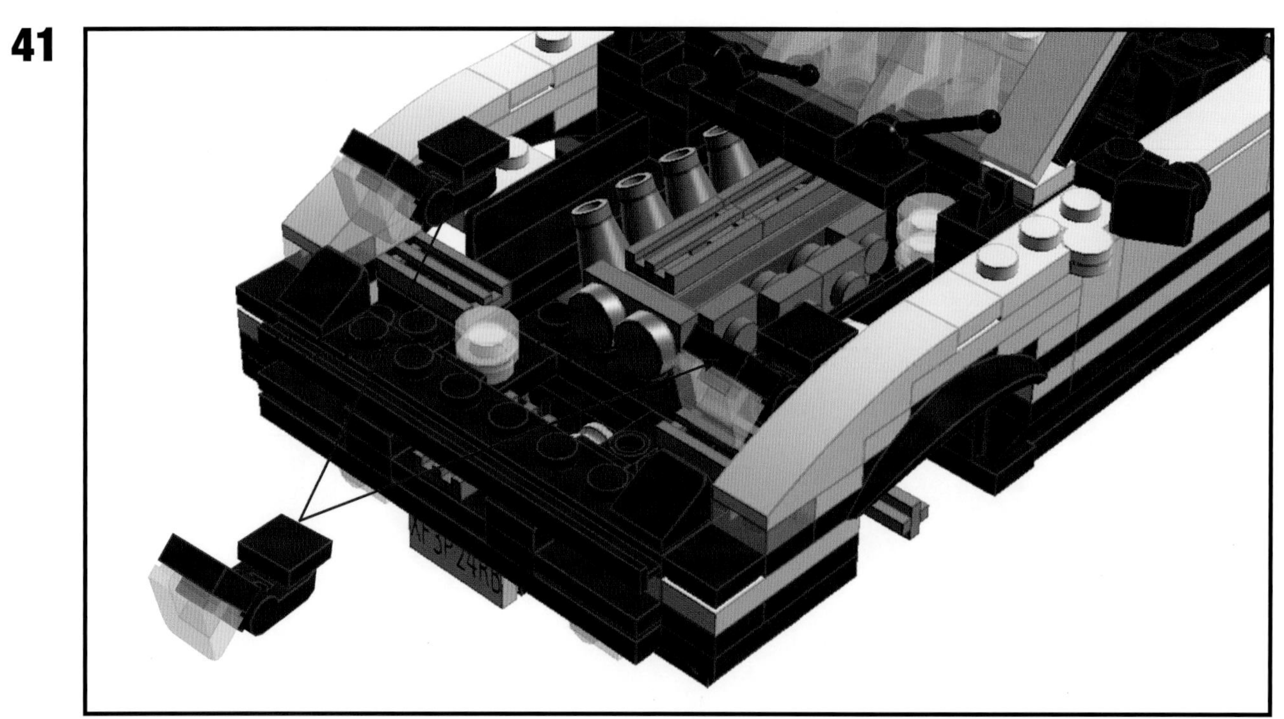

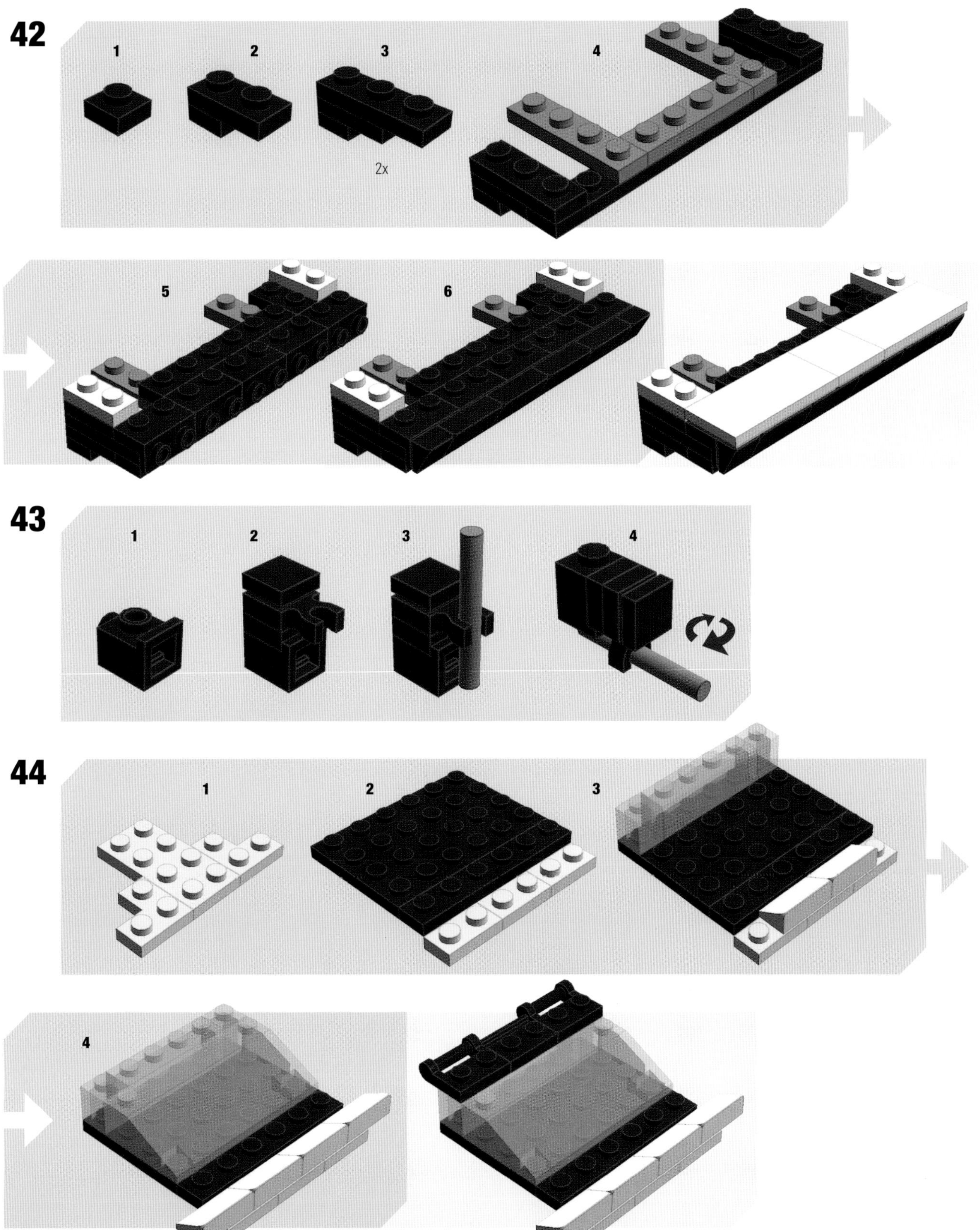
42
1
2
3
2x
4
5
6
43
1
2
3
4
44
1
2
3
4

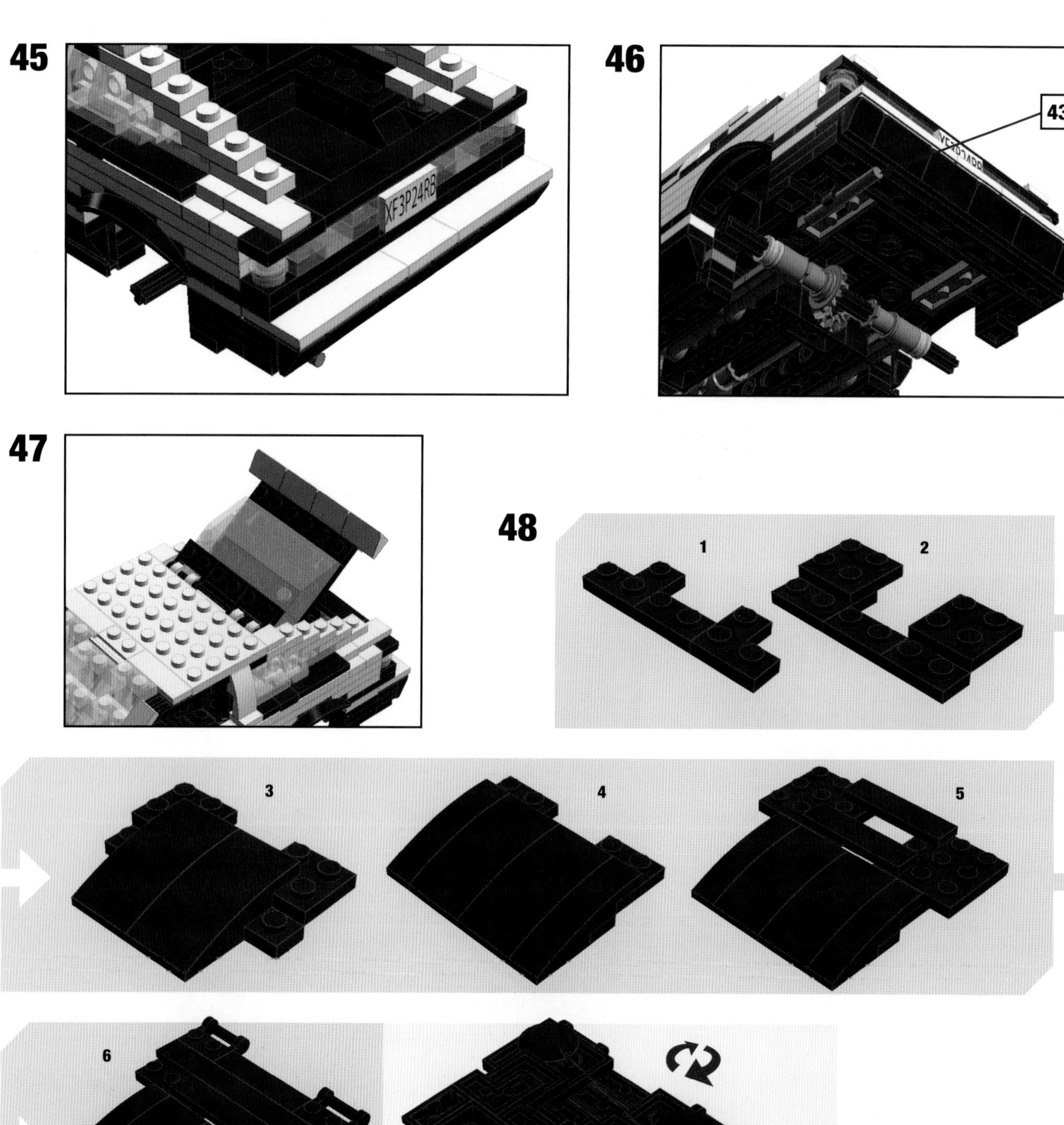
45
XF3P24RB
46
43
47
48
1
2
3
4
5
6
2x

49

50

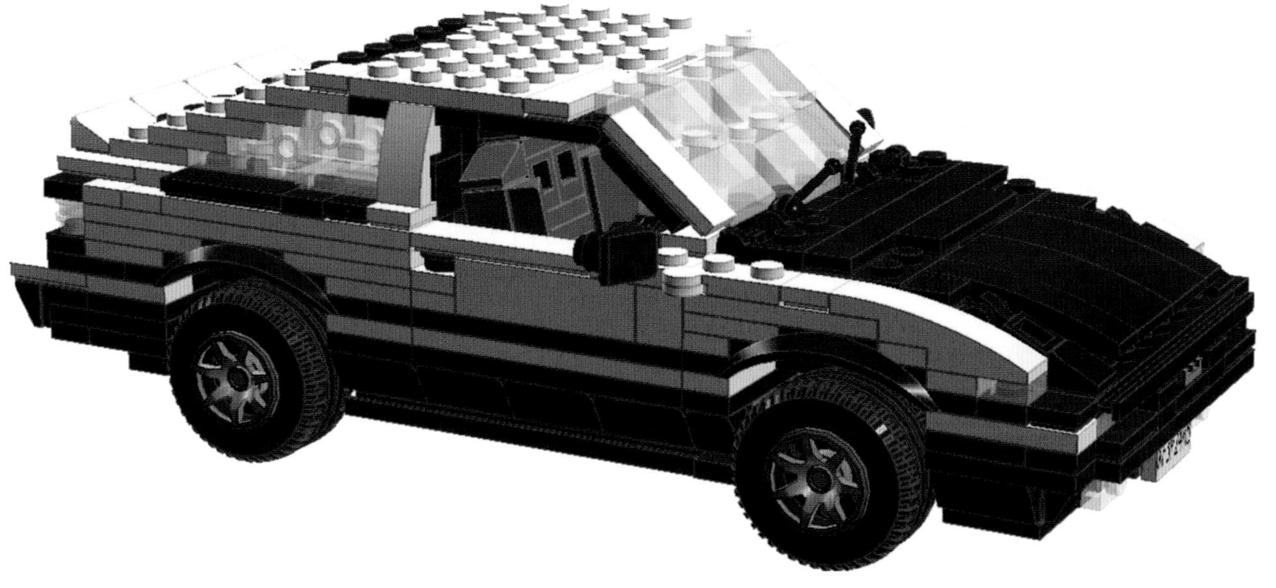

CHAPTER 8

FERRARI 308 GTS
MAGNUM P.I.

Ferraris do not need to feature in TV and film to be considered objects of desire. If anything, the reverse is true—they add cachet to their screen companions. The Ferrari 308 GTS Targa certainly helped actor Tom Selleck's character Thomas Magnum and his trademark moustache in the TV series *Magnum P.I.* Filmed in Hawaii, the series ran from 1980 to 1988. The Ferrari 308 featured in the show was replaced each season with a new car; differences can be seen season to season as Ferrari updated the model.

The 308 was the first Ferrari to pass the 10,000-unit production barrier, close to the total of all previous models combined. The 308 also had a long production life with regular updates. The first cars, from 1975 in GTB (Berlinetta) specification only, had bodies made of fiberglass (which changed to steel in mid-1977 after 808 cars had been built). These early cars are highly coveted today, partly for the 330 lb (150 kg) lighter weight and partly due to pre-1980 vehicles producing an extra 41 hp (31 kW). All 308 GTS models had steel bodies and were built from 1977 on.

The Ferrari 308 styling was created at Italian coachbuilder Pininfarina under acclaimed designer Leonardo Fioravanti. They set a new Ferrari design aesthetic with the 308 GTS and also the two-year-earlier 365 GT4 BB: low and wedgy with hidden headlamps and open rear buttresses.

COUNTRY OF ORIGIN:	Italy
PRODUCTION:	1977–1985
NUMBER MADE:	Approx. 12,200 (all types)
LAYOUT/DRIVE:	Mid-engine, Rear-wheel-drive
ENGINE:	2.9 liter, 8 cylinders, Vcc
POWER TORQUE:	202 hp (151 kW) / 179 lb-ft (243 Nm) 1980–82
CONSTRUCTION/DOORS:	Tubular Steel Spaceframe Steel Panels, two-door Targa Top
TV/FILM APPEARANCES:	*Magnum P.I.* (1980–1988), *Cannonball Run* (198

HAWAII 81
ROBIN · 1
ALOHA STATE

Despite a ten-year production run, the core shape survived an additional four years in the form of the Ferrari 328. Key visual differences were revised body-color bumper, front and rear, along with a 3.2 L version of the mid-engine V8 with 270 bhp (201 kW).

A reboot of the television show *Magnum P.I.* aired in late 2018, the new lead character driving a current-model Ferrari 488 Spider after the iconic 308 GTS is destroyed by a truck in the first episode. Thankfully the 308 is CGI and not the real thing.

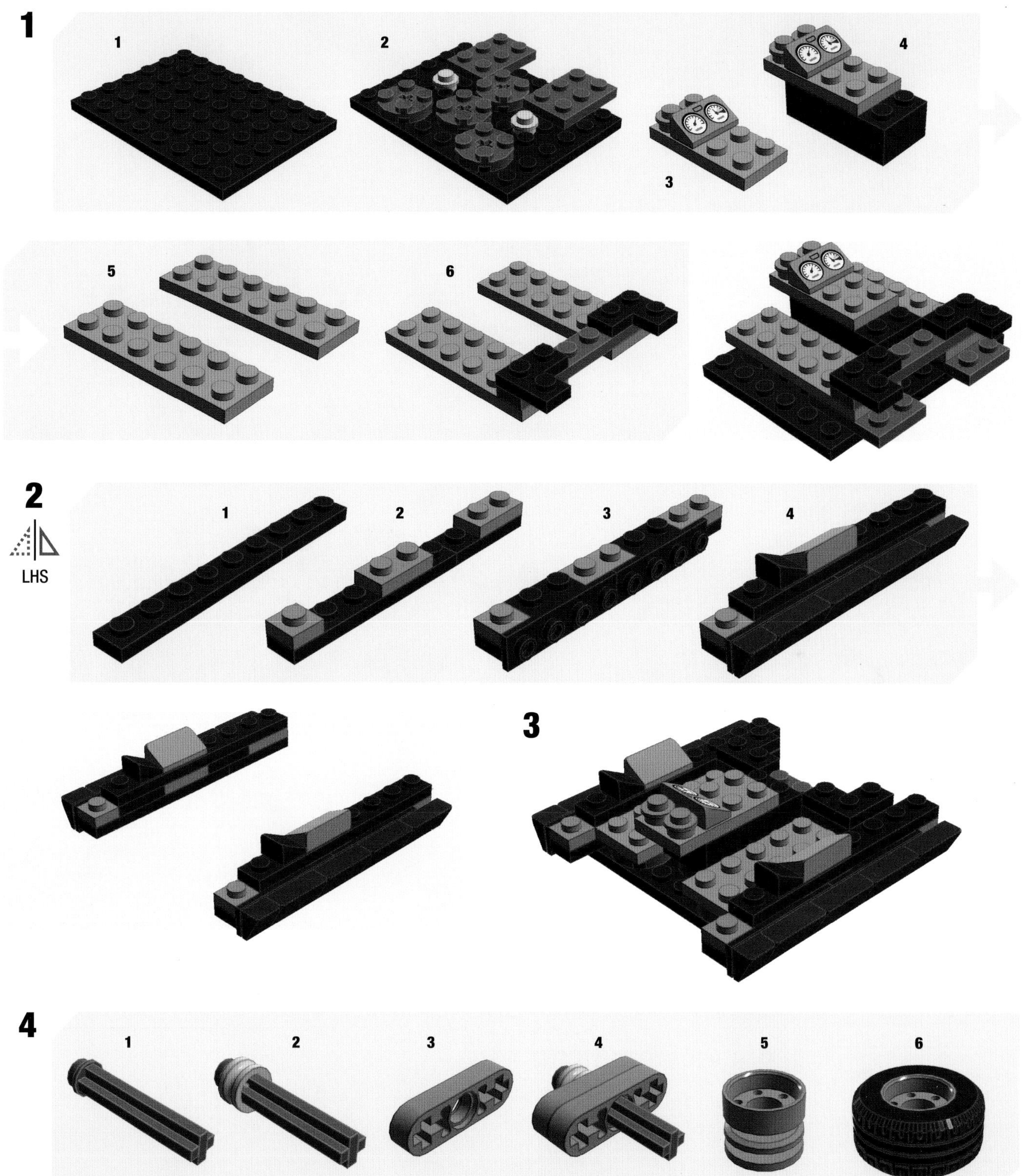
1
1
2
3
4
5
6
2
1
2
3
4
LHS
3
4
1
2
3
4
5
6

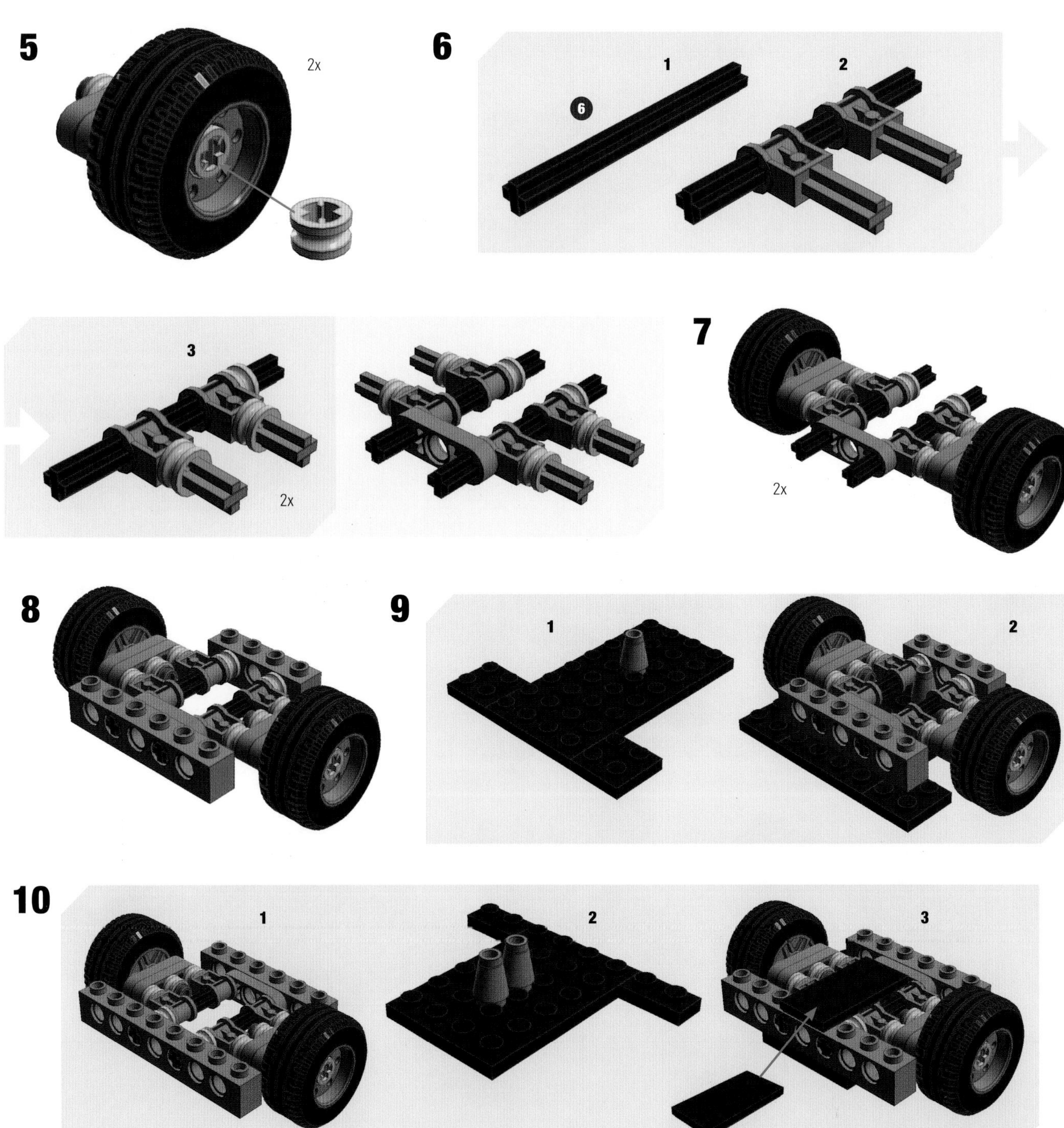
5
2x
6
1
6
2
3
2x
7
2x
8
9
1
2
10
1
2
3

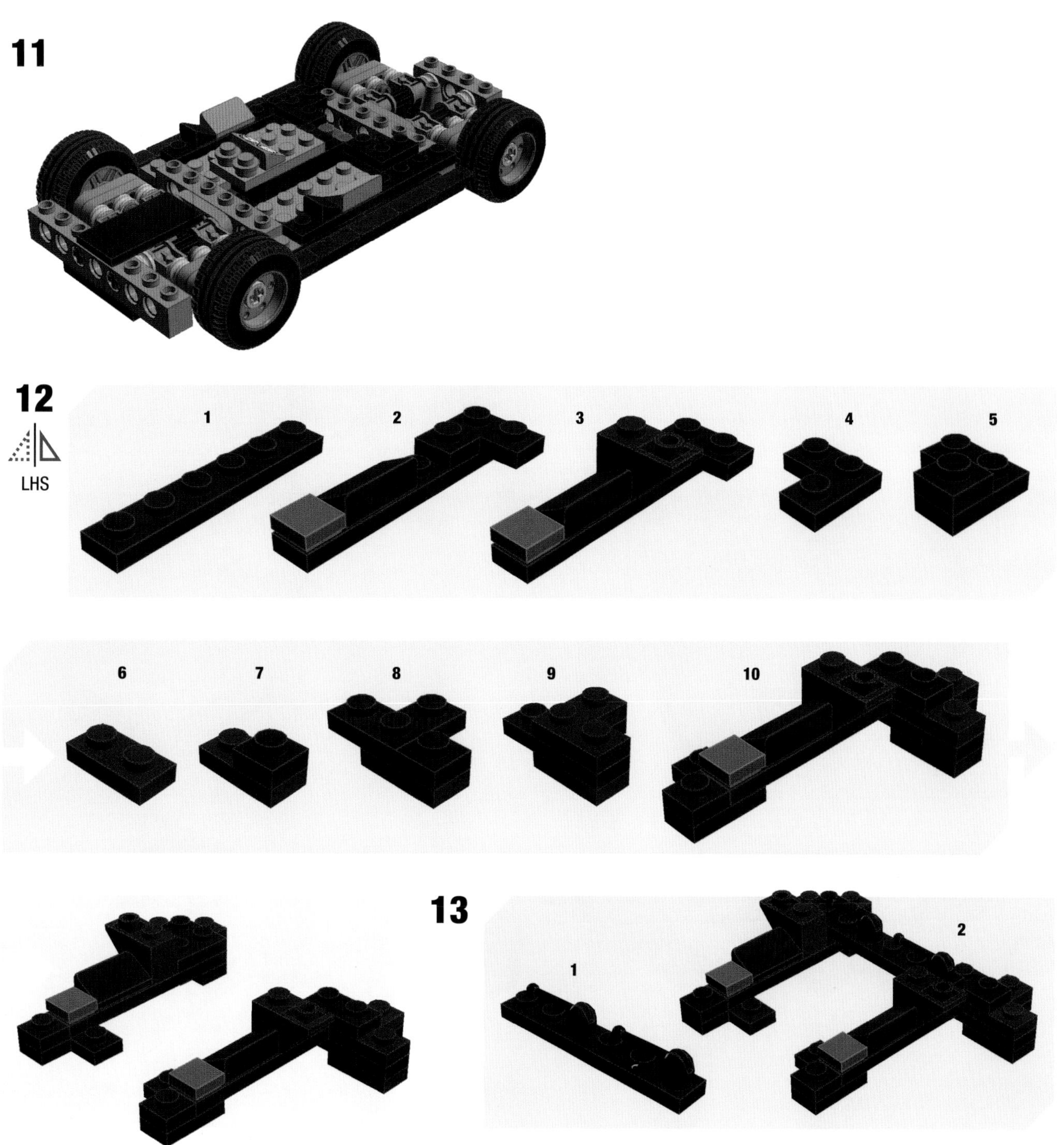
11
12
LHS
1
2
3
4
5
6
7
8
9
10
13
1
2

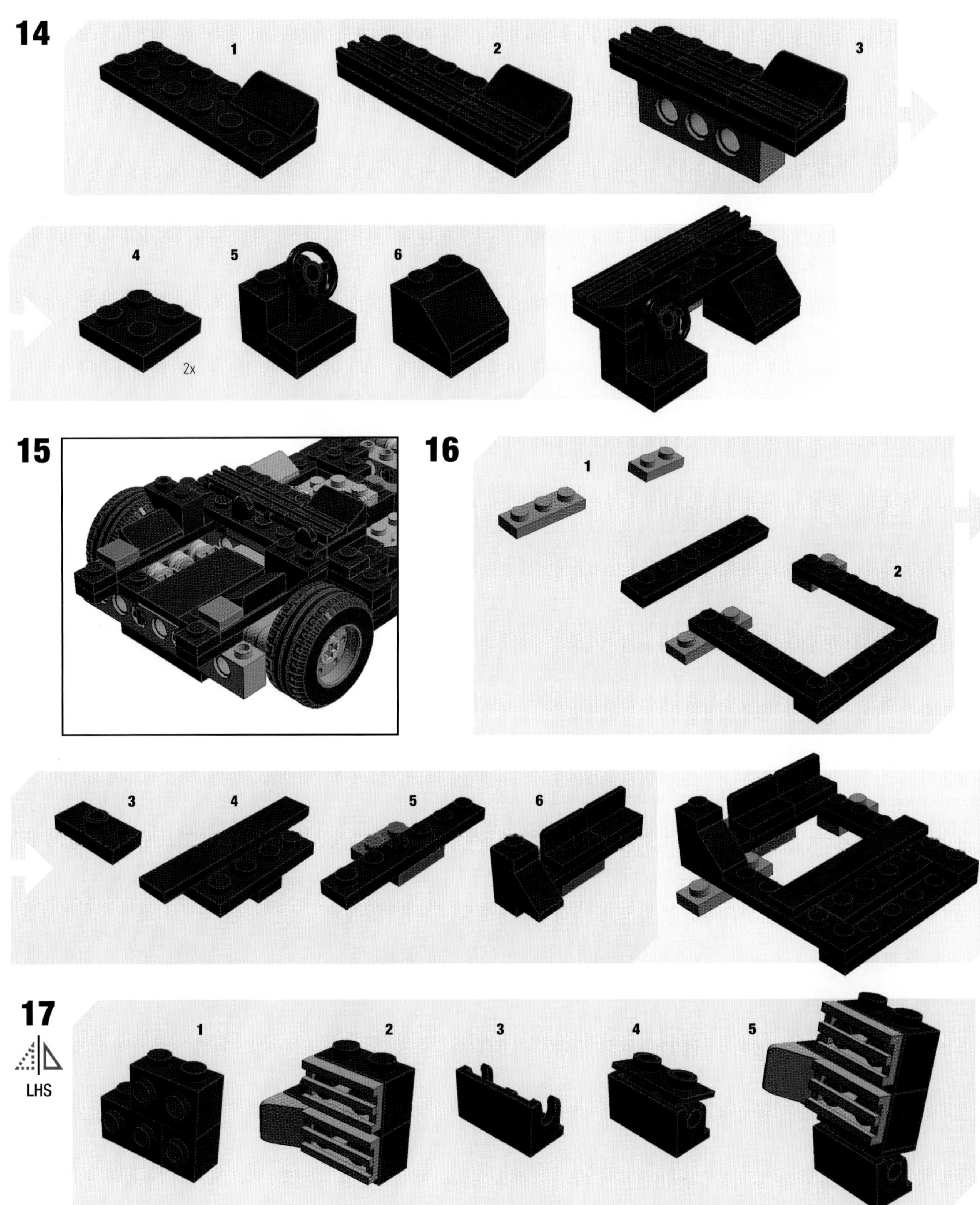
14
1
2
3
4
5
6
2x
15
16
1
2
3
4
5
6
17
1
2
3
4
5
LHS

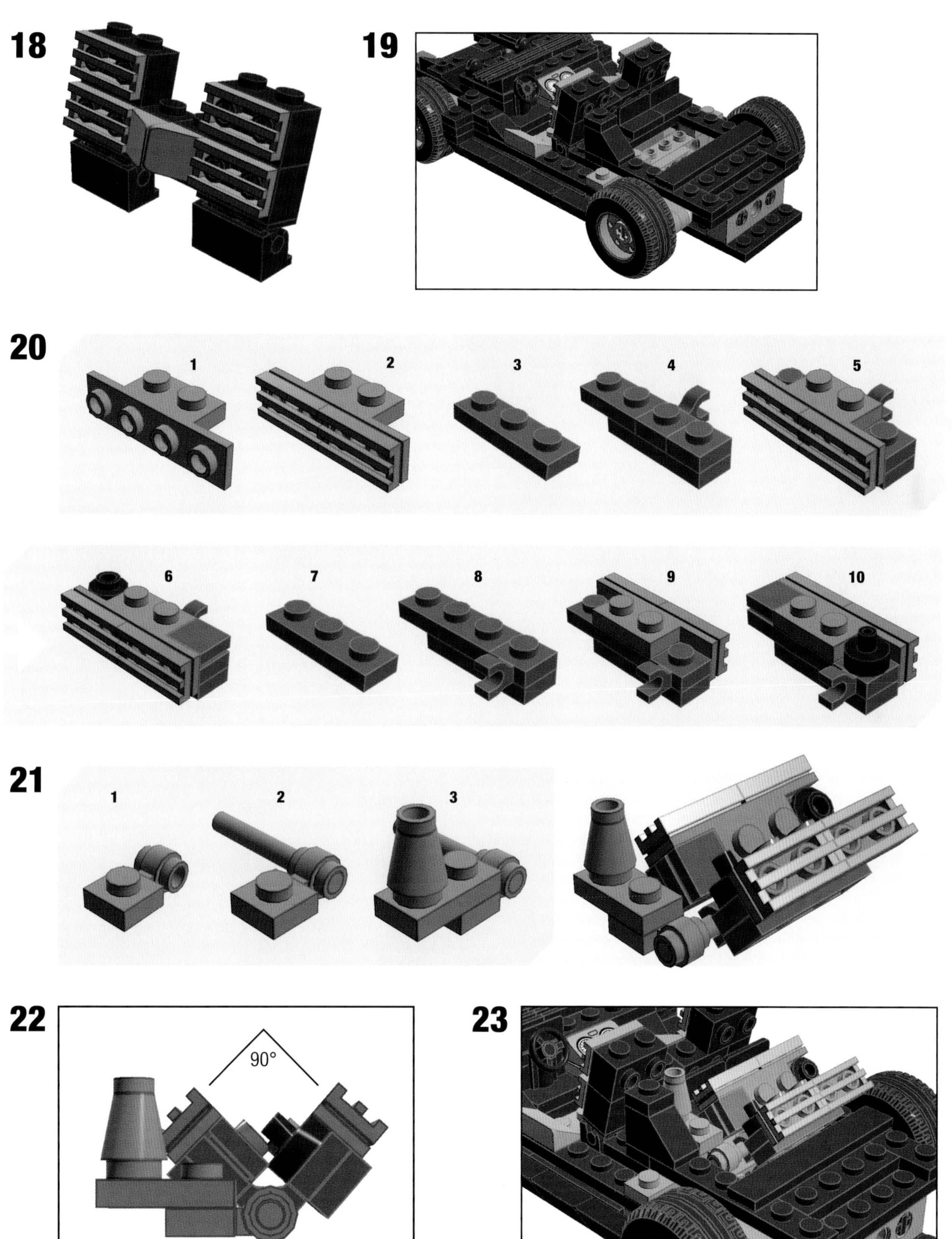
18
19
20
1
2
3
4
5
6
7
8
9
10
21
1
2
3
22
90°
23

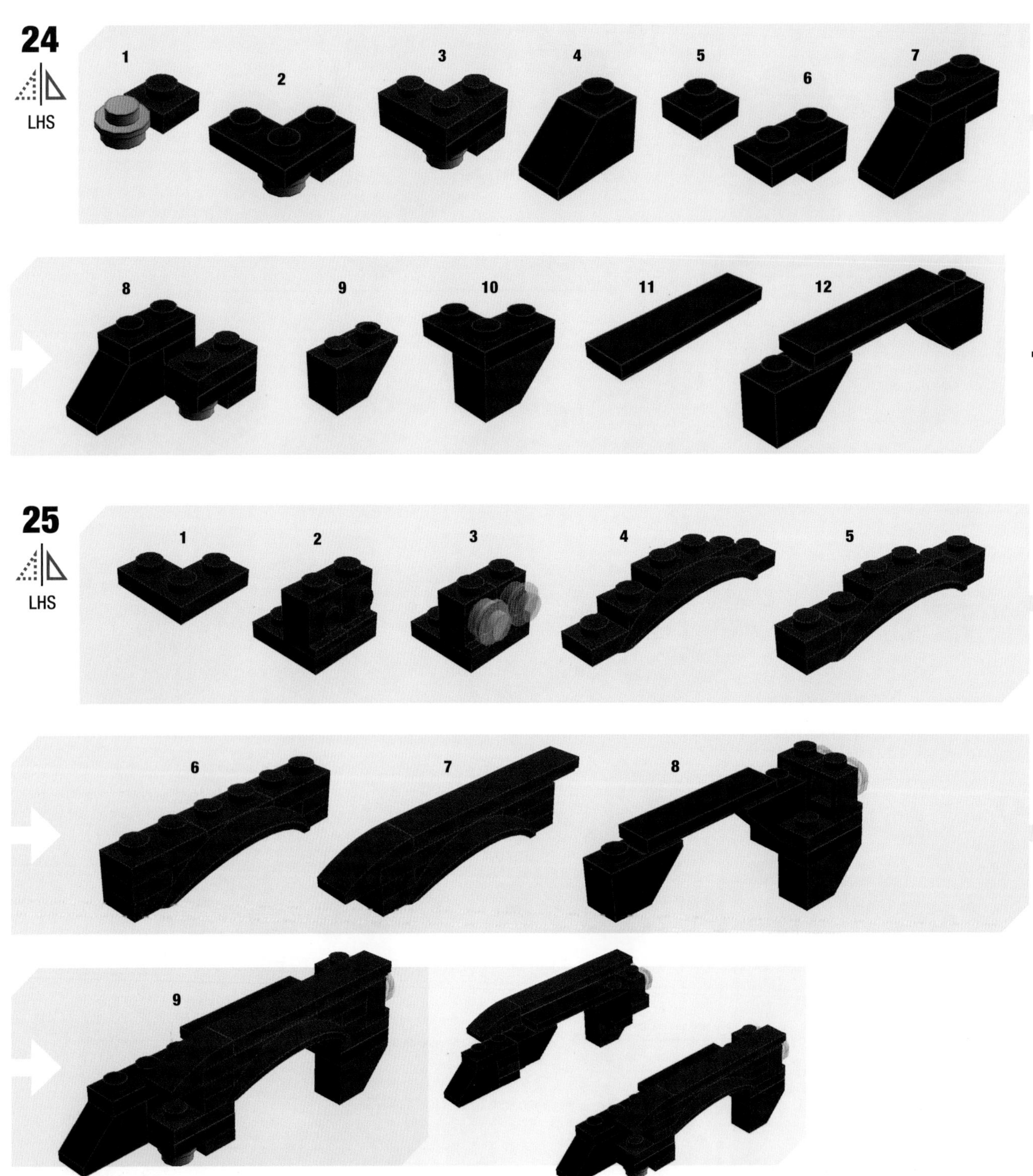

24
LHS
1
2
3
4
5
6
7
8
9
10
11
12
+
25
LHS
1
2
3
4
5
6
7
8
9

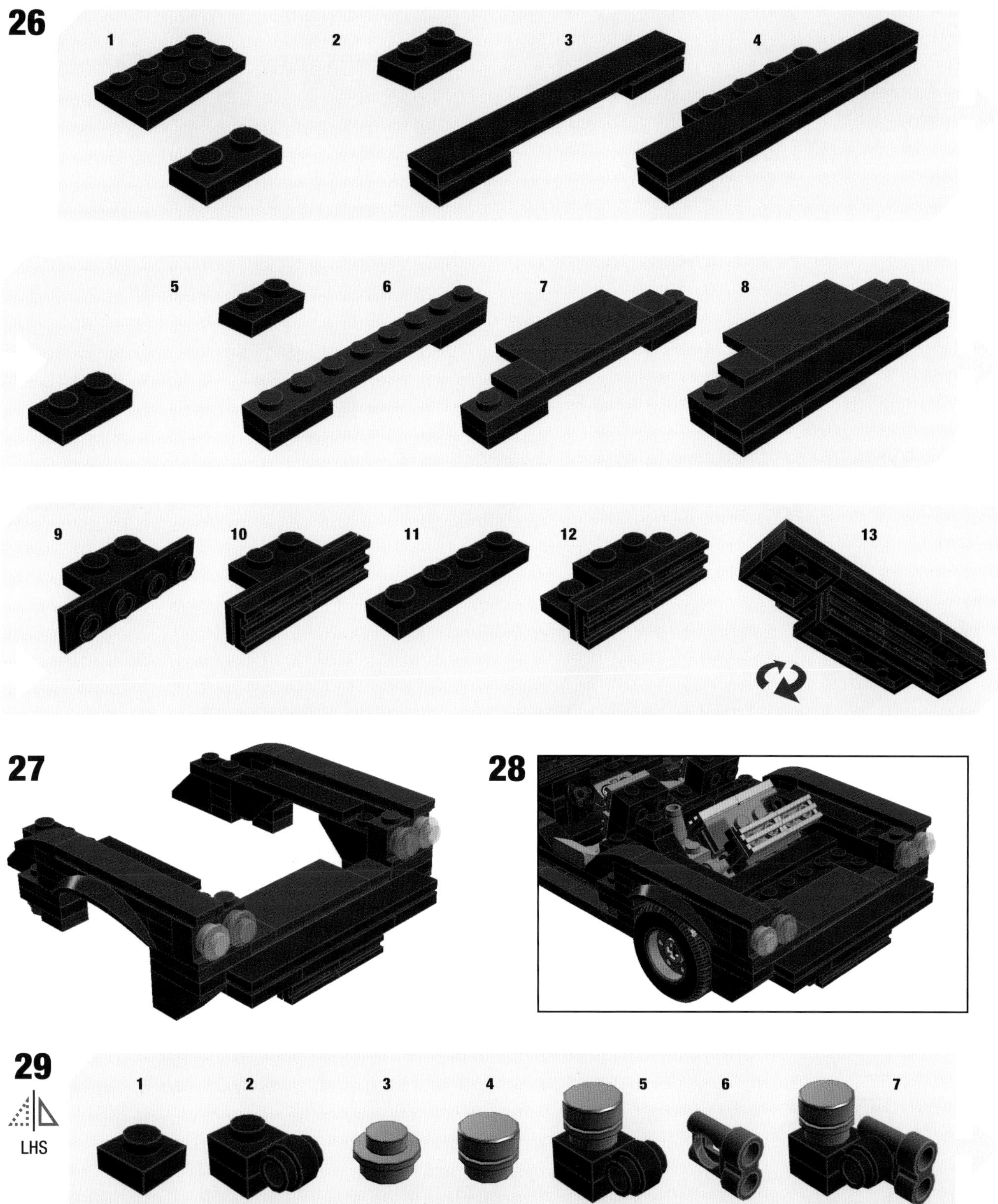
26
1
2
3
4
5
6
7
8
9
10
11
12
13
27
28
29
1
2
3
4
5
6
7
LHS

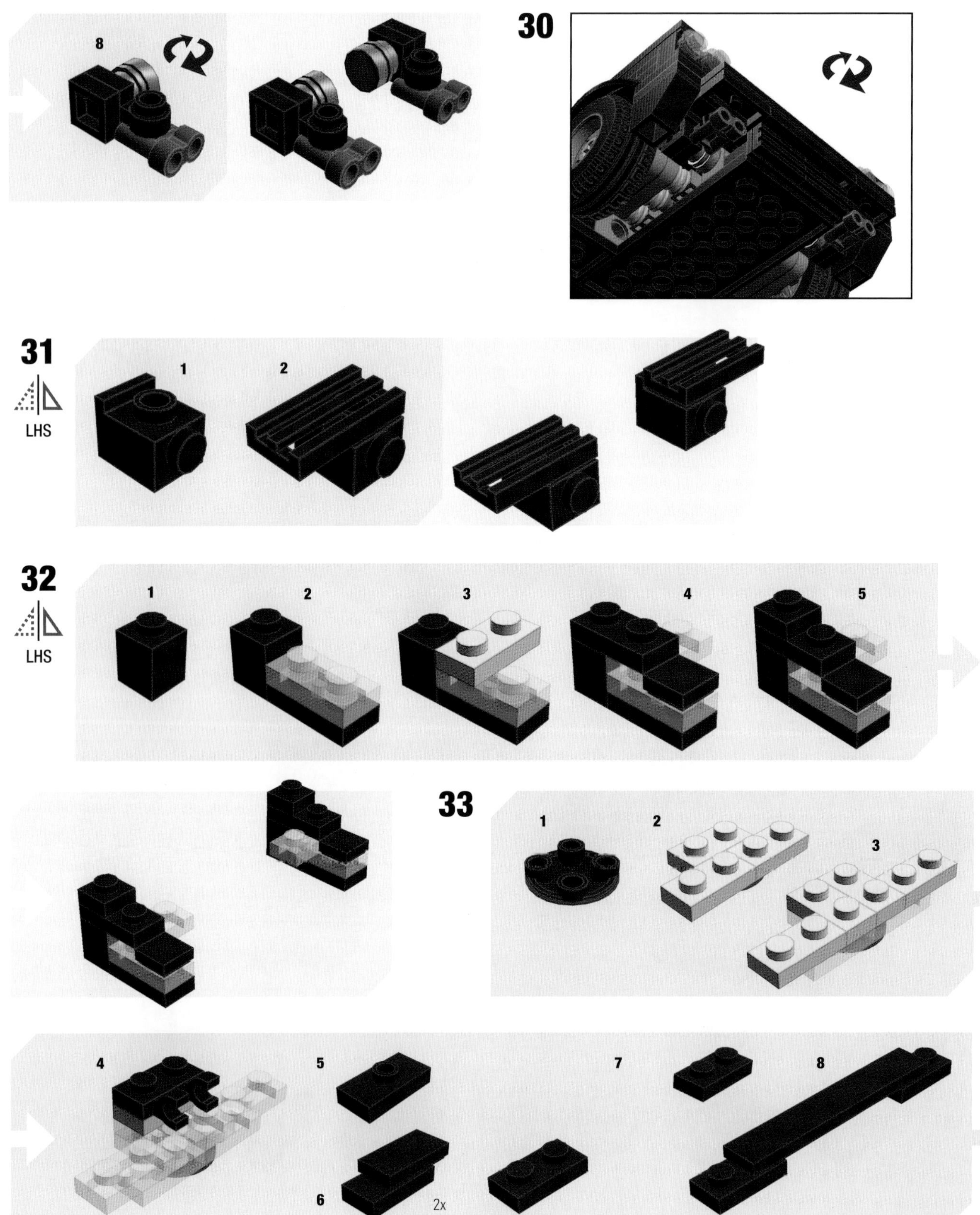

8
30
31
1
2
LHS
32
1
2
3
4
5
LHS
33
1
2
3
4
5
7
8
6
2x

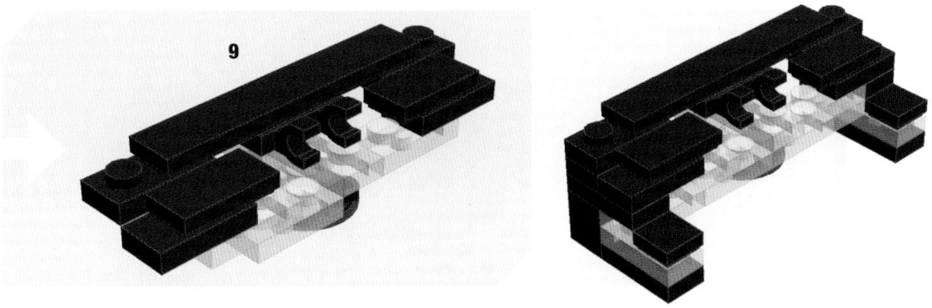

9

34

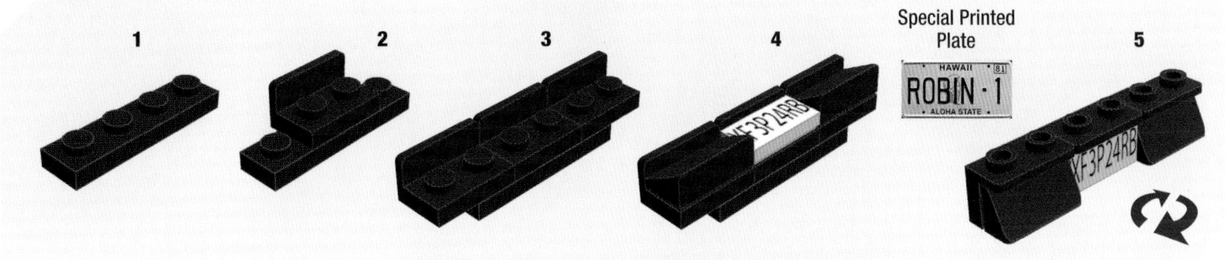

1 2 3 4

Special Printed Plate

HAWAII 81
ROBIN · 1
ALOHA STATE

5

XF3P24RB

35

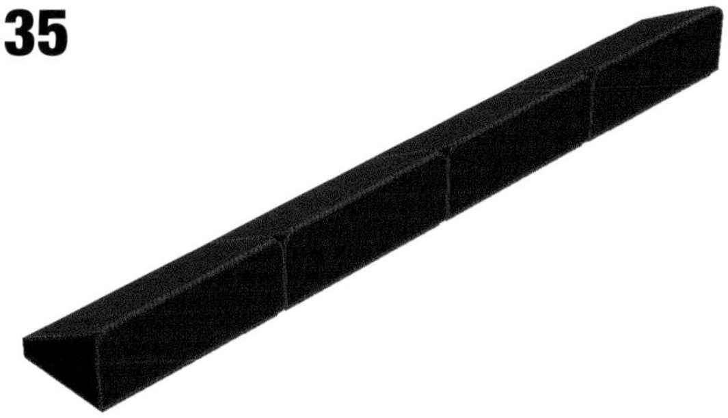

36

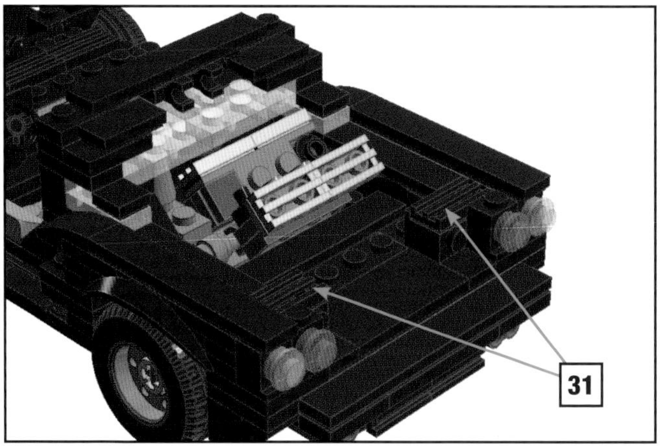

31

37

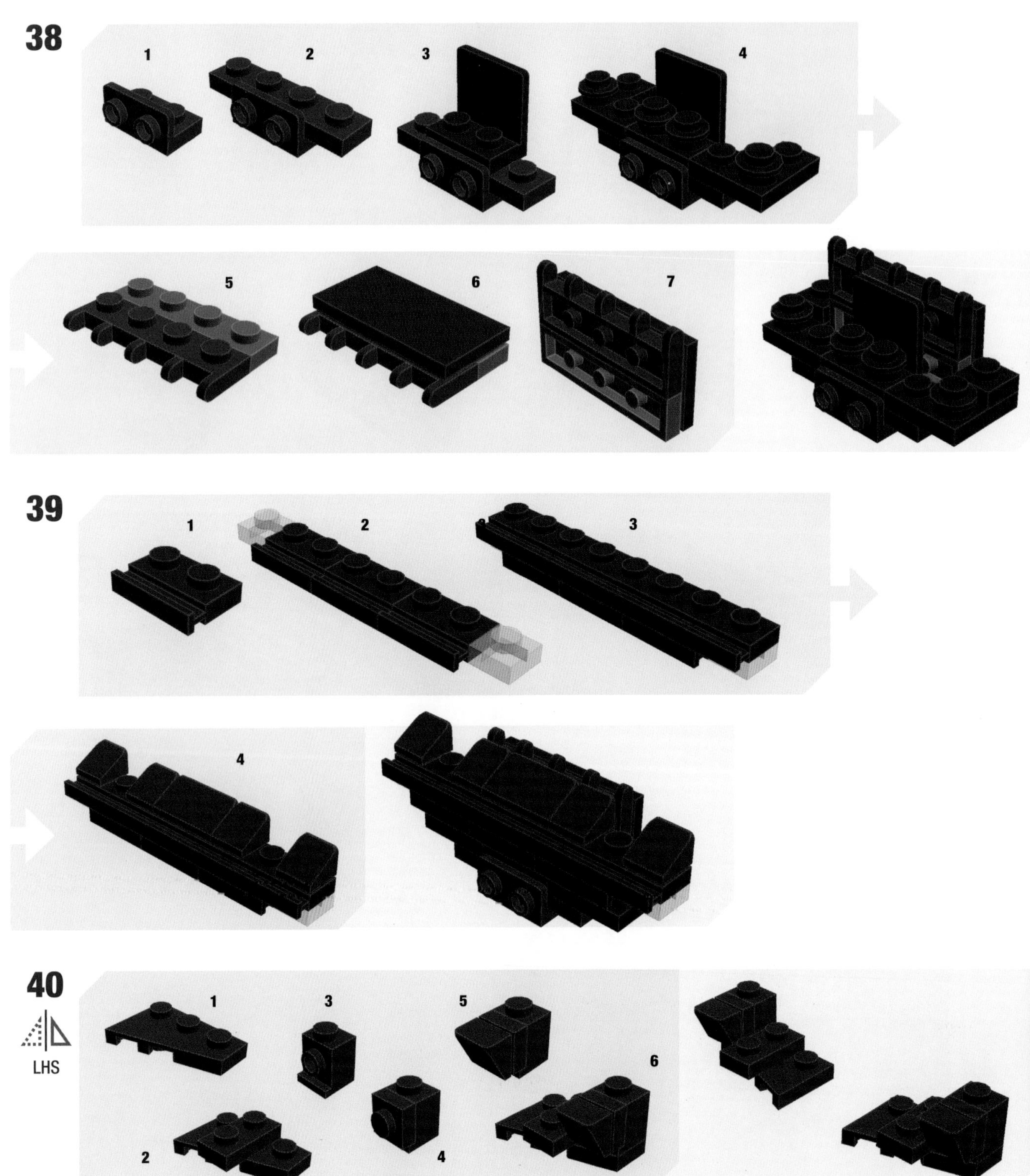
38
1
2
3
4
5
6
7
39
1
2
3
4
40
1
2
3
4
5
6
LHS

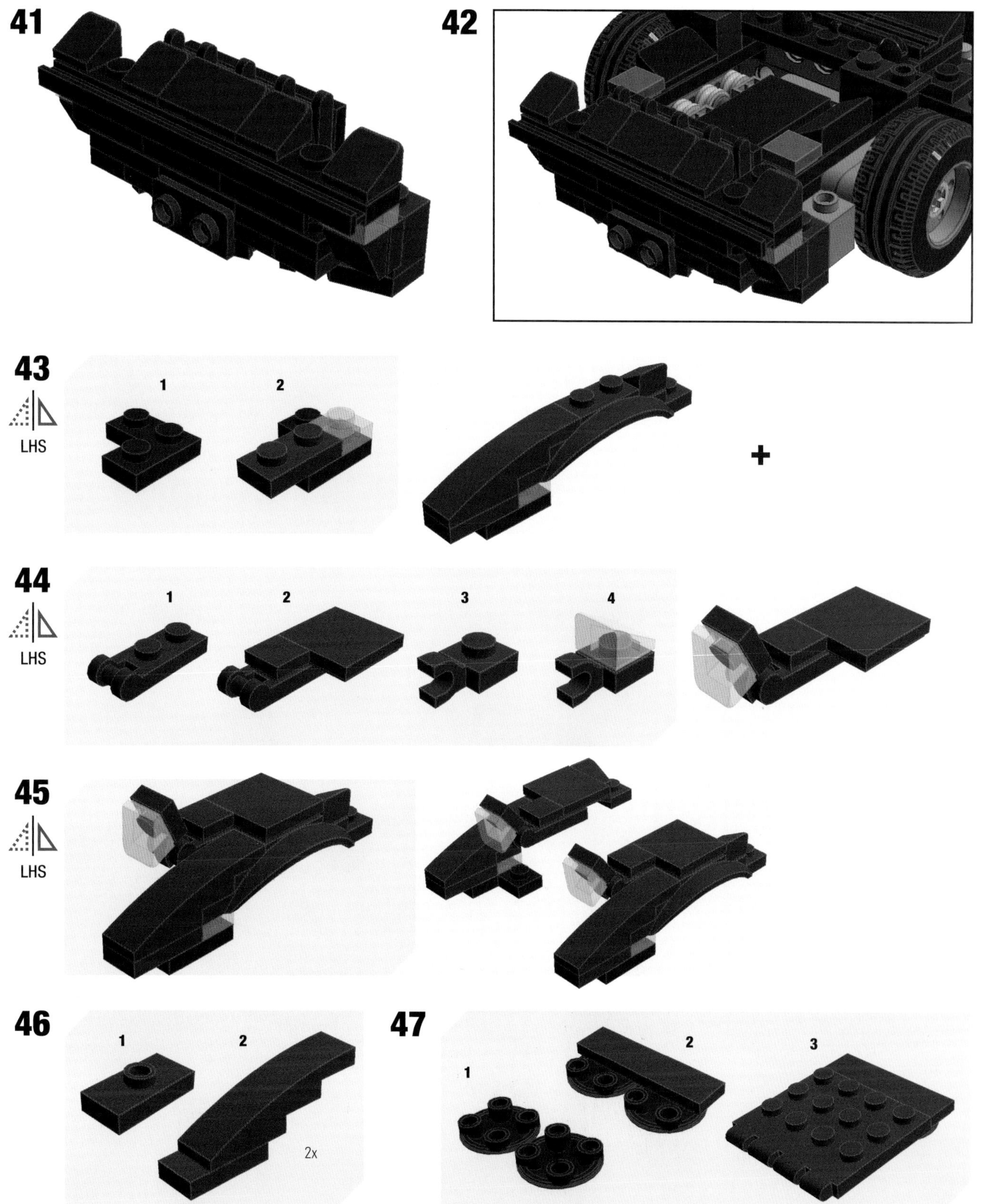
41
42
43
LHS
1
2
+
44
LHS
1
2
3
4
45
LHS
46
1
2
2x
47
1
2
3

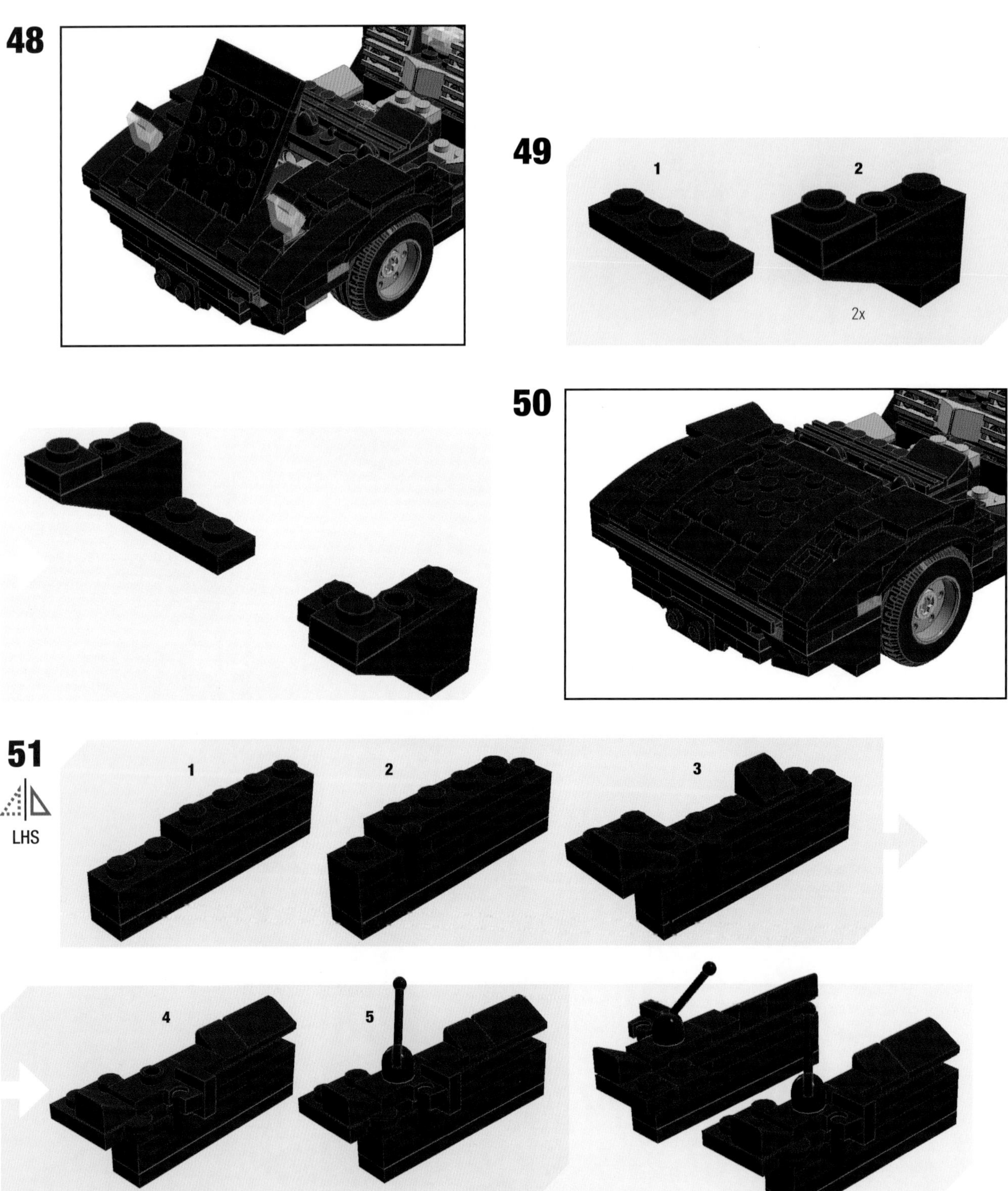
48
49
1
2
2x
50
51
LHS
1
2
3
4
5

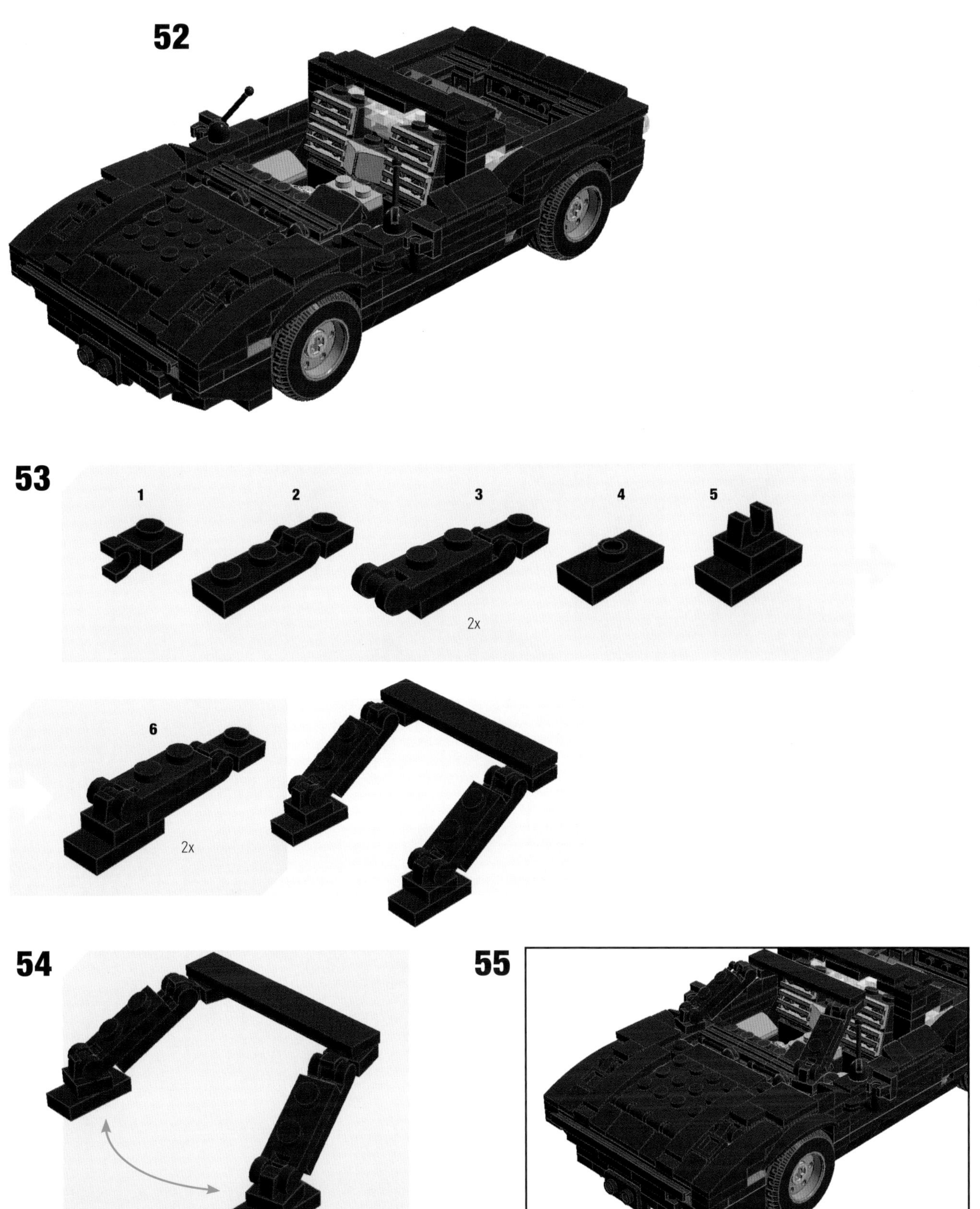
52
53
1
2
3
4
5
2x
6
2x
54
55

56

1 2 3

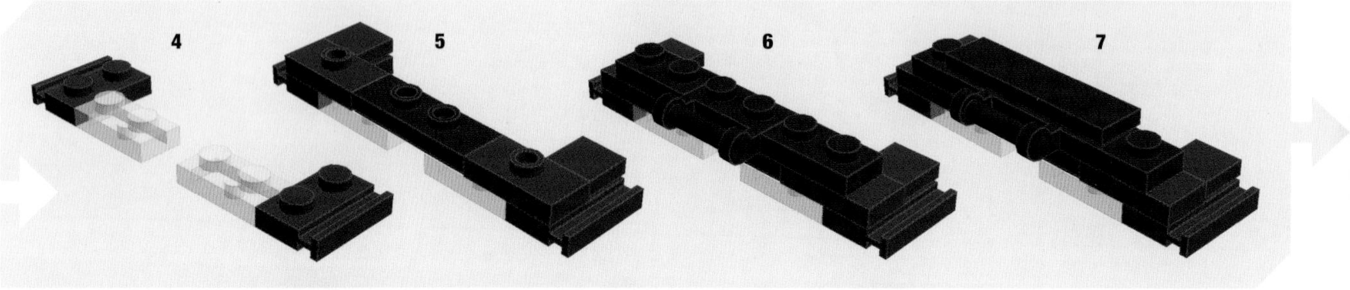

4 5 6 7

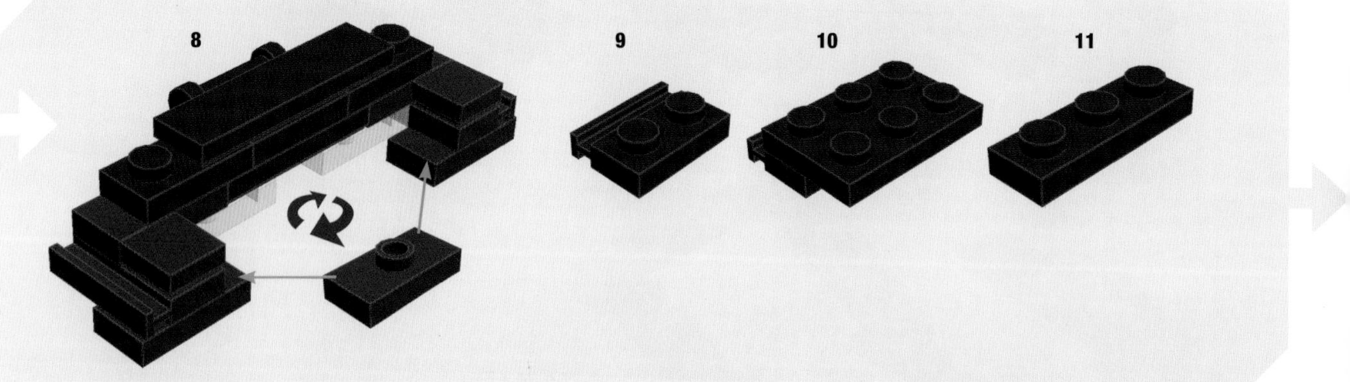

8 9 10 11

12

CHAPTER 9

LOTUS ESPRIT
JAMES BOND 007: THE SPY WHO LOVED ME

Fictional British Spy James Bond, known as 007, hasn't always driven British lead cars, but they feature prominently in the series. The character in the novels occasionally drives a Bentley, and the films have featured various Aston Martin models. The wildest Bond car, though, is arguably the Lotus Esprit S1 from *The Spy Who Loved Me*.

Lotus Esprits are cool—wedgy, exotic, Giugiaro-esque cool. They even look futuristic (at least they did back in 1977). A break away from old-school Astons gave the producers an opportunity to do something special with the car. Thus Wet Nellie was created: a powered submarine version of the Lotus that had the ability to function underwater. The film included a stunt where Bond, played by Roger Moore, drives off the end of a pier into the ocean. At this point, the car transforms into the submarine and glides off silently (if somewhat bubbly).

Wet Nellie cost around $100,000 to build at the time and was sold at auction in 2013 to tech-inventor Elon Musk for £550,000. Musk has said he plans to rebuild the car into a working model, powered by some of the electric-vehicle technologies developed at Tesla.

In submarine mode, the Bond-mobile is powered by a series of propellers at the rear of the vehicle and is steered by rear rudders and a series of horizontal planes where one would normally find the wheel wells.

Even as a car, though, the Esprit would still be cool. Bond had another two Lotus Esprits, turbo models, in the 1981 film *For Your Eyes Only*. The first car shown, a white one, is destroyed by an explosion in Spain and is replaced by a bronze model at a ski resort in northern Italy.

PPW 306R

PPW 306R

COUNTRY OF ORIGIN: Great Britain

PRODUCTION: 1976–1978

NUMBER MADE: 718

LAYOUT/DRIVE: Front engine, Rear-wheel-drive

ENGINE: 1,973 cc, 4 cylinders

POWER TORQUE: 162 hp (119 kW) / 140 lb-ft (142 Nm)

CONSTRUCTION/DOORS: Back-bone Chassis, Glass-fiber panels, two-door

TV/FILM APPEARANCES: *The Spy Who Loved Me* (1977), *For Your Eyes Only* (1981)

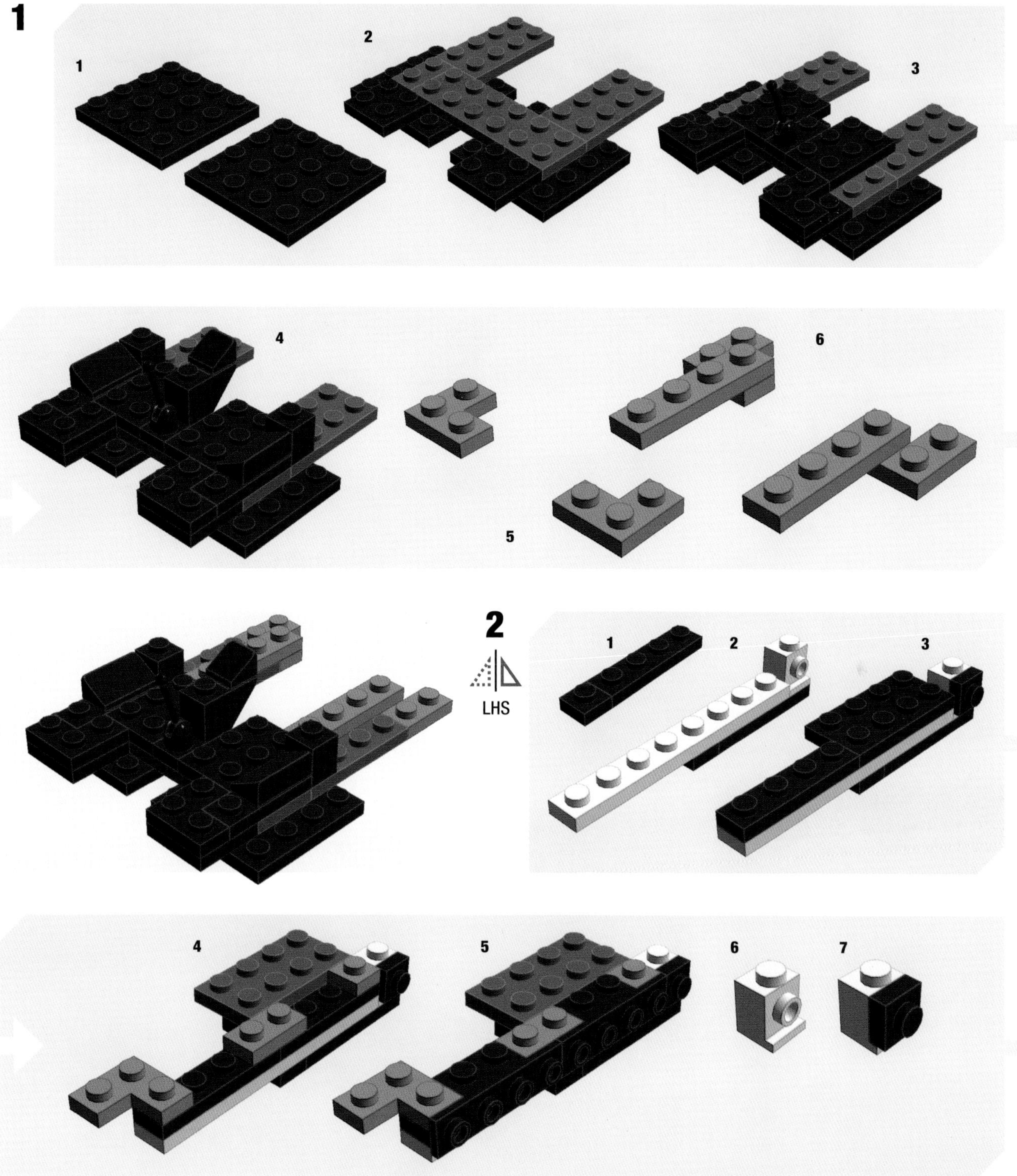
1
1
2
3
4
5
6
2
LHS
1
2
3
4
5
6
7

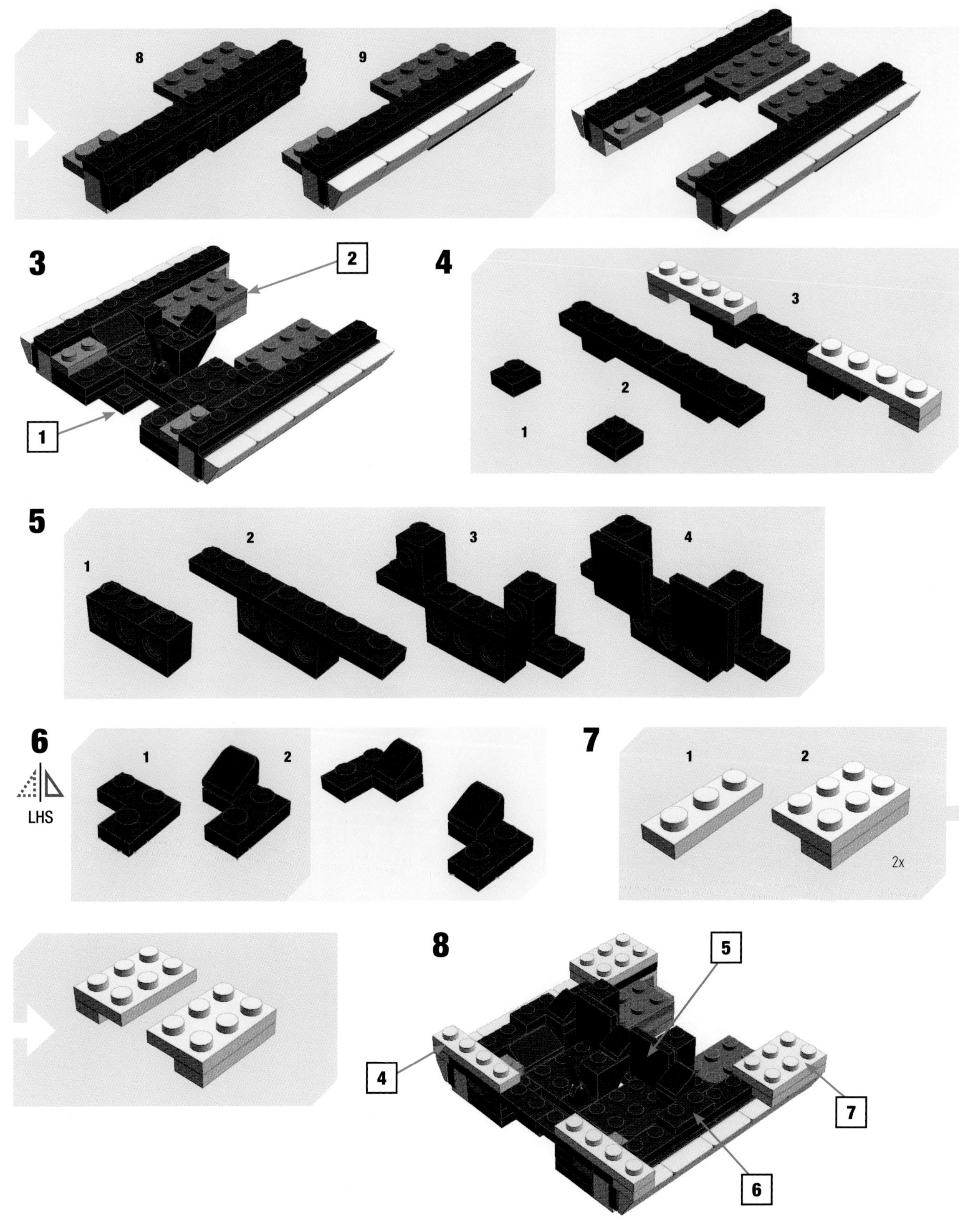
8
9
3
2
1
4
3
2
1
5
1
2
3
4
6
1
2
LHS
7
1
2
2x
8
5
4
7
6

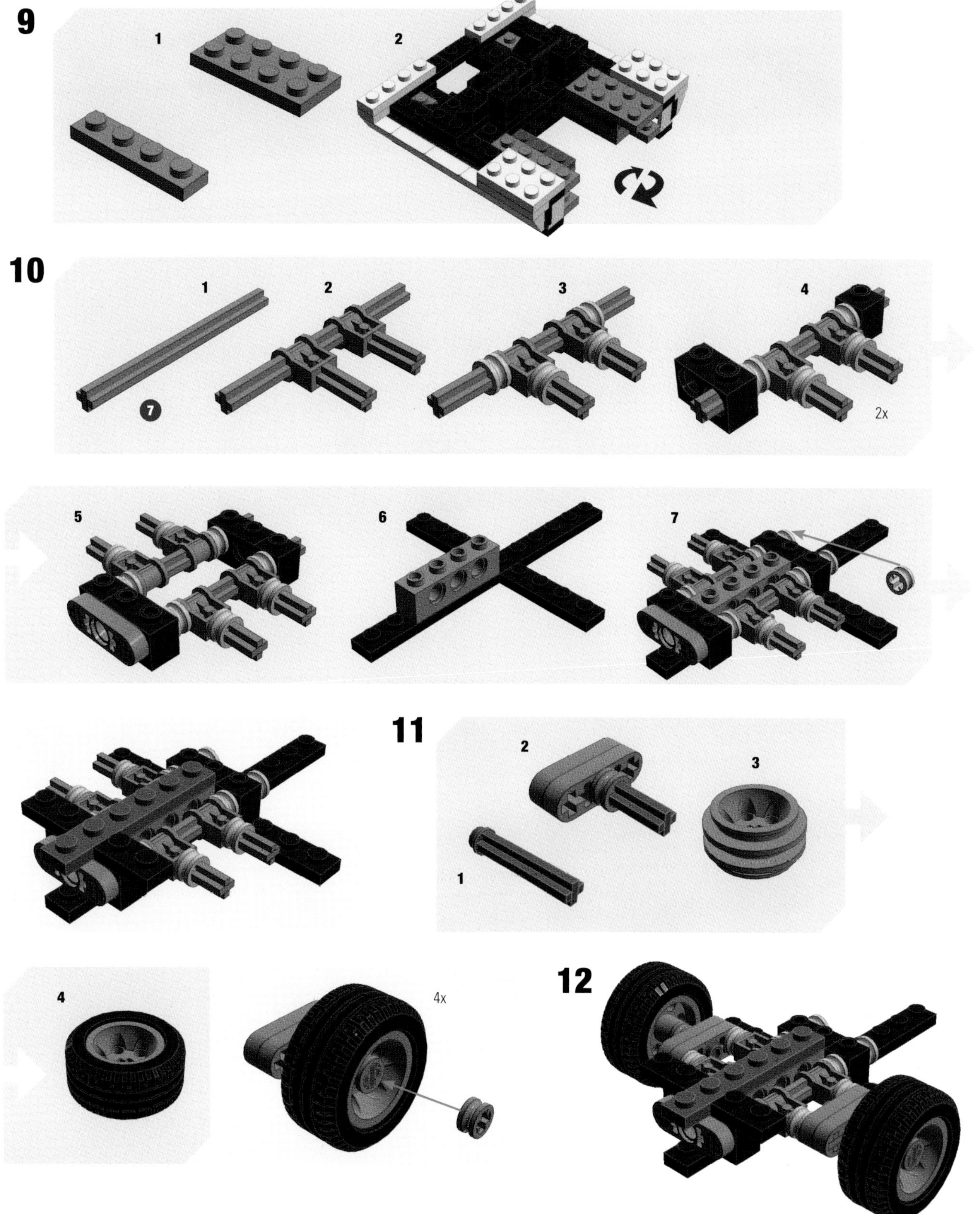
9
1
2
10
1
2
3
4
2x
5
6
7
11
2
3
1
4
4x
12

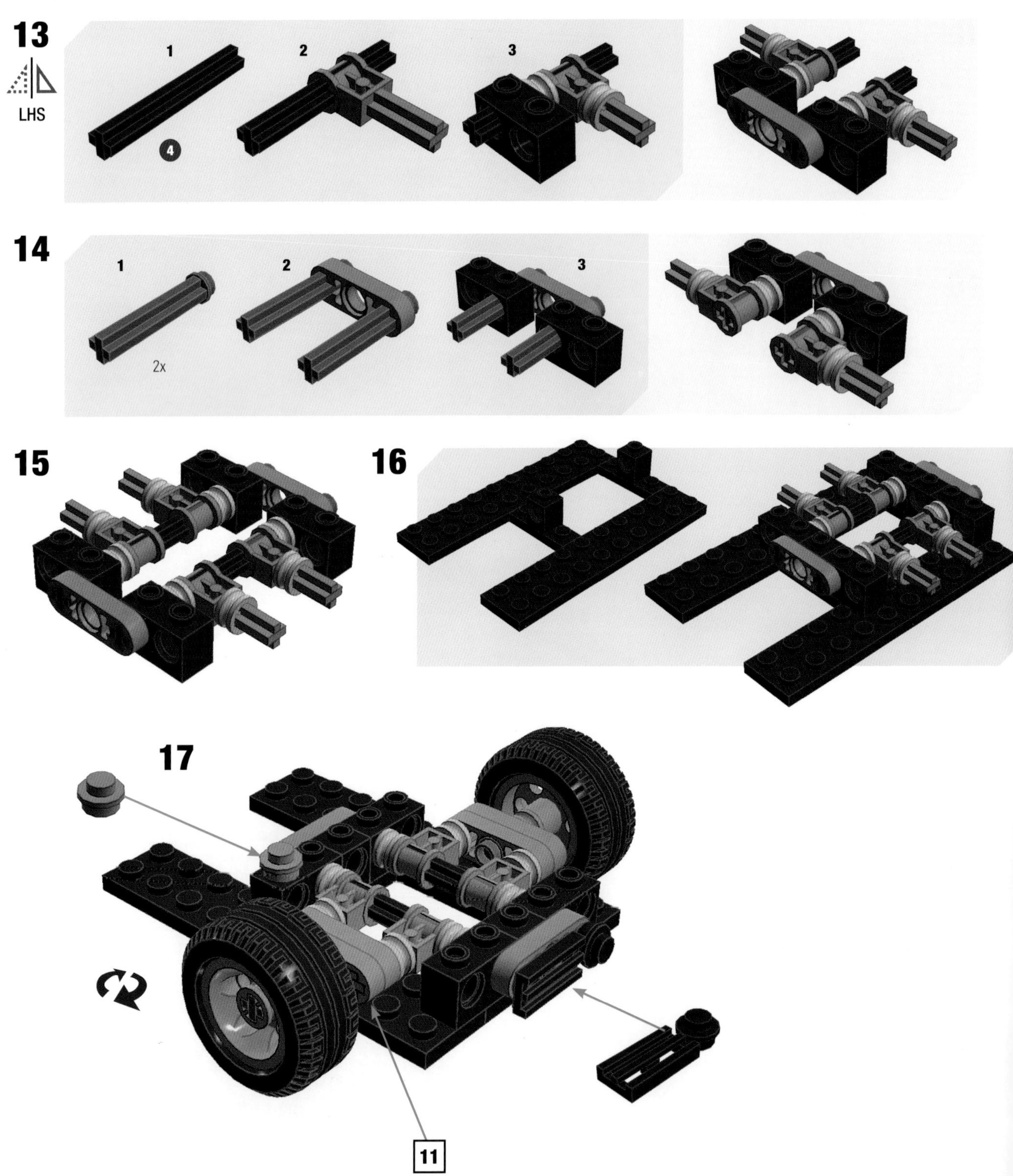
13
1
2
3
4
LHS
14
1
2
3
2x
15
16
17
11

18

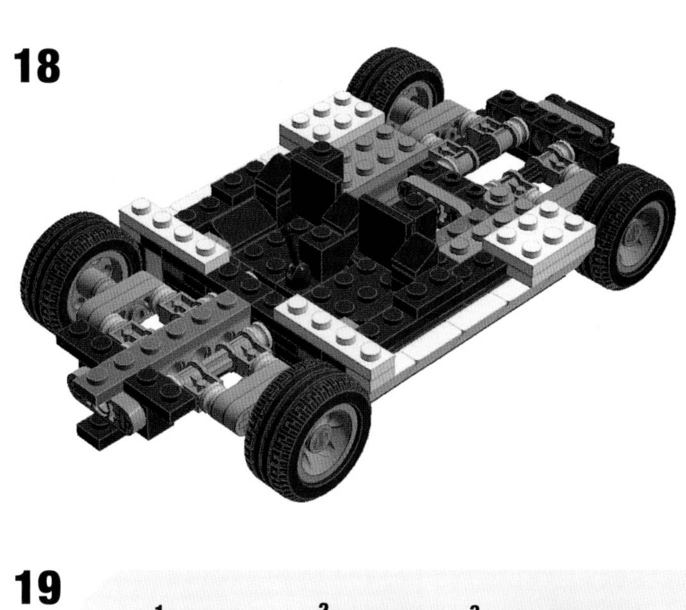

19

1 2 3 4x 4 5

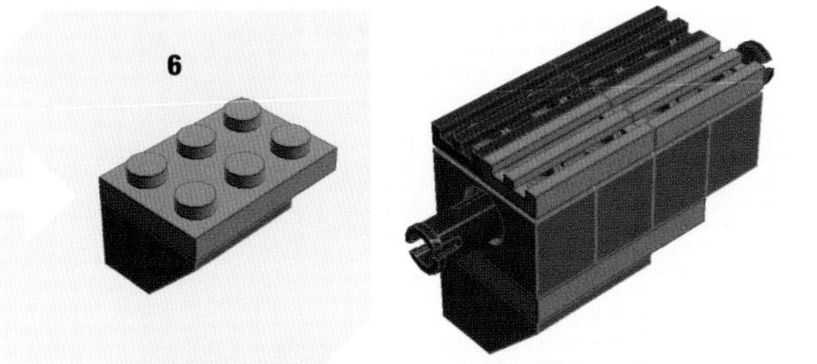

6

20

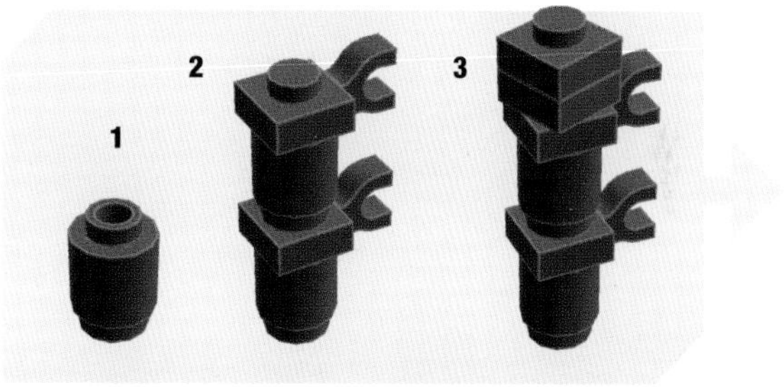

1 2 3

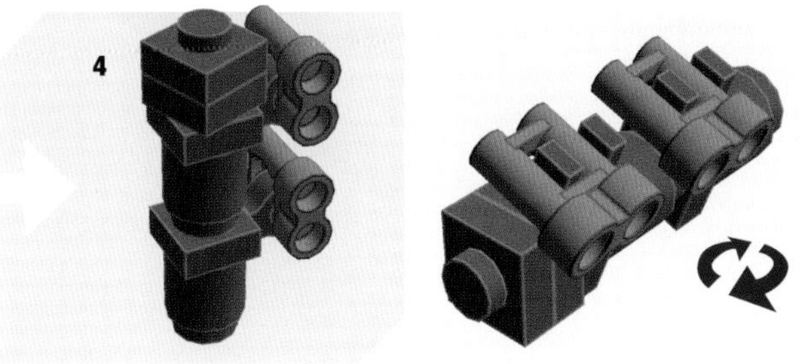

4

21

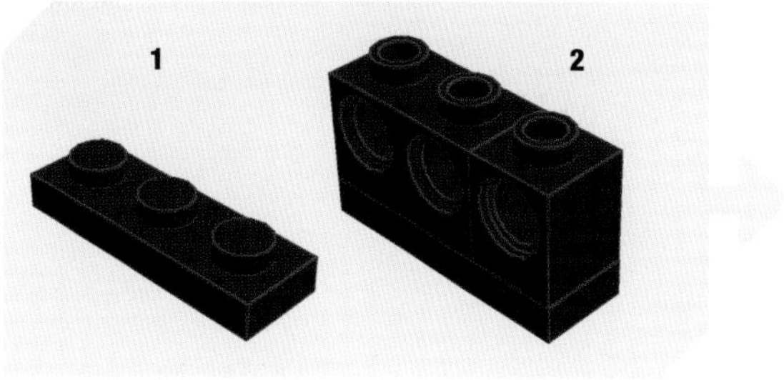

1 2

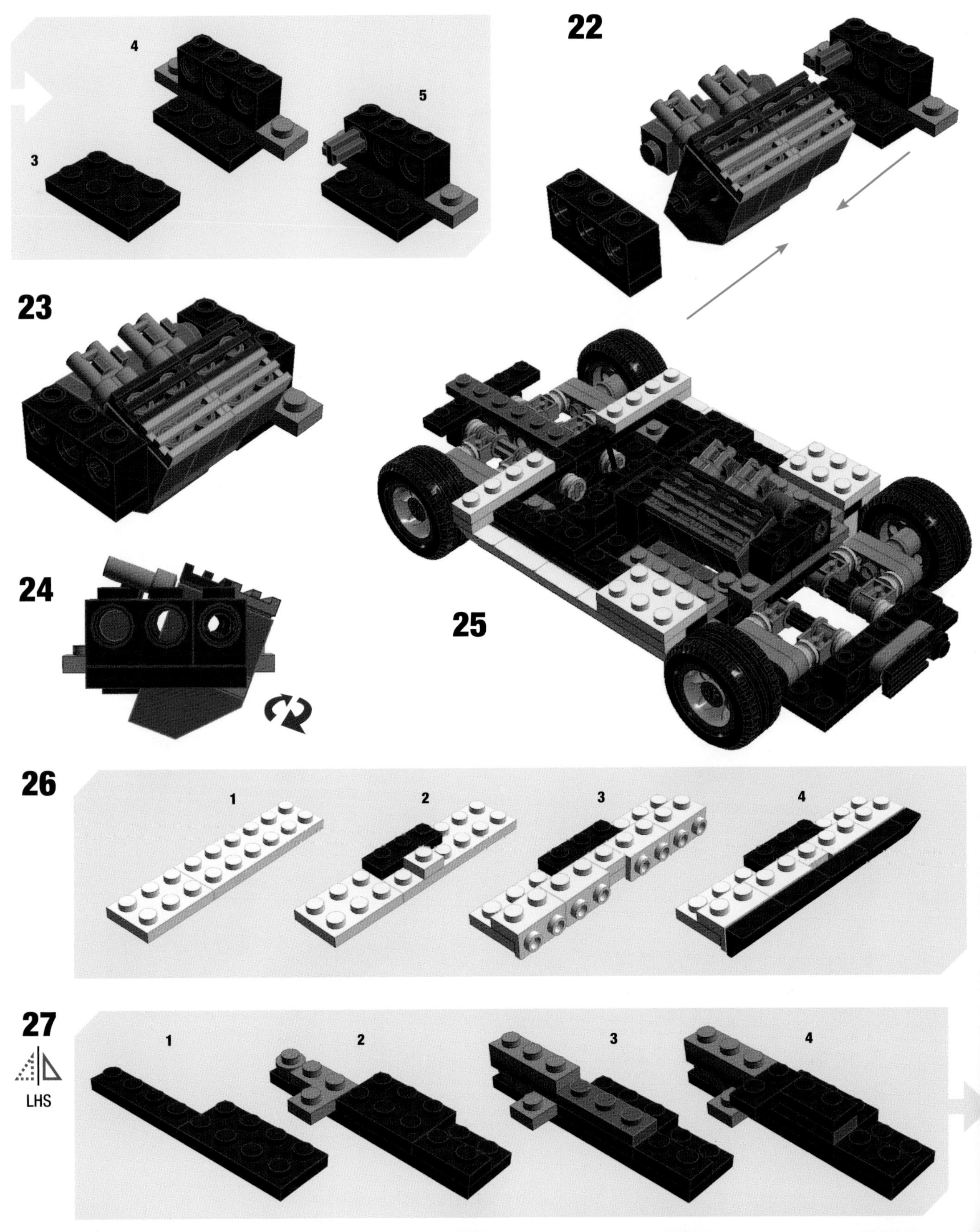
4
5
3
22
23
25
24
26
1
2
3
4
27
LHS
1
2
3
4

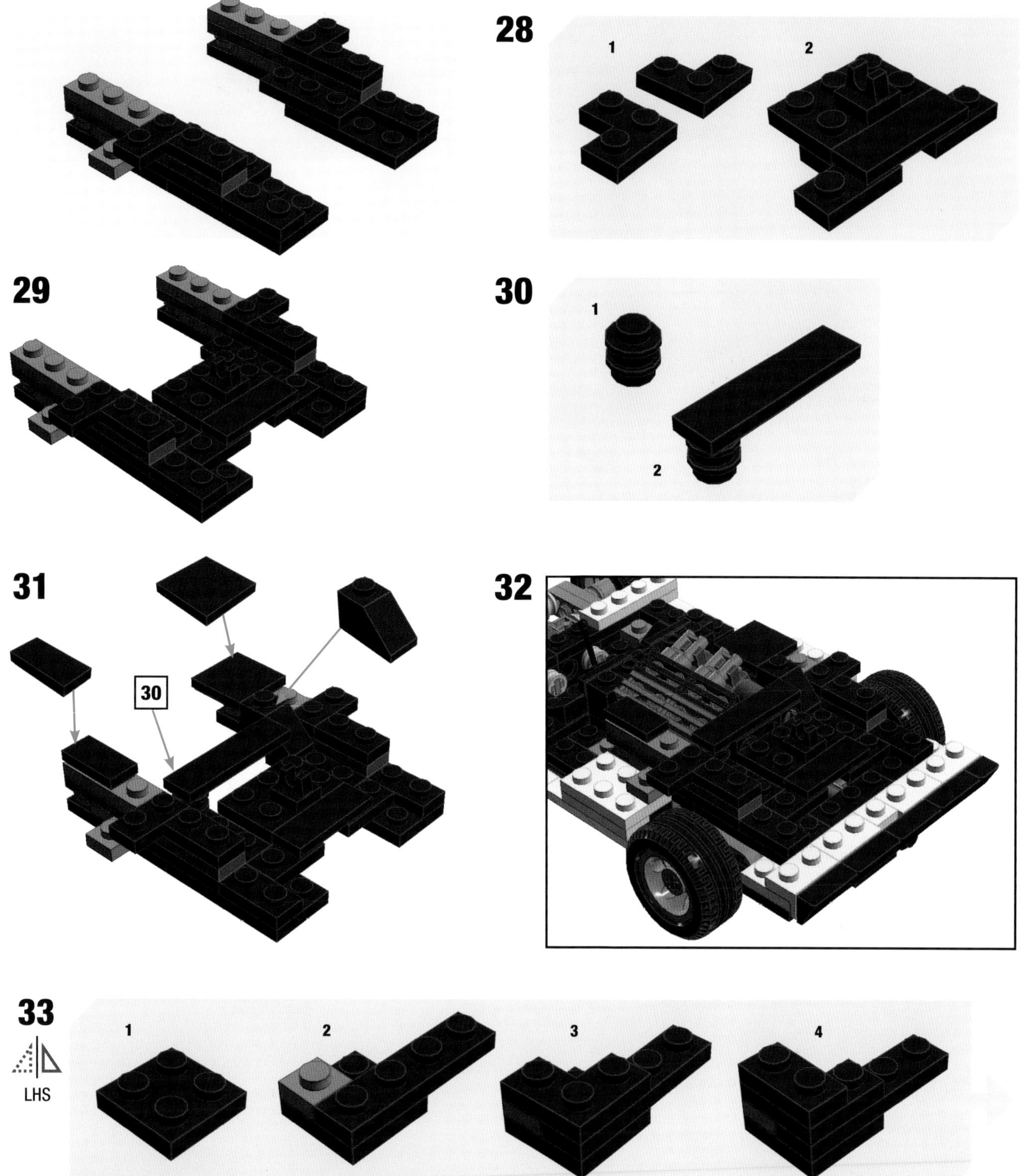

33

1

2

3

4

LHS

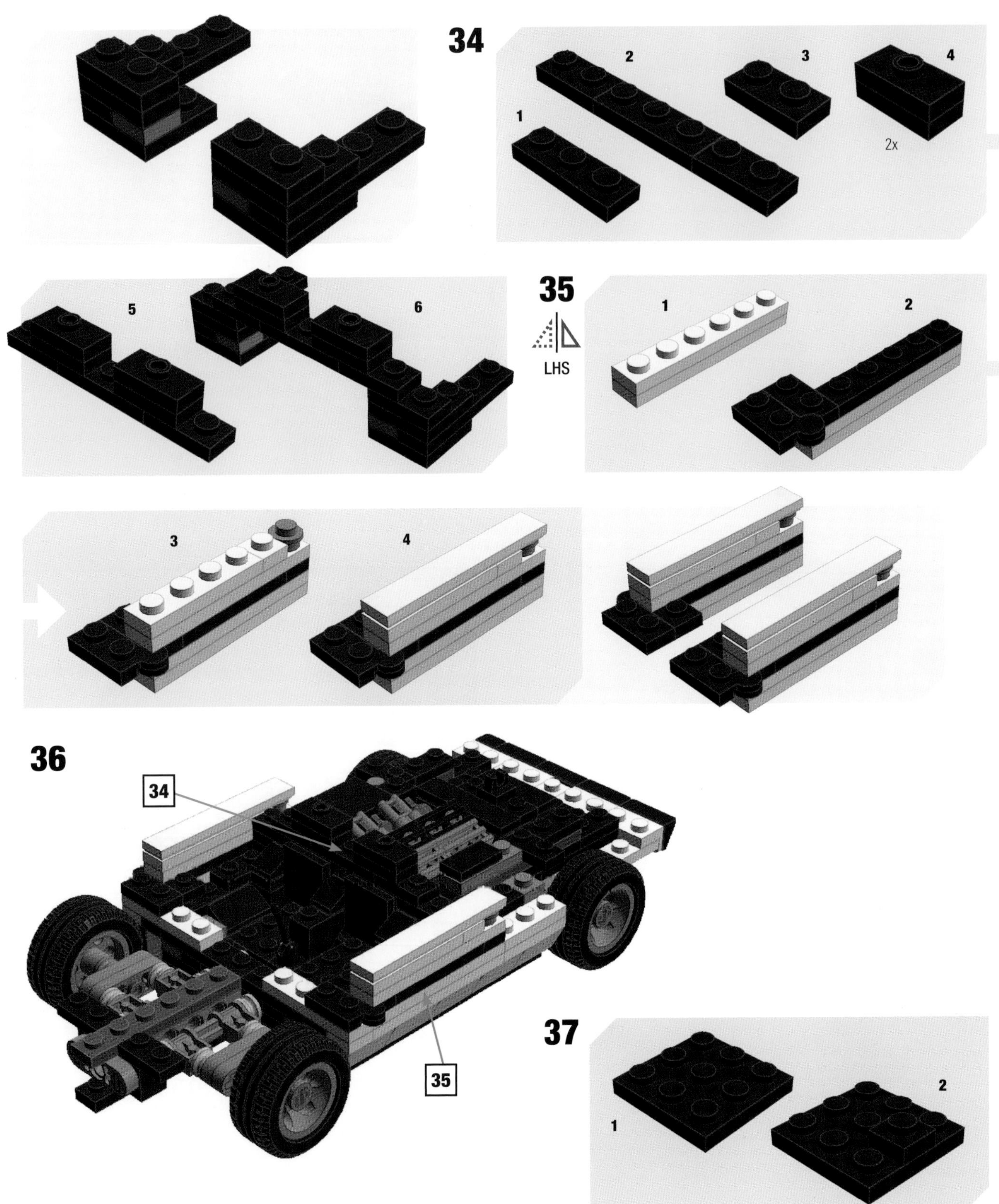
34
1
2
3
4
2x
5
6
35
LHS
1
2
3
4
36
34
35
37
1
2

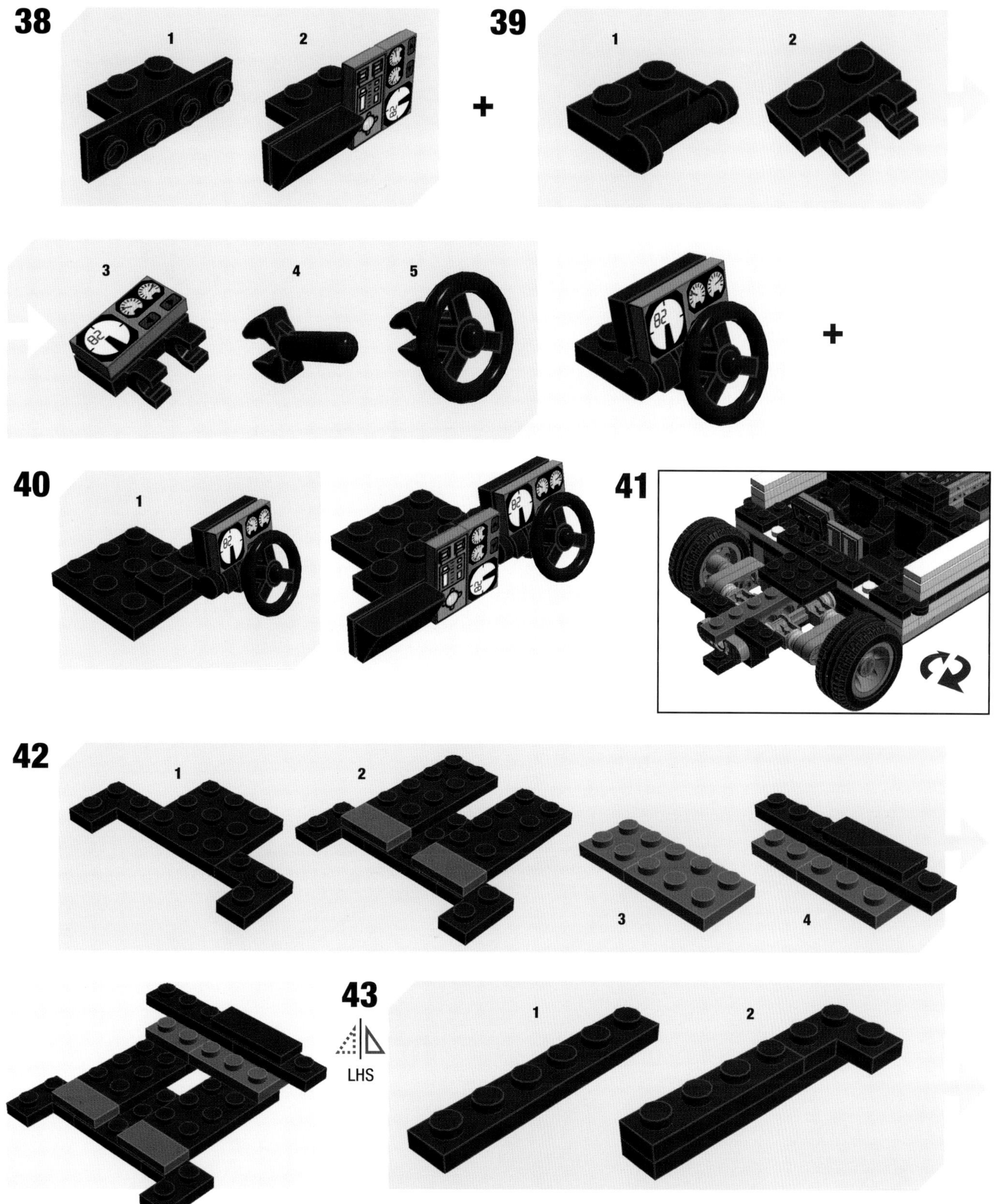
38
1
2
+
39
1
2
3
4
5
+
40
1
41
42
1
2
3
4
43
LHS
1
2

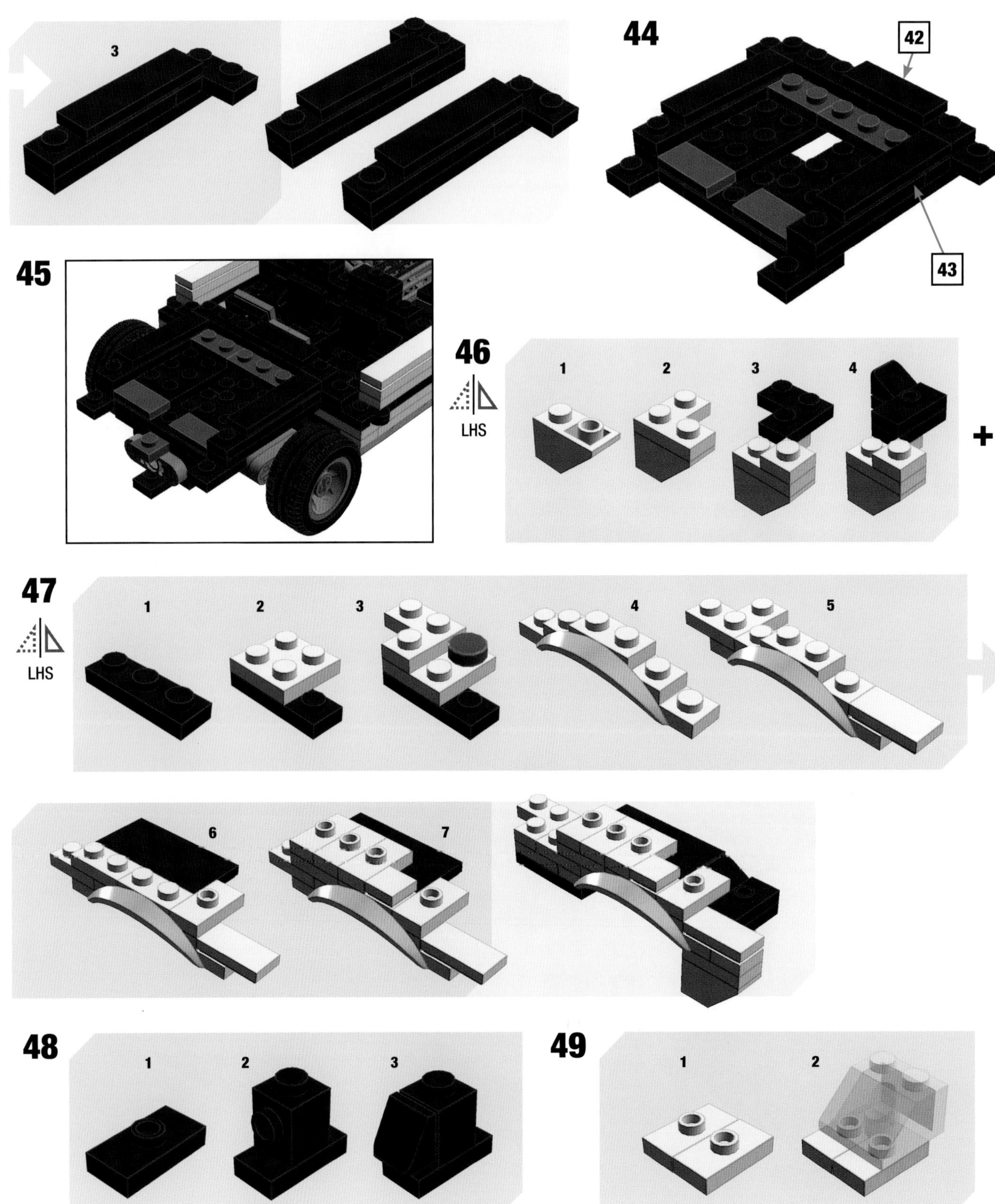
3
44
42
43
45
46
LHS
1
2
3
4
+
47
LHS
1
2
3
4
5
6
7
48
1
2
3
49
1
2

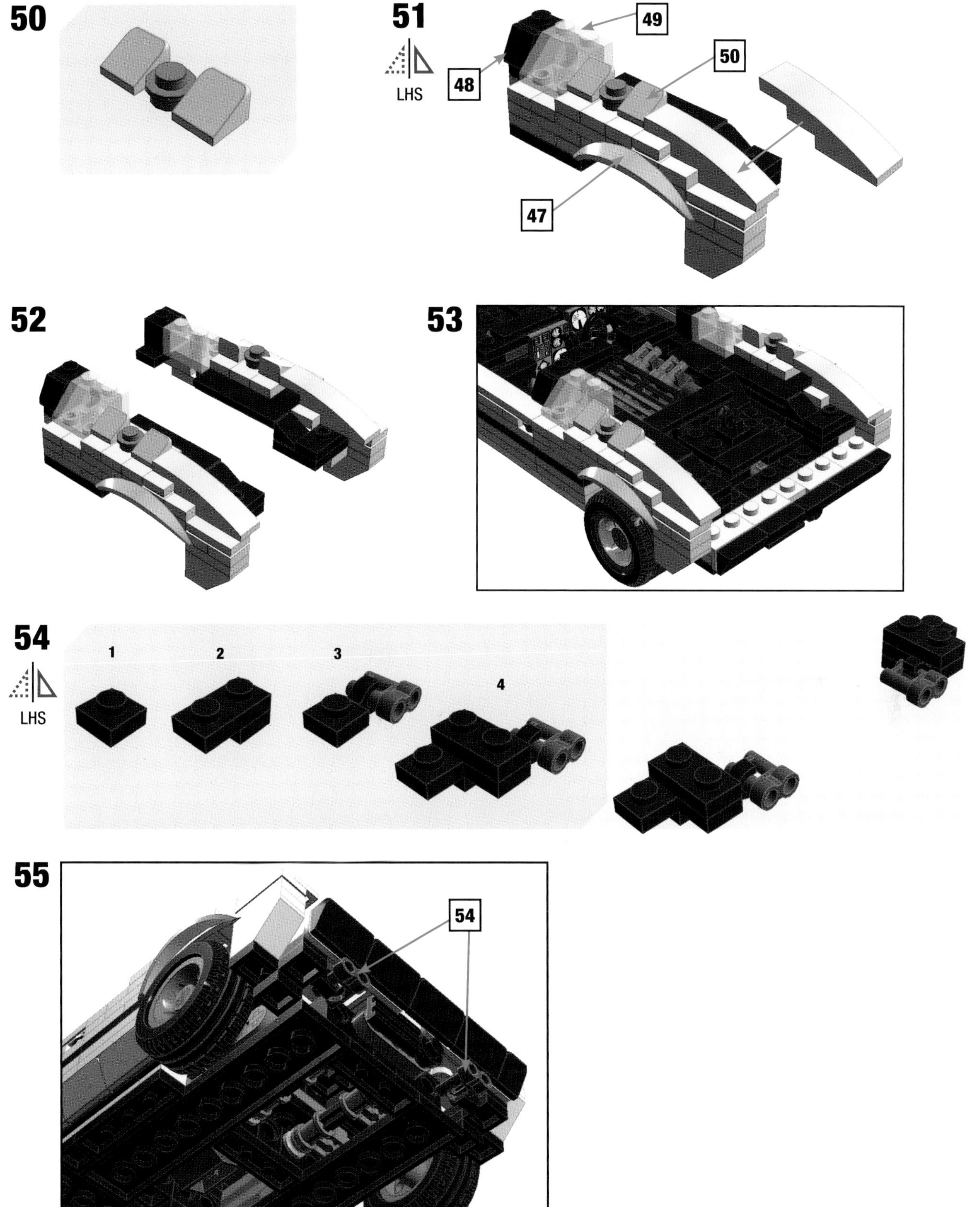
50
51
LHS
49
48
50
47
52
53
54
LHS
1
2
3
4
55
54

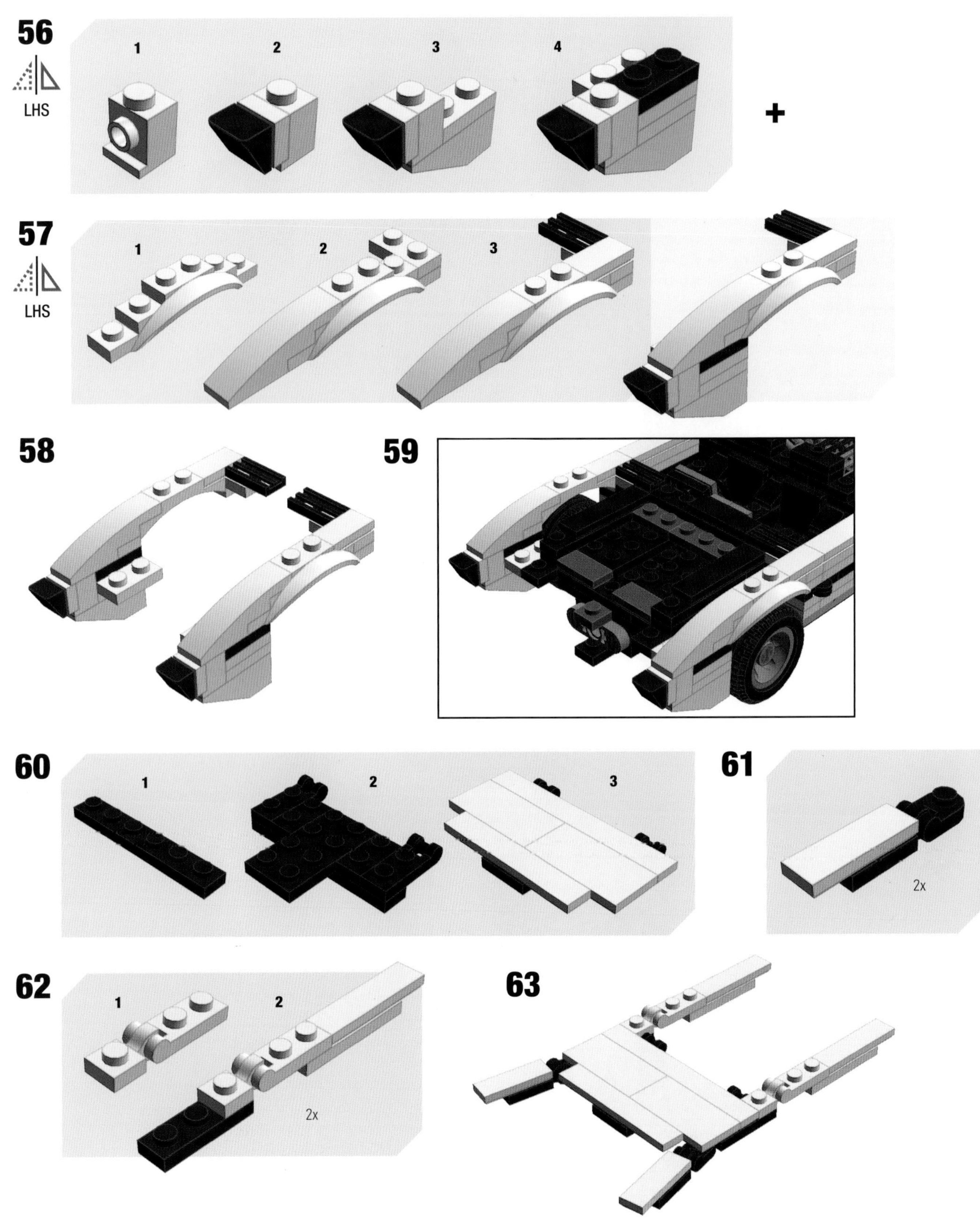
56
LHS
1
2
3
4
+
57
LHS
1
2
3
58
59
60
1
2
3
61
2x
62
1
2
2x
63

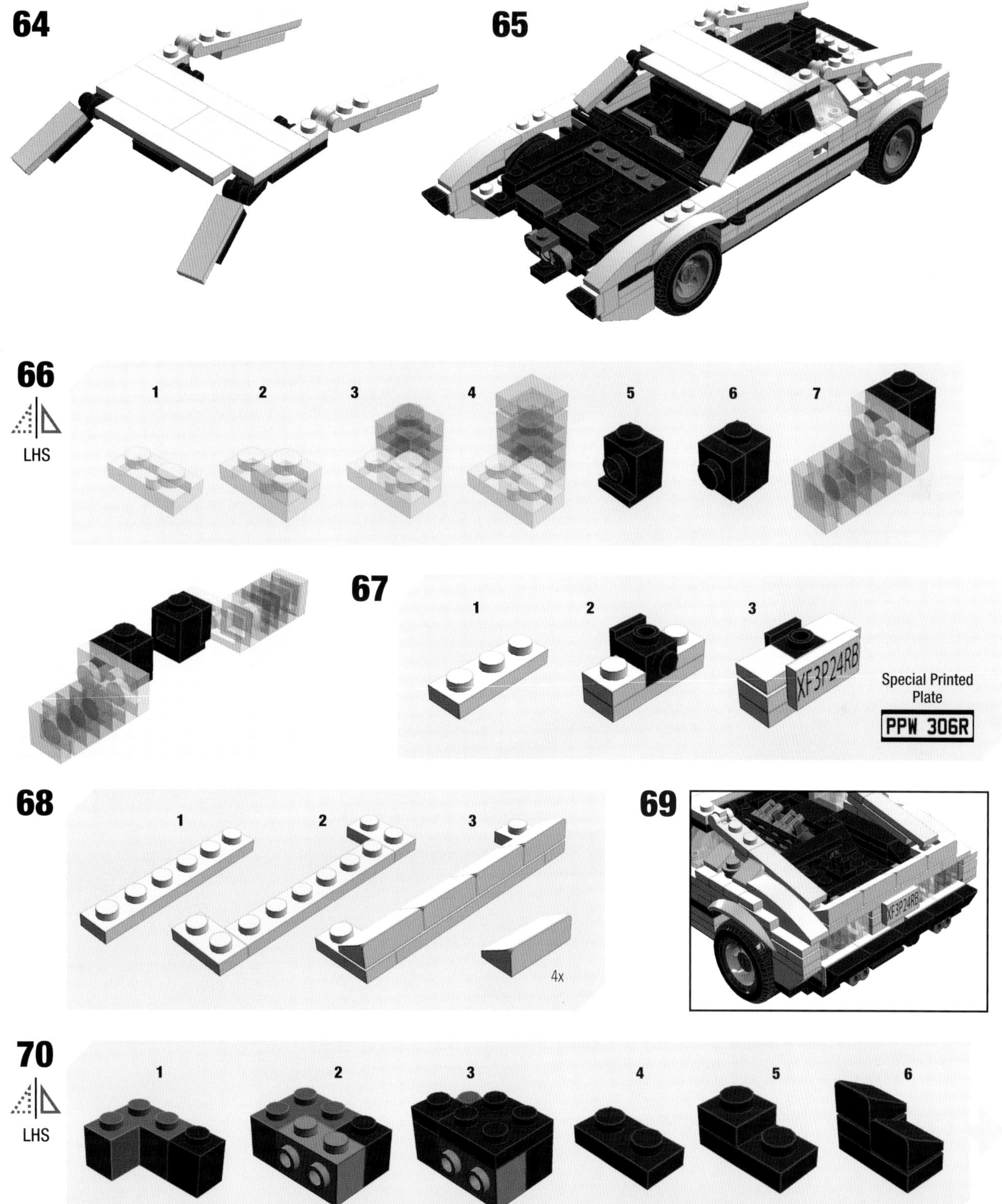
64
65
66
LHS
1
2
3
4
5
6
7
67
1
2
3
XF3P24RB
Special Printed Plate
PPW 306R
68
1
2
3
4x
69
XF3P24RB
70
LHS
1
2
3
4
5
6

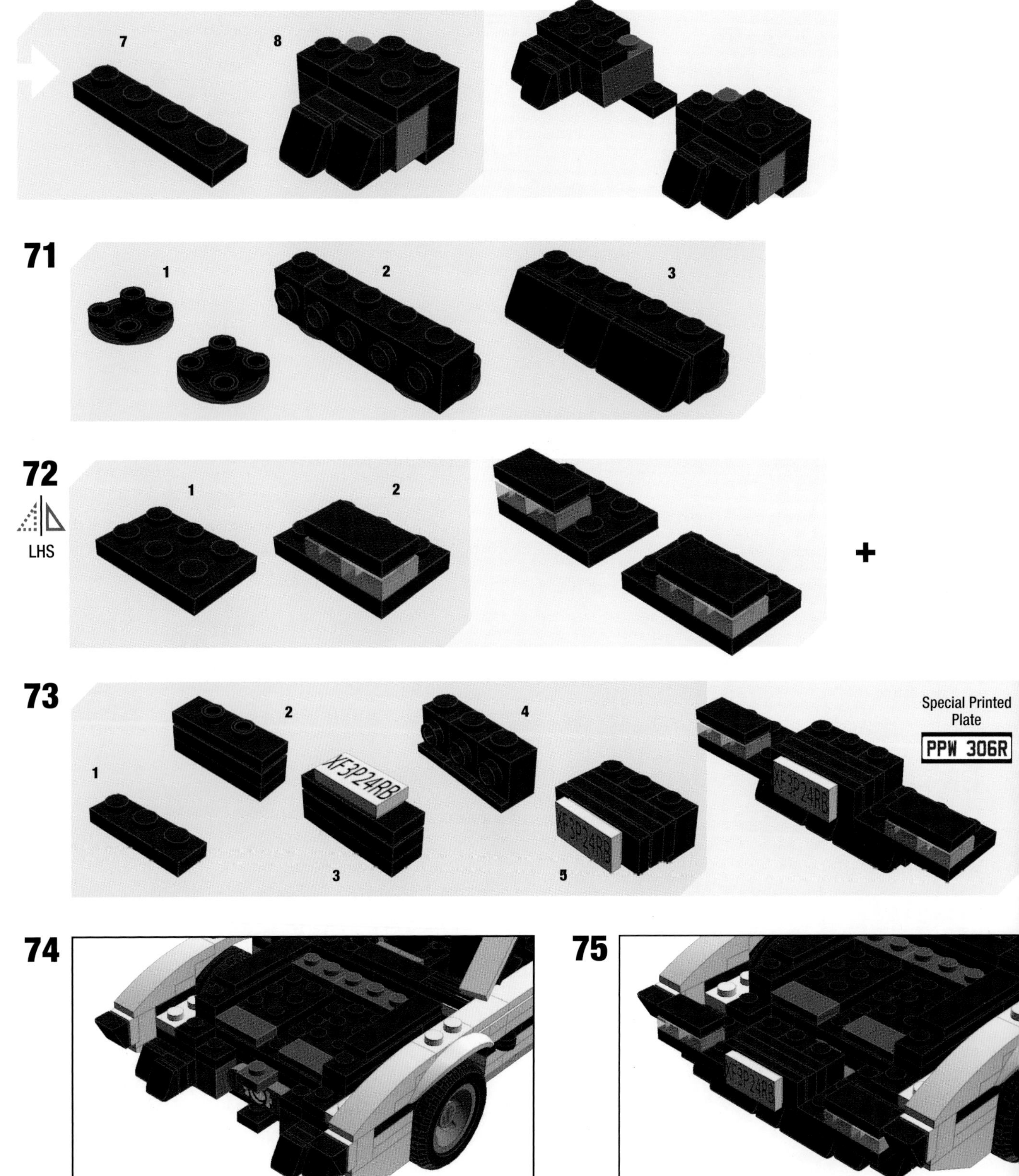
7
8
71
1
2
3
72
1
2
LHS
+
73
2
4
1
XF3P24RB
3
XF3P24RB
5
XF3P24RB
Special Printed Plate
PPW 306R
74
75
XF3P24RB

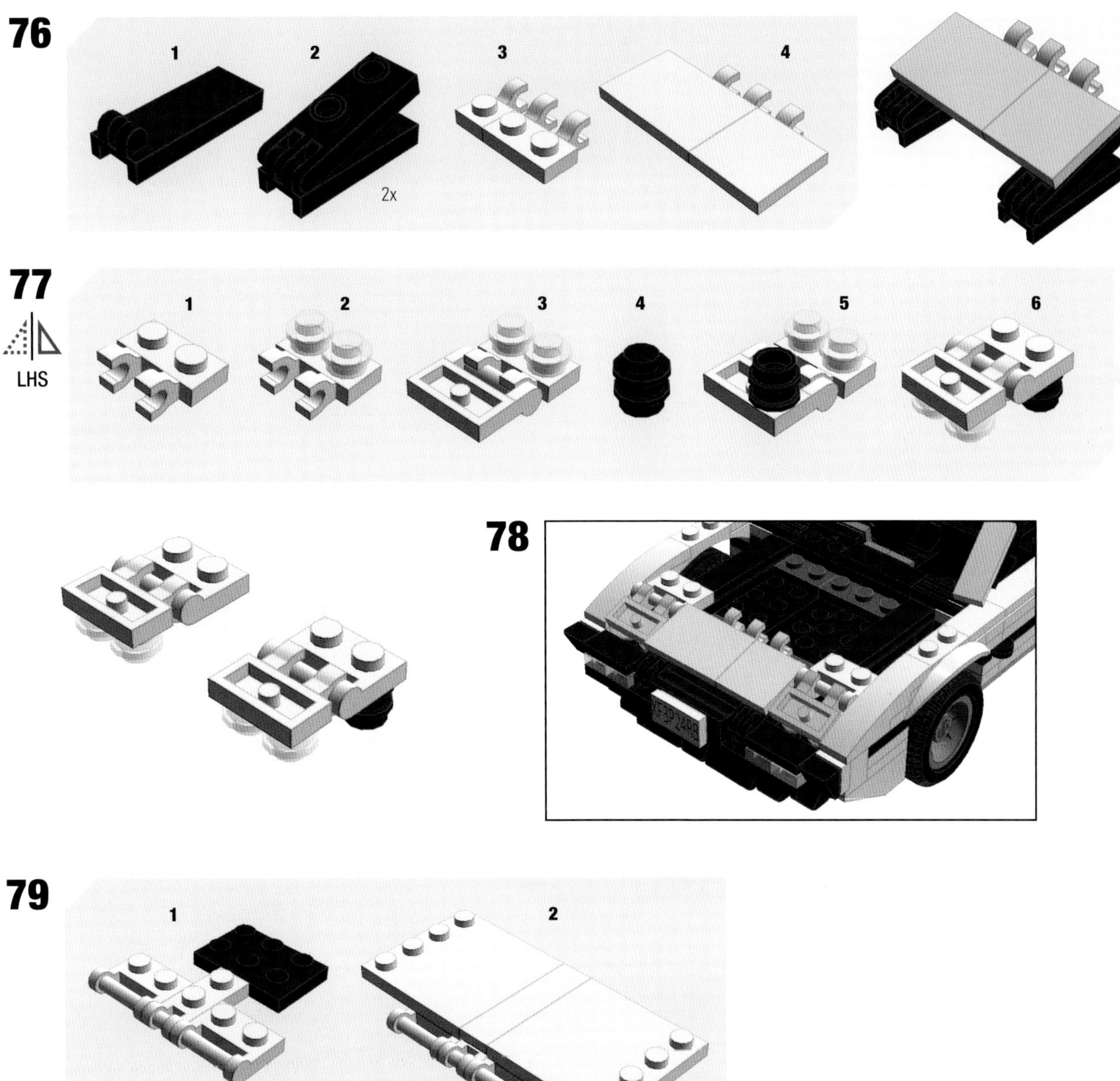
76
1
2
3
4
2x
77
1
2
3
4
5
6
LHS
78
79
1
2

80

1 2 3 4 5

81

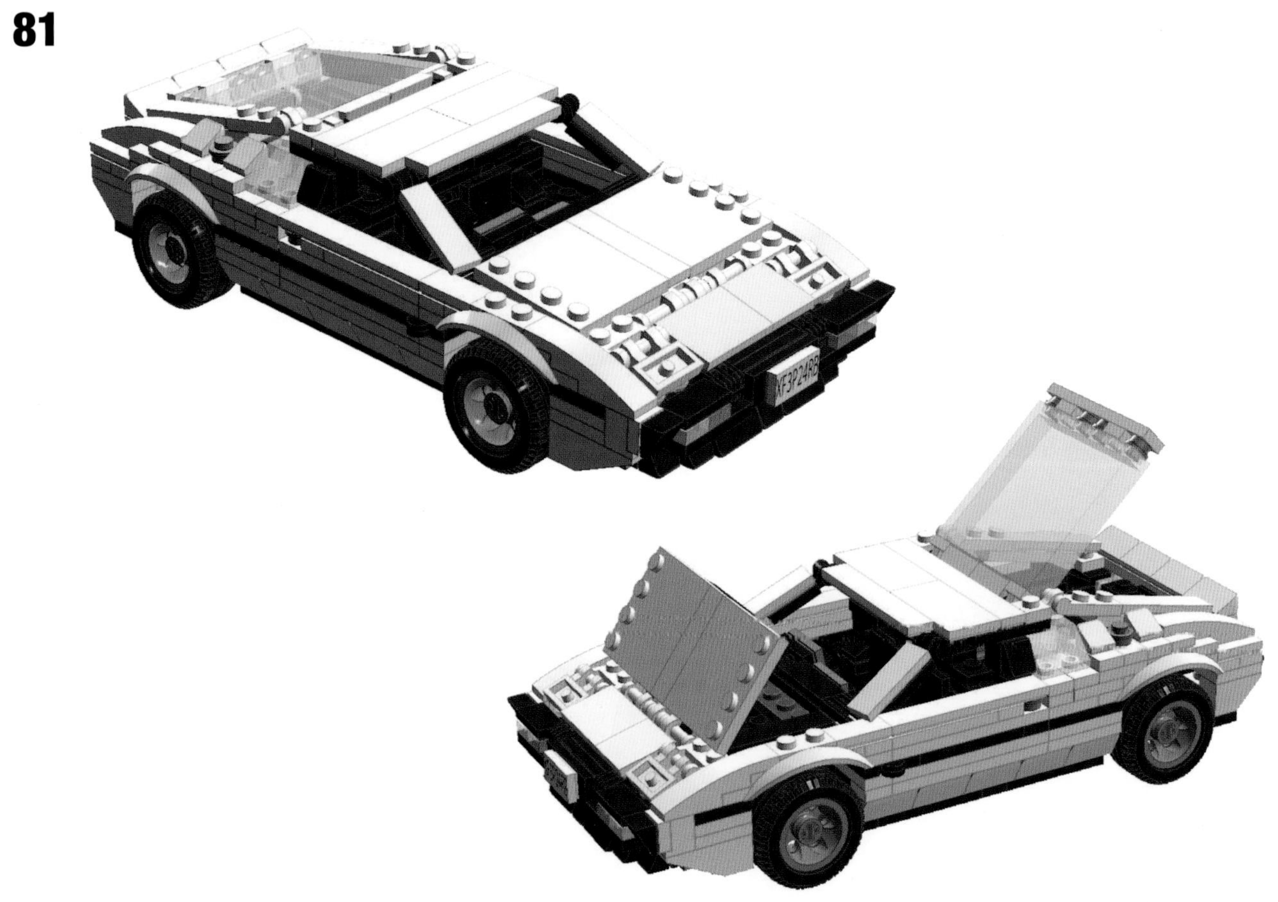

CONVERT TO SUBMARINE

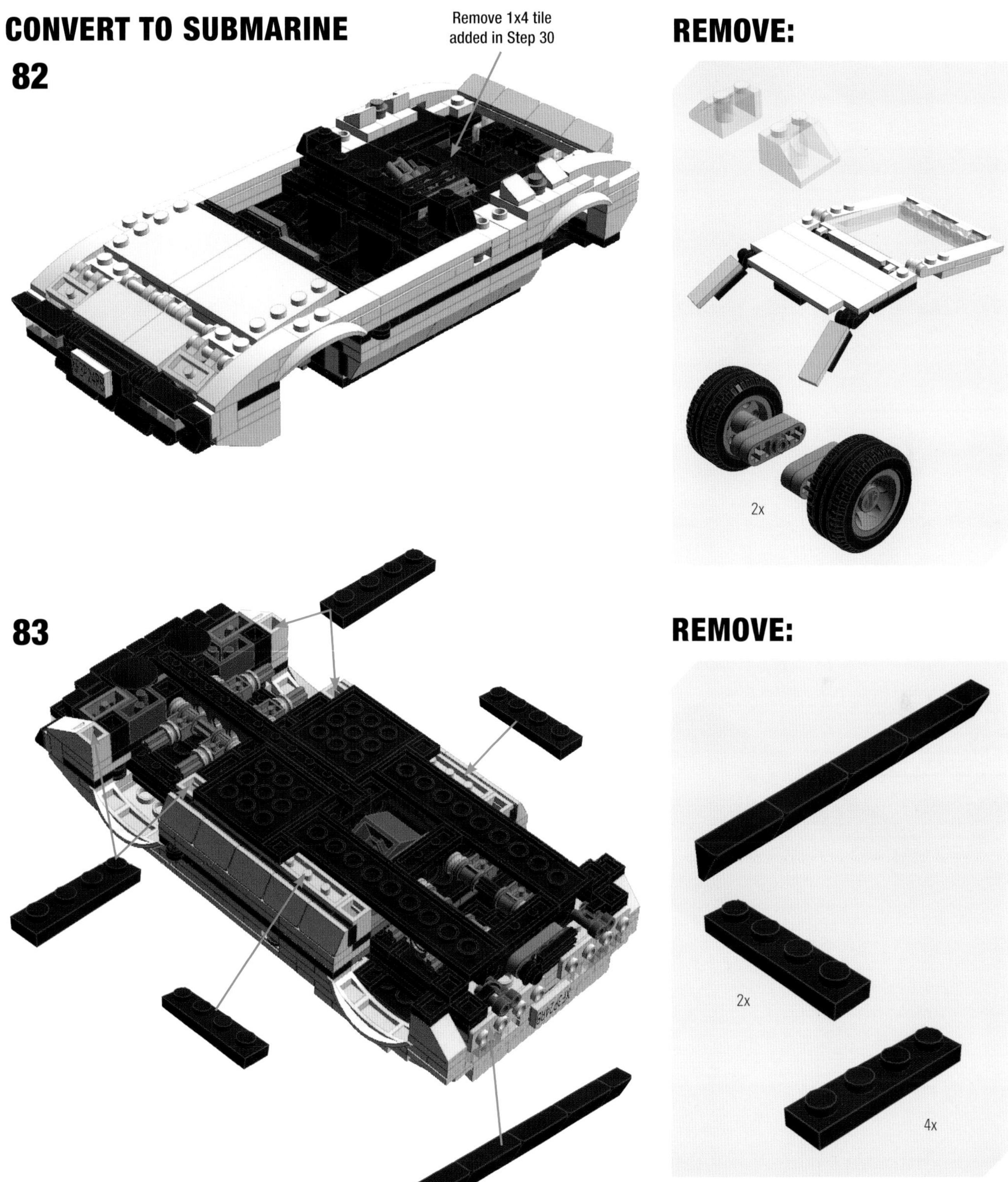

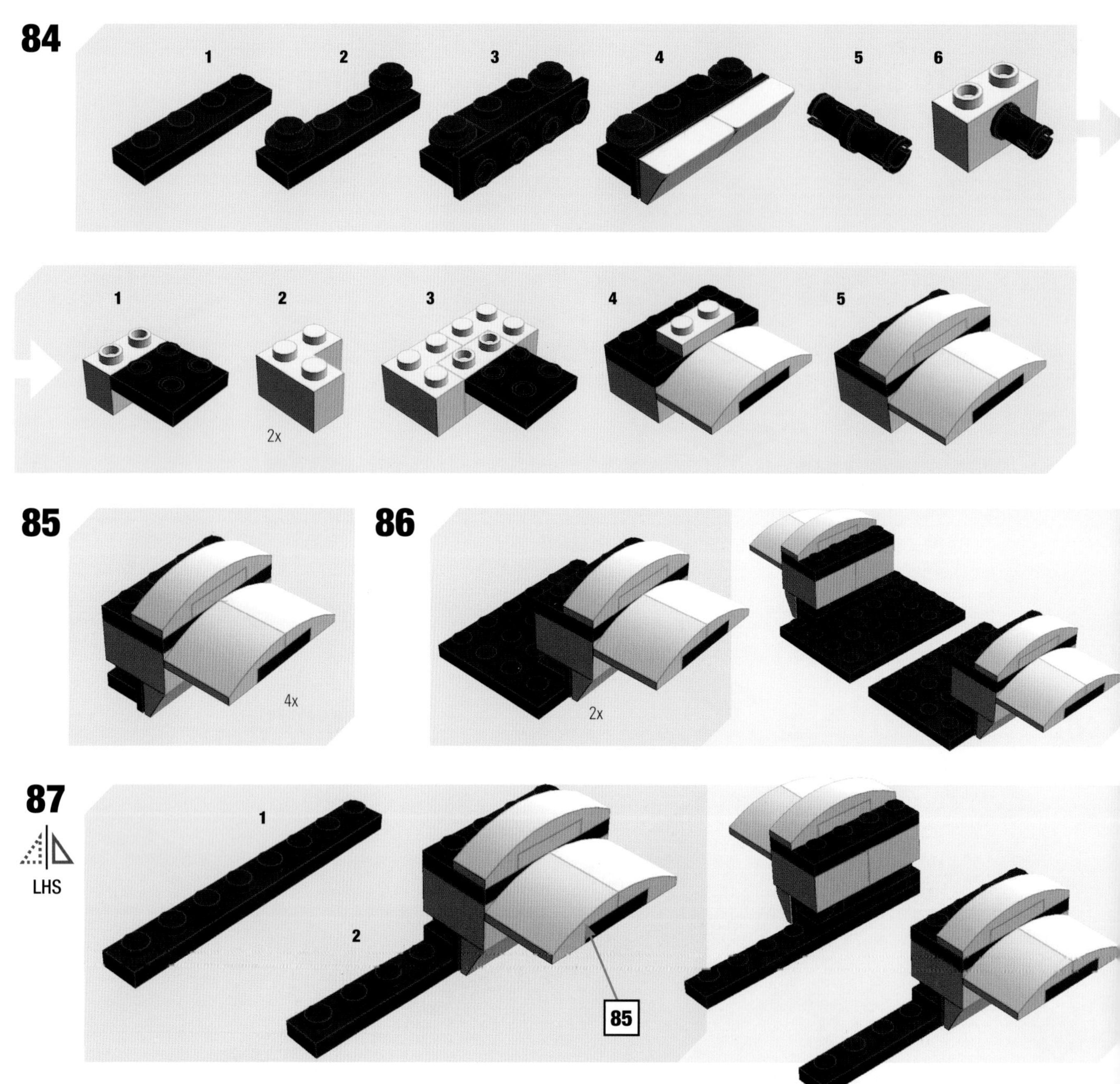

84
1
2
3
4
5
6
1
2
3
4
5
2x
85
4x
86
2x
87
LHS
1
2
85

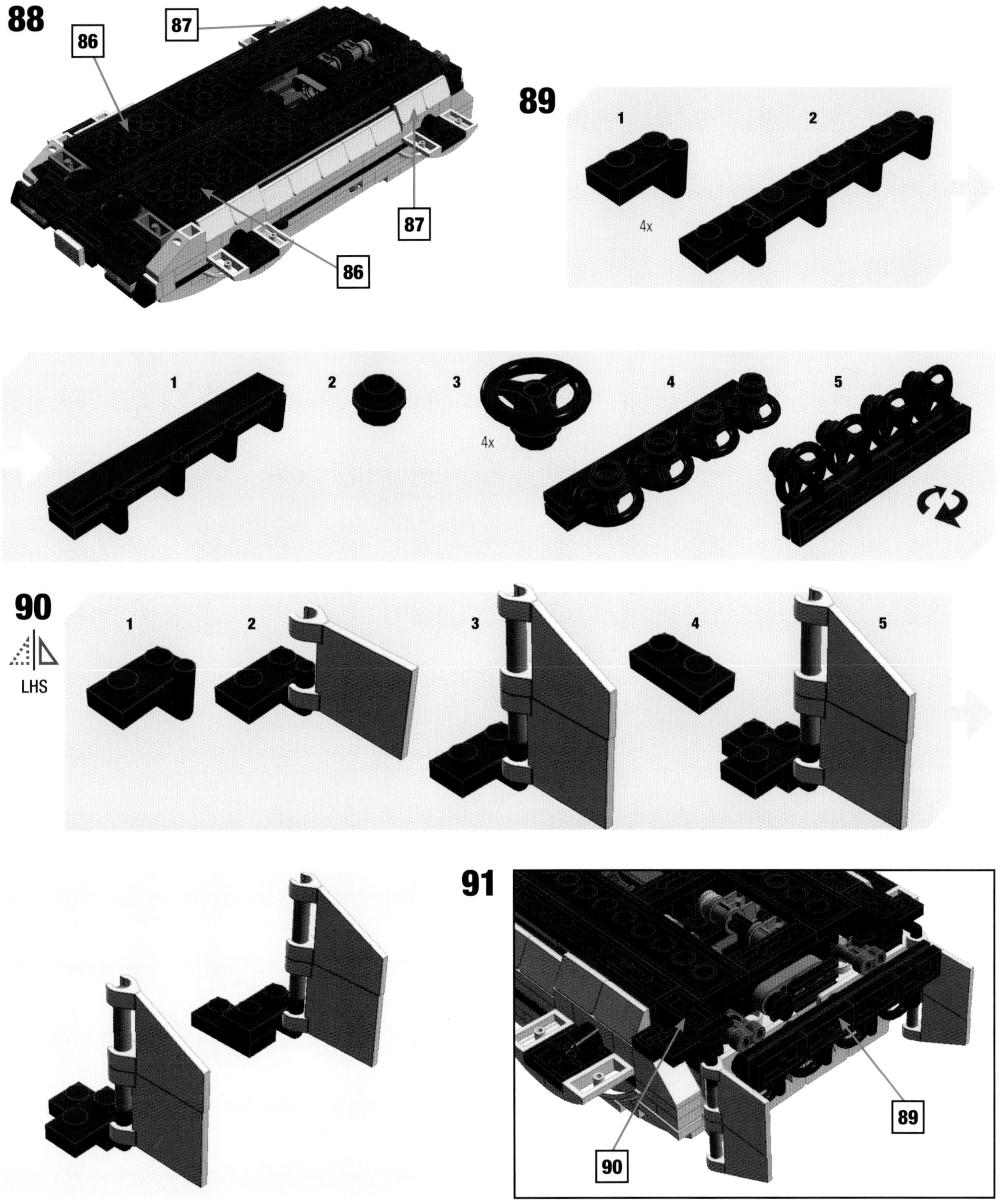
88
86
87
87
86
89
1
2
4x
1
2
3
4x
4
5
90
LHS
1
2
3
4
5
91
90
89

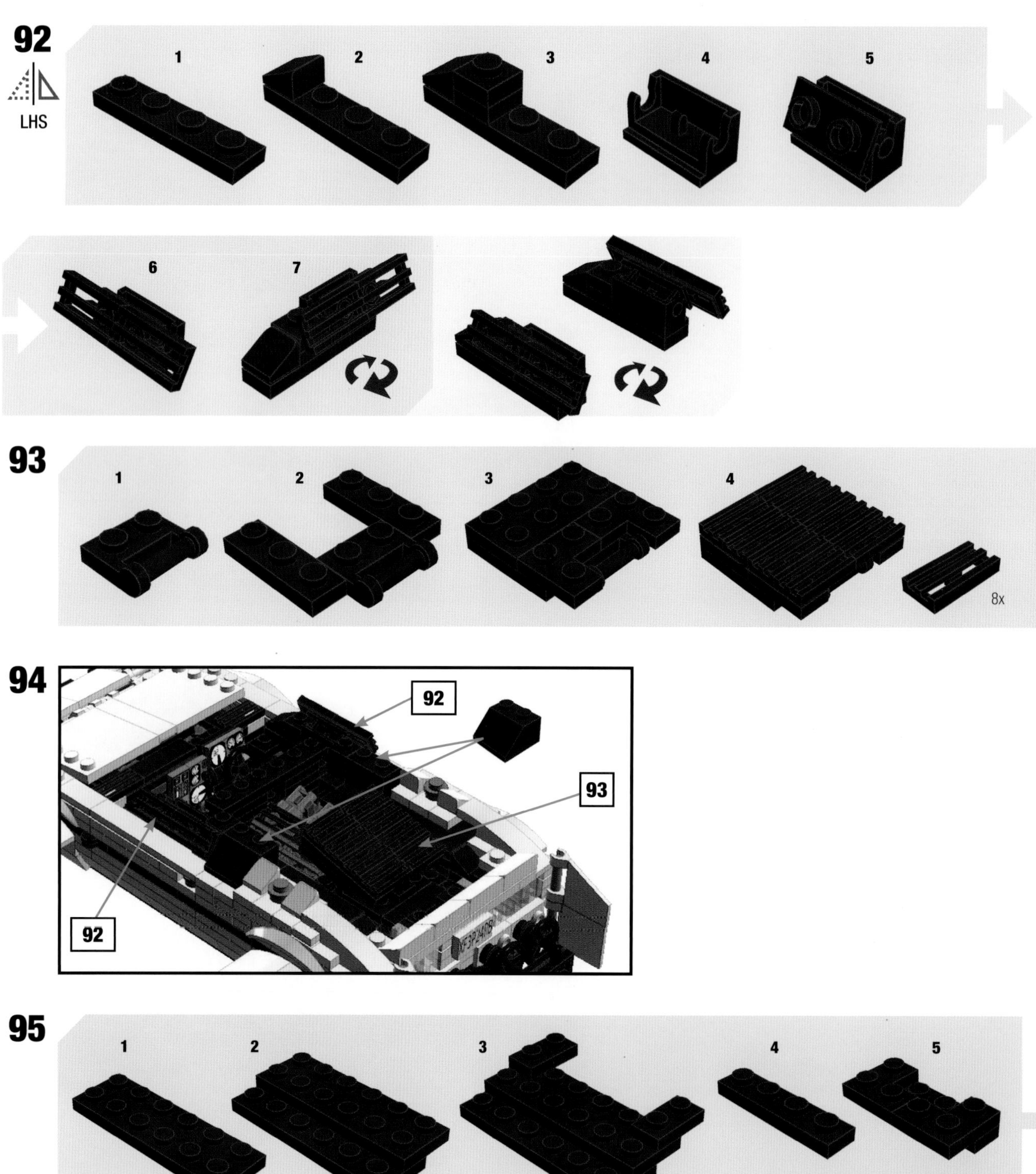
92
LHS
1
2
3
4
5
6
7
93
1
2
3
4
8x
94
92
93
92
95
1
2
3
4
5

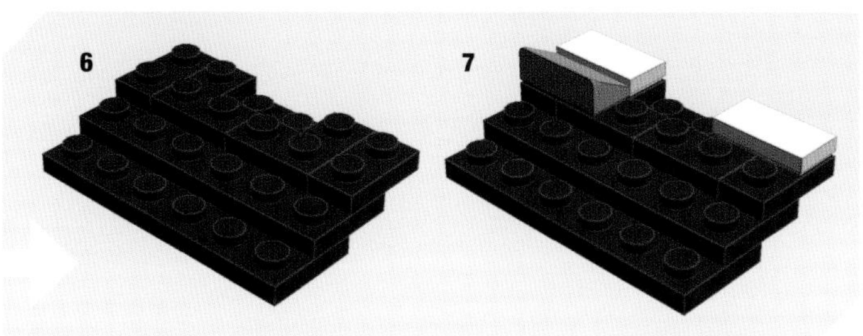

96

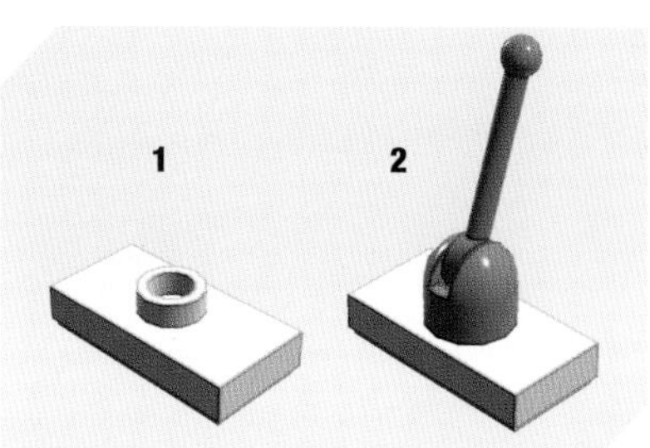

97

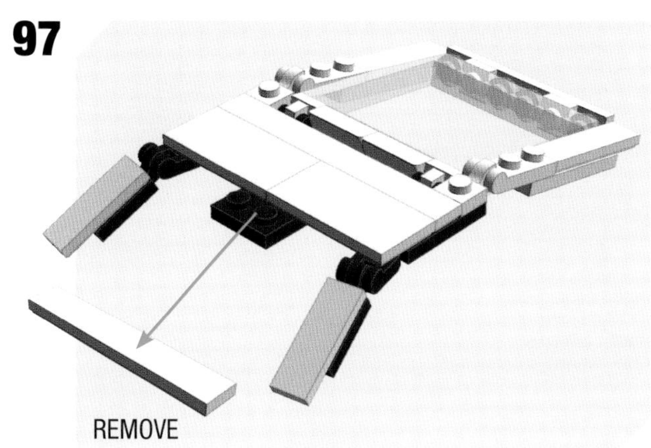

98

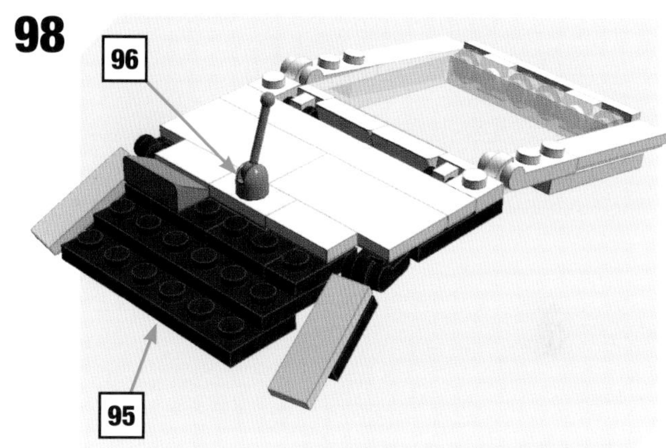

99

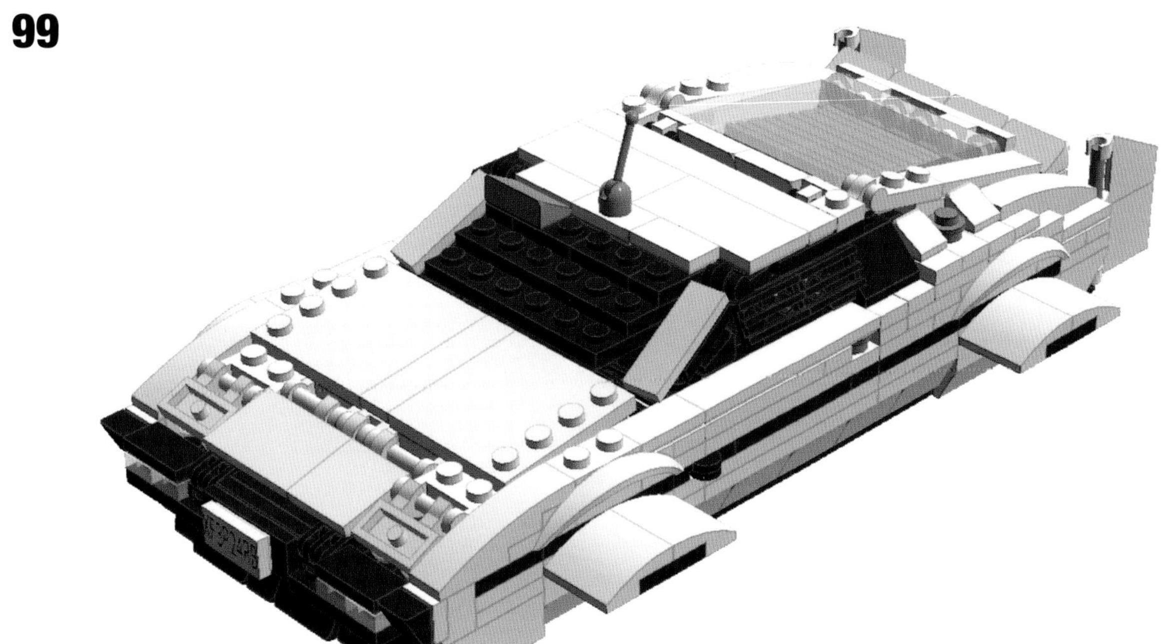

SECTION 3

ADVANCED

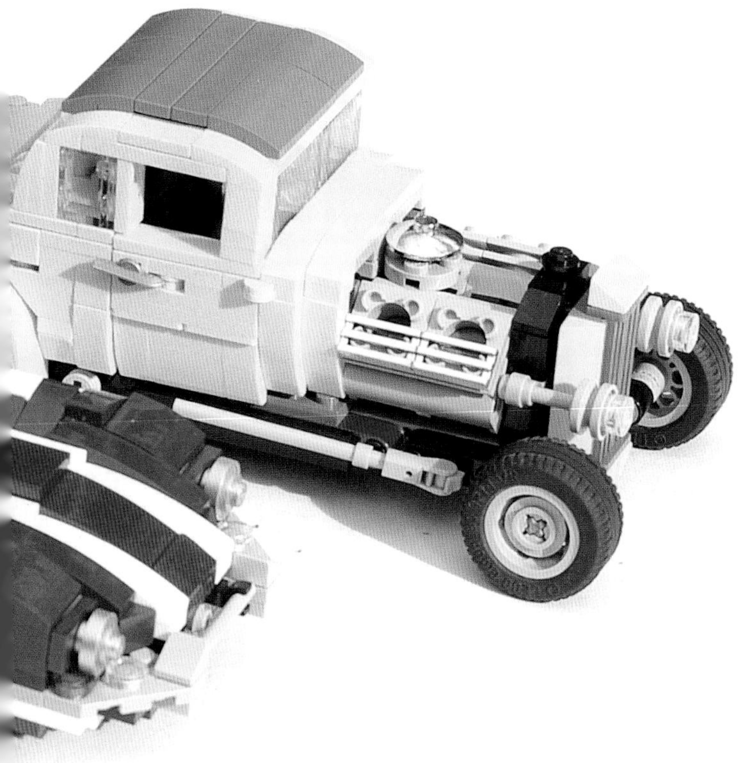

Each of the cars here represents speed and performance. During the classic period that most of the cars in this book come from, this was achieved through big engines and sleek bodywork. All three cars have these characteristics. The Ford V8 from 1932 was a taste of affordable performance from day one and has been frequently tuned to performance cars even through to today. The *Mad Max* Interceptor, designed to chase down villains on Australia's outback roads, deployed an even bigger engine fitted with a supercharger. The E-Type, classically beautiful, was nonetheless fast, and the Austin Powers car here is a real challenge for model-builders with its wild paintwork.

These models are again presented in Miniland scale but include more detailed chassis and moving engines, utilising LEGO's Technic theme parts. As builders assemble these models, they will experience constructing major systems as they exist in real machines. These cars are classics, and designs for these are often requested by people who follow my work.

Once builders have completed all the cars from the book, they should be well-placed to create their own models using some of the techniques presented.

CHAPTER 10

FORD 1932 COUPE HOT ROD
AMERICAN GRAFFITI

Like many of the films featured in this book because of their noteworthy cars, *American Graffiti* has a cult following. Set in 1962 in Modesto, California, the film's beat is a mix of period tunes and the rumble of V8 engines that made up the cruising culture of the time. Directed by George Lucas, who would go on to greater fame with the Star Wars® franchise, *American Graffiti* was a much more autobiographic work and a reflection of his love of cars.

The film centers on a number of chief automotive protagonists. The car modelled here is the yellow 1932 Ford coupe hot rod driven by John Milner (played by Paul Le Mat), which features prominently throughout the film. The deuce coupe sets much of the tone of the film as a model of vehicle that would have been accessible to the youth during the period; the cars were inexpensive and could be modified easily as an outward expression of an individual's self-image.

COUNTRY OF ORIGIN: United States

PRODUCTION: 1932

NUMBER MADE: 298,647

LAYOUT/DRIVE: Front engine, Rear-wheel-drive

ENGINE: 283 ci (4.6 liter), 8 cylinders, Vee

POWER TORQUE: N/A

CONSTRUCTION/DOORS: Steel Separate Chassis, two-door

TV/FILM APPEARANCE: *American Graffiti*

The 1932–34 Fords, featuring Flathead V8 engines, typify this customizing culture, though earlier Model T and Model A Fords along with Chevrolets and other US makes from this period were often crafted into modified performance machines. Though there is some debate, the "Milner Coupe" was said to be powered by a Chevrolet 283 ci V-8.

American Graffiti is set on the last night of summer break. After finishing high school, two of the characters, Curt Henderson (Richard Dreyfuss) and Steve Bolander (Ron Howard) are due to leave for college the following day while their peers appear destined to remain in their small-town lives.

Just as street racing was part of the scene during this era, a number of small traffic-light drag racers break up the frustration and tension of the film. The climax features Bob Falfa (Harrison Ford), driving a 1955 Chevrolet 150 coupe, racing Milner's 1932 Ford on the edge of town along Paradise Road, culminating in a crash and explosion.

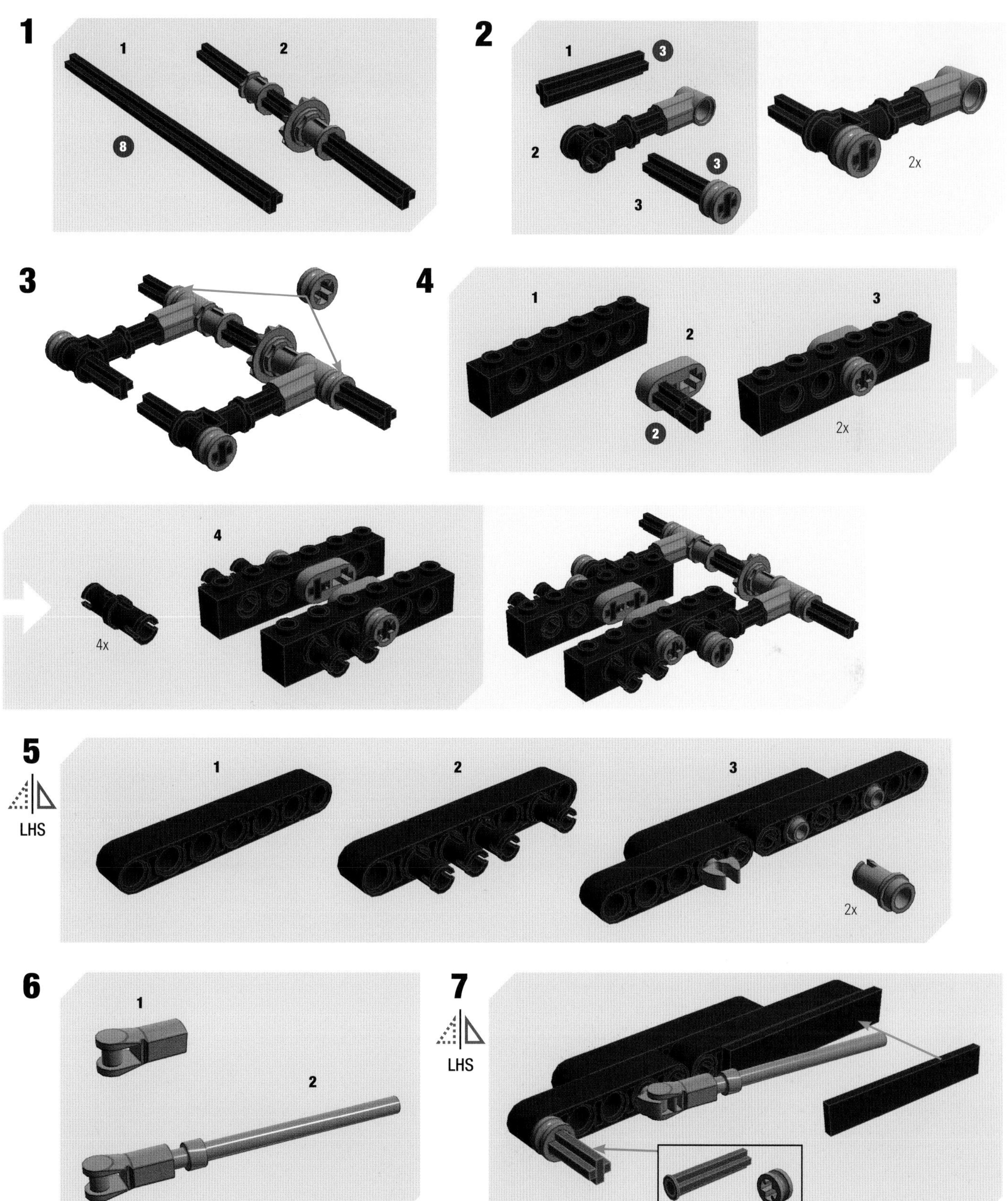
1
1
2
8
2
1
3
2
3
3
2x
3
4
1
2
3
2
2x
4
4x
5
1
2
3
LHS
2x
6
1
2
7
LHS

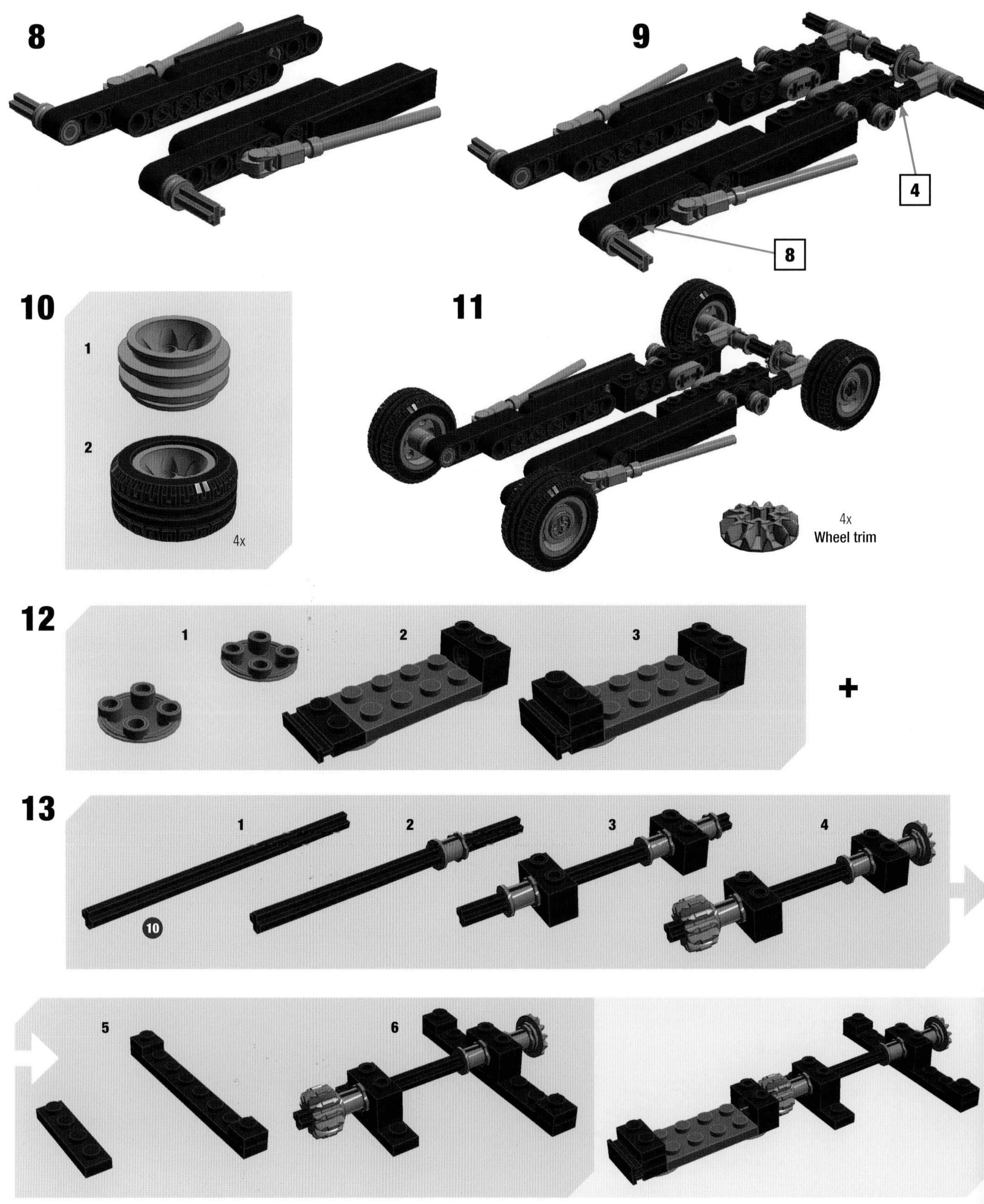
8
9
4
8
10
1
2
4x
11
4x
Wheel trim
12
1
2
3
+
13
1
2
3
4
10
5
6

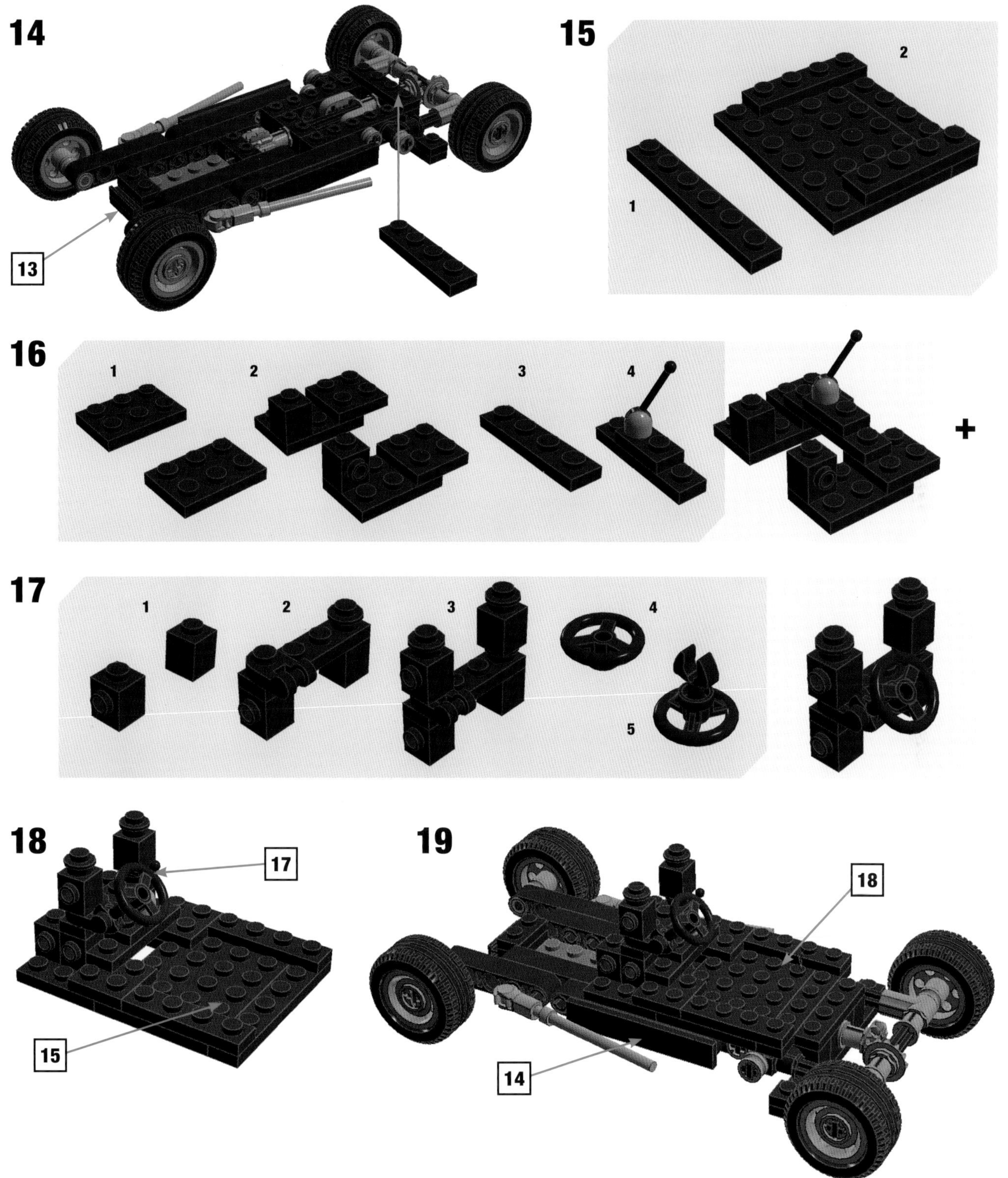
14
13
15
2
1
16
1
2
3
4
+
17
1
2
3
4
5
18
17
15
19
18
14

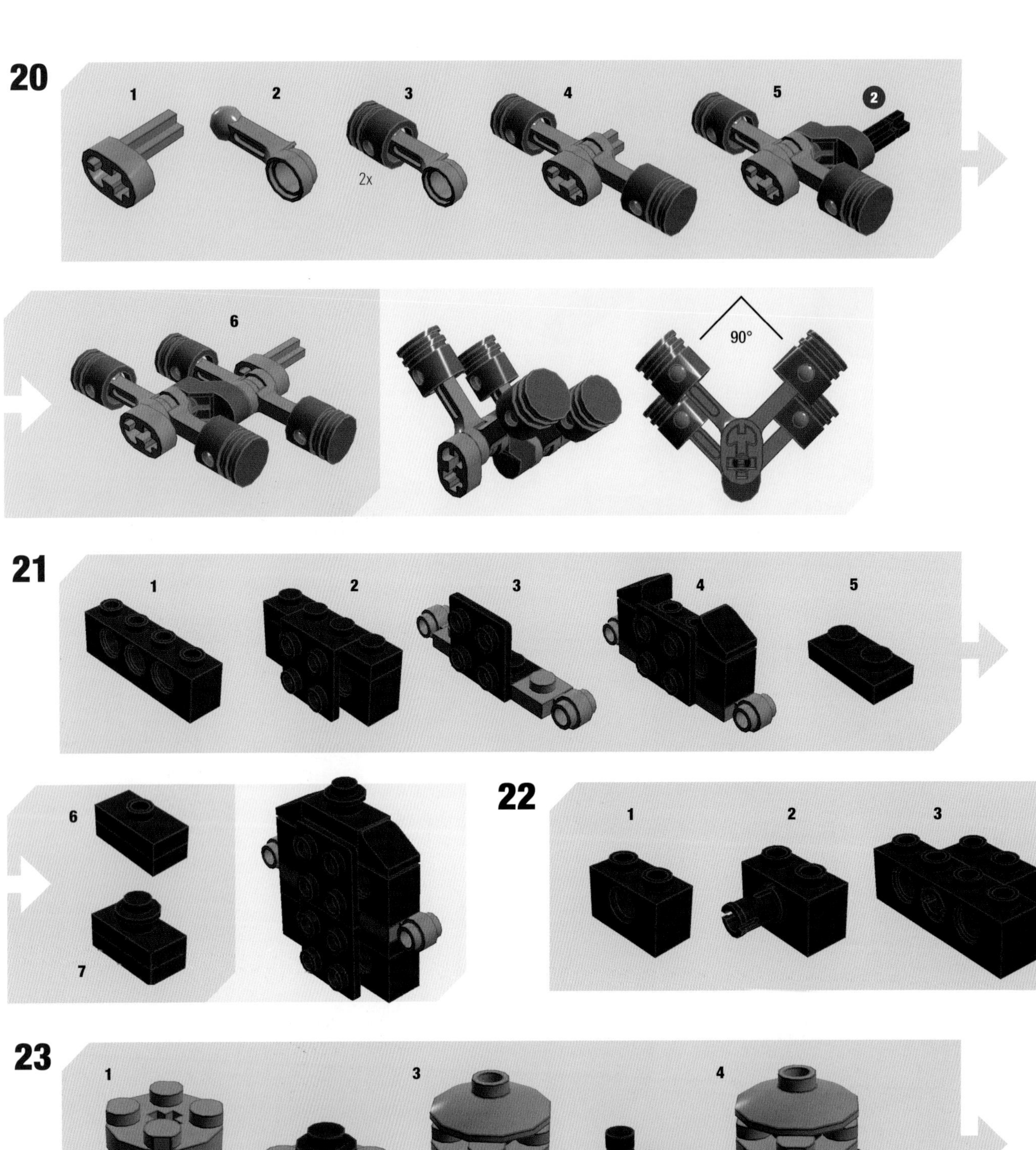
20
1
2
3
4
5
2
2x
6
90°
21
1
2
3
4
5
6
7
22
1
2
3
23
1
2
3
4

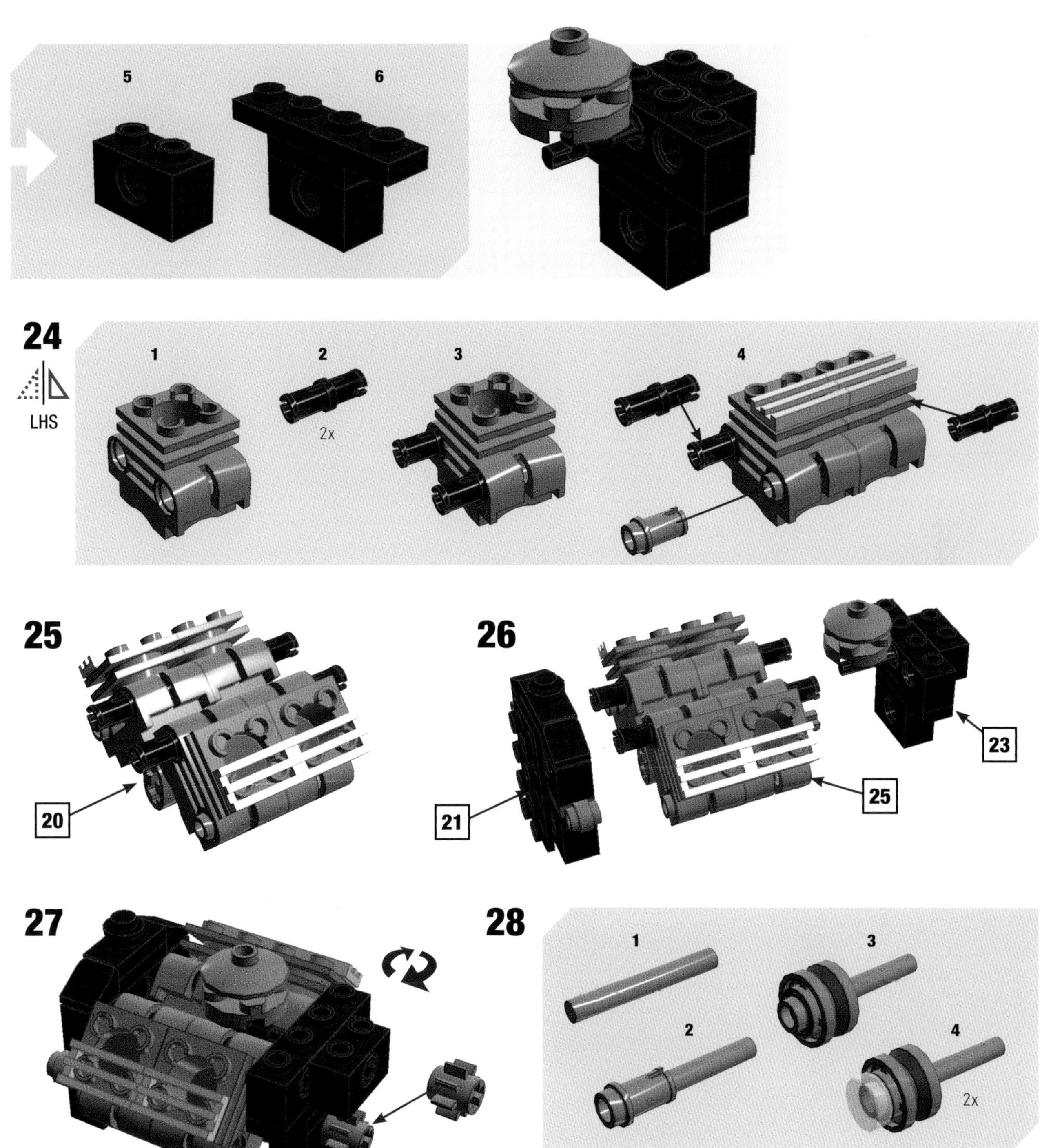

5
6
24
LHS
1
2
2x
3
4
25
20
26
21
25
23
27
28
1
3
2
4
2x

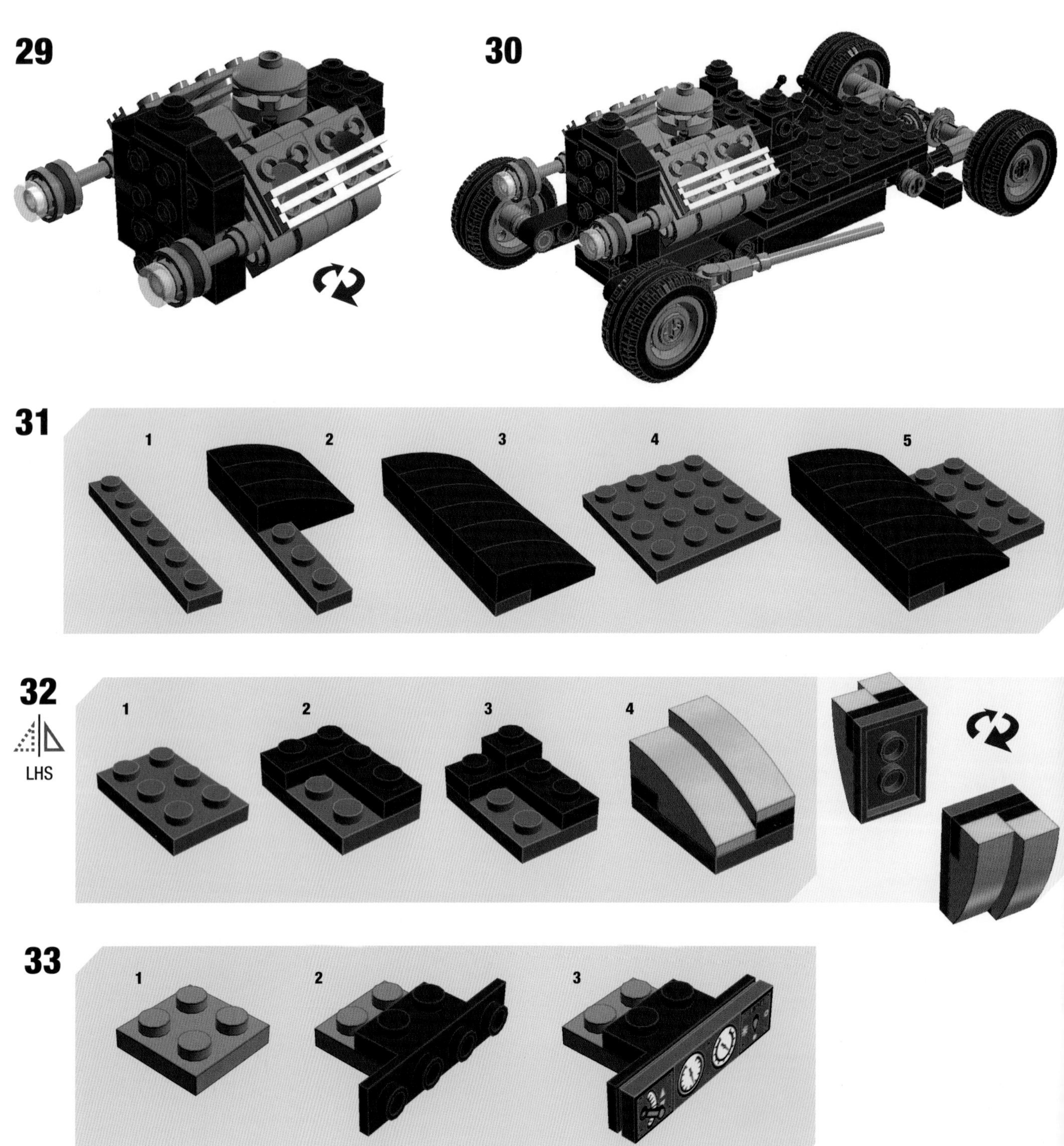
29
30
31
1
2
3
4
5
32
LHS
1
2
3
4
33
1
2
3

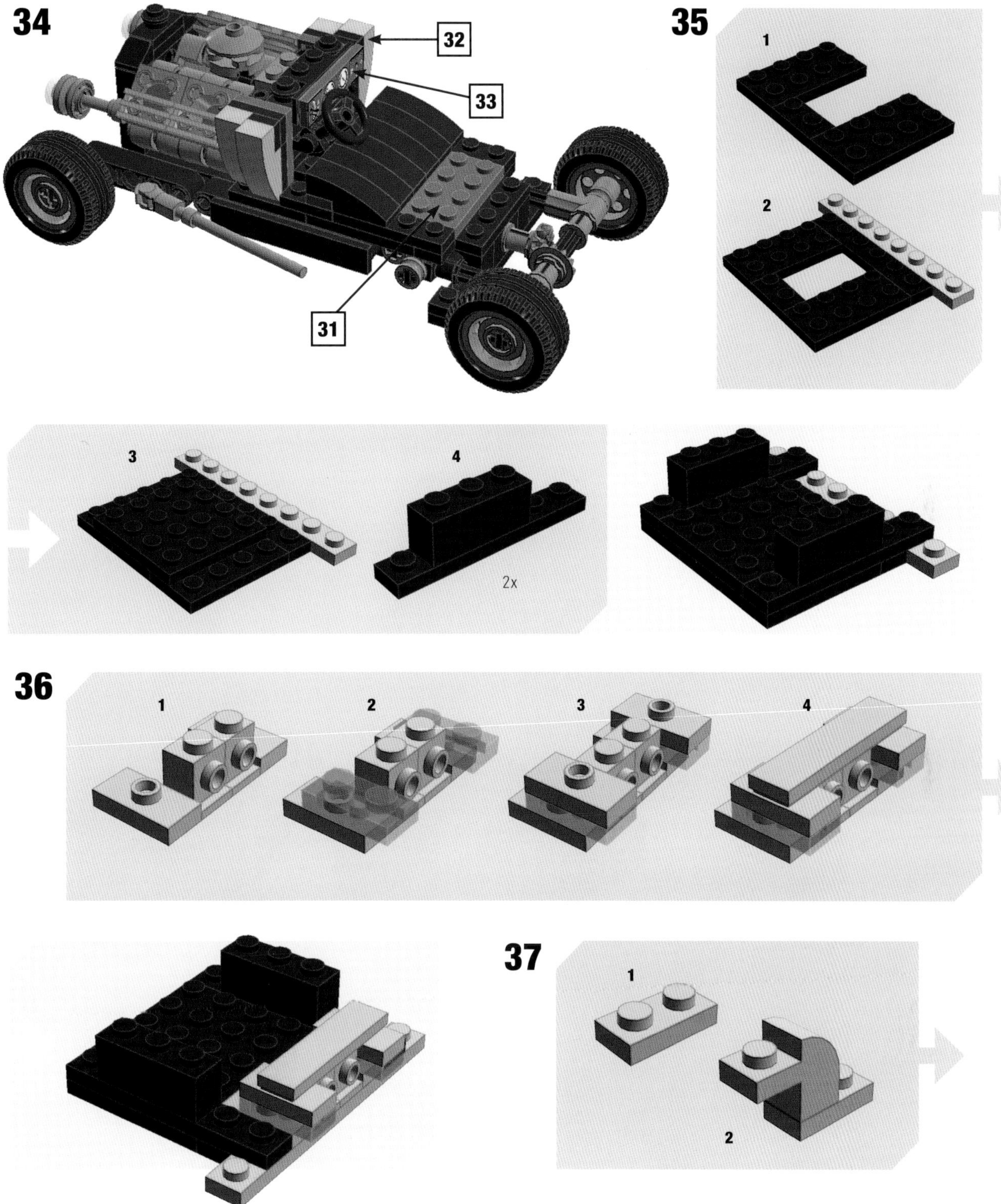
34
32
33
31
35
1
2
3
4
2x
36
1
2
3
4
37
1
2

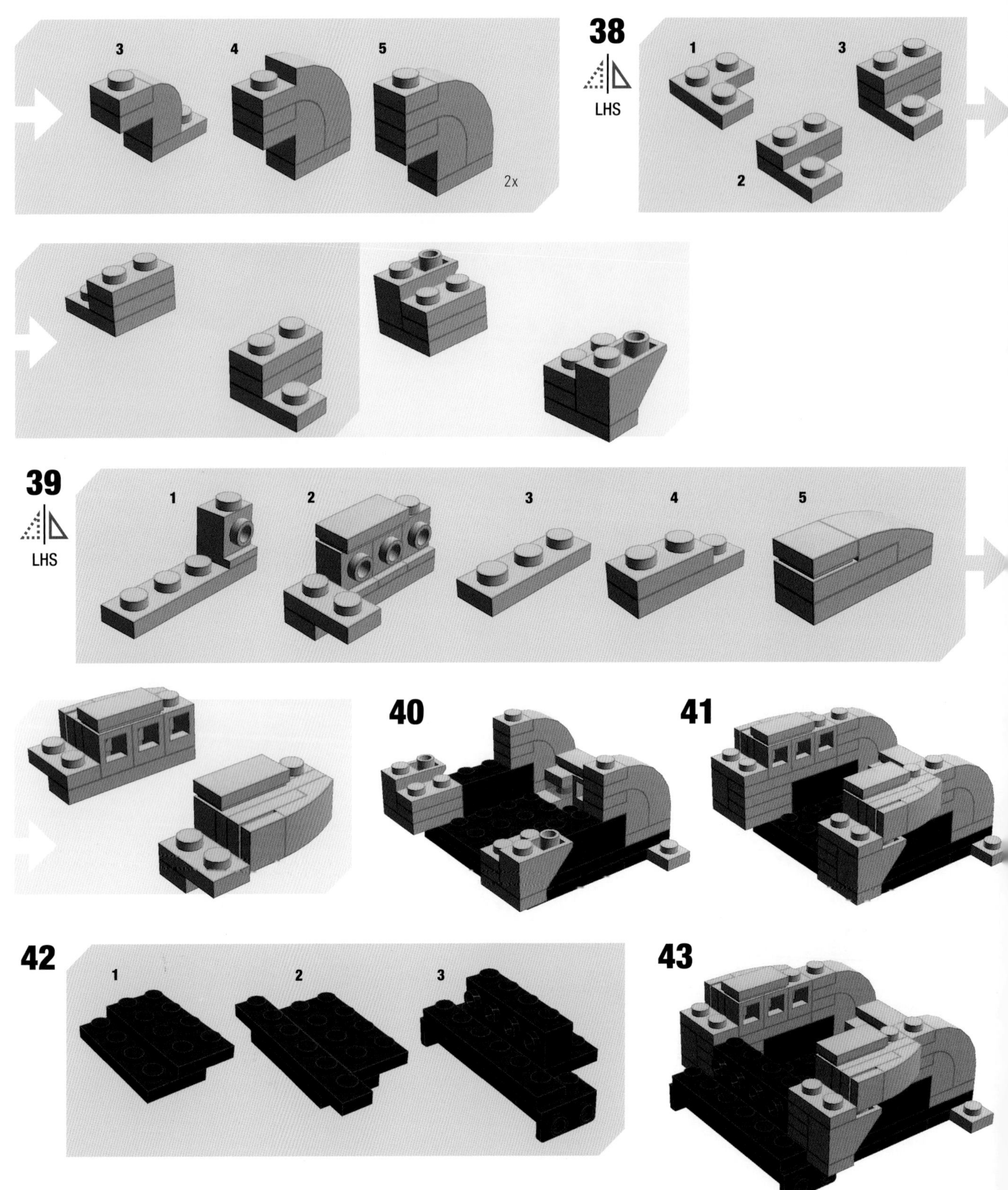
3
4
5
2x
38
LHS
1
3
2
39
LHS
1
2
3
4
5
40
41
42
1
2
3
43

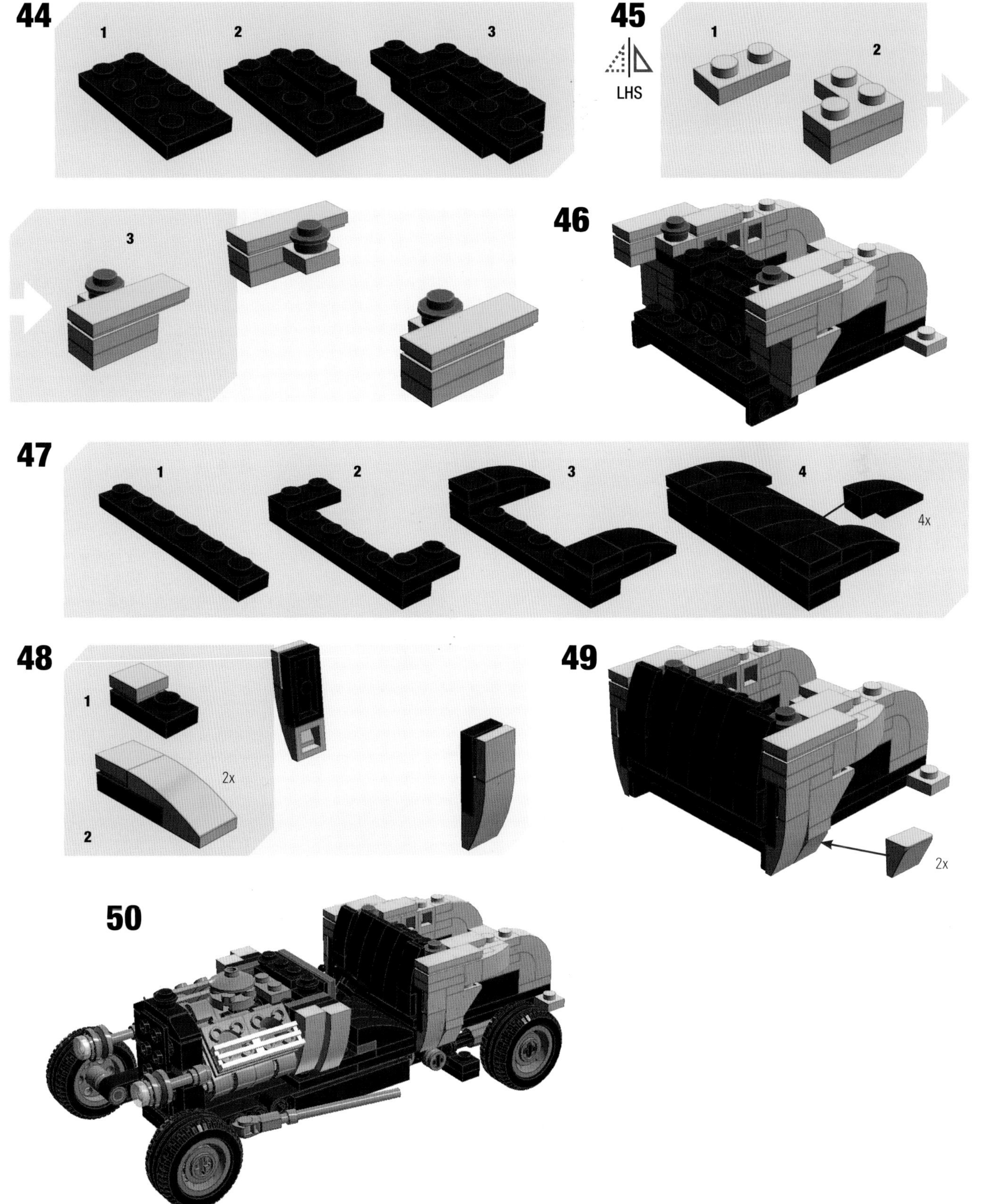
44
1
2
3
45
LHS
1
2
3
46
47
1
2
3
4
4x
48
1
2x
2
49
2x
50

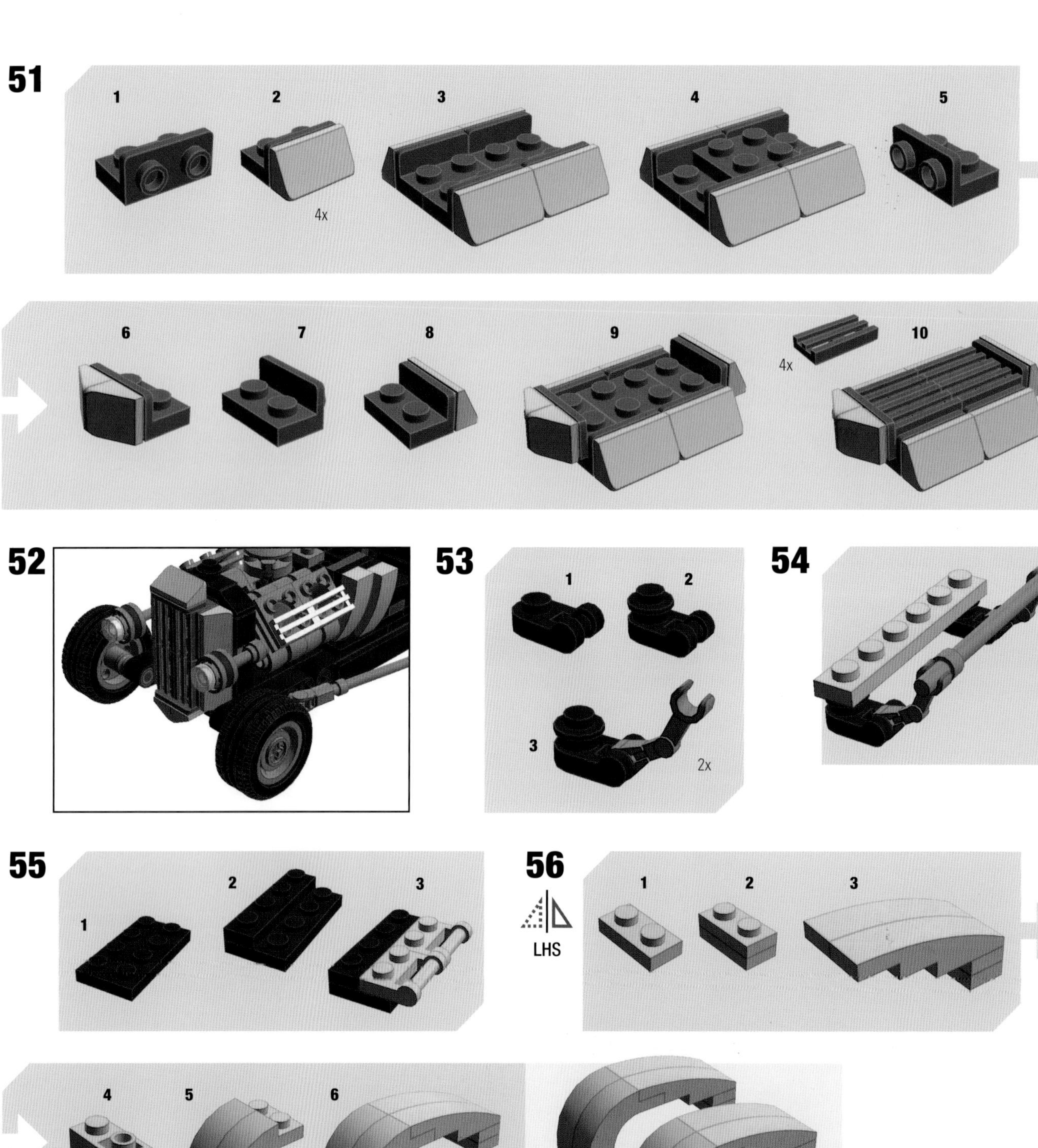
51
1
2
4x
3
4
5
6
7
8
9
4x
10
52
53
1
2
3
2x
54
55
1
2
3
56
LHS
1
2
3
4
5
6

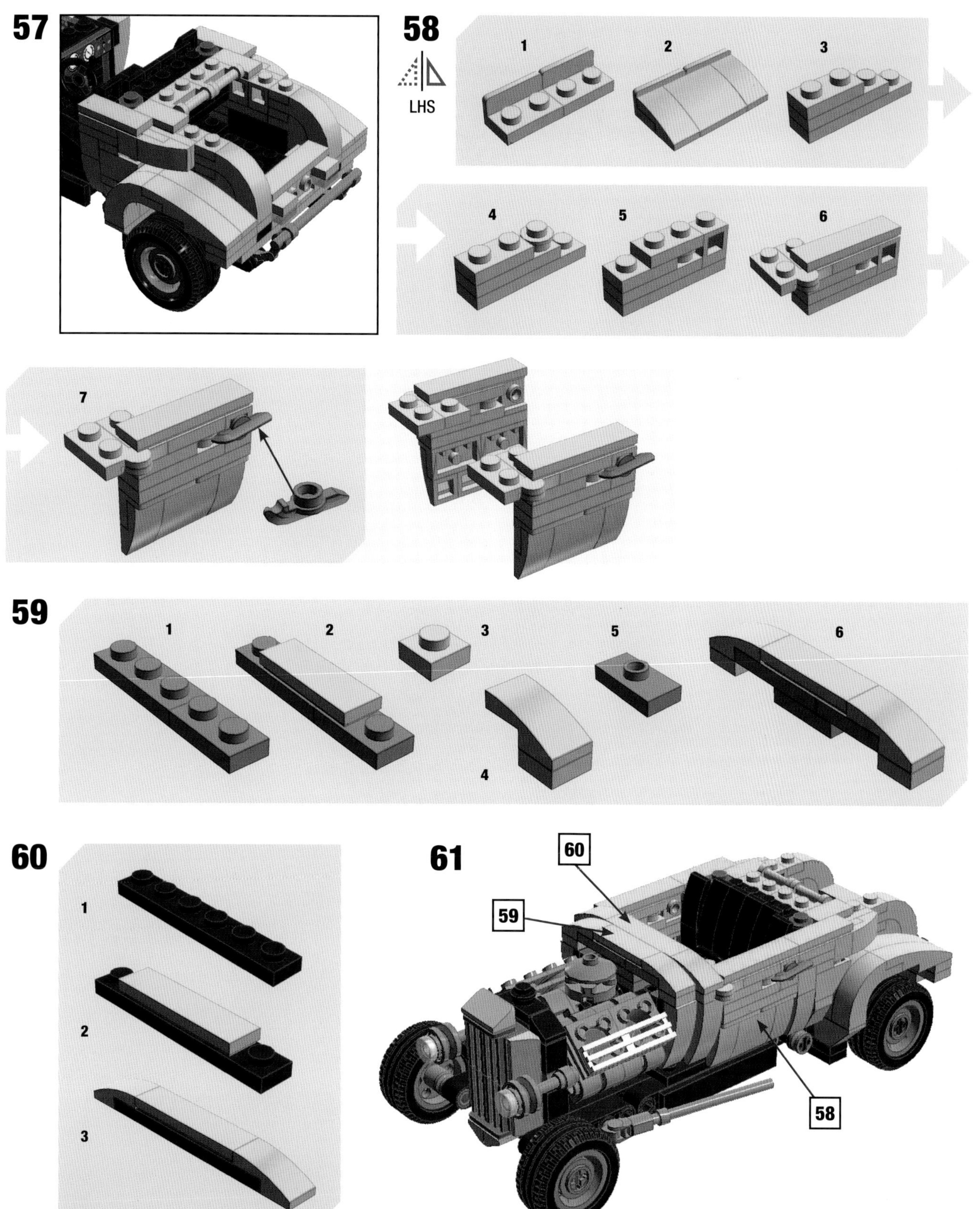

57
58
LHS
1
2
3
4
5
6
7
59
1
2
3
4
5
6
60
1
2
3
61
60
59
58

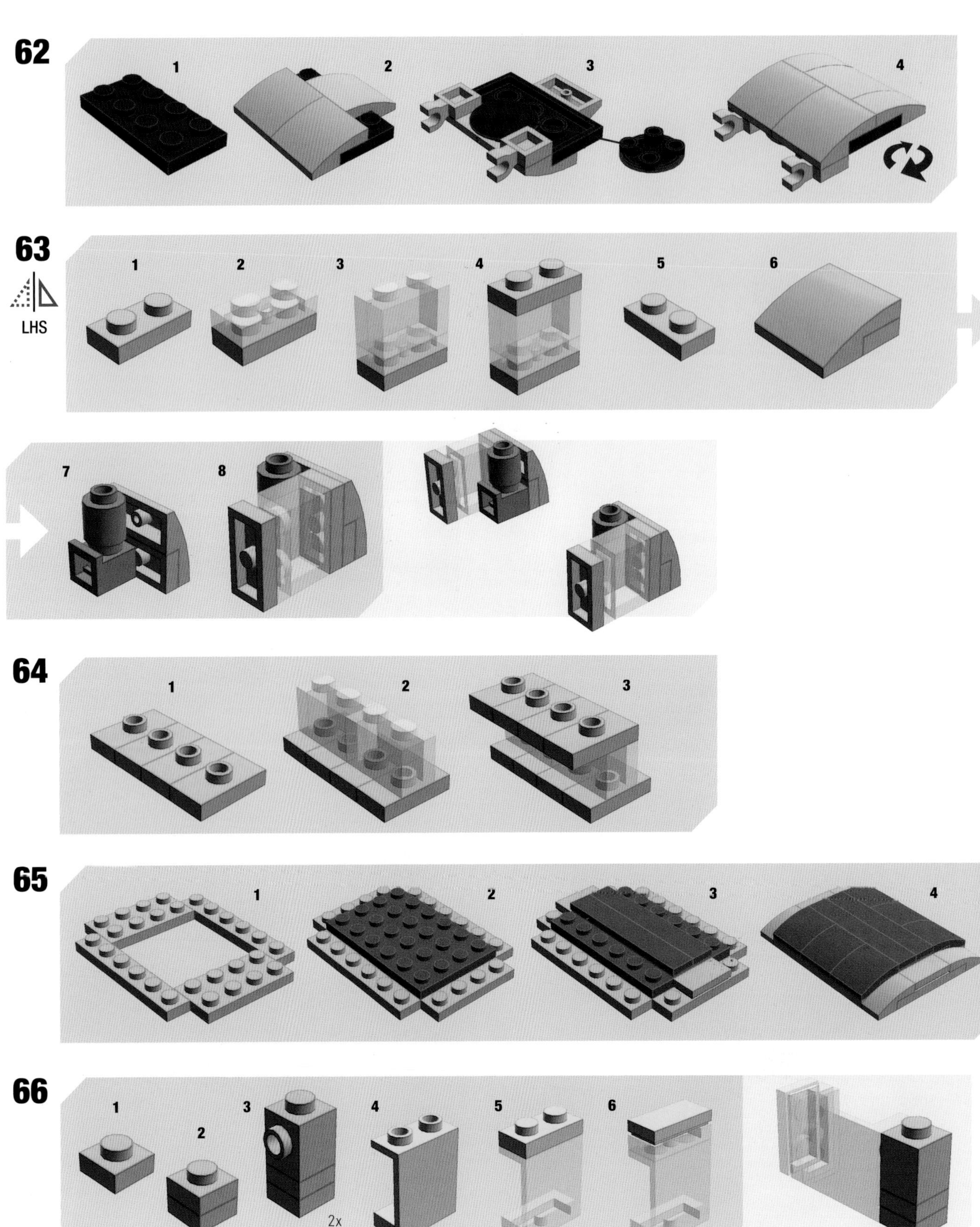
62
1
2
3
4
63
LHS
1
2
3
4
5
6
7
8
64
1
2
3
65
1
2
3
4
66
1
2
3
4
5
6
2x

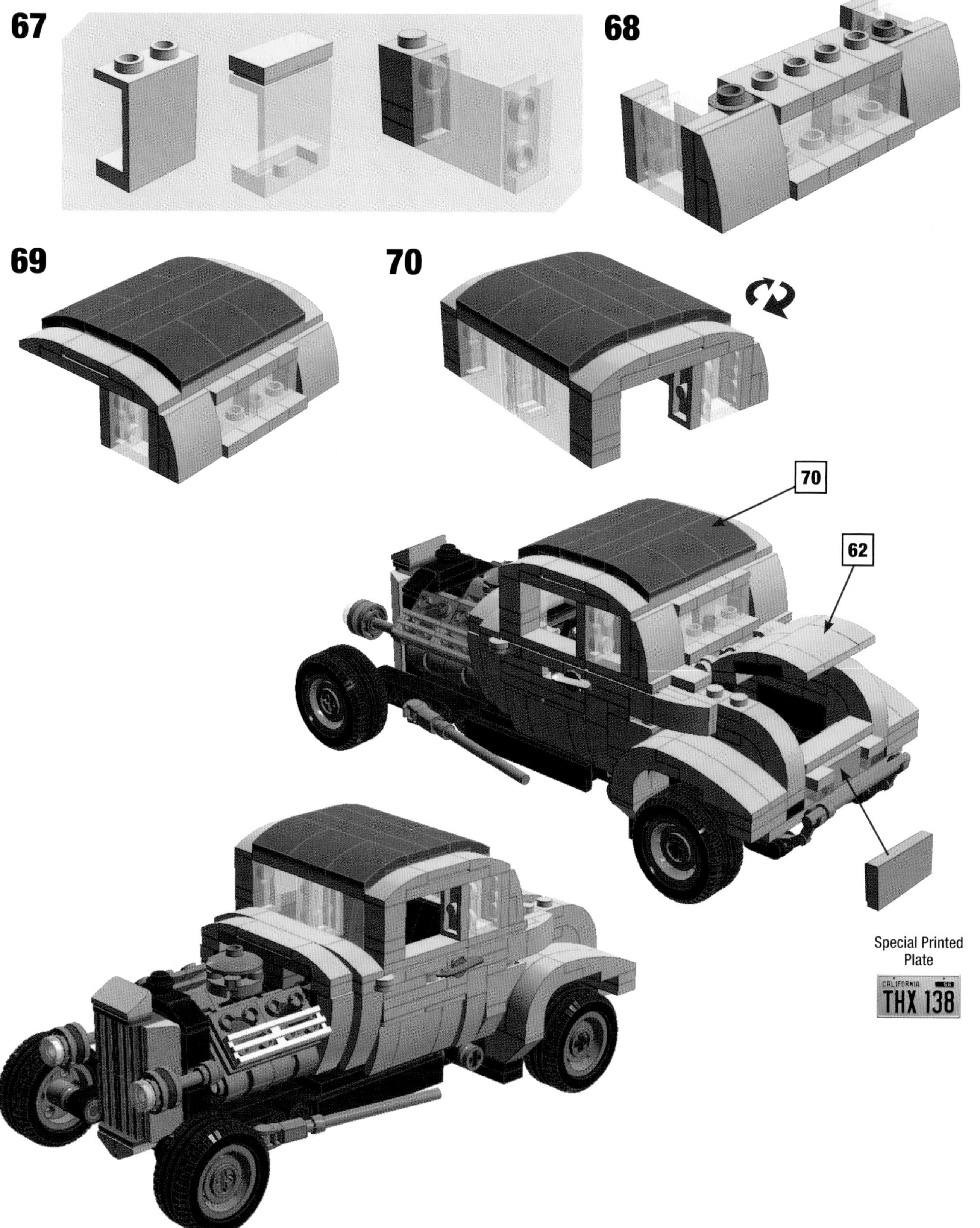
67
68
69
70
70
62
Special Printed Plate
CALIFORNIA
THX 138

CHAPTER 11

FORD FALCON V8 INTERCEPTOR
MAD MAX

There is only one Australian road movie and one road movie car: *Mad Max* (1979) and the Ford XB V8 Interceptor coupe. *Mad Max* is a film lamenting the decline of society and glorification of speed and violence. Set on the edge of civilization in an imagined post-apocalyptic world, the reality is that this was just the real-life landscape between Melbourne and Geelong (where I live).

The film heavily features cars—chief among them the XB Interceptor. This car has been modified from a standard model with the fitment of the large mechanical supercharger emerging from the hood—though this was not functional in the film. The car features a custom "Concorde'" nose cone designed by Peter Arcadipane while working for Ford Australia. The standard car's 351 cubic inch (5.8 liter) V8 Cleveland produced 300 hp (224 kW) (Australia produced its own version of this engine during this period.)

Whereas the United States experienced their muscle car era during the late 1960s, this did not occur in Australia until the 1970s, and this aligns with the use of cars as tools of intimidation both by antisocial citizens and the police who deal with them in the film.

Other Falcon models are featured as standard V8 police cars, along with a black Holden Monaro Interceptor.

COUNTRY OF ORIGIN:	Australia
PRODUCTION:	1973–1976
NUMBER MADE:	211,971 (all types)
LAYOUT/DRIVE:	Front engine, Rear-wheel-drive
ENGINE:	351 ci (5.8 liter), 8 cylinders, Vee
POWER TORQUE:	300 hp (224 kW) / 380 lb-ft (515 Nm)
CONSTRUCTION/DOORS:	Steel Monocoque / two-door
TV/FILM APPEARANCES:	*Mad Max* (1979), *Mad Max 2* (1981), *Mad Max: Fury Road* (2015), *Love the Beast* (2009)

MFP

Mad Max is a violent film and was banned or released with an R (Restricted) rating in a number of countries at its debut. Suffice it to say that there are several large motor vehicle accidents that graphically depict human damage along with more deliberate acts of violence.

The V8 Interceptor would reappear in *Mad Max 2* (1981) and when the franchise was rebooted in 2015 with *Mad Max: Fury Road*, the Interceptor was silver from the sandblasting of life in the desert.

Of all the films, the original *Mad Max* best captures the raw essence of a crumbling world at the individual and societal level.

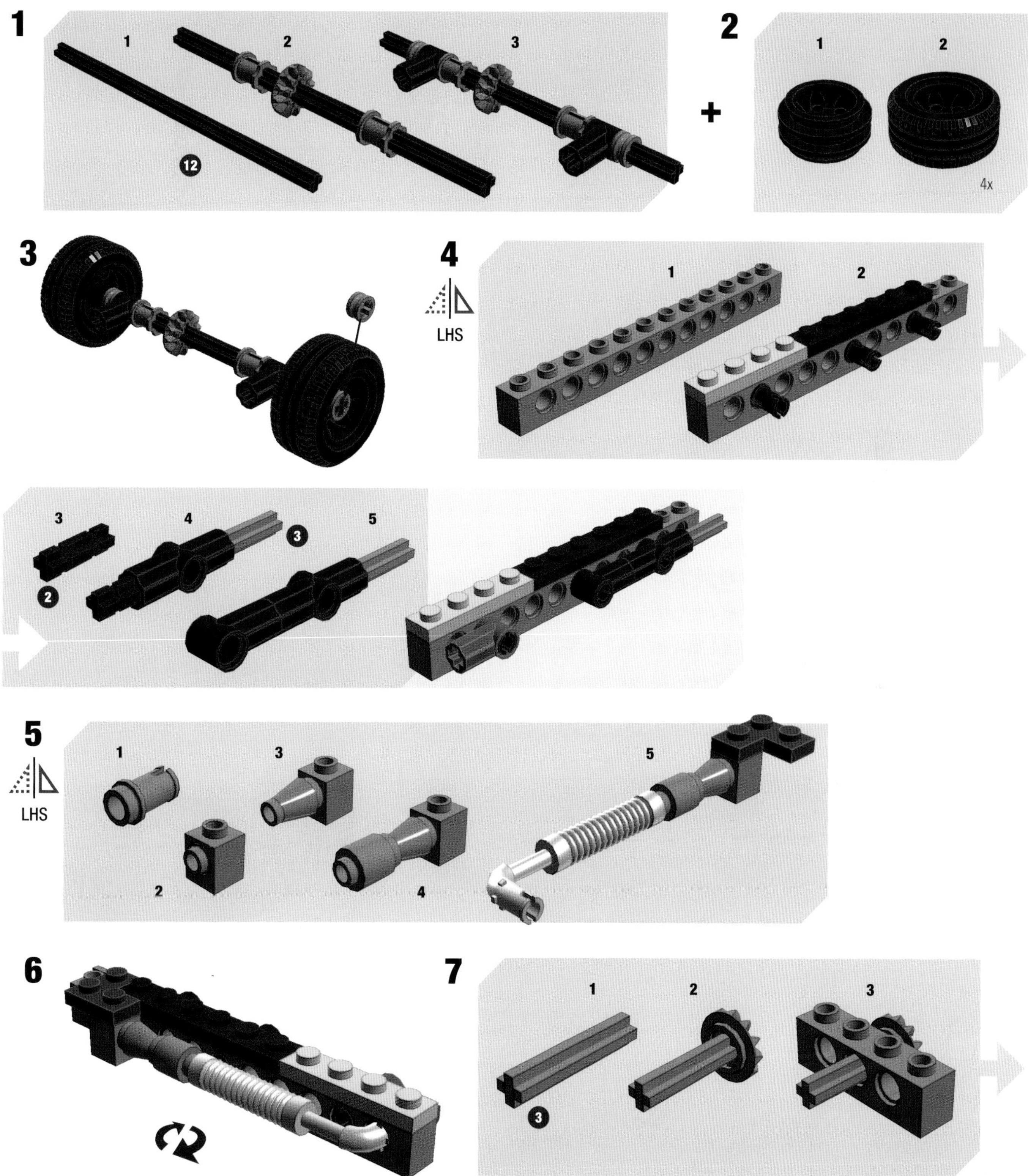
1
1
2
3
12
2
1
2
+
4x
3
4
LHS
1
2
3
4
5
3
2
5
LHS
1
3
5
2
4
6
7
1
2
3
3

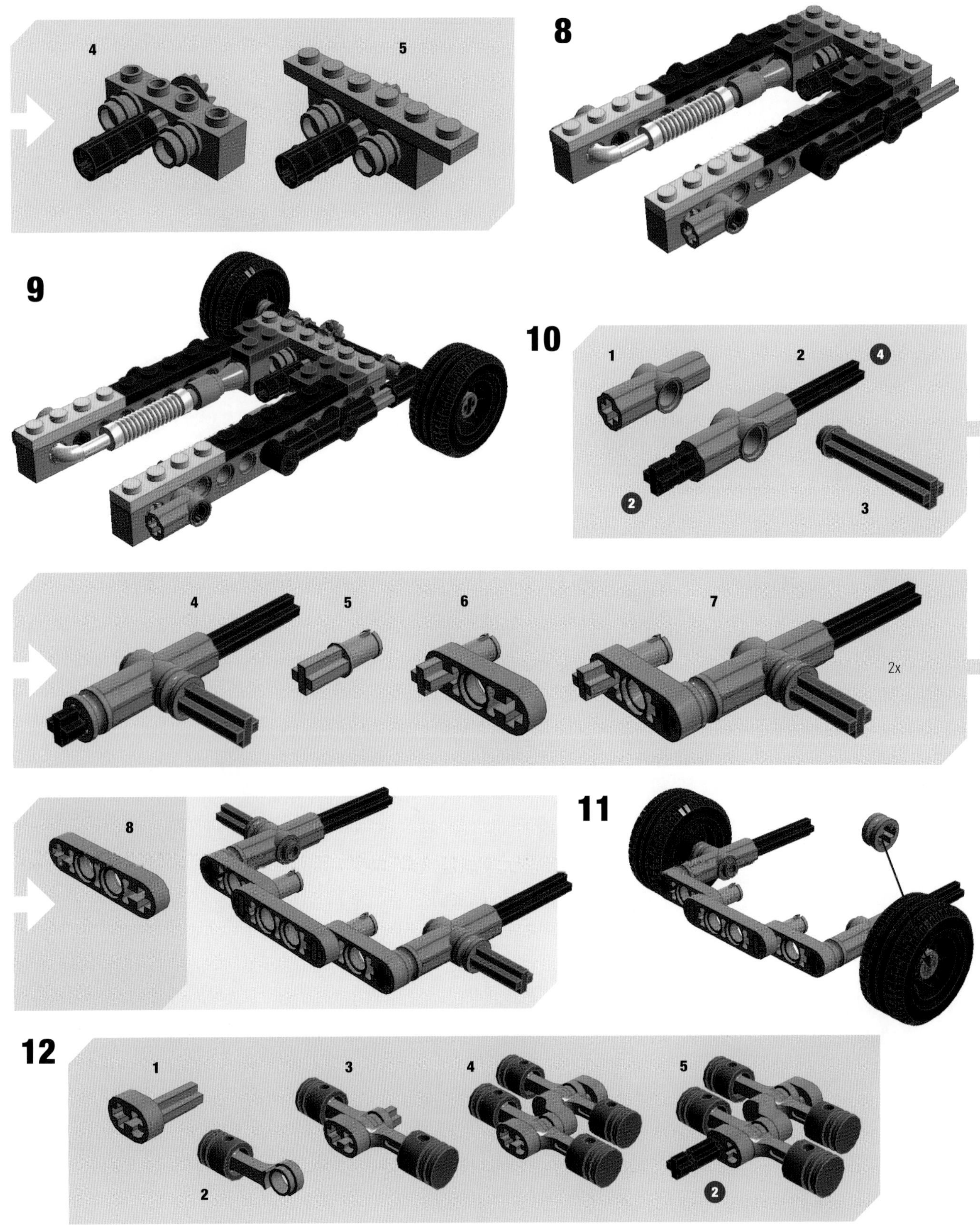
4
5
8
9
10
1
2
4
2
3
4
5
6
7
2x
8
11
12
1
2
3
4
5
2

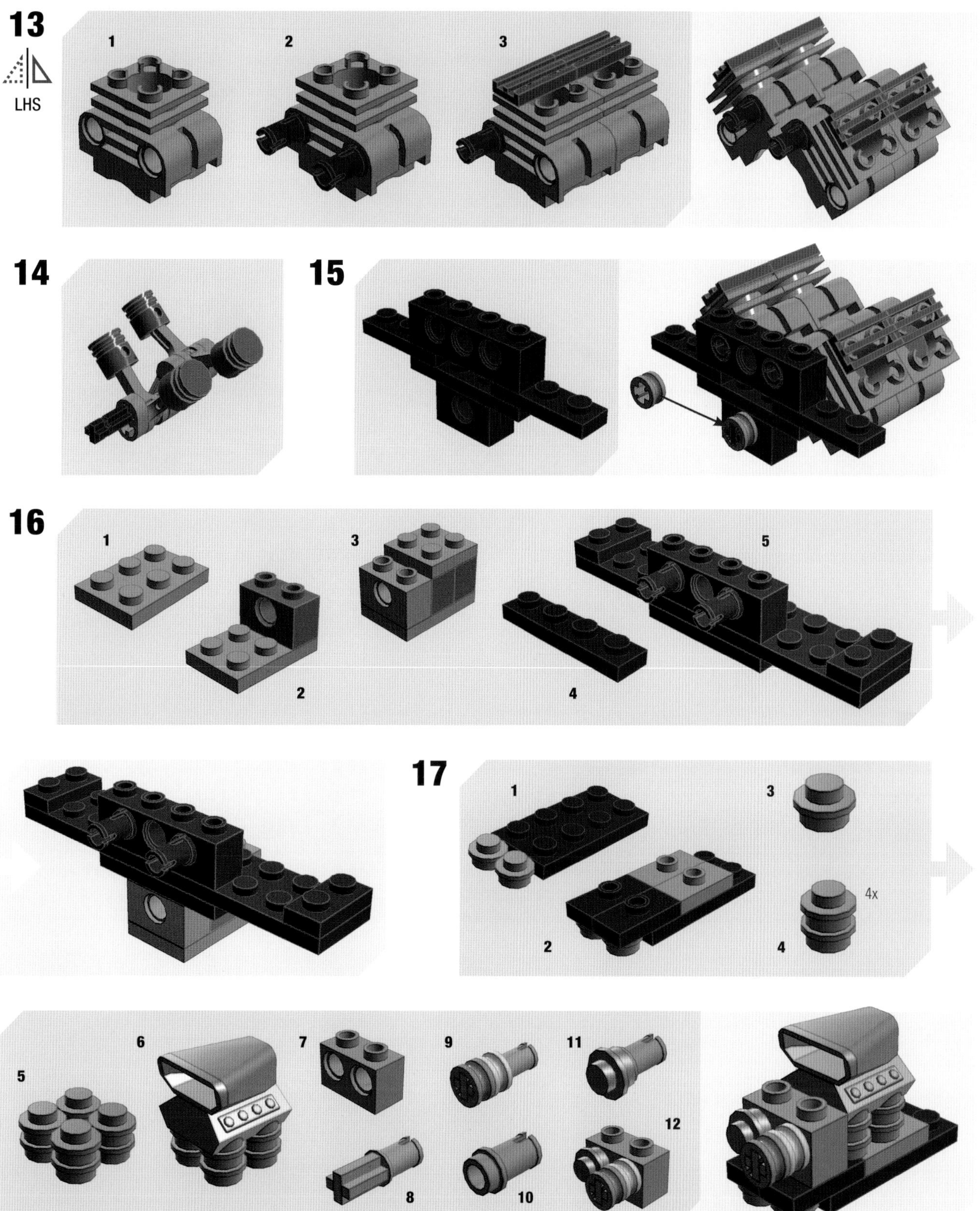
13
LHS
1
2
3
14
15
16
1
2
3
4
5
17
1
2
3
4
4x
5
6
7
8
9
10
11
12

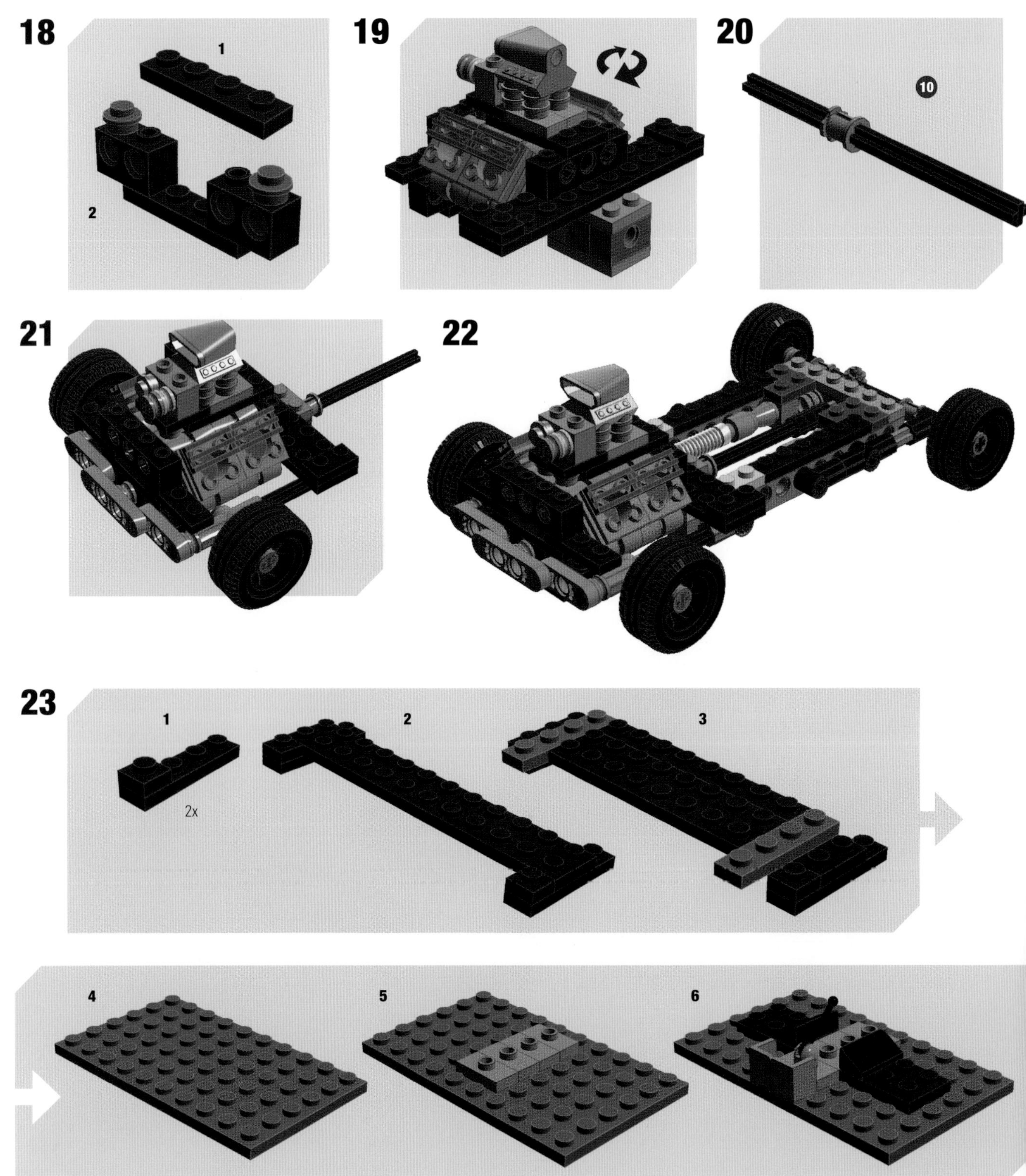
18
1
2
19
20
10
21
22
23
1
2x
2
3
4
5
6

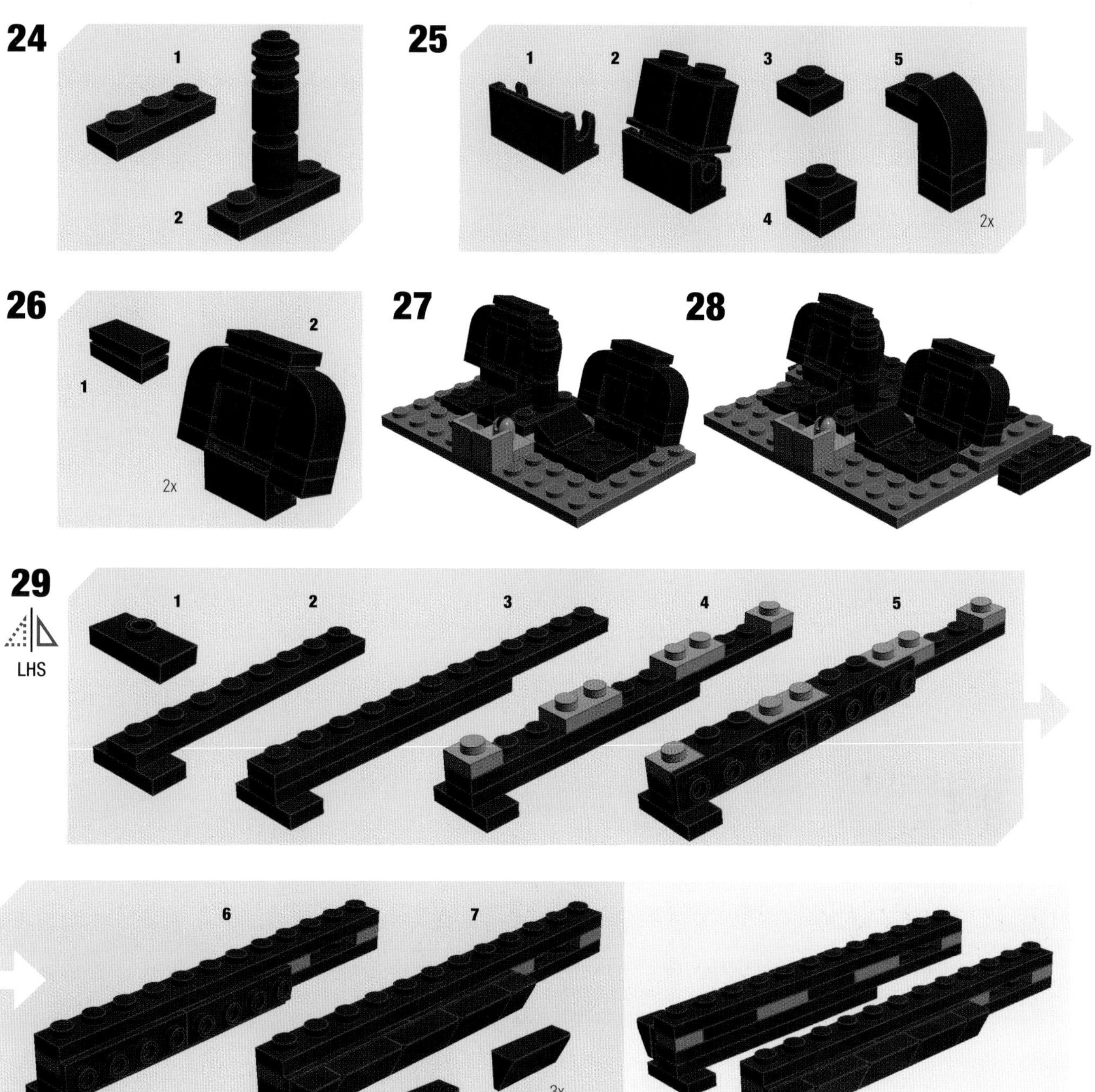
24
1
2
25
1
2
3
4
5
2x
26
1
2
2x
27
28
29
LHS
1
2
3
4
5
6
7
2x
3x

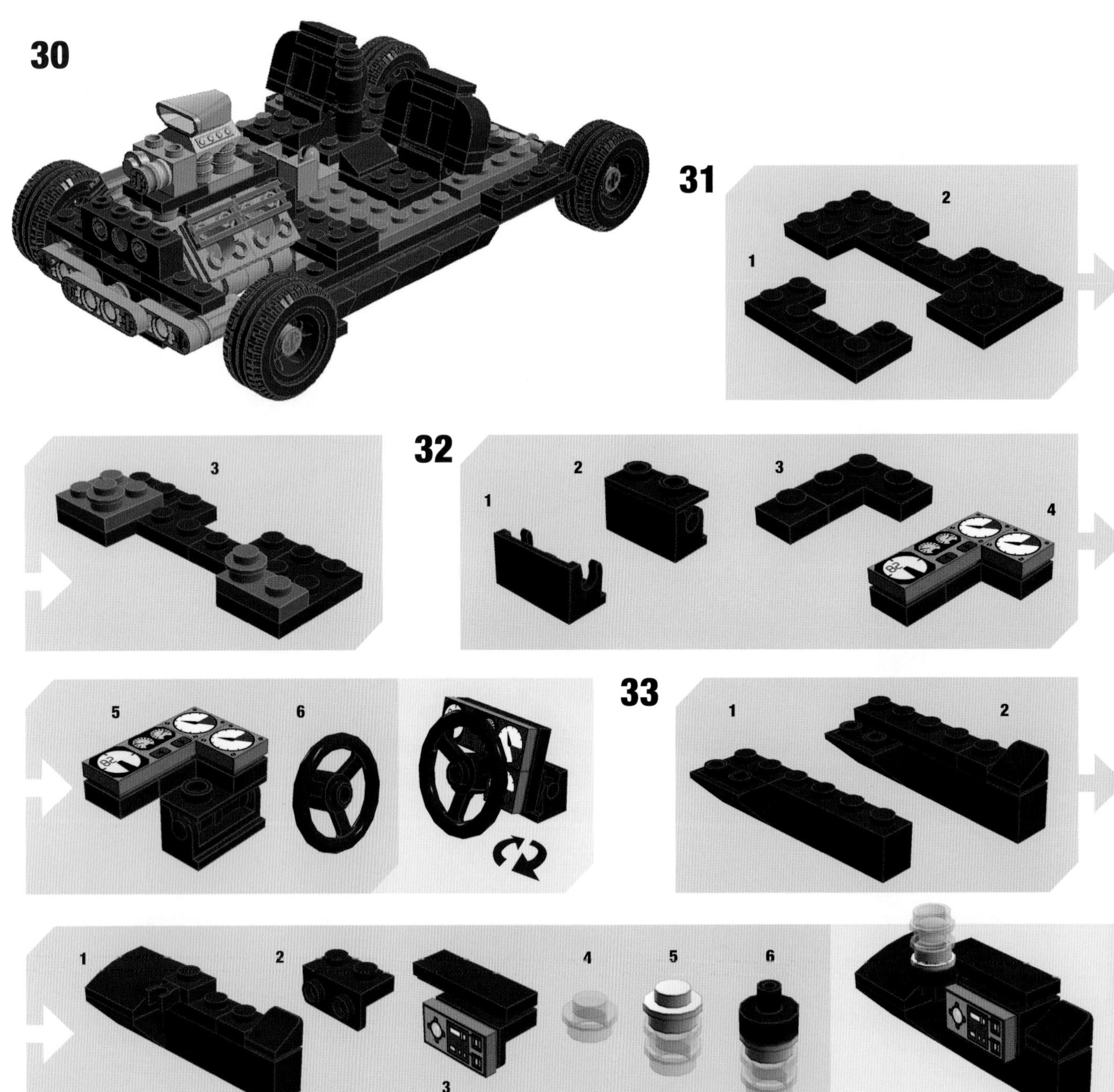
30
31
1
2
3
32
1
2
3
4
5
6
33
1
2
1
2
3
4
5
6

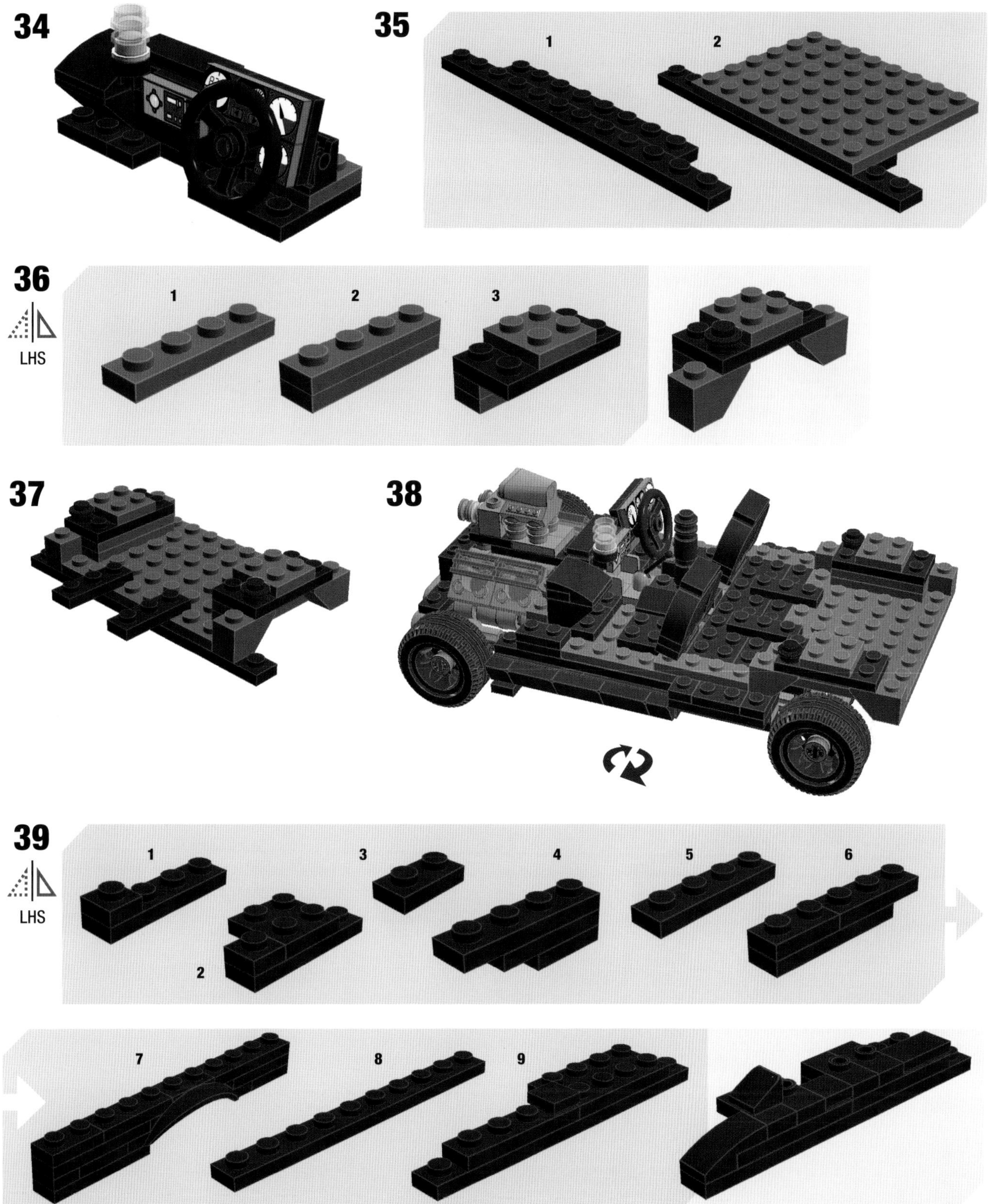
34
35
1
2
36
1
2
3
LHS
37
38
39
1
2
3
4
5
6
LHS
7
8
9

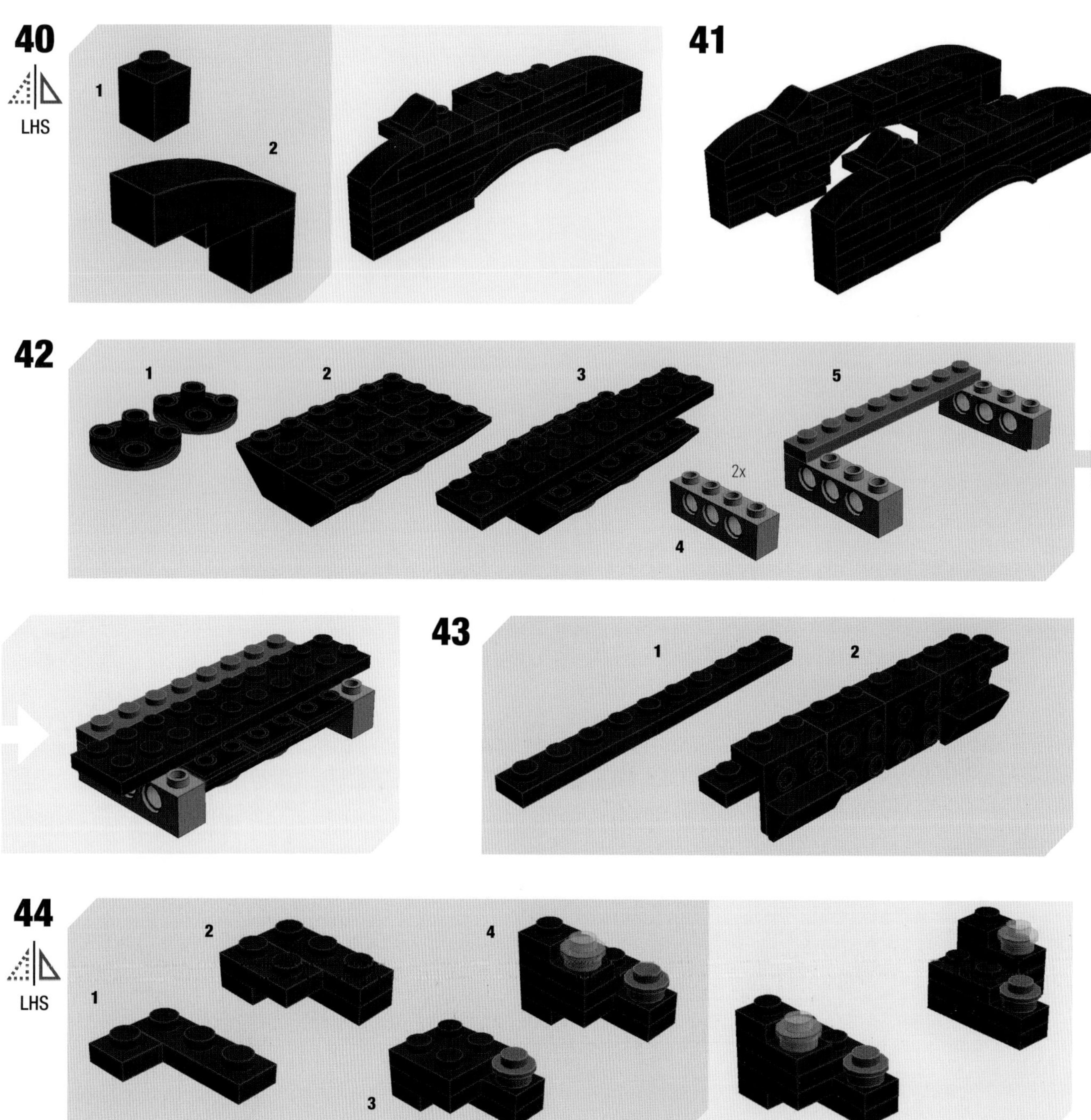
40
LHS
1
2
41
42
1
2
3
5
2x
4
43
1
2
44
LHS
2
4
1
3

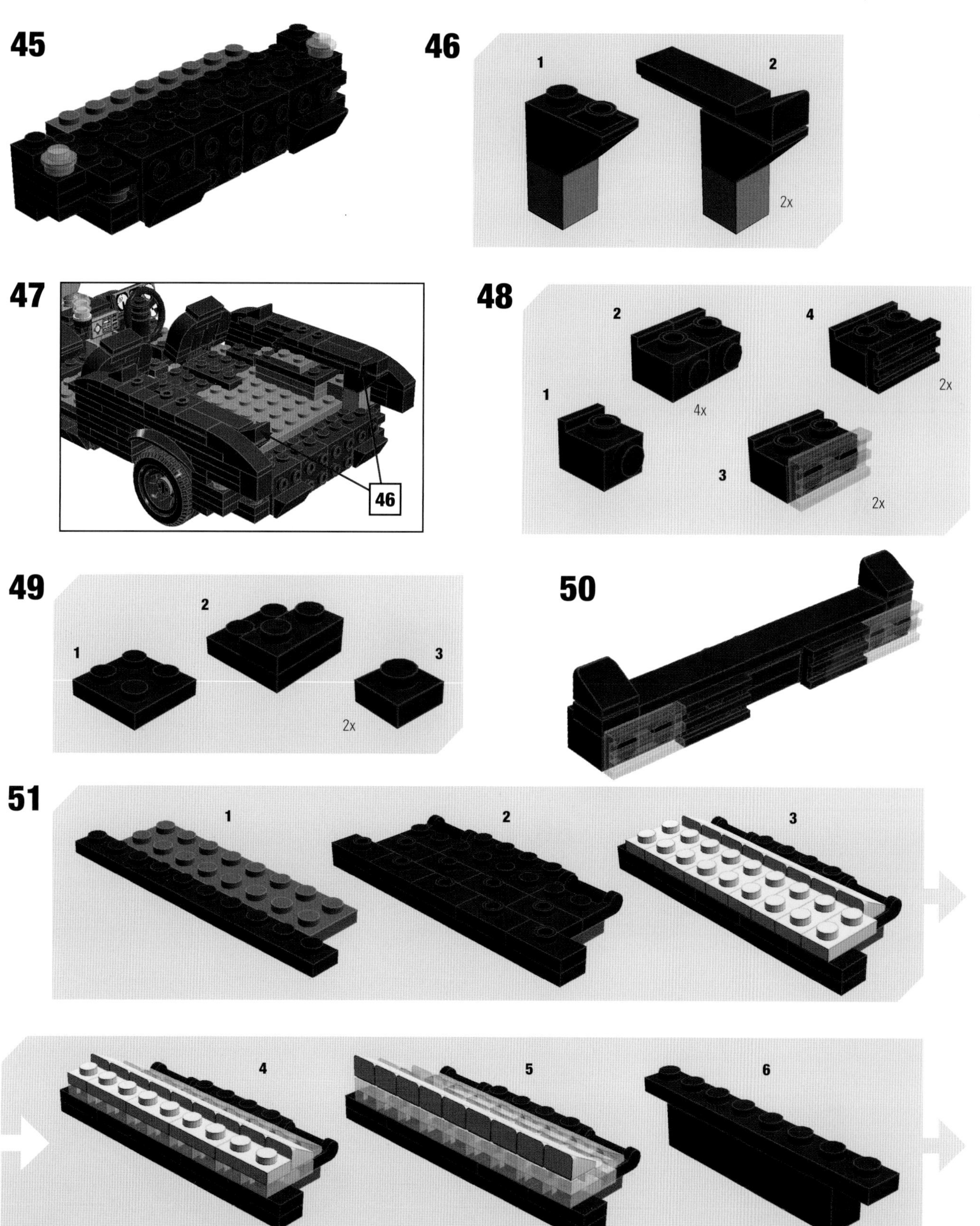
45
46
1
2
2x
47
46
48
2
4
1
4x
2x
3
2x
49
2
1
3
2x
50
51
1
2
3
4
5
6

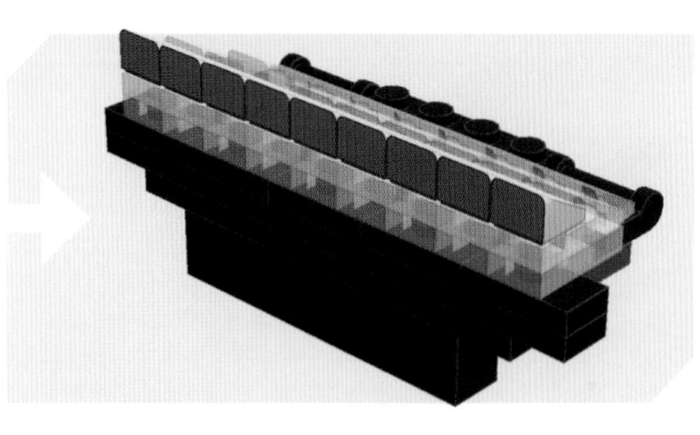

52

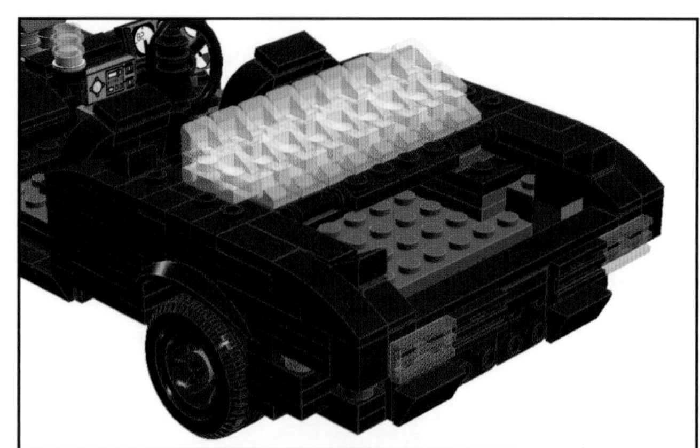

53

LHS

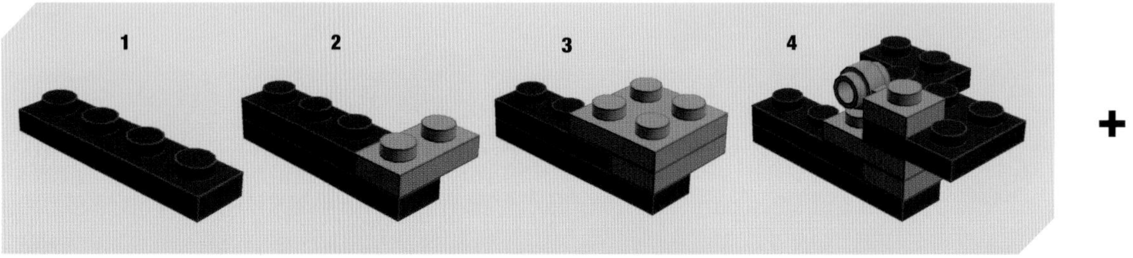

1 2 3 4

+

54

LHS

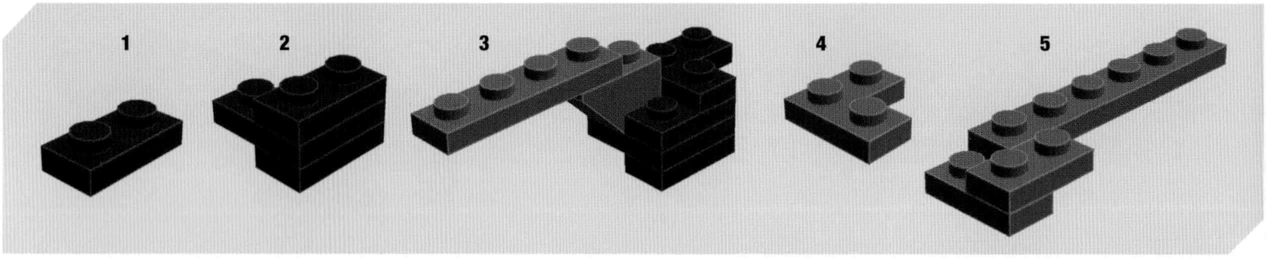

1 2 3 4 5

55

LHS

56

LHS

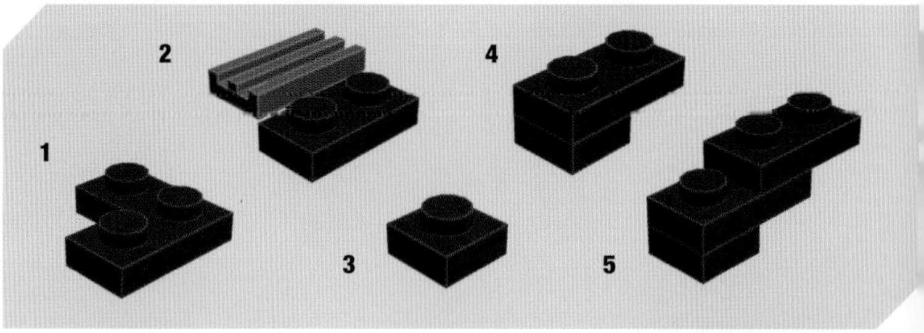

1 2 3 4 5

57

LHS

1 2 3 4

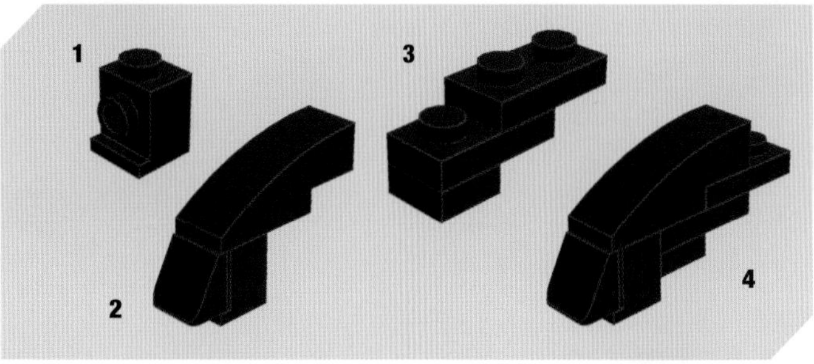

58

LHS

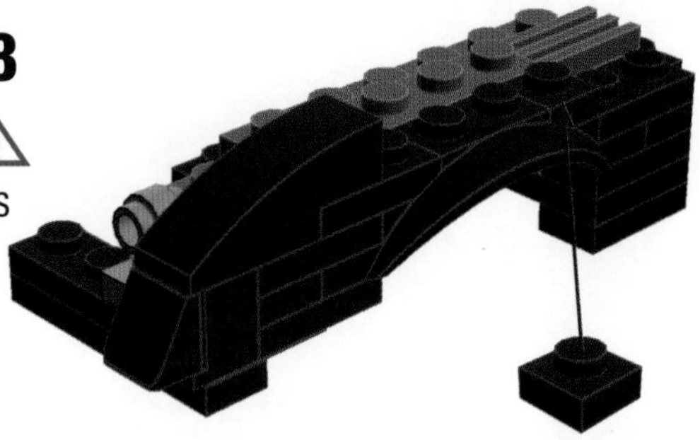

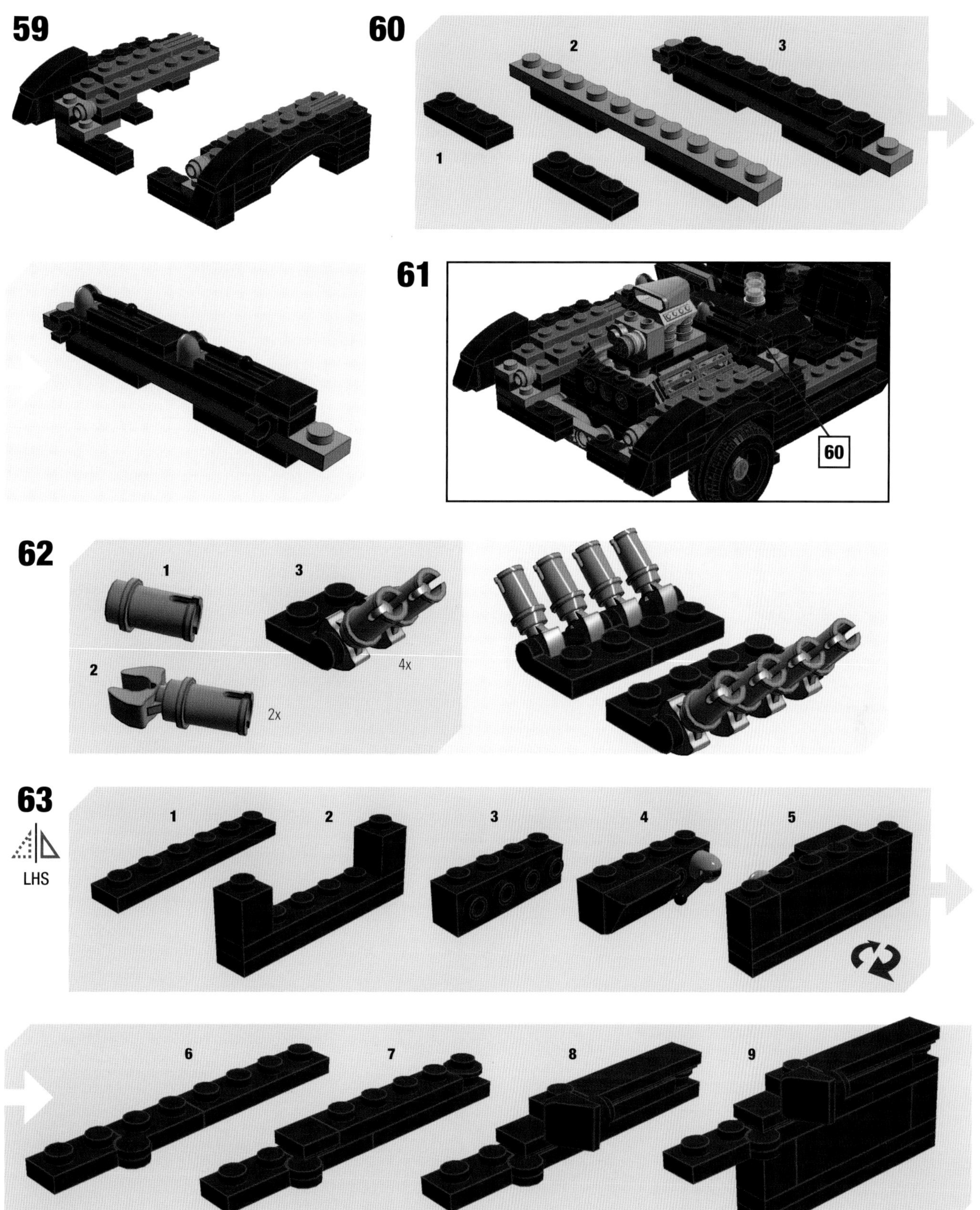
59
60
1
2
3
61
60
62
1
2
3
2x
4x
63
LHS
1
2
3
4
5
6
7
8
9

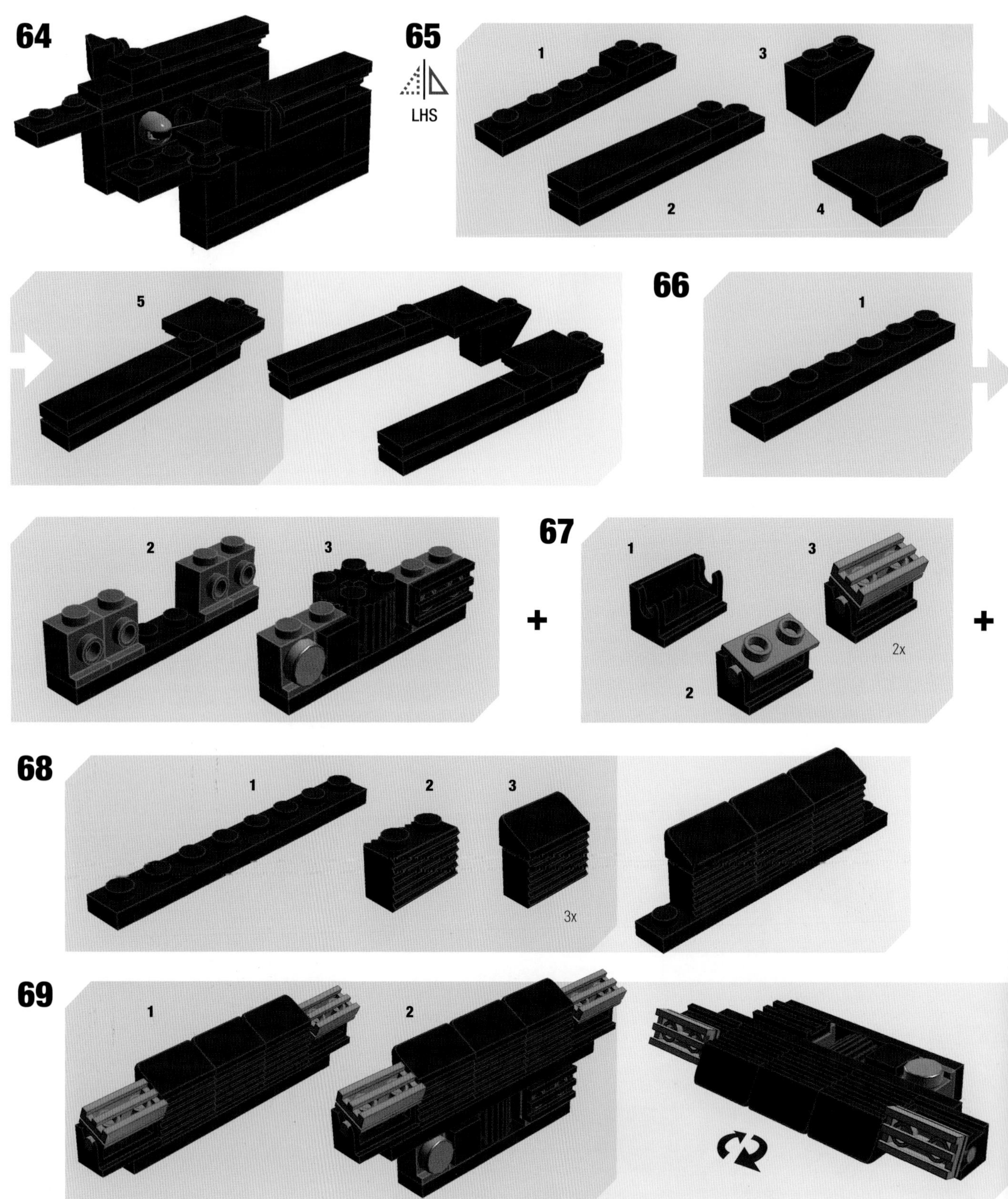
64
65
LHS
1
3
2
4
5
66
1
2
3
+
67
1
3
2
2x
+
68
1
2
3
3x
69
1
2

70

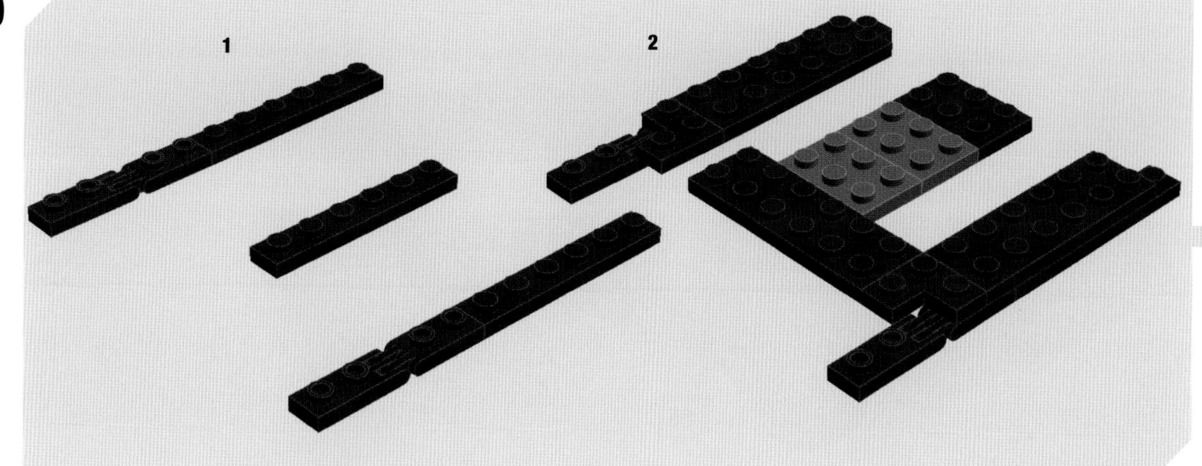

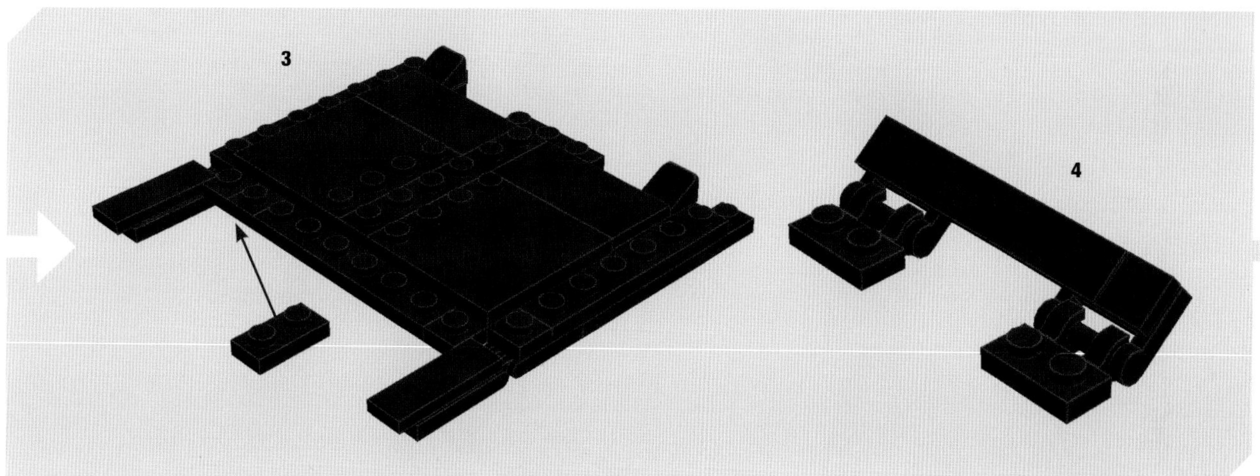

71

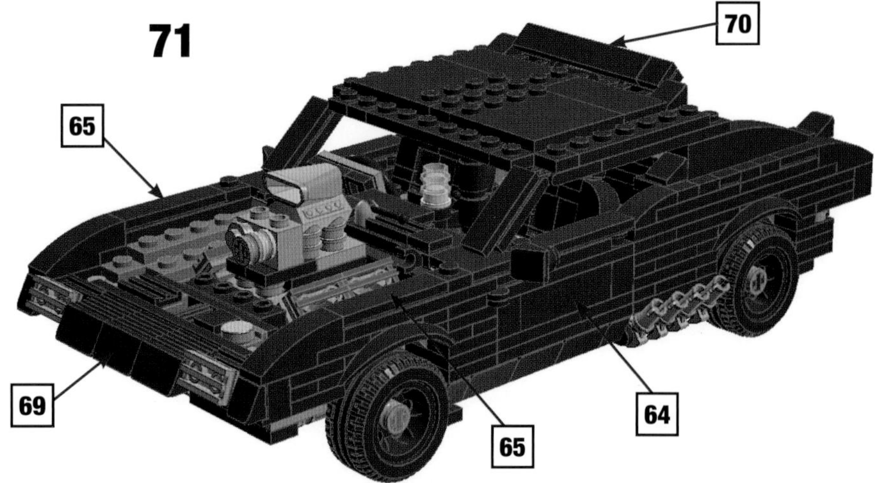

72

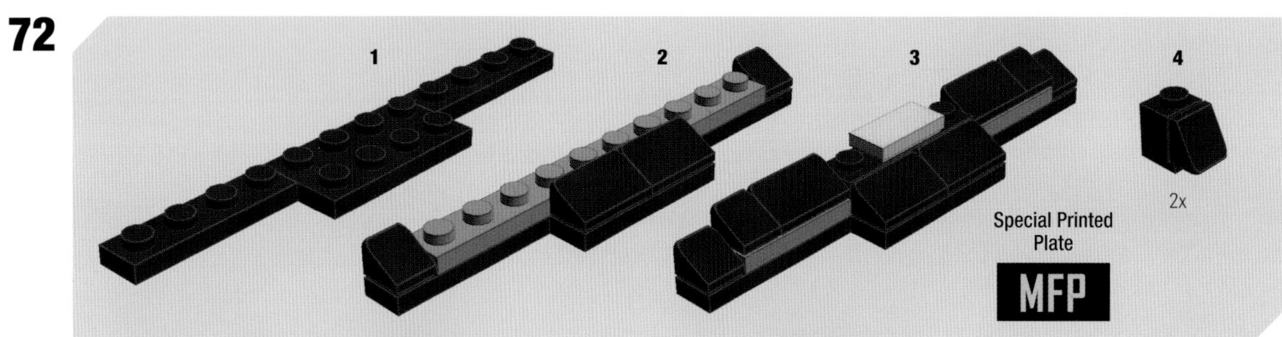

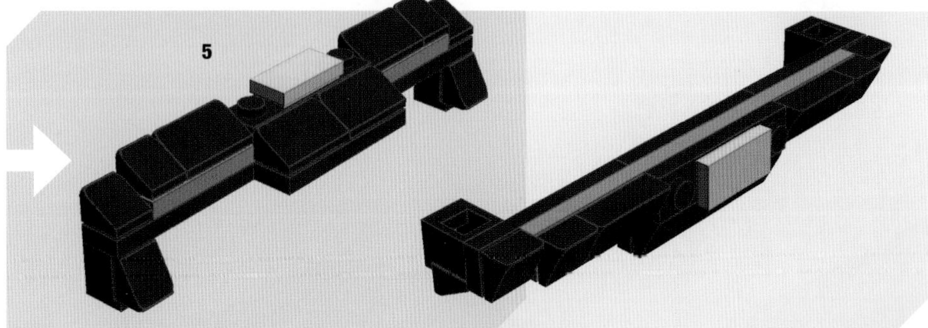

73

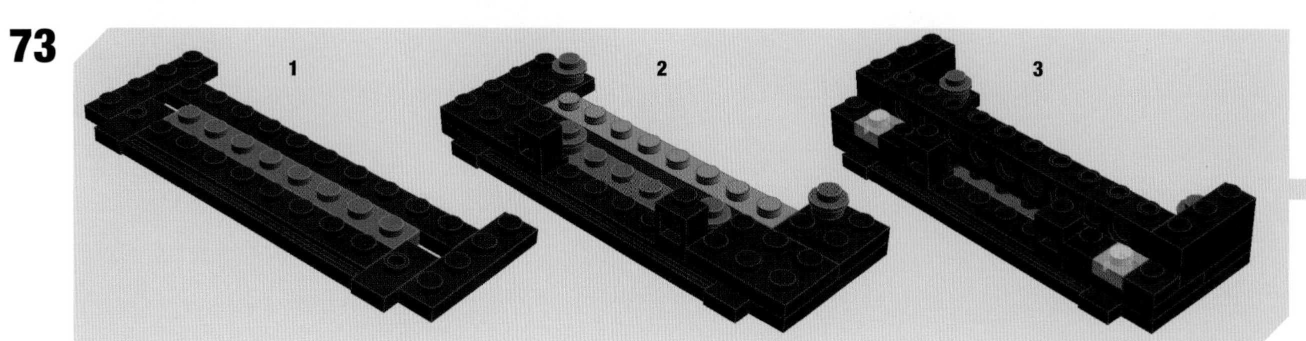

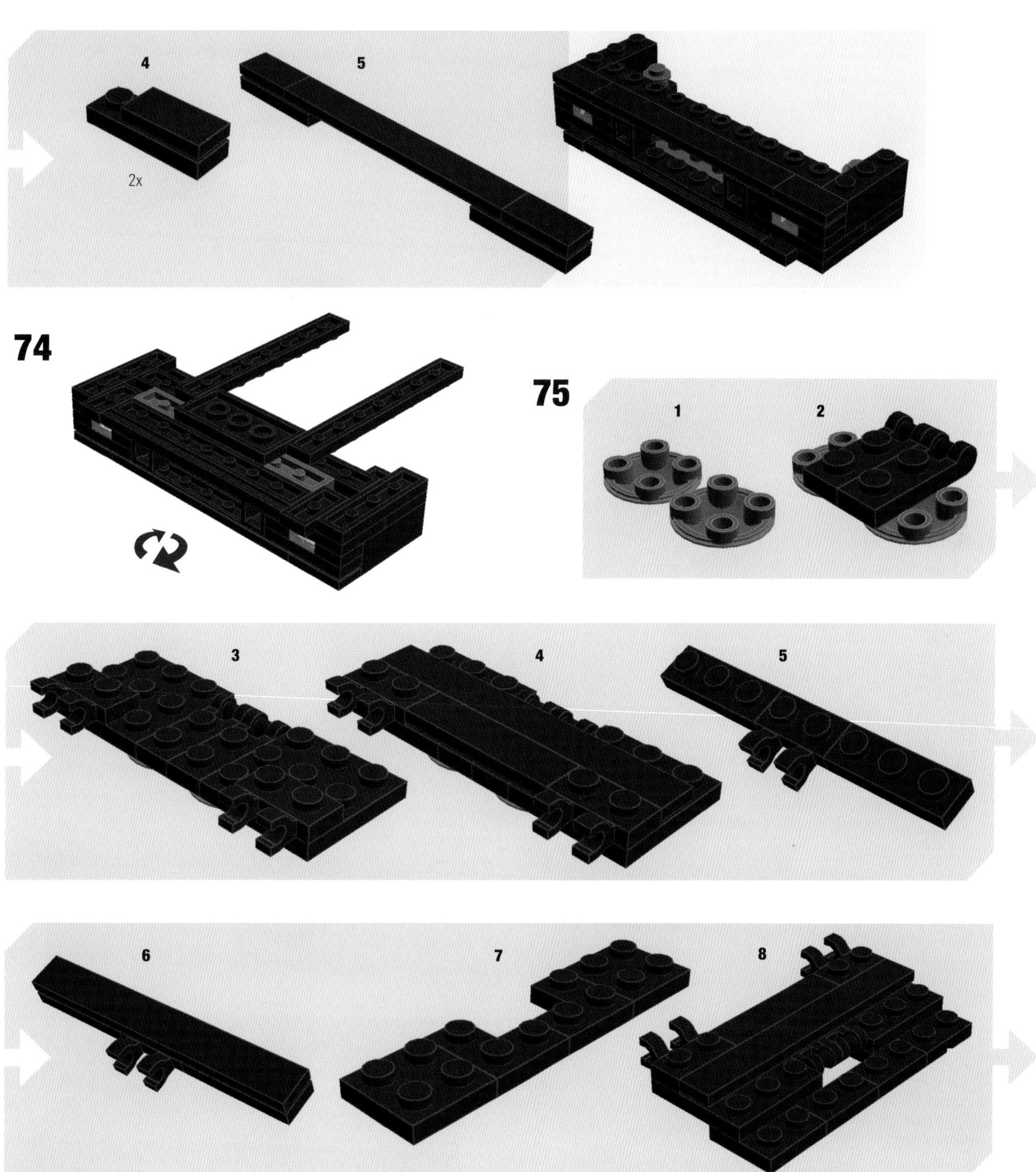
4
5
2x
74
75
1
2
3
4
5
6
7
8

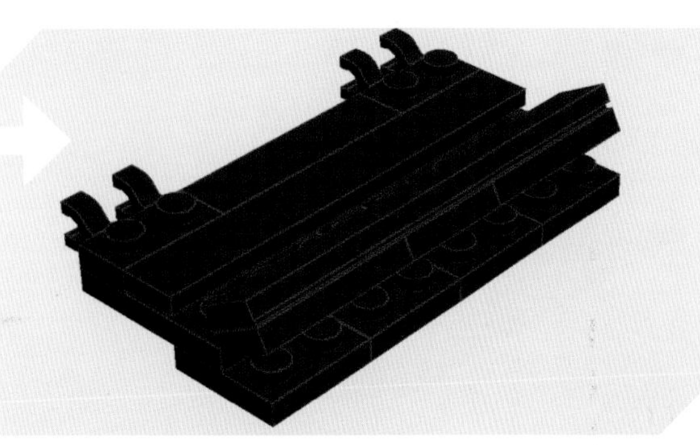

76

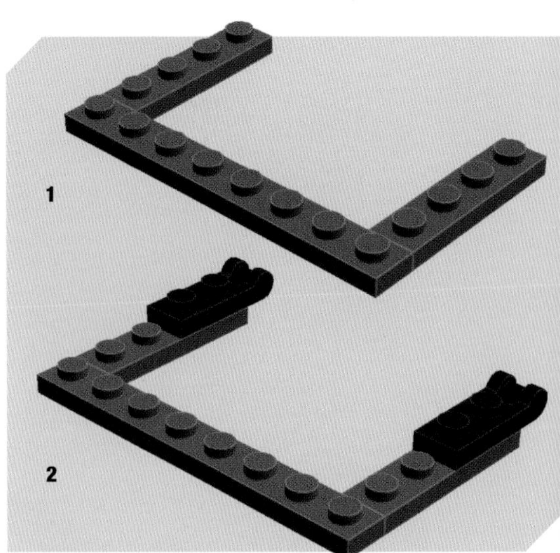

77

LHS

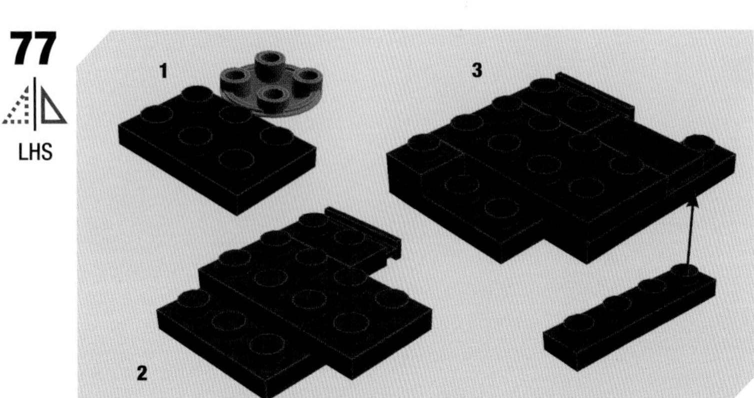

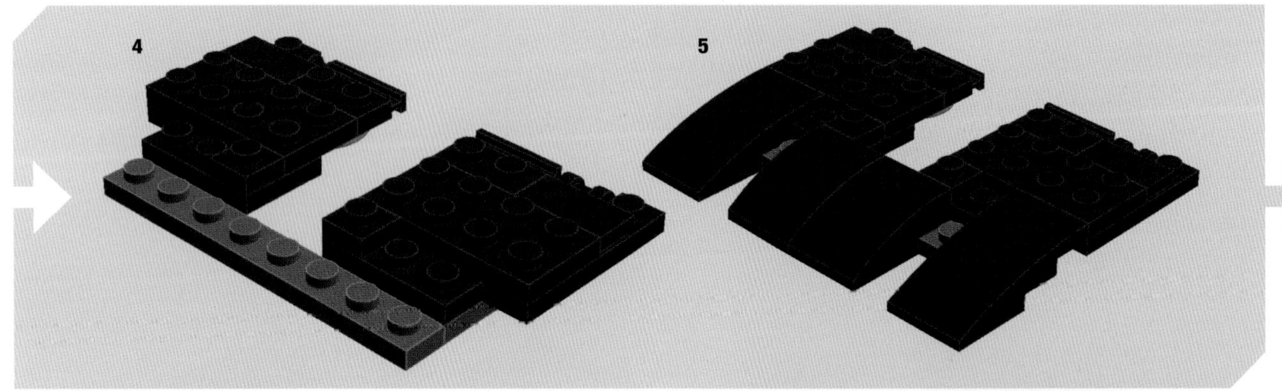

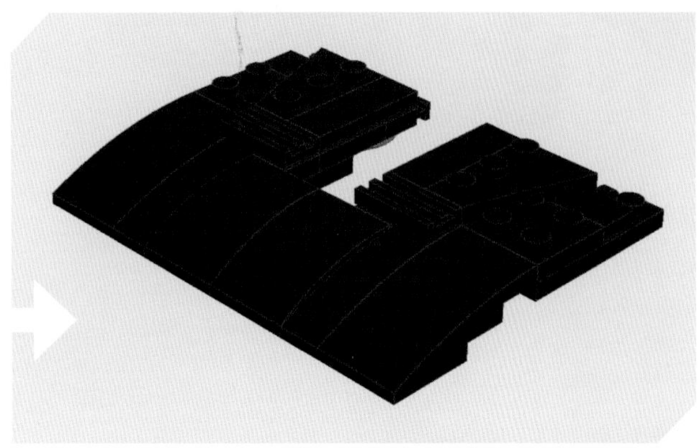

78

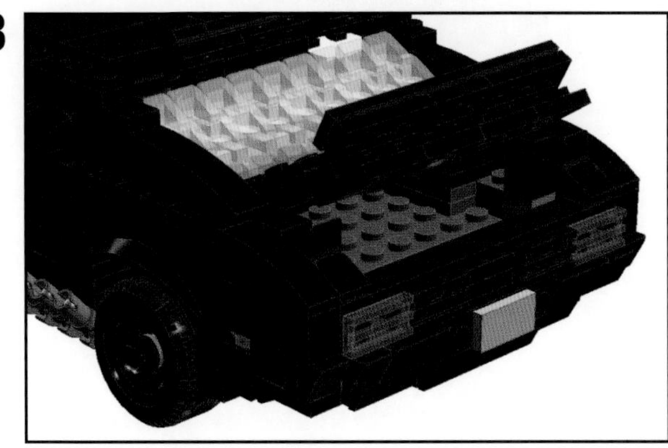

79

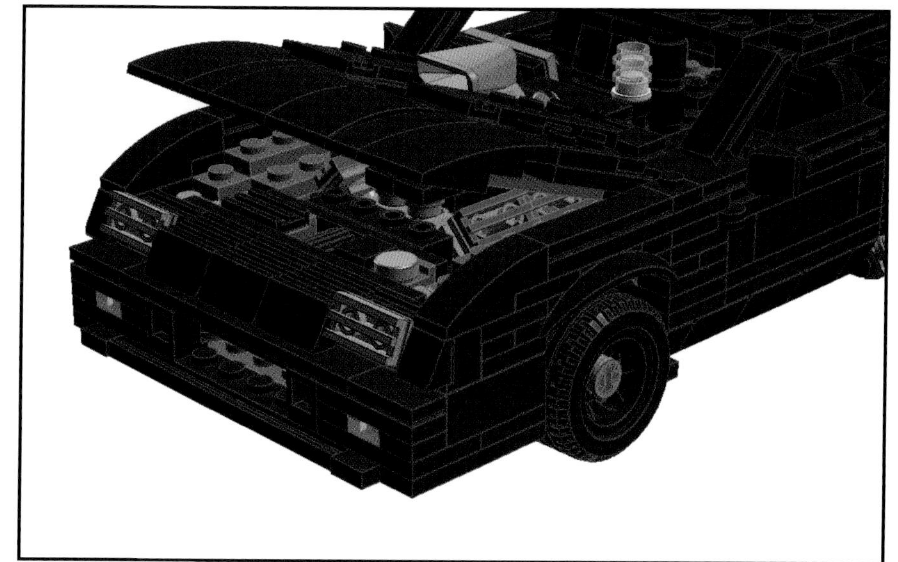

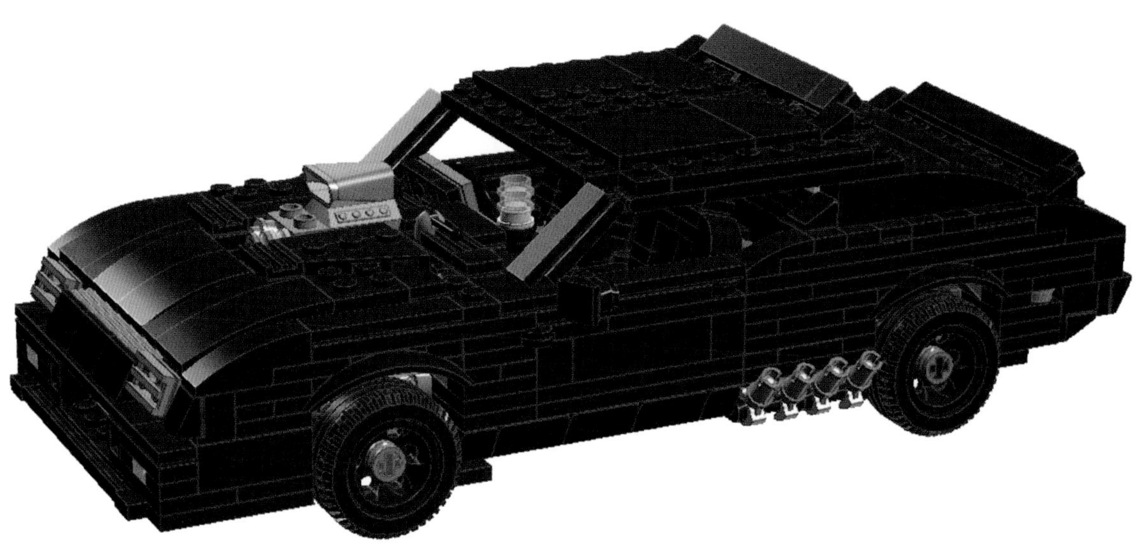

JAGUAR E-TYPE "SHAGUAR"
AUSTIN POWERS IN GOLDMEMBER

"Yeah Baby, Yeah!"

The Austin Powers films took a humorous jab at action spy films of the preceding decades, notably those to do with James Bond. Writer, producer, and star Mike Myers played both hero Austin Powers and villain Dr. Evil. Whereas most Bond films are played fairly straight by their principal actors, sometimes they would get a bit silly—and this is exactly where Myers takes the characters in his Austin Powers films.

An action hero needs an action car, and Powers gets his in the form of the "Shaguar," a 1961 Jaguar E-type emblazoned with the Union Jack across the bodywork. Jaguars have a reputation for being driven by "ladies' men," and Myers plays on this in most of his characterization. Interestingly, this power-position is exchanged in the video clip for the Madonna song "Beautiful Stranger" which was featured in the 1999 film *The Spy Who Shagged Me*.

The Jaguar E-Type would make a great agent car due to its high performance—the car is powered by a 3.8 liter (raised to 4.2 liters for 1965), Twin-cam six producing 265 bhp (198 kW)—and racy looks. The long hoodline serves as one of the main gag-lines as part of the innuendo imagery associated with many props of the Austin Powers films. The Shaguar's license plate reads "SWINGER," and in a subsequent film, a 2001 Jaguar XK8 convertible, also featuring Union Jack paintwork, uses "SWINGER2."

In all, the films are silly good fun, though highly suggestive.

And the Shaguar is "a bit of all right."

SWINGER

SHAGUAR

COUNTRY OF ORIGIN:	Great Britain
PRODUCTION:	1961–1975
NUMBER MADE:	7,828 3.8L S1 Roadsters, (75,515 all types)
LAYOUT/DRIVE:	Front engine, Rear-wheel-drive
ENGINE:	3.8 liter, 6 cylinders
POWER TORQUE:	265 hp (198 kW) / 240 lb-ft (325 Nm)
CONSTRUCTION/DOORS:	Steel Monocoque with tubular steel subframe, two-door
TV/FILM APPEARANCES:	*Austin Powers: International Man of Mystery* (1997), *Austin Powers: The Spy Who Shagged Me* (1999), *Austin Powers in Goldmember* (2002)

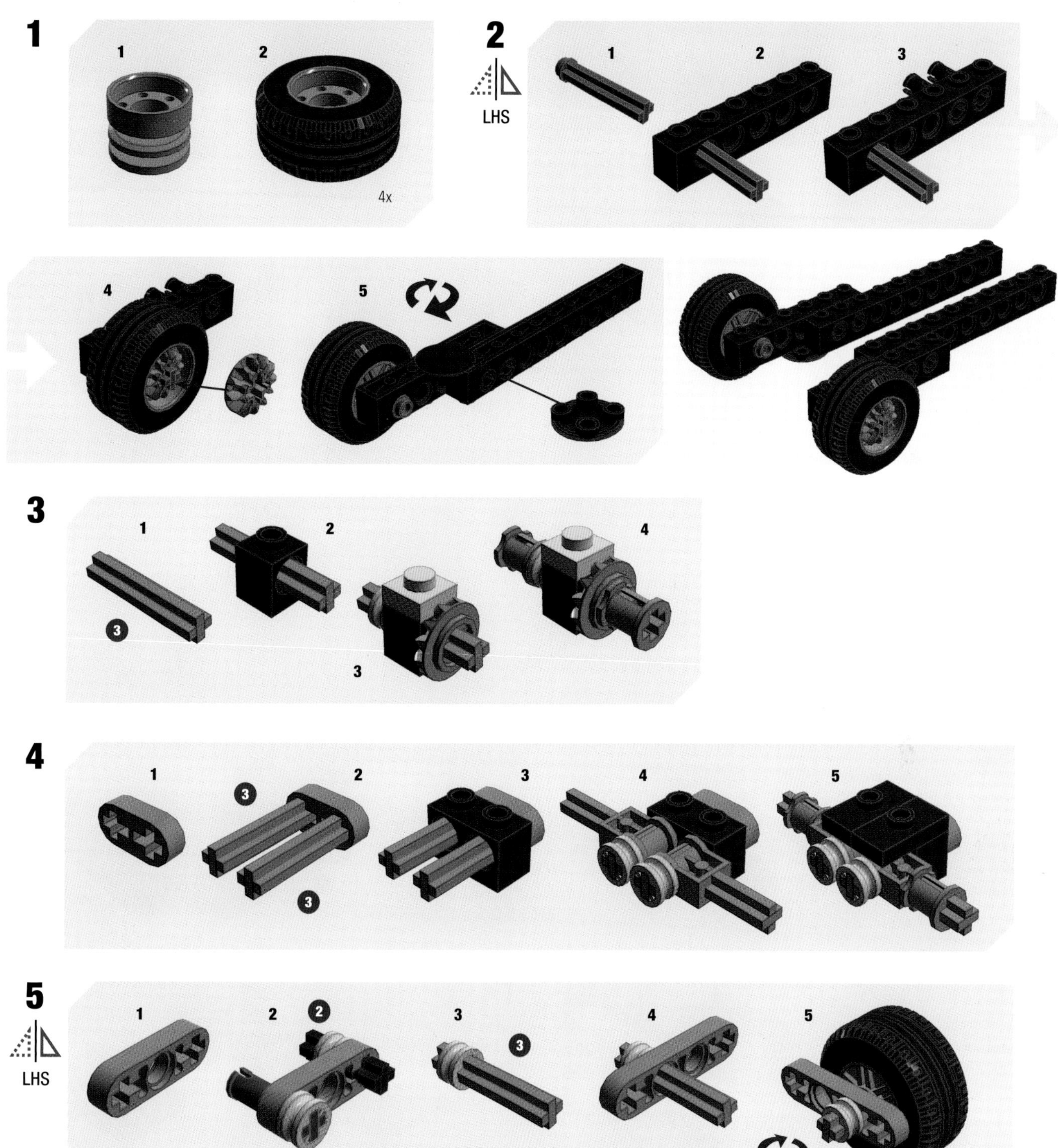
1
1
2
4x
2
LHS
1
2
3
4
5
3
1
2
3
3
4
4
1
3
2
3
4
5
3
5
LHS
1
2
2
3
3
4
5

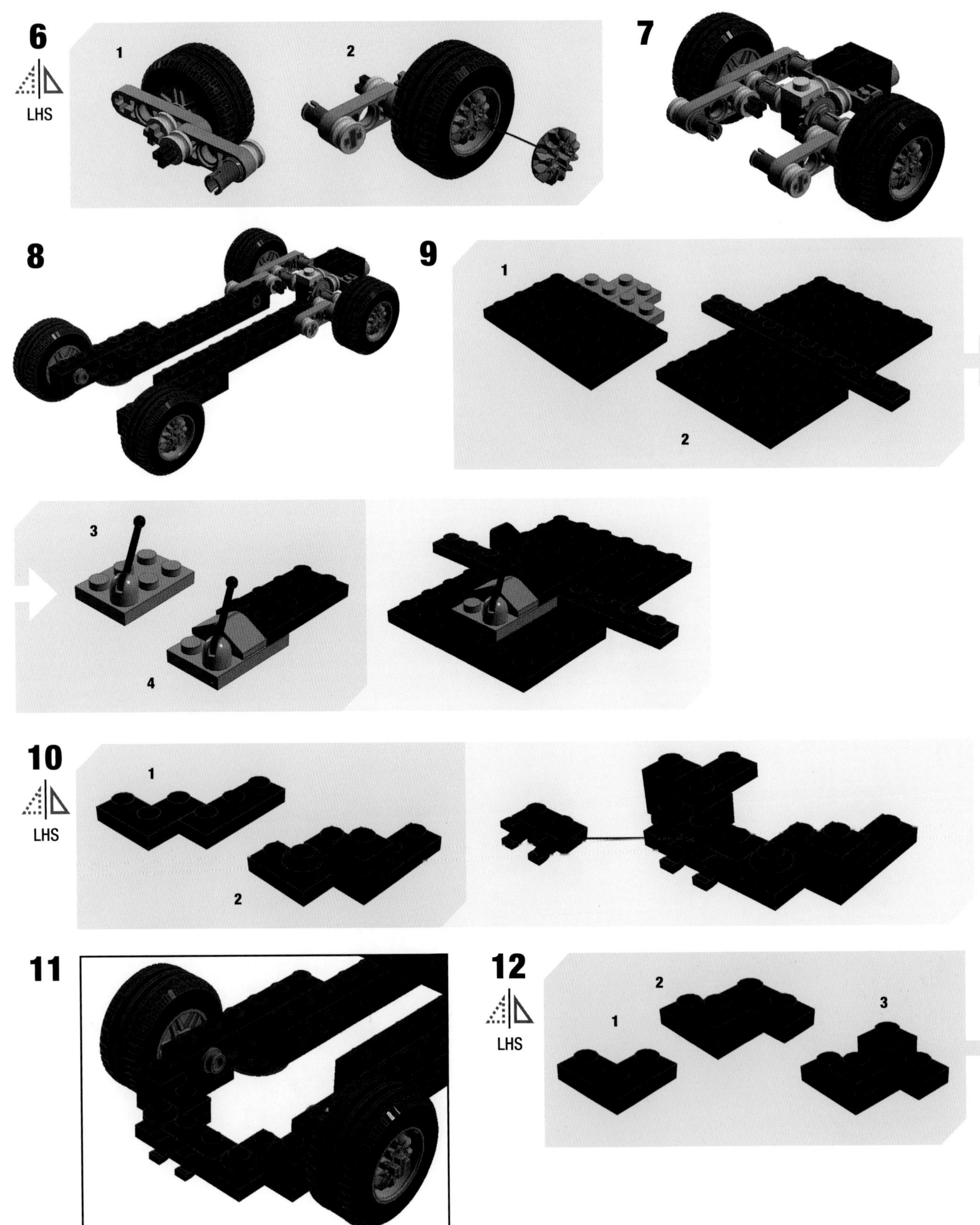
6
1
2
LHS
7
8
9
1
2
3
4
10
1
2
LHS
11
12
1
2
3
LHS

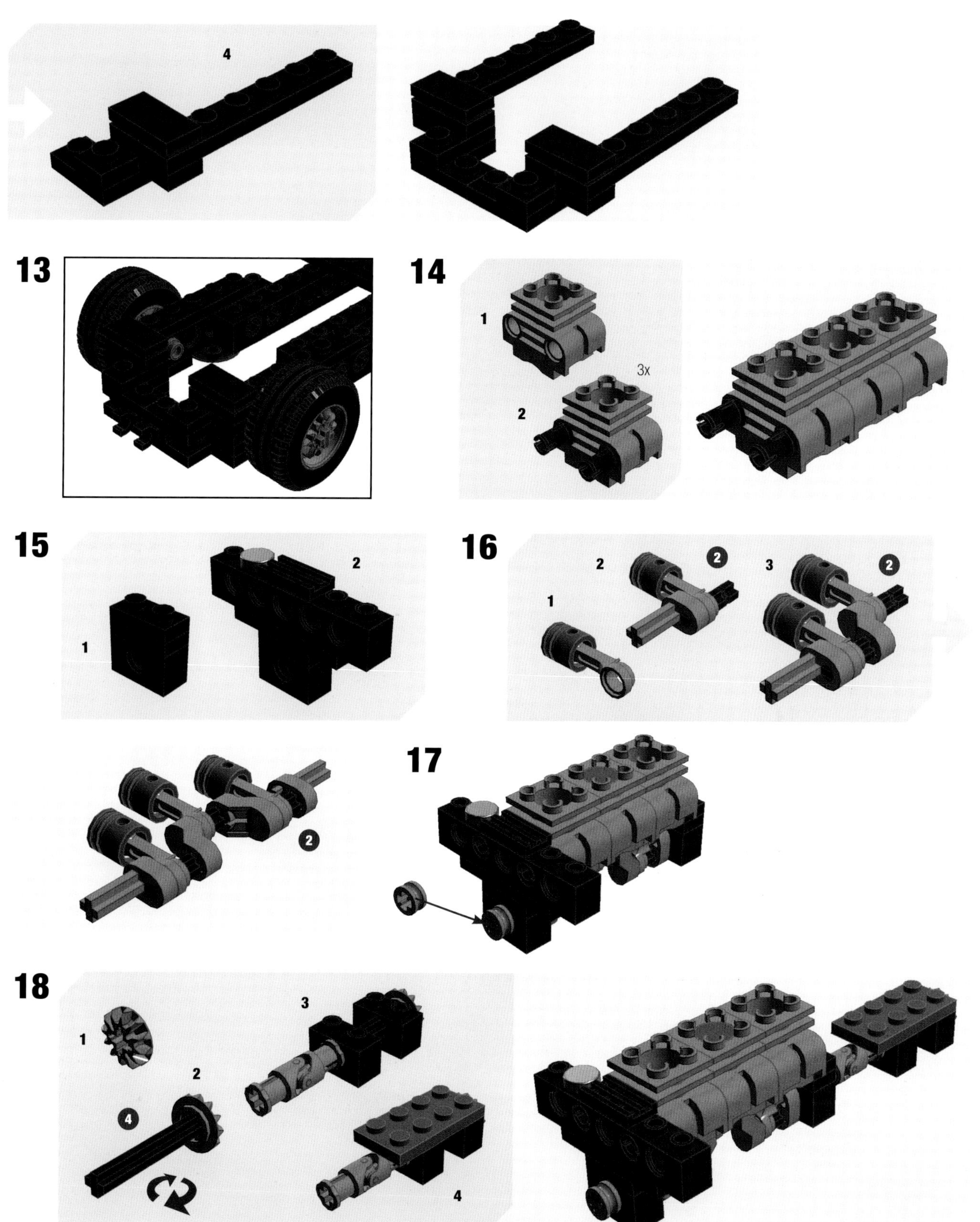
4
13
14
1
3x
2
15
2
1
16
2
2
3
2
1
2
17
18
3
1
2
4
4

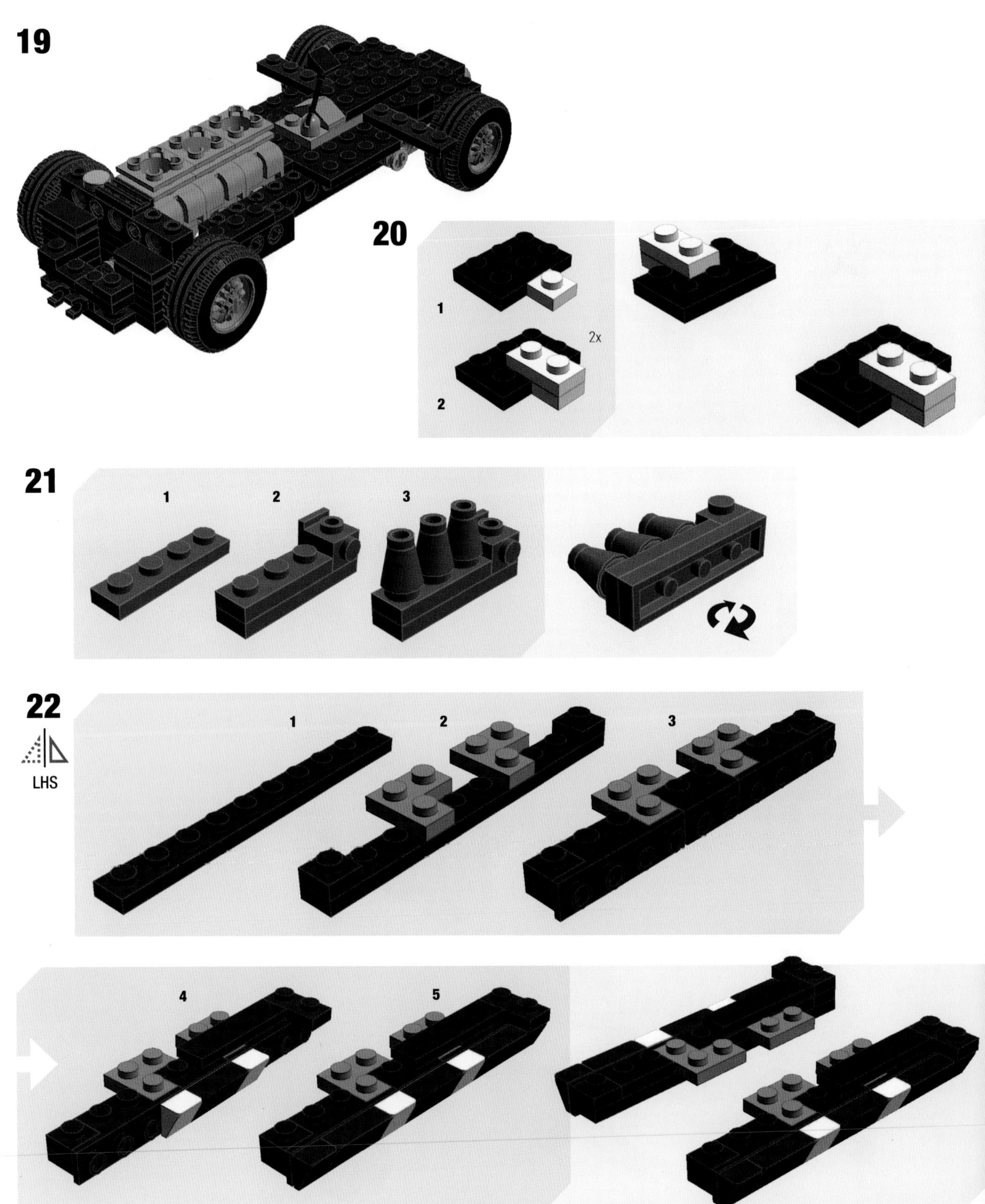
19
20
1
2
2x
21
1
2
3
22
LHS
1
2
3
4
5

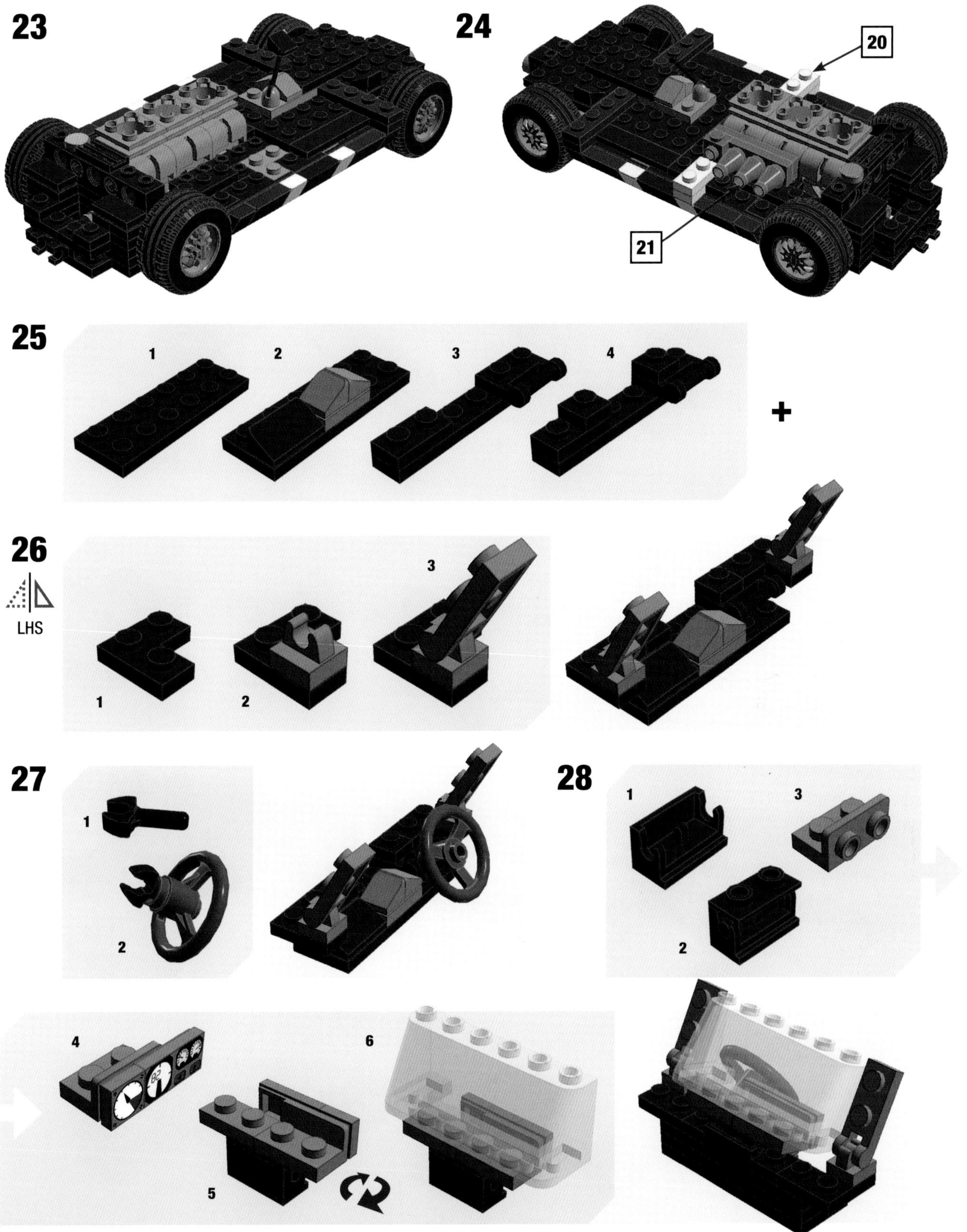
23
24
20
21
25
1
2
3
4
+
26
LHS
1
2
3
27
1
2
28
1
3
2
4
6
5

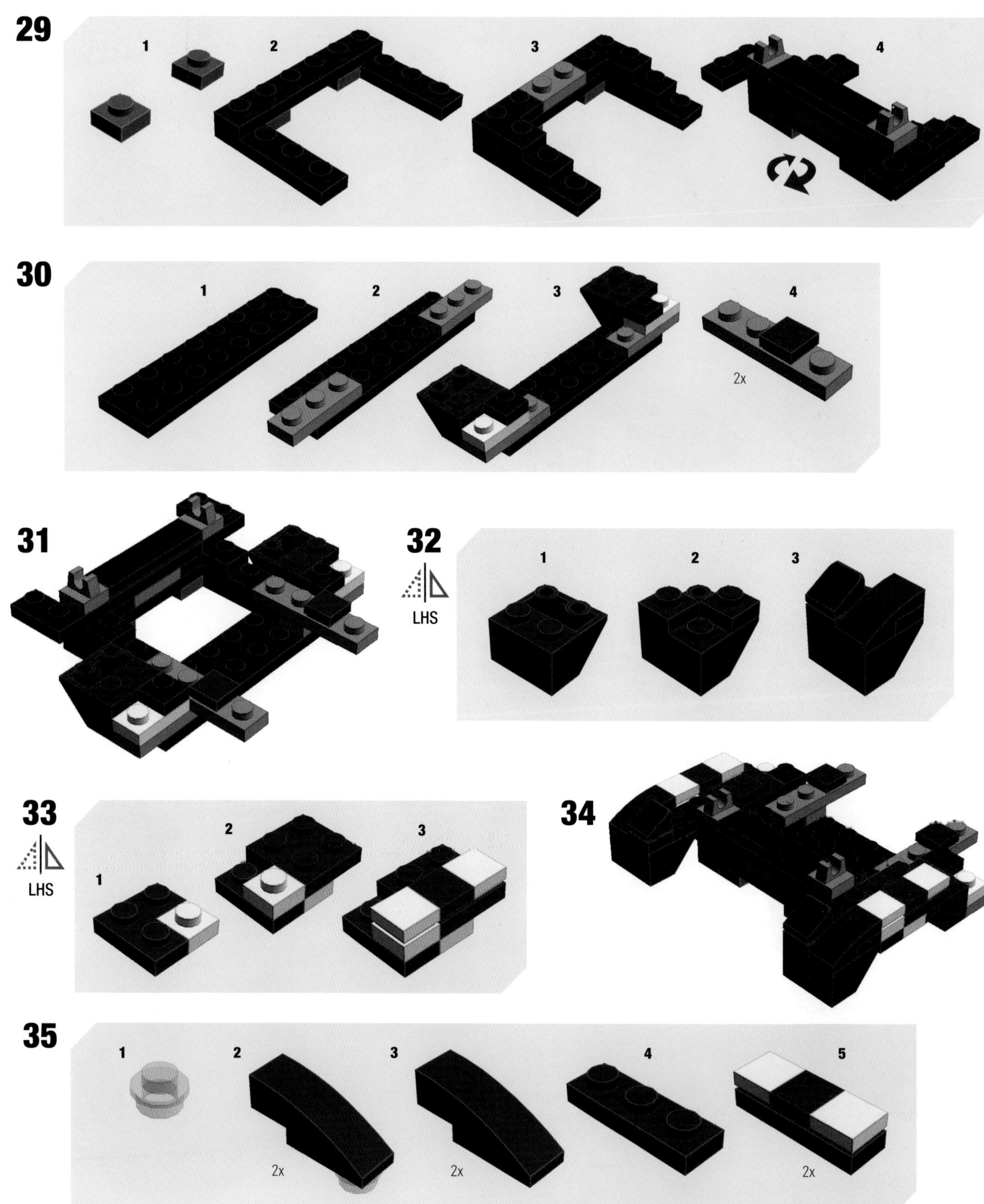
29
1
2
3
4
30
1
2
3
4
2x
31
32
LHS
1
2
3
33
LHS
1
2
3
34
35
1
2
3
4
5
2x
2x
2x

36

37

LHS

1

2

3

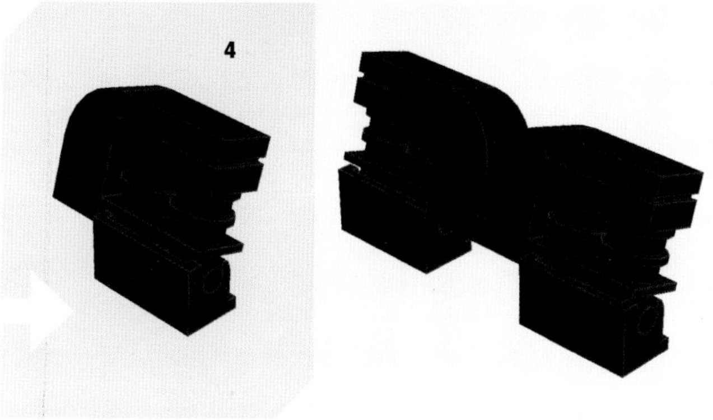

4

38

39

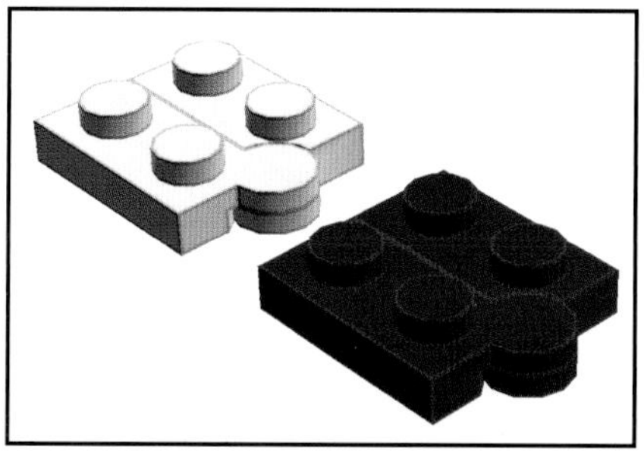

Split one red and one white hinge and rebuild as shown to the right

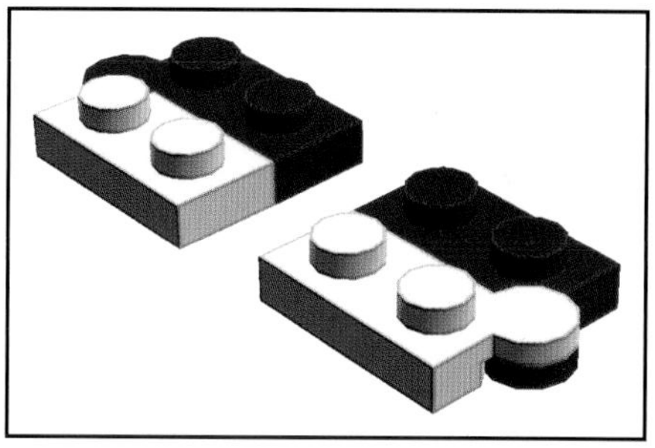

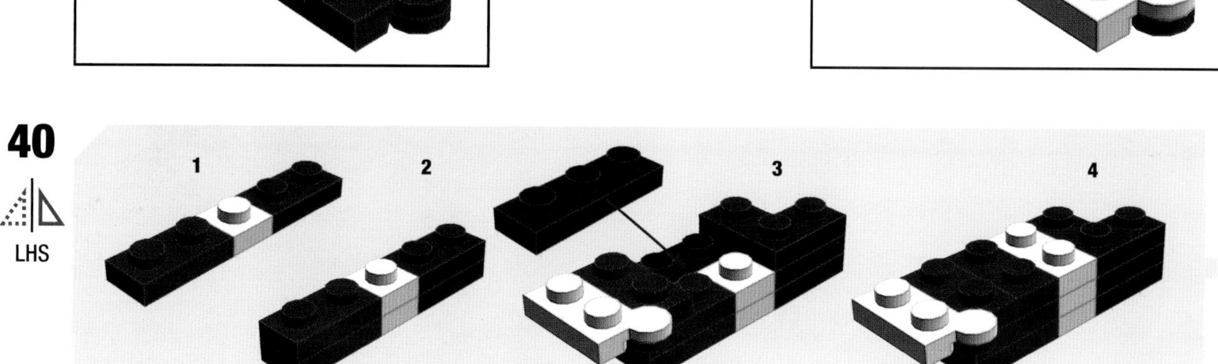

40

LHS

1

2

3

4

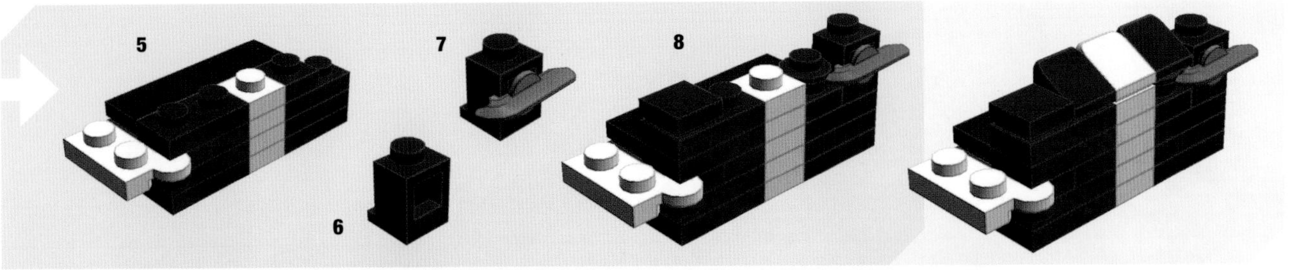

5 7 8

6

41

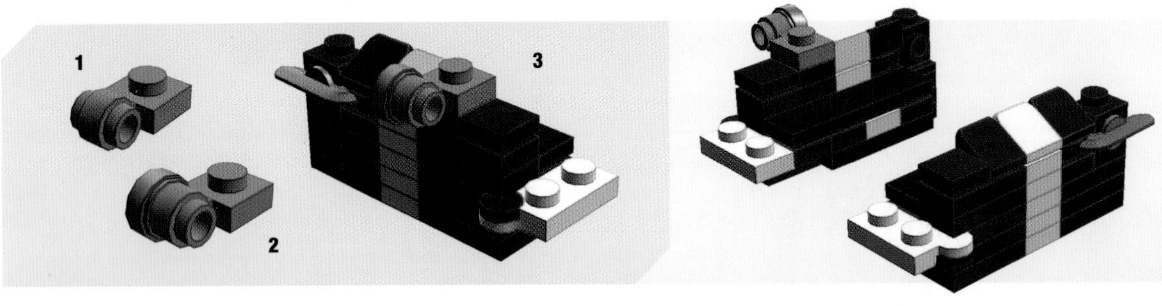

1 3

2

42

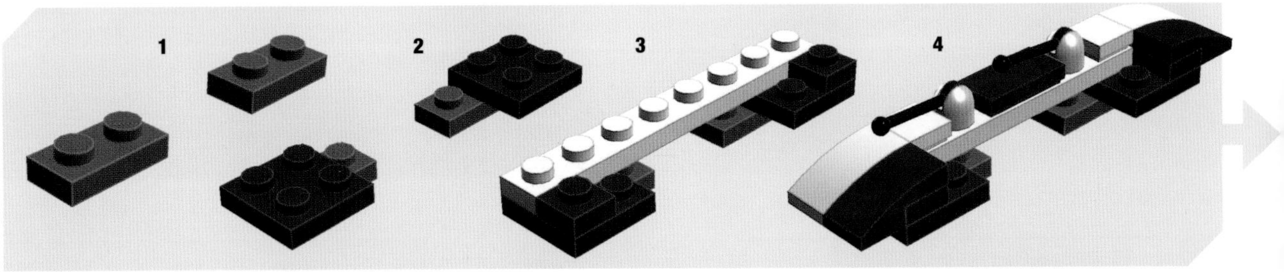

1 2 3 4

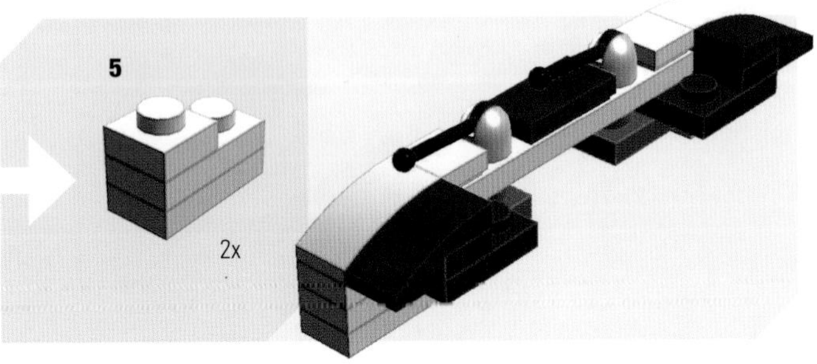

5

2x

43

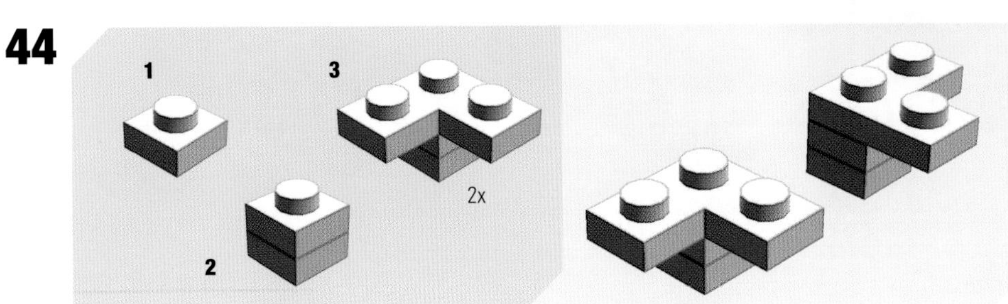

44

1 3

2x

2

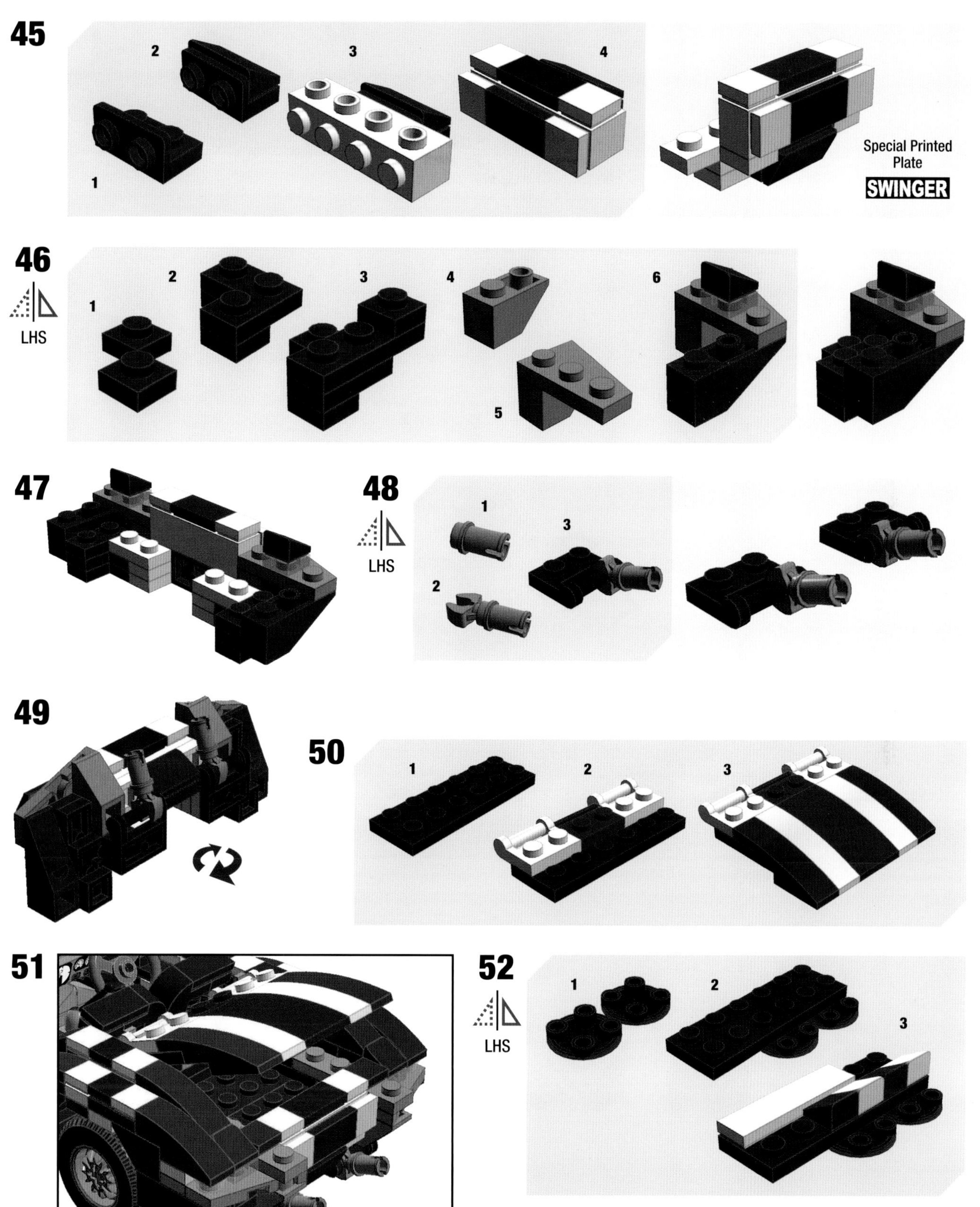
45
1
2
3
4
Special Printed
Plate
SWINGER
46
LHS
1
2
3
4
5
6
47
48
LHS
1
2
3
49
50
1
2
3
51
52
LHS
1
2
3

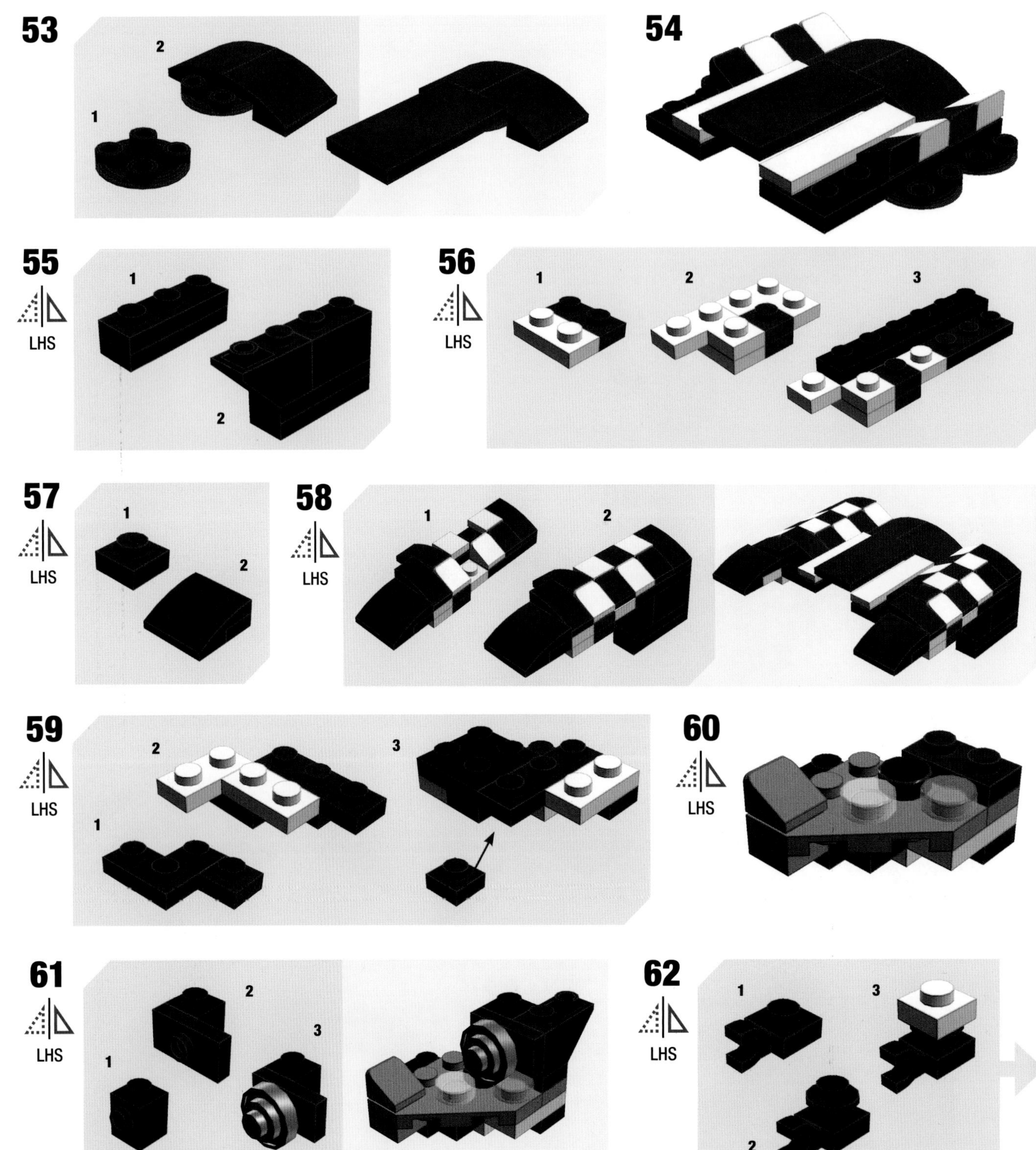
53
2
1
54
55
LHS
1
2
56
LHS
1
2
3
57
LHS
1
2
58
LHS
1
2
59
LHS
2
3
1
60
LHS
61
LHS
2
3
1
62
LHS
1
3
2

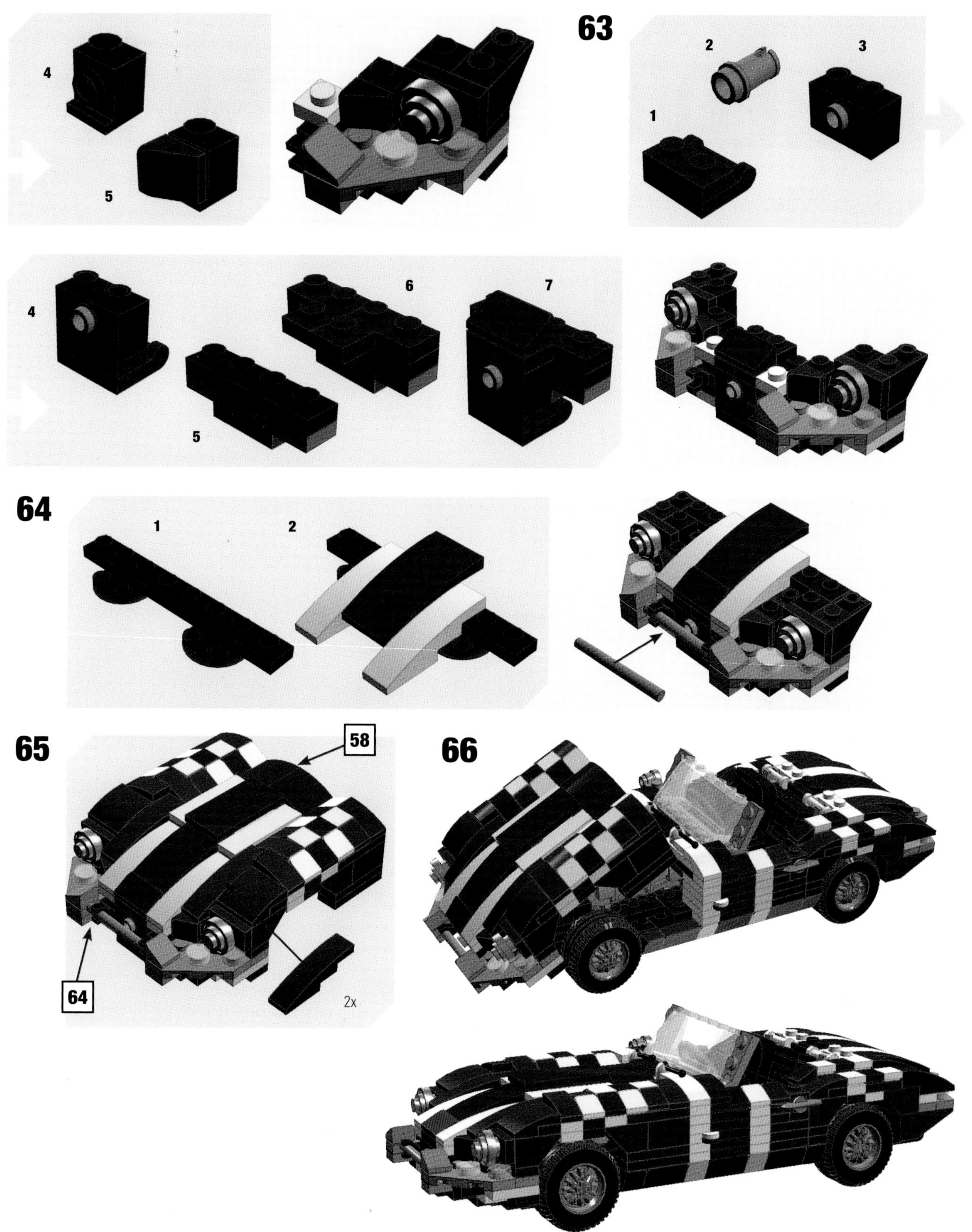
4
5
63
2
3
1
4
6
7
5
64
1
2
65
58
64
2x
66

APPENDIX I
BUILD COMPONENTS

LEGO COLOR CODES:

1
White

2
Old Gray

5
Brick Yellow

21
Bright Red

23
Bright Blue

24
Dark Yellow

26
Black

28
Dark Green

40
Transparent

41
Transparent Red

47
Transparent Fluorescent
Red Orange

111
Transparent Brown

138
Sand Yellow

140
Earth Blue

141
Earth Green

151
Sand Green

154
New Dark Red

182
Transparent Fluorescent
Red Orange

192
Reddish Brown

194
Medium Stone Gray

199
Dark Stone Gray

315
Silver Metallic

PART	COLOR	QUANTITY
2420-	26	3
3020-	199	3
3021-	199	2
3023-	26	4
	111	3
	199	2
3024-	26	4
	41	1
3034-	26	1
3622-	199	1
3623-	26	2
	199	2
	194	2
3710-	26	2
	199	2
4070-	26	6
	199	2
6157-	26	2
11477-	26	3
15068-	26	6

PART	COLOR	QUANTITY
15573-	26	2
	199	4
24299-	26	1
29119-	26	2
29120-	26	2
30414-	199	2
50945-	26	4
54200-	26	6
	111	13
63864-	26	1
87087-	26	1
93594-	315	4
99780-	26	2
99781-	26	2
3068b-	26	3
3069b-	26	2
	111	1
3070b-	26	1
	194	1

PONTIAC FIREBIRD TRANS AM

KNIGHT RIDER

FERRARI 250 GT SWB CALIFORNIA SPIDER

FERRIS BUELLER'S DAY OFF

PART	COLOR	QUANTITY
2420-	5	4
	21	8
	26	3
2540-	5	2
2555-	21	3
	26	2
2654-	26	6
3005-	194	2
3021-	5	2
	21	3
	26	4
	194	2
	199	1
3022-	21	2
	26	3
3023-	21	6
	26	6
	40	9
	199	3

PART	COLOR	QUANTITY
3024-	21	8
	26	16
	40	2
	194	2
	199	1
3460-	199	1
3623-	21	8
	26	6
	194	1
	199	1
3700-	199	4
3710-	5	1
	26	4
	194	1
3749-	5	4
3832-	26	2
4070-	5	2
	21	6
	26	4

PART	COLOR	QUANTITY
	40	2
4073-	26	16
	194	6
6091-	5	1
6636-	21	1
11211-	21	2
11212-	26	1
	194	1
11477-	21	12
	194	2
15068-	21	2
15573-	21	2
	26	1
	194	1
18974-	21	4
18976-	315	4
18977-	26	4
26047-	26	1
	194	2

PART	COLOR	QUANTITY
30162-	199	2
30374-	194	1
32028-	194	4
34103-	26	2
43722-	194	1
43723-	194	1
48336-	26	1
54200-	5	1
	21	12
	26	1
	40	12
	41	2
60478-	21	3
61252-	21	1
	194	2
61678-	21	2
63864-	21	3
85861-	194	3
85984-	21	14

PART	COLOR	QUANTITY
87087-	21	1
	194	3
98138-	26	2
	315	1
99780-	26	6
2412b-	5	2
	26	4
	194	1
3062b-	194	2
3069b-	*1	1
	21	2
3070b-	21	4
	194	1
3829c01-	26	1
4081b-	21	2
4592co2-	26	1
60470b-	21	1

*exchange custom printed 3069b- "NRVOUS"

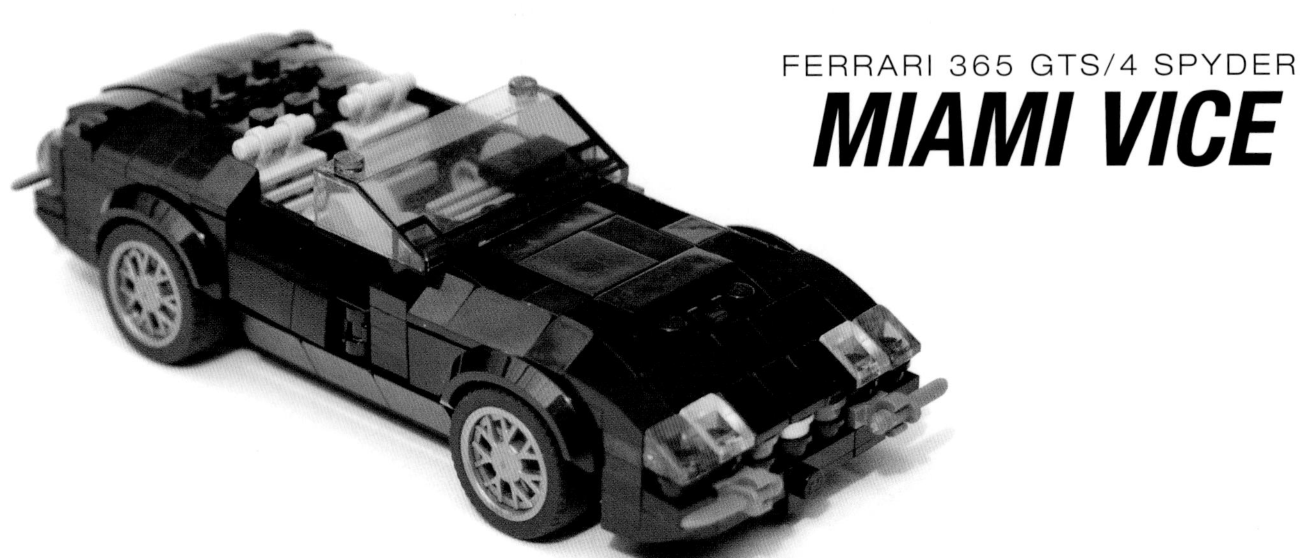

FERRARI 365 GTS/4 SPYDER

MIAMI VICE

PART	COLOR	QUANTITY
2420-	5	2
	26	11
	199	4
2540-	5	2
2555-	26	5
2654-	5	2
3021-	26	5
	194	1
	199	1
3022-	5	2
	26	7
3023-	26	19
	194	3
	199	5
3024-	5	2
	26	26
	40	1
	182	2
	199	1
3062-	21	2
3460-	194	1
3623-	21	1
	26	10
	199	2
3665-	26	4
3666-	26	1
3700-	199	4
3710-	5	1
	26	6
	199	1
3749-	5	4
3832-	26	2
4070-	5	4
	199	1
4073-	5	2
	23	2
	26	9
	41	4
	194	8
	199	2
	315	3
6091-	5	1
11212-	194	2
11477-	26	19
15068-	26	2
15573-	26	3
18976-	315	4
18977-	26	4
24201-	26	8
26047-	26	1
26603-	26	1
30162-	199	2
30374-	194	1
34103-	26	2
48336-	26	1
54200-	26	15
	40	2
	182	2
	194	2
58181-	111	1
60478-	26	3
61252-	26	1
	194	2
	199	4
63864-	26	2
85984-	26	11
87087-	26	1
	194	5
98138-	21	2
98282-	26	4
99780-	194	6
2412b-	5	3
	194	2
	315	4
3069b-	26	1
	*1	1
3070b-	26	6
3829c01-	26	1
4081b-	26	2
44658a-	199	4
4592c02-	26	1
60470b-	26	1

* exchange custom printed 3069b- “ZAQ 178”

MINI COOPER S

THE ITALIAN JOB

PART	COLOR	QUANTITY
2420-	21	4
	26	4
	194	2
	199	4
2431-	21	2
	26	1
	194	1
2540-	21	1
	199	2
2555-	21	4
	26	4
2654-	26	3
3004-	26	1
3005-	21	2
3010-	21	2
	199	1
3020-	26	2
	194	2
3021-	21	2
	26	1
	151	1
3022-	21	2
	26	1
3023-	21	11
	26	4
	40	15
	151	1
	194	2
	199	4
3024-	21	34
	26	5
	40	5
	194	2
3031-	26	2
3036-	26	1
3460-	21	1
3623-	21	7
	194	2
3666-	26	2
	199	1
3710-	21	4
	26	5
	194	4
	199	1
3747-	194	1
3749-	194	4
3795-	194	1
4032-	21	2
4070-	26	4
	40	1
	199	4
4073-	23	3
	40	3
	182	2
	199	2
6081-	21	2
6091-	21	2
6191-	21	2
11477-	21	9
	26	2
15068-	21	6
15573-	21	15
	26	4
	199	10
18976-	315	4
18977-	26	4
30136-	194	1
30357-	21	4
30374-	26	1
	194	4
30377-	26	2
30663-	26	2
32018-	26	2
32028-	26	2
	194	2
48336-	26	1
	194	2
54200-	21	6
54200-	40	14
61252-	26	1
	194	1
63864-	21	3
85861-	194	6
87087-	21	2
	26	2
	194	1
87552-	40	2
87580-	26	1
87994-	26	1
91049-	315	2
92280-	26	1
98138-	*1	1
	26	5
98282-	199	4
99780-	26	1
99781-	199	1
2412b-	315	3
2429c01-	21	2
2436b-	26	1
3062b-	21	2
3069b-	21	7
	199	5
3069px5-	**1	2
	***26	2
3070b-	21	2
	26	2
	41	2
3070pb07-	194	3
4081b-	194	2
4589b-	26	2
4592c02-	194	1
	26	1
4865b-	26	2
48729b-	26	1
60470b-	26	1

* or custom printed 98138- "GB"

** or 2x 3069

*** with printed plates. "ITLN JOB", "HMP 729G", "GPF 146G", "LGW 809G"

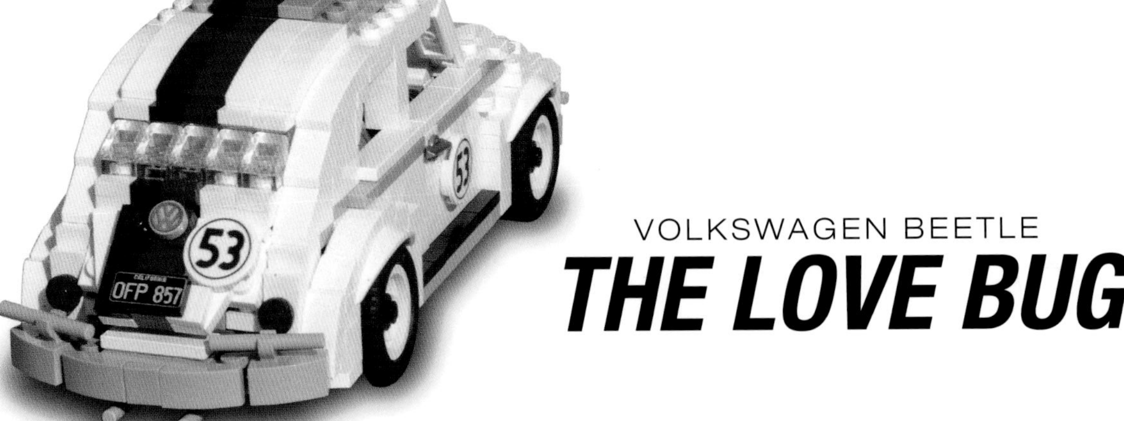

VOLKSWAGEN BEETLE

THE LOVE BUG

PART	COLOR	QUANTITY
2412b-	194	4
	199	2
	315	1
2420-	1	10
	26	4
	140	1
	194	2
2431-	1	2
	21	1
	140	1
	194	1
2555-	26	4
2994-	1	4
3004-	1	10
3005-	1	2
	26	2
3020-	1	2
	26	2
	194	1
3021-	1	3
	26	9
	194	2
3022-	1	4
	26	4
	194	5
3023-	1	16
	26	4
	40	9
	194	3
	199	2
3024-	1	28
	21	3
	26	10
	40	2
3024-	140	4
	194	10
3031-	26	1
3032-	26	1
3040-	1	4
3069b-	1	2
	26	2
	140	3
3070b-	1	8
	26	2
	140	1
	194	4
3460-	1	1
	26	4
3622-	194	1
3623-	1	7
	21	1
	26	5
	194	6
3665-	26	1
3666-	1	2
	26	3
	194	3
3701-	26	2
3707-	26	4
3710-	1	10
	21	1
	26	5
	140	1
	194	3
15573-	1	23
	21	3
	26	5
	140	3
	194	6
3795-	26	6
4070-	1	7
	26	1
	199	4
4085d-	194	1
4150/14769-	1	4
61252-	26	1
	194	4
4073-	1	2
	21	2
	23	1
	26	5
	40	4
	41	2
	194	5
6553-	194	4
6578-	26	4
6587-	199	4
6632-	194	8
6636-	194	1
11212-	26	2
11477-	1	5
	21	1
	140	1
	194	8
15573-	26	1
30663-	194	1
26047-	1	1
29119-	1	1
29120-	1	1
30414-	26	1
32013-	194	4
32062-	21	4
4265c-	194	12
32828-	194	1
41677-	194	4
43722-	1	2
43723-	1	2
47905-	199	1
48336-	26	1
	194	4
48729b-	26	1
54200-	1	10
	21	1
	26	4
	40	5
50950-	21	1
60470b-	1	1
60478-	1	2
	21	1
	194	4
4085d-	26	2
61252-	21	1
	194	6
11153-	1	4
	21	1
	140	2
62361-	1	4
63864-	1	5
63868-	1	2
	21	1
4592c02-	194	3
	26	3
2429c01-	1	2
85984-	1	1
	26	2
87079-	26	2
87087-	1	6
	26	2
	194	3
87904	194	7
93555-	315	2
93606-	1	2
98138-	23	1
	26	1
	194	4
	***315	4

* custom printed with "HERBIE" or "OFP 857"
** custom printed "53"
*** 2x printed 98138pr0012
2x Custom Printed logo "VW"

FORD MUSTANG
BULLITT

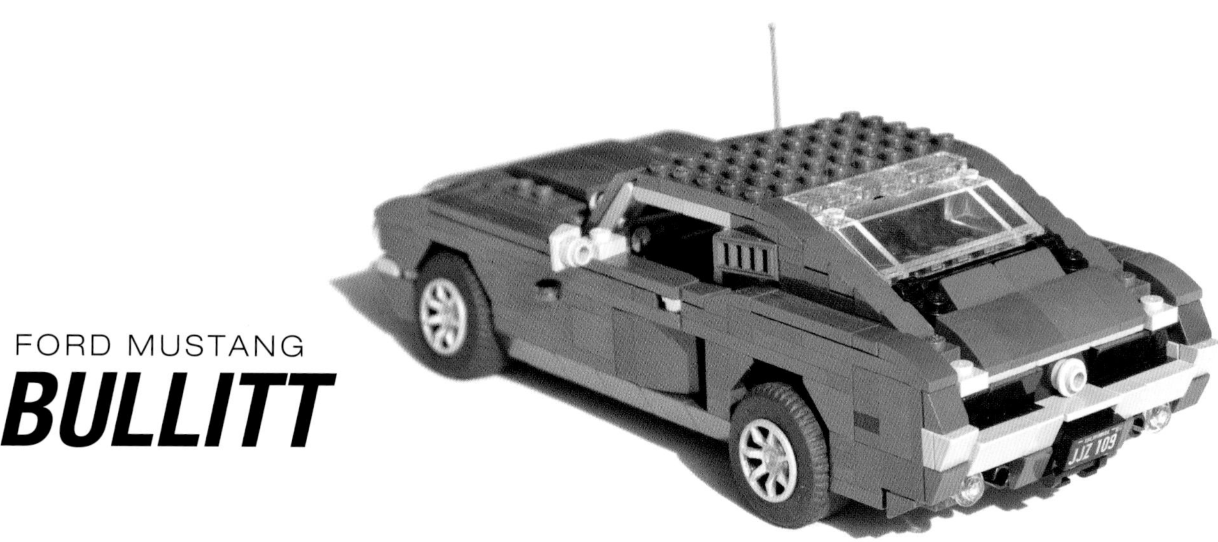

PART	COLOR	QUANTITY
2420-	26	8
	194	2
2431-	141	3
2555-	26	4
2654-	26	2
	40	2
	194	1
	199	1
2780-	26	7
3004-	141	4
3005-	141	2
3010-	26	2
3020-	26	11
	141	8
3021-	26	4
	141	10
3022-	26	4
	194	1
3023-	26	20
	40	2
	141	32
	194	6
	199	8
3024-	26	14
	40	1
	41	2
	141	12
	194	2
3034-	26	2
3035-	141	1
3036-	26	1

PART	COLOR	QUANTITY
3038-	26	1
3040-	26	1
3460-	26	8
3623-	26	11
	141	12
	194	3
3660-	141	6
	199	1
3665-	141	6
3666-	26	7
	141	6
	194	1
3700-	26	1
	194	1
	199	2
3701-	194	2
3705-	26	2
3710-	23	2
	26	7
	141	2
	194	1
3713-	194	2
3737-	26	1
3749-	5	1
	23	4
3795-	26	2
	199	3
3894-	26	2
3937-	23	4
	26	2

PART	COLOR	QUANTITY
3938-	23	4
	26	2
4032-	194	1
4070-	26	14
4073-	26	3
	40	8
	194	4
	315	3
4275-	194	2
4276-	194	2
4477-	26	2
4519-	194	4
6231-	194	2
6541-	26	2
6558-	26	1
6587-	199	2
6589-	194	2
6636-	141	2
11477-	141	6
	194	2
15068-	141	5
15535-	26	1
15573-	26	7
	141	2
26047-	26	2
30136-	194	2
30663-	26	1
32000-	26	4
32013-	194	4
32028-	26	2
	194	2

PART	COLOR	QUANTITY
32034-	194	4
32062-	21	4
34103-	26	2
41677-	194	6
41769-	141	1
41770-	141	1
43722-	194	1
43723-	194	1
44294-	194	1
44728-	26	2
	194	3
48336-	26	5
50950-	141	6
54200-	26	4
	41	2
	141	20
	194	6
55982-	26	4
58090-	26	4
58181-	40	1
58367-	194	1
61409-	141	2
62359-	315	4
63864-	141	3
63868-	26	4
85861-	194	1
85984-	26	7
	141	14
	194	4
87079-	26	2
	141	6

PART	COLOR	QUANTITY
87087-	26	4
	141	10
93550-	315	1
93606-	141	2
98138-	40	1
	315	
99780-	26	4
99781-	26	2
2412b-	26	4
	141	2
	315	1
2429c01-	141	2
2436b-	26	4
3069b-	1	1
	26	4
	40	3
	141	2
3069pbc1 x1-	194	1
3069pbx19 x1-	194	1
3070b-	141	11
4081b-	194	1
4085d-	194	1
4265c-	194	7
4589b-	26	1
4592c02-	194	1
	26	2
4865b-	194	3
60470b-	26	2
6252c01-	194	1
9037pb01-	26	1
	315	1

* replace with custom print 3069b- 26 "JJZ 109"

TOYOTA AE86 TRUENO

INITIAL D

PART	COLOR	QUANTITY
2420-	1	6
	26	11
	154	1
	194	6
2431-	1	2
	26	2
2540-	26	1
2555-	26	2
2654-	26	2
2780-	26	5
3004-	26	4
3005-	1	2
	26	2
	111	2
3009-	192	1
3010-	*1	2
3020-	1	1
	26	3
	154	2
3021-	26	2
3022-	26	3
3023-	1	20
	26	19
	41	2
	111	2
	154	1
	194	7
	199	4
3024-	1	8
	26	16
	40	2
	41	6
	44	2
	111	2
	182	4
	192	2
	194	2
	199	2
	315	2
3032-	26	1
3034-	26	1
3035-	1	1
3036-	26	1
3039-	40	6
3040-	26	2
3066-	111	1
3460-	1	2
	26	5
	154	1
3623-	1	6
	26	16
	154	4
	199	2
3665-	26	4
3666-	1	4
	26	15
	199	4
3700	26	2
3701-	26	1
3706-	26	1
3710-	1	2
	26	5
	154	1
	194	3
	199	3
3713-	194	4
3737-	26	1
3749-	5	2
3795-	26	1
3894-	26	2
3937-	26	2
3938-	26	2
4070-	26	9
	40	6
	199	2
4073-	21	2
	26	2
	40	3
	182	4
	194	2
	315	2
4162-	26	1
4275-	26	2
4276-	26	2
4477-	26	1
4510-	26	3
4519-	194	1
6541-	26	1
	194	1
6589-	194	2
6636-	26	1
11211-	194	1
11212-	26	2
11477-	1	2
15573-	1	6
	26	12
26047-	26	2
27940-	199	2
30413-	26	2
30414-	26	1
30663-	26	1
32000-	26	2
32013-	194	4
32028-	1	2
	26	1
32034-	194	2
32062-	21	6
32064-	26	2
41677-	26	2
	194	4
44294-	194	2
47905-	26	2
48336-	26	4
	194	2
49668-	315	4
52107-	26	2
54200-	26	12
	40	2
	111	6
	154	4
	199	3
55982-	26	4
58090-	26	4
58181-	111	1
61252-	26	2
61678-	26	2
	1	2
62359-	315	4
62361-	26	4
63864-	1	4
	26	2
85861-	26	1
85984-	1	4
	26	14
	154	1
	192	2
	199	3
87079-	1	2
	26	4
87087-	26	2
	194	1
	199	2
87580-	26	1
87994-	194	1
93606-	26	2
98138-	40	2
	315	2
99781-	26	5
2412b-	26	1
	154	1
	194	2
	315	3
2429c01-	1	2
2436b-	26	5
3068b-	1	1
3069b-	**1	4
	26	2
	111	2
	199	1
3069bpc1-	199	1
3070b-	1	8
	26	7
4081b-	26	2
4085d-	26	1
4265c-	24	6
4589b-	315	4
4592c02-	26	3
48729b-	26	5
60470b-	1	2
6252c01-	194	1
6538b-	194	2

* custom print 3010 (Japanese Text)

** 2x 3069- 1 custom Japanese "13.654"

FERRARI 308 GTS

MAGNUM P.I.

PART	COLOR	QUANTITY
2420-	21	6
	26	16
2431-	21	1
	26	3
2555-	26	4
2654-	26	3
3001-	26	1
3004-	26	1
3005-	26	2
3020-	5	1
	26	2
3021-	26	1
	199	2
3022-	26	4
	199	1
3023-	21	12
	26	14
	40	14
	194	6
	199	1
3024-	21	8
	26	15
	182	4
	194	2
	199	1
3032-	26	1
3034-	21	1
3035-	26	1
3036-	26	1
3039-	26	1
3040-	26	3
3460-	21	1
	26	2
3623-	21	2
	26	3
	194	1
	199	3
3665-	21	4
	26	4
3666-	21	4
	26	11
	199	1
3701-	194	2
3702-	194	1
3706-	26	4
3710-	21	7
	26	2
	199	1
3795-	5	2
	26	1
3894-	194	2
3937-	26	2
3938-	26	2
4032-	199	4
4070-	21	6
	26	2
4073-	24	2
	26	4
	41	2
	182	2
	194	2
	315	4
4162-	26	1
4213-	21	1
4287-	21	2
4315-	21	1
4510-	26	1
6553-	194	8
6587-	199	4
6632-	194	10
6636-	21	4
	26	1
11477-	21	2
15573-	21	10
	26	3
20482-	26	1
30162-	199	2
32028-	21	2
	26	4
34103-	26	1
43722-	21	1
43723-	21	1
48336-	26	1
52107-	26	4
54200-	5	2
	21	14
	26	2
	40	2
55982-	194	4
58090-	26	4
60478-	21	4
	26	2
61252-	26	2
	21	2
	199	2
61678-	21	4
62361-	21	4
85861-	26	1
85984-	5	2
	21	17
	26	3
87079-	21	1
	26	2
87087-	26	2
87994-	194	1
88072-	21	2
98138-	315	2
99207-	26	1
99780-	21	4
2412b-	5	4
	26	11
	315	4
2429c01-	21	2
2436b-	26	5
	194	2
3068b-	21	3
3069b-	*1	1
	21	4
3070b-	21	8
	26	2
	199	4
3829c01-	26	1
4081b-	26	2
	194	1
4265c-	24	20
4589b-	194	1
	194	3
4592c02-	26	4
4865b-	26	2
60470b-	26	1
85984pb100-	199	

* custom printed 3069b- 1 "ROBIN 1"

LOTUS ESPRIT

JAMES BOND 007
THE SPY WHO LOVED ME

PART	COLOR	QUANTITY
2357-	1	8
	199	2
2420-	1	6
	26	18
	194	6
2431-	1	3
	26	3
2444-	26	4
2555-	1	2
	26	1
2654-	26	2
2780-	26	4
2994-	194	4
3005-	26	4
3020-	26	12
	194	1
	199	4
3021-	1	3
	26	9
	194	1
	199	1
3022-	1	4
	26	6
	199	1
3023-	1	12
	26	29
	40	2
	194	3
	199	1
3024-	1	13
	26	25
	40	4
	41	6
	182	4
	194	4
	199	2
3031-	26	2
3032-	26	2
3039-	26	2
	40	2
3040-	26	1
3460-	1	2
	26	2
3623-	1	3
	26	18
	194	3
3660-	199	1
3665-	1	2
	26	1
3666-	1	8
	26	3
	199	3
3700-	1	4
	199	4
3701-	194	1
3705-	26	2
3710-	1	6
	26	26
	194	3
3795-	1	1
	26	2
	199	1
3832-	26	2
3937-	26	2
3938-	26	2
4070-	1	6
	26	6
4073-	21	8
	26	11
	40	4
	194	3
	315	8
4162-	1	1
	26	1
4275-	26	2
4287-	1	2
4477-	26	2
4531-	26	2
6179-	1	2
6541-	26	7
6553-	194	8
6558-	26	2
6578-	26	4
6587-	199	6
6632-	194	11
6636-	1	3
11211-	194	2
11212-	26	2
15068-	1	8
15573-	1	12
	26	6
	1	2
26047-	26	2
26603-	1	1
30162-	194	2
	199	2
30414-	26	1
30663-	26	5
32000-	26	9
34103-	26	1
43093-	23	1
44294-	194	2
44676-	1	2
48336-	1	4
	26	2
54200-	1	4
	26	17
59349-	40	1
60478-	1	3
	26	2
60479-	26	1
60779-	1	2
61252-	1	3
	199	2
	26	2
61678-	1	4
62361-	1	4
63864-	1	2
	*26	2
63868-	26	2
85984-	1	24
	26	9
	194	1
87079-	1	2
	26	2
87087-	26	5
87994-	194	2
88072-	26	6
93273-	1	4
98138-	199	2
99781-	1	4
2412b-	21	2
	26	15
	315	2
2429c01-	26	2
2436b-	26	9
3062b-	199	2
3068b-	1	1
	26	3
3069b-	**1	8
	26	3
	***199	3
3069pbx19-	****194	2
3070b-	1	4
	182	2
4265c-	24	18
	194	8
4592c02-	26	1
4592c03-	194	1
48729b-	26	1
60470b-	1	3
	26	1

* add additional 2x 63864 Cusptom Print "PPW 306R"

** substitute two for custom number plate prints

*** Printed 3069bpc1- 199 x 1

****printed x2

FORD 1932 COUPE HOT ROD

AMERICAN GRAFFITI

PART	COLOR	QUANTITY
2420-	24	4
	26	2
2431-	24	4
2654-	26	1
	199	2
2780-	26	21
2850-	194	4
2851-	199	4
2852-	194	4
2853-	194	2
2854-	199	1
2994-	194	4
3020-	24	2
	26	7
	199	1
3021-	26	2
	199	2
3022-	26	2
	194	1
	199	1
3023-	24	26
	26	14
	40	3
	41	2
	194	1
3024-	24	10
	26	6
3031-	26	1
	199	1
3032-	26	1
	199	1
3065-	40	4
3460-	24	1
	26	1
3622-	26	2
3623-	24	4
	194	1
3647-	194	1
3665-	24	4
3666-	24	3
	26	7
	199	1
3700-	26	5
3701-	26	3
3710-	24	4
	26	8
3713-	194	5
3737-	26	2
3894-	26	2
4032-	194	1
4070-	24	10
	194	2
4073-	24	
	26	7
	199	2
4274-	194	8
4519-	26	4
4740-	194	1
6005-	24	6
6091-	24	2
6578-	26	4
6587-	199	2
6589-	194	6
6636-	26	2
	199	2
11153-	24	4
11477-	24	18
	26	2
15068-	24	7
	199	6
15573-	24	12
	26	1
	194	1
23443-	194	2
26047-	26	3
30377-	194	2
30414-	26	1
30663-	26	1
32013-	194	2
32028-	26	2
32039-	26	2
32062-	26	3
32270-	194	1
32316-	26	2
32524-	26	4
41677-	194	2
42610-	194	2
44728-	26	1
48336-	24	2
50950-	24	4
	26	10
54200-	24	4
	26	2
58367-	26	1
61252-	24	2
63864-	24	3
63965-	194	3
85984-	24	5
87087-	24	2
	26	6
87552-	40	2
87994-	194	2
93555-	315	2
98138-	40	2
99207-	26	1
99780-	24	4
	199	6
99781-	26	2
2412b-	199	4
	309	4
2429c01-	24	2
2431px17-	*199	1
2436b-	26	1
3062b-	194	2
3069b-	24	4
	40	2
	**191	1
3070b-	24	4
	26	2
4081b-	194	2
4265c-	194	8
4592c02-	194	1
	26	1
48729b-	26	1
	194	2

* printed

** Flame Yellowish Orange or custom printed "THX 138" or "GRAFFITI"

FORD FALCON V8 INTERCEPTOR

MAD MAX

PART	COLOR	QUANTITY
2420-	23	2
	26	15
	199	2
2431-	26	5
2445-	26	1
2654-	26	2
	199	4
2730-	26	1
2780-	26	14
2819-	26	1
2850-	194	4
2851-	199	4
2852-	194	4
2853-	194	2
2854-	194	1
2877-	26	3
2994-	26	4
3005-	26	6
	194	2
3009-	26	1
3010-	26	1
3020-	26	10
3021-	26	9
	194	1
	199	2
3022-	26	11
	194	3
	199	3
3023-	26	21
	40	13
	140	1
	194	6
	199	3
3024-	26	32
	40	3
	194	4
3033-	199	1
3034-	26	1
	199	1
3036-	199	1
3460-	26	8
	194	1
	199	3
3622-	26	2
3623-	26	20
	192	1
3660-	26	7
3665-	26	4
	199	6
3666-	5	1
	21	2
	26	12
	199	2
3700-	26	1
	194	1
	199	2
3701-	26	2
	194	3
3705-	26	2
3708-	26	1
3710-	24	2
	26	27
	199	10
3713-	194	3
3737-	26	1
3795-	26	3
3832-	26	2
3895-	194	2
3937-	26	5
3938-	26	3
	194	2
4070-	26	14
	199	4
4073-	21	2
	43	2
	182	2
	194	4
	199	10
	309	1
	315	11
4162-	26	4
4274-	194	11
4275-	26	2
4276-	26	2
4477-	26	5
	194	2
4510-	26	1
4519-	194	3
6091-	26	4
6179-	26	2
6231-	194	2
6541-	194	2
6562-	5	3
6578-	26	4
6587-	199	2
6589-	194	2
6632-	194	2
6636-	26	1
7073-	26	4
11212-	26	2
11477-	26	2
15068-	26	1
15573-	26	18
	194	10
20482-	26	1
24309-	26	2
30136-	26	2
30414-	26	2
32000-	26	2
	194	1
32013-	26	4
	194	2
32028-	26	2
32034-	26	2
	194	2
32062-	21	4
	26	1
32449-	194	1
42022-	26	2
43722-	26	1
43723-	26	1
44728-	26	4
48336-	26	8
50943-	315	1
50950-	26	4
54200-	26	23
	40	26
60478-	26	4
60479-	26	5
61252-	26	2
61678-	26	2
62361-	26	4
63864-	26	7
85984-	26	19
87079-	26	2
92947-	26	1
93606-	26	2
98138-	315	1
99781-	26	1
2412b-	5	2
	23	4
	26	7
	41	2
	199	2
2429c01-	26	2
2436b-	26	4
3062b-	26	2
	194	2
3068b-	26	2
3069b-	*24	1
	26	8
3069pbx19-	**194	2
3070b-	26	9
3070pb07-	**194	2
4081b-	26	2
	194	2
4085d-	26	1
4265c-	24	1
	194	12
4589b-	194	2
4592c02-	194	5
	26	5
48729b-	315	8
60470b-	26	5
6538b-	26	1
71137b-	309	2

* replace with custom print 3069b- 26 "MFP" or "MAD MAX"

** printed

JAGUAR E-TYPE "SHAGUAR"

AUSTIN POWERS IN GOLDMEMBER

PART	COLOR	QUANTITY
2420-	1	6
	21	2
	26	12
	140	
	194	6
2431-	1	2
	*26	5
2450-	194	2
2555-	194	4
2654-	21	1
	26	8
2730-	26	2
2780-	26	10
2819-	217	1
2850-	194	3
2851-	199	3
2852-	194	3
2853-	194	2
2854-	194	2
3004-	140	2
3020-	26	1
	199	1
3021-	26	2
	140	2
	194	1
3022-	21	2
	26	2
	140	2
3023-	1	18
	21	13
	26	9
	140	8
	194	5
	199	3
3024-	1	22
	21	5
	24	1
	26	16
	41	2
	140	18
	194	2
	199	2
3032-	26	2
3034-	26	1
3460-	1	1
	26	1
3623-	21	2
	26	4
	140	10
	194	2
	199	1
3660-	21	2
	140	2
3665-	140	4
	194	2
3666-	26	6
3700-	26	5
3705-	26	1
3710-	26	5
	194	3
	199	1
3713-	194	4
3795-	26	4
3894-	26	3
3937-	26	3
3938-	26	3
4070-	26	2
	140	2
	199	1
4073-	26	12
	140	2
	182	2
	199	2
4081-	194	1
4176-	40	1
4274-	19	3
4287-	21	2
4477-	26	2
	140	1
4519-	194	5
6091-	26	2
6541-	26	1
6553-	194	2
6587-	199	2
6589-	194	6
6632-	194	2
11477-	1	2
	21	2
	140	8
15068-	21	2
	140	2
15573-	26	2
	140	2
30374-	194	1
30414-	1	1
32000-	26	1
32028-	21	1
32062-	21	2
	26	3
32449-	194	2
41677-	194	1
43093-	23	2
43722-	194	1
43723-	194	1
48336-	1	2
	21	1
	26	3
50950-	140	4
54200-	1	14
	21	5
	26	2
	140	16
	194	6
55982-	194	4
58090-	26	4
60478-	194	2
61252-	26	2
61678-	1	4
	140	4
85984-	21	4
	26	1
	140	4
87079-	21	1
87087-	26	2
91049-	315	2
93555-	315	2
93606-	21	2
98138-	26	2
	40	2
	182	2
	315	2
99780-	21	1
	194	1
99781-	26	2
2412b-	26	1
2429c01-	1	1
	21	1
2436b-	26	4
3069b-	21	2
	26	5
3069bpx19-	**194	1
3070b-	1	18
	21	8
	140	2
3070pb07-	**194	1
4265c-	24	9
	194	1
4589b-	199	3
4592c02-	194	3
	26	3
48729b-	26	1
	194	2
60470b-	26	1
6252c01-	194	1

* plus additional 2431- 26 Custom printed "SHAGUAR" or "SWINGER"
** printed

APPENDIX II

PARTS INDEX

Not to scale

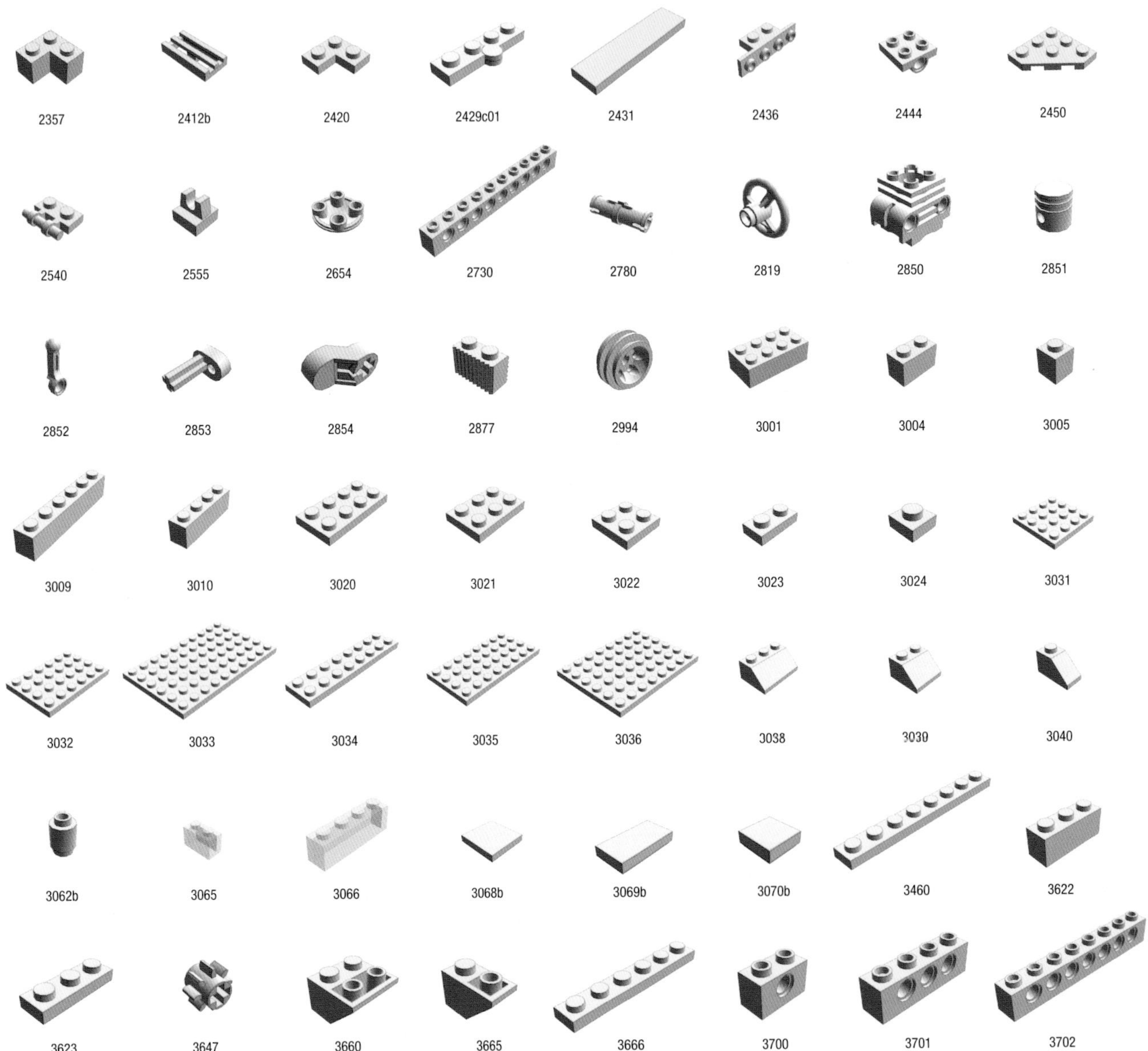

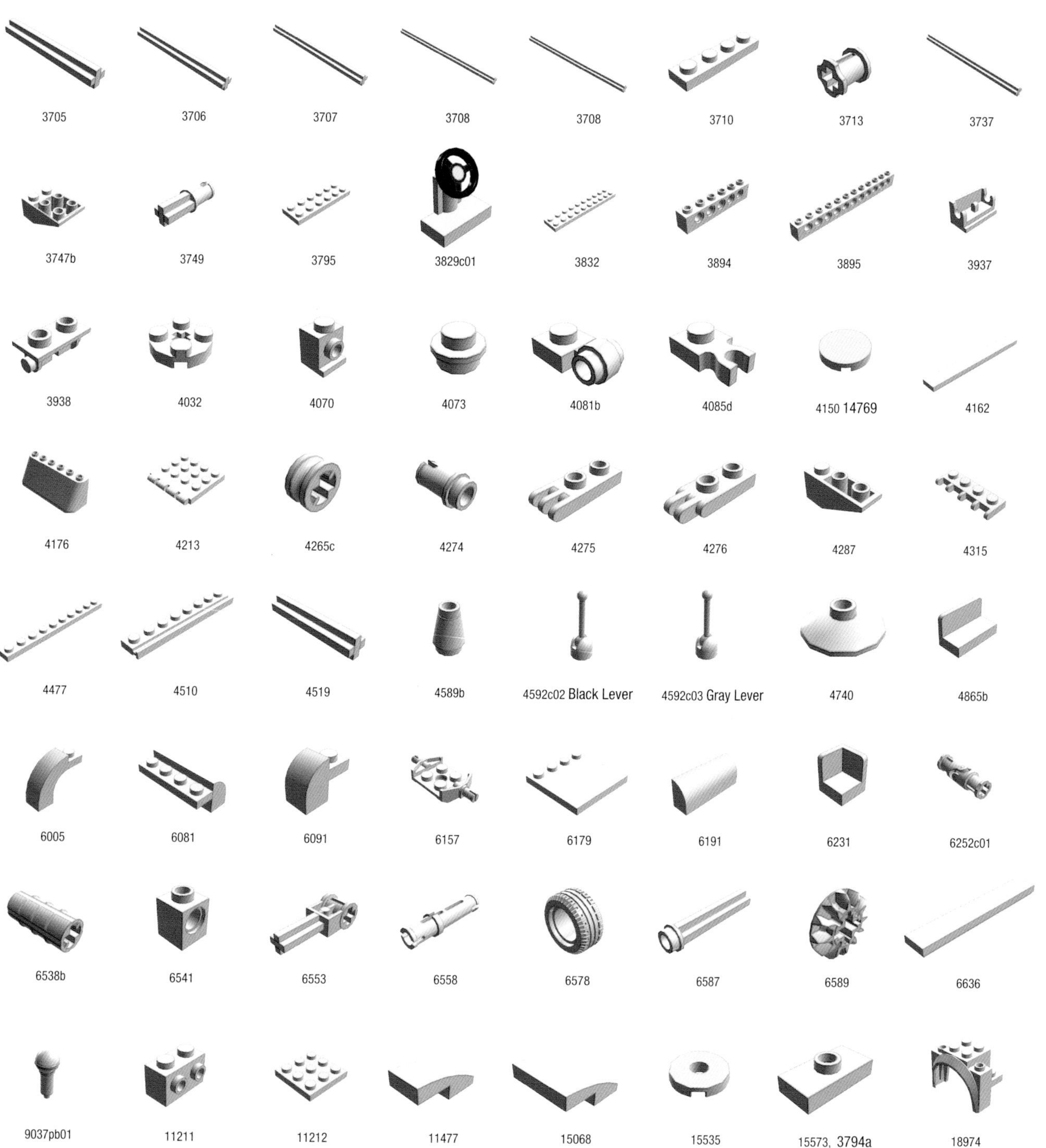

3705
3706
3707
3708
3708
3710
3713
3737
3747b
3749
3795
3829c01
3832
3894
3895
3937
3938
4032
4070
4073
4081b
4085d
4150 14769
4162
4176
4213
4265c
4274
4275
4276
4287
4315
4477
4510
4519
4589b
4592c02 Black Lever
4592c03 Gray Lever
4740
4865b
6005
6081
6091
6157
6179
6191
6231
6252c01
6538b
6541
6553
6558
6578
6587
6589
6636
9037pb01
11211
11212
11477
15068
15535
15573, 3794a
18974

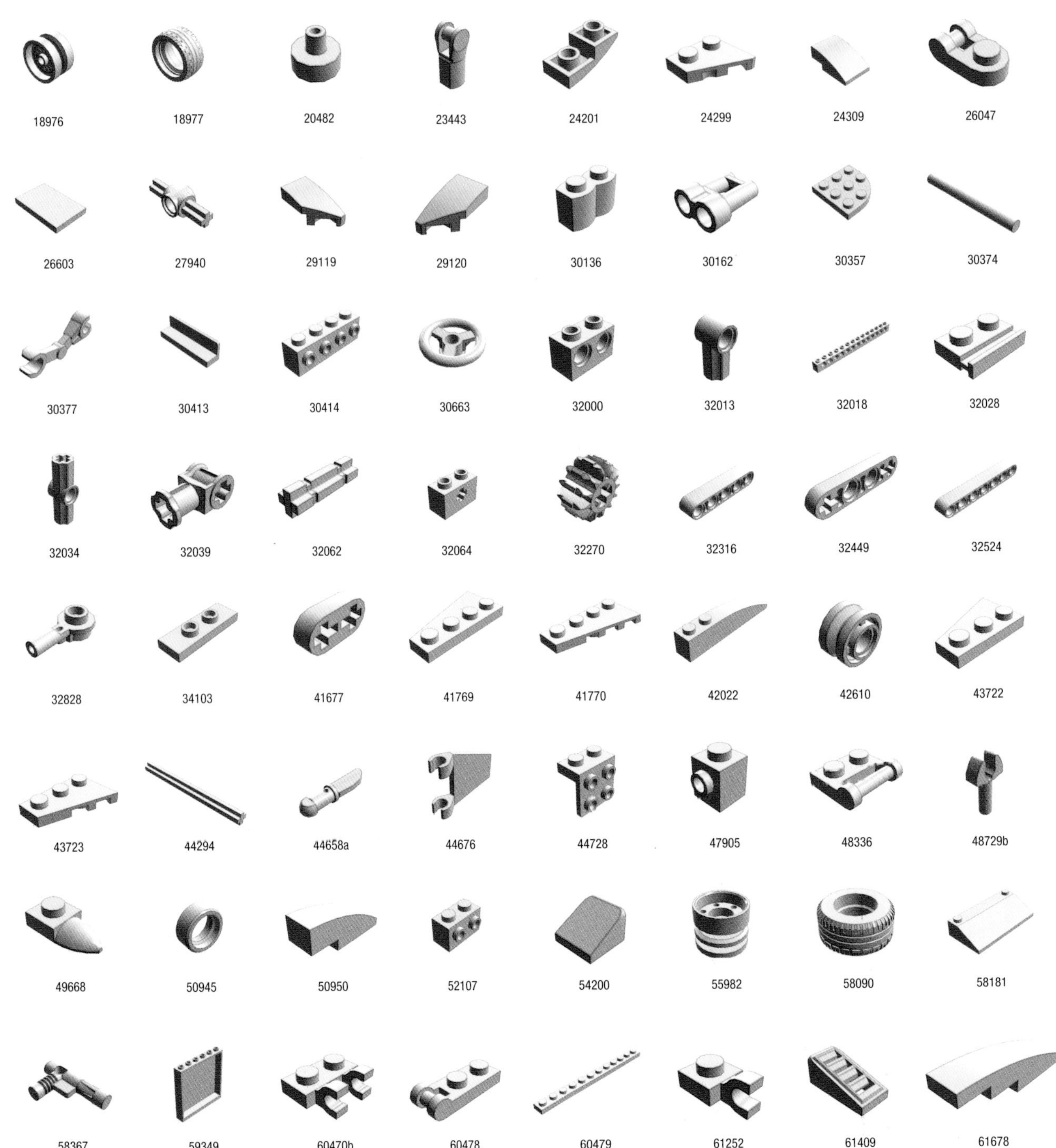
18976
18977
20482
23443
24201
24299
24309
26047
26603
27940
29119
29120
30136
30162
30357
30374
30377
30413
30414
30663
32000
32013
32018
32028
32034
32039
32062
32064
32270
32316
32449
32524
32828
34103
41677
41769
41770
42022
42610
43722
43723
44294
44658a
44676
44728
47905
48336
48729b
49668
50945
50950
52107
54200
55982
58090
58181
58367
59349
60470b
60478
60479
61252
61409
61678

62359
62361
63864
63868
63965
71137
85861
85984
87079
87087
87552
87580
87994
88072
91049
92280
92947
93273
93550
93555
93594
93606
98138
98282
99207
99780
99781

APPENDIX III

PRINTED PARTS INDEX

Not to scale

3069b-1

3069b-1

3069b-26

3069b-26

3069b-26

3069b-26

98138-1

3069b-26

3069b-26

14769

98138-194

3069b-26

3069b-26

3069b-26

3069b-1

3010-1

3069b-1

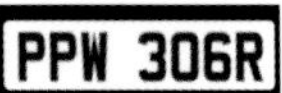

63864-26

63864-26

3069b-191

3069b-191

3069b-26

3069b-26

SWINGER

2431-26

SHAGUAR

2431-26

ACKNOWLEDGMENTS

I WANT TO THANK Motorbooks for the opportunity to create this book project and share my models with the world. Thanks to my project manager Jessi Schatz for keeping me moving along and my publisher Zack Miller. Most special to me are my family, particularly my wife Jeana—thank you for letting me do another book. And to my three kids, I hope that this inspires you to follow your dreams with all your energy.

ABOUT THE AUTHOR

PETER BLACKERT is the most prolific vehicle builder in the LEGO community. He has built thousands of cars from LEGO over the years, drawing on his experience as a Powertrain & Chassis Systems Engineering Architect for the Ford Motor Company. His Bugatti Veyron, featured in his first Motorbooks title *How to Build Brick Cars*, was listed #5 in *TopGear* magazine's "Ten Greatest Replica LEGO Cars" in 2014. His work also has featured regularly in articles on LEGO fan sites, such as brothers-brick.com and TheLegoCarBlog.com, and car-club magazines. Peter's work can be found on Flickr under the username lego911 and on Instagram under lego__911. His second Motorbooks title *How to Build Brick Airplanes* published in 2018. He lives near the beach in Australia with his wife and three kids—and a large room full of LEGO bricks.

ALSO AVAILABLE FROM MOTORBOOKS:

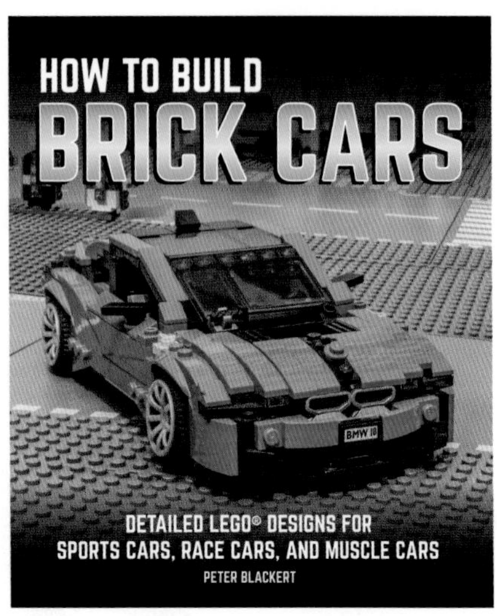

How to Build Brick Cars
By Peter Blackert
978-0-7603-5265-6

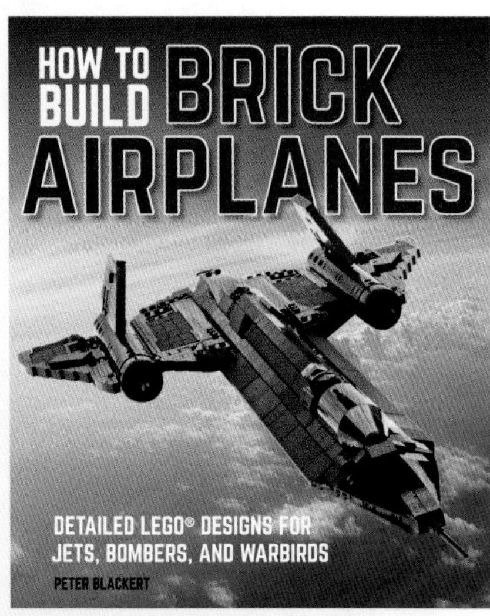

How to Build Brick Airplanes
By Peter Blackert
978-0-7603-6164-1